MODERNIST ANTHROPOLOGY

MODERNIST ANTHROPOLOGY

FROM FIELDWORK TO TEXT

Edited and with an Introduction
by Marc Manganaro

PRINCETON UNIVERSITY PRESS PRINCETON, NEW JERSEY

Published by Princeton University Press, 41 William Street,
Princeton, New Jersey 08540
In the United Kingdom: Princeton University Press, Oxford

Library of Congress Cataloging-in-Publication Data

Modernist anthropology : from fieldwork to text / edited and with an introduction by Marc Manganaro.
p. cm.
Includes bibliographical references.
ISBN 0-691-06846-1 (alk. paper) — ISBN 0-691-01480-9
(alk. paper)
1. Anthropology—Field work. 2. Anthropology—Methodology.
3. Literature and anthropology. 4. Anthropologists' writings.
I. Manganaro, Marc, 1955– . II. Title.
GN33.M58 1990
306'.072—dc20 89-77333

This book has been composed in Linotron Palatino

Princeton University Press books are printed on acid-free paper, and meet the guidelines for permanence and durability of the Committee on Production Guidelines for Book Longevity of the Council on Library Resources

Printed in the United States of America by Princeton University Press, Princeton, New Jersey

10 9 8 7 6 5 4 3 2 1

(Pbk.)
10 9 8 7 6 5 4 3 2 1

Contents

Preface vii

Acknowledgments xi

INTRODUCTION

Marc Manganaro
Textual Play, Power, and Cultural Critique: An Orientation to Modernist Anthropology 3

FRAZER: TEXTUAL REEVALUATIONS

John B. Vickery
Frazer and the Elegiac: The Modernist Connection 51

Marty Roth
Sir James Frazer's *The Golden Bough*: A Reading Lesson 69

Marilyn Strathern
Out of Context: The Persuasive Fictions of Anthropology
Comments by I. C. Jarvie; Stephen A. Tyler and George E. Marcus 80

ETHNOGRAPHY AS DISCOURSE: THE ERA OF THE MONOGRAPH

Arnold Krupat
Irony in Anthropology: The Work of Franz Boas 133

Deborah Gordon
The Politics of Ethnographic Authority: Race and Writing in the Ethnography of Margaret Mead and Zora Neale Hurston 146

Richard Handler
Ruth Benedict and the Modernist Sensibility 163

ANTHROPOLOGICAL MODERNISM: LANGUAGE, THEORY, AND PRAXIS

Michèle Richman
Anthropology and Modernism in France: From Durkheim to the *Collège de sociologie* 183

Francesco Loriggio
Anthropology, Literary Theory, and the Traditions of Modernism 215

Robert Sullivan
Marxism and the "Subject" of Anthropology 243

Steven Webster
The Historical Materialist Critique of Surrealism and Postmodernist Ethnography 266

Vincent Crapanzano
Afterword 300

Notes on Contributors 309

Bibliography 311

Index 329

Preface

IN A SEMINAL ESSAY, "From Work to Text," Roland Barthes makes the distinction between the "work," which is "concrete, occupying a portion of book-space," and the "text," which, "on the other hand, is a methodological field" (Barthes 1979, 75). The distinction between the material, empirical notion of a "work" ("held in the hand") and the eminently interpretive and discursive conception of a "text" ("held in language," existing "only as discourse") (Barthes 1979, 75) proves useful when approaching the relation between the discourses of anthropology and literature. Now anthropological texts have never been viewed solely as collections of facts, yet the subtitle of this work borrows from Barthes to exemplify a recent qualitative shift in perspective—toward anthropology as textual form in which facts culled from the field are not only inextricably bound up within the discursive process we call text-making, but are themselves at times seriously put into question. At the least, the subtitle asserts that the pressing reality of anthropological fact should never simply be isolated from, and privileged above, the formal and ideological features of anthropological writing.

Other recent books have considered questions of the literary and discursive nature of anthropological writing, perhaps most notably James Clifford and George Marcus's *Writing Culture* and Clifford Geertz's *Works and Lives: The Anthropologist as Author*. This collection makes no claim to opening up the discussion on anthropology as text, but instead applies notions of the discursiveness of anthropology to anthropological writings of the first half of this century, the time frame traditionally referred to as the modernist period. The primary title of this book, *Modernist Anthropology*, constitutes a claim that anthropology vitally participated in the century's most important cultural and (more specifically, in this context) literary movement. In the process of interpreting the relation of anthropological writing to the fundamental although highly ambiguous concept of modernism, the contributors to this volume significantly add to, question, and even alter the terms of the debate on the role of discourse in the science of culture.

The impetus within the volume to suggest the pan-disciplinary nature of modernism as a cultural force that has spilled over institutional boundaries is reflected in the various affiliations of the contributors. Four of the contributors (including me) hold positions in English departments; two work in Comparative Literature or Romance Language departments; three hold positions in departments of Anthropology; one is affiliated with both a Comparative Literature program *and* an Anthropology department; and one has done her training in a program that has abandoned traditional academic divisions altogether. As Barthes says in "From Work to Text," "interdisciplinary work is not a peaceful operation: it begins *effectively* when the solidarity of the old disciplines breaks down" (1979, 73). This collection does not amount to a unanimous call by its contributors for the dismantling of the traditional academic institutions, but, as editor, I know that no one institutional field could have adequately supplied the expertise and insight necessary to do justice to the subject of the volume. That fact has served for me as both a warning against disciplinary over-specialization and an encouraging word in favor of cross-disciplinary pursuit.

This work did not originate from a conference or symposium (although two of the essays appeared in early stages in a session I organized on Frazer for the 1987 Modern Language Association convention in San Francisco); and only two of the ten essays were previously published. The essays do not function as parts of the same roundtable discussion, nor do the essayists together comprise a coherent school or movement: the backgrounds, theoretical assumptions, and aims of the various contributors often differ radically. Indeed, only after they completed their own essays were the contributors given the opportunity to read the other essays that would appear in the volume and make relevant cross-references. I hope to establish, in my Introduction, why these essays are brought together. Indeed, the essays themselves ought to function collectively as a commentary upon the intertwining issues of modernism as cultural movement and anthropology as writing: but it is important, indeed critical, to recognize that no tidy consensus is reached on these issues (it is indicative in this respect that the author of the Afterword refuses to furnish a consensual site, refuses to "represent" the views of the authors grouped under this title).

There are more people to thank than there is space, and yet there are a good number who absolutely *must* be acknowledged. I am very grateful to George Marcus and George Stocking who, early on in this project, suggested a few contributors who have made their way into the volume. And thanks to Clifford Geertz for gracious words of encouragement when the book was still an idea. I also would like to thank James Clifford, Henry Louis Gates, William Harmon, Denis Hollier, Paul Rabinow, Tzvetan Todorov, Marianna Torgovnick, and

Stephen Tyler, for their willingness to share writings and ideas. My thanks also to those contributors to the volume—Richard Handler, Robert Sullivan, Steven Webster, and especially Michèle Richman—who suggested revisions to the Introduction and to other essays in the collection. I am also very grateful to Craig Howes, Mary Elizabeth (Beth) Tobin, Joseph Tobin, and Rob Wilson, former colleagues at the University of Hawaii, for reading early versions of parts of the work (and to Jeff Tobin, for help with the title). And thanks to Greta Anderson at Rutgers for assembling the final bibliography.

Much thanks goes to the Department of English at the University of Hawaii, especially to Joseph Kau, Chair. I am also grateful to the Department of English at Rutgers University (New Brunswick), particularly to Thomas Van Laan and Barry Qualls. I am indebted to Robert Brown, editor at Princeton University Press, for his confidence and capability. And, needless to say, I appreciate the punctuality, patience, and good graces of all of the volume's contributors.

Finally, for unceasing love and support, I need to thank my parents, Ross and Alice Manganaro, and grandmother, Nettie Manganaro; my father- and mother-in-law, Elie and Phyllis Salem; and my wife Lisa, without whom little would be possible.

Acknowledgments

ARNOLD KRUPAT'S essay "Irony in Anthropology: The Work of Franz Boas" appeared, in very different form, as "Anthropology in the Ironic Mode: The Work of Franz Boas" in *Social Text*, 19/20 (Fall 1988), to whom we acknowledge thanks for permission to reprint. We are also grateful to the editors of *Current Anthropology*, the Wenner-Gren Foundation for Anthropological Research, and the University of Chicago Press for granting us permission to reprint, unchanged, Marilyn Strathern's essay "Out of Context: The Persuasive Fictions of Anthropology," © 1987 by The Wenner-Gren Foundation for Anthropological Research (all rights reserved), and two of the responses included in *Current Anthropology*'s June 1987 issue (vol. 28).

For permission to quote material held in copyright, we are indebted to the following:

Excerpt from *W. H. Auden: Collected Poems,* edited by Edward Mendelson. (Copyright © 1976 by Edward Mendelson, William Meredith, and Monroe K. Spears, Executors of the Estate of W. H. Auden.) Reprinted by permission of Random House, Inc.

Excerpt from "The Waste Land" in *Collected Poems, 1909–1962* by T. S. Eliot, copyright 1936 by Harcourt Brace Jovanovich, Inc., copyright © 1964, 1963 by T. S. Eliot, reprinted by permission of the publisher.

Excerpts from *Absalom, Absalom!* by William Faulkner. (Copyright 1936 by William Faulkner and renewed 1964 by Estelle Faulkner and Jill Faulkner Summers.) Reprinted by permission of Curtis Brown, London, and Random House, Inc.

Excerpt from *Creation and Evolution in Primitive Cosmogenies* by Sir James Frazer. Reprinted by permission of A. P. Watt Limited on behalf of Trinity College, Cambridge.

Excerpts from *Ulysses* by James Joyce. (Copyright 1914, 1918 by Margaret Caroline Anderson. Copyright renewed, 1942, 1946, by Nora Joseph Joyce. Copyright, 1934, by Modern Library, Inc. Copyright renewed, 1961, by Lucia and George Joyce.) Reprinted by permission of Random House.

"Elegy" by W. S. Merwin. (Copyright 1967, 1968, 1969, 1970 by W. S. Merwin.) Reprinted by permission of Atheneum Publishers, an imprint of Macmillan Publishing Company, from *The Carrier of Ladders* by W. S.

Merwin. Also reprinted by permission of Georges Borchardt Inc. and the author.

Excerpts from *The Cantos of Ezra Pound* by Ezra Pound. (Copyright 1934, 1959 by Ezra Pound.) Reprinted by permission of New Directions Publishing and Faber & Faber.

INTRODUCTION

Textual Play, Power, and Cultural Critique: An Orientation to Modernist Anthropology

MARC MANGANARO

THIS ANTHOLOGY is born out of a number of critical developments in the past twenty-five years that have brought about, among other things, a coalescence of anthropology and current theories on discourse emerging from literary and other cultural studies. Perhaps most important, recent anthropological writing has called into question the legitimacy with which we represent the "Other" in cultural written accounts. Indeed, insights gained into the nature of representation and power relations have made impossible the comfortable assumption that other cultures can be grasped, categorized, and put on paper. The recognition that cultural representation is inherently problematic is of course hardly confined to anthropological study. Indeed, a sign of the increasing reciprocity of anthropology and other discourses on culture is the appearance of such studies from outside the discipline, particularly literary theory, that have made a significant impact upon how anthropologists view their own activities: Edward Said's *Orientalism* is a prominent example of a text illustrating the uses and abuses of the cultural Other by Western institutions.

Recent criticism of the treatment of the cultural Other—the *subject*, *native*, or *savage*, as that figure has variously been termed—forges an integral tie between the appropriation of Other and the discursive forms that contain the act of appropriation. The borrowing of anthropological concepts by literary theorists (as in the case of the literary uses of Lévi-Strauss's brand of structuralism), has reversed, so that anthropological theorists have adopted literary criticism's orientation toward the "text." The result has been a textualization of social science, what James Clifford (1986c, 2) terms a "focus on text making and rhetoric" that "serves to highlight the constructed, artificial nature of cultural accounts."

Contemporary ideas on alterity, power relations, and representation, brought to the forefront by theorists such as Tzvetan Todorov, Michel Foucault, and Hayden White, have dramatically altered our perspective on anthropology as an activity. This volume is a concerted effort to relate those recent developments to texts written or influenced by anthropologists between 1900 and 1945, the years that by a traditional consensus frame what literary scholars have referred to as the modernist period. The primary aims of the volume are to understand better the discursive and political dimensions of anthropologically oriented texts of the period, and in the process to illustrate how those texts were inextricably related to literary and other artistic manifestations of that time frame; also, we hope to understand some of the ways in which these texts act as cultural products that not only reflect but also anticipate changes in contemporary and perhaps future social-cultural formations. In fact, the book's organization moves both chronologically and according to discourse type: from Frazer's comparativist text, to the era of the monograph, then on to French ethnographic surrealism. At the same time, the orientation of the book shifts from essays that primarily approach anthropology from the vantage points of literariness and power, to the essays in the last section, that contemplate what bearing the juncture of theory and anthropology can have upon present and future social institutions. All the while, the book shuttles back and forth in time, from present to past, in the continual application of recent literary and cultural theory to the anthropology of the century's first half.

Why an emphasis upon the first fifty years of this century? To begin with, these years saw the formation of anthropology as an autonomous discipline. Certainly Frazer's *The Golden Bough* gave fame to anthropology as an exhilarating scholarly pursuit, but it was the work of people such as Franz Boas in the United States, Bronislaw Malinowski in England, and Marcel Mauss in France that, in part through an emphasis on fieldwork methods, brought about the emergence of anthropology as a scientific and academic discipline. It is the assumptions of that discipline, especially as developed in England and the U.S. that recent anthropology and anthropological theory is resisting and insisting upon reformulating.

Why modernism? For one, there are strong influences at work in the relation between modern anthropology and modernist literature: the impact of Frazer's *The Golden Bough* upon works such as Eliot's *The Waste Land* and Joyce's *Ulysses* is a reminder of that borrowing. In fact, it was halfway through the literary modernist period that the rather dramatic appearance of Malinowski's monograph sounded a death knell for Frazer's comparativist form of anthropological discourse.[1] Indeed, 1922, the year of the publication of Malinowski's *Ar-*

[1] Malinowski's *Argonauts* had a dramatic effect upon the way anthropologists in En-

gonauts of the Western Pacific, also marks the advent of literary high modernism, for it was in that year that *The Waste Land* and *Ulysses* exploded upon the cultural scene. This is not to suggest that, on the other hand, Malinowski and other writers of monographs had no literary inclinations or implications. Indeed, as several essays in this volume testify, in the years after 1922 anthropologists often performed dual roles as students of culture and artists: witness Ruth Benedict's work as a practicing poet, and the French phenomenon that Clifford calls ethnographic surrealism, practiced in the 1920s and 1930s by Georges Bataille, Roger Caillois, and other members of what would become the Collège de Sociologie. Still others, such as Malinowski, worked as anthropologists but conceived of themselves as author figures; both Clifford and Stocking refer to Malinowski's claim, that "[W.H.R.] Rivers is the Rider Haggard of anthropology; I shall be the Conrad" (Stocking 1983, 104).

Some anthropologists complain that the use of the term *modernism* is simply a valorization of aesthetics over social science, and in a sense that objection is undeniable. However, so symbiotic has the relationship become between artistic theory and anthropology that a focus upon modernism can no longer be seen as simply the privileging of literature, say, over social science. The increasing number of references made by anthropologists to anthropology's modernist and postmodernist stages does indicate at least a limited recognition within the field that anthropology is a discursive category, a type or group of types of writing that have important filiations to other modern cultural and academic fields. But more important, the very terms *modernism* and *postmodernism* have been progressively modified to encompass larger areas of culture. Modernism, in other words, is not

---

gland and the United States shaped their texts. Doubtless it was the most important monograph in the shaping of that form. Still, it would be a gross oversimplification to suggest that Malinowski single-handedly brought the monograph into being. Among others, Franz Boas, with his diffusionist fieldwork studies, had been highly critical of the evolutionary comparativist text for forty years before the appearance of Malinowski's *Argonauts,* and trained a generation of prominent students from his fieldwork-oriented perspective. In fact, the essays in the second section of this volume deal with what has been called the Boasian school: Boas, Mead, Hurston, and Benedict.

Although Frazer's comparativist discursive form found few important followers in anthropology after Malinowski, it is important to note that comparativism itself hardly died with the emergence of the monograph. Lévi-Straussian structuralism is obviously comparativist in many of its assumptions and methods. Also, although Frazer's method was fairly rapidly abandoned within the field of anthropology, his comparativist discursive form and the rhetoric emerging from it had a fundamental impact upon the texts of other disciplines, such as literary criticism, classical studies, and mythology. My own book, *A Modernist Will to Power: The Rhetoric of Anthropological Authority* (forthcoming), deals with the legacy of this particular discursive form.

valid any longer as *only* a term descriptive of literary texts written between 1900 and 1945, or even as a term used to characterize all of the arts in that period. It has become, rather, a term variously employed to define a variety of cultural manifestations that are not even *necessarily* bound to the first half of the twentieth century.

Labeling a modernism of anthropology is an extremely contestatory act. Noting that Anglo-American literary modernism peaked at the juncture of two anthropological periods does not mean that all the essayists in this volume would concur that the chronology of an anthropological modernism matches that of literary modernism. Indeed, Marcus and Fischer's borrowing of the term *modernist* to apply to anthropological texts is meant "as a parallel reference to allude to the late nineteenth- and early twentieth-century literary movement in reaction to realism" (Marcus & Fischer 1986, 69); however, the anthropology they have in mind has largely been written within the past ten to fifteen years. The properties of those contemporary texts—dialogue, discourse, cooperative texts, and surrealism—are all anticipated, according to the authors, in one form or another by literary modernist texts of one half-century before.

Anthropologist Edward Ardener is speaking of this interdisciplinary lag when he claims that the periodization of the various disciplines is often quite confusing, not only because the term *modernism* is used in different disciplines for different purposes, but also because in a specific time period two disciplines may well be involved in quite different activities using radically varying methodologies. Referring to the "out-of-phaseness of such developments," Ardener (1985, 51) maintains, for one, that what can be called modernism in anthropology begins in 1920 (roughly, with the advent of Malinowski's version of the monograph) and ends in 1975 (with the beginnings of postmodern anthropology) and contains distinct movements that have no direct chronological relation to developments within literary modernism.

Although the contributors to this volume might all agree with the Ardener's claim of "out-of-phaseness," they would not all adhere to the notion that modernism in anthropology necessarily constitutes the period from 1920 to 1975. This lack of consensus reflects current critical musings on the nature of modern periodization, brought to the forefront of theoretical discussions in the compelling debate over the relation of modernism to postmodernism. If we consider Fredric Jameson's enunciation of the issue, modernism must be seen as an overarching cultural phenomenon, not confined to characterizing artistic achievement and indeed very much tied to what Jameson terms "the classic age of competitive classicism" (1983, 115). That means, of course, that anthropological texts first *must* be seen not as mere *influences* upon the mighty literary canon but as equally legitimate manifestations of culture that are, like literature, integrally tied to the capitalist schema.

Jameson's discussion of the distinction between modernism and postmodernism has very illuminating parallels to anthropology, correspondences that have been explored by several theorists of anthropology. According to Jameson, high or classical modernism set itself in opposition to the society into which it was born and hence "emerged within the business society of the gilded age as scandalous and offensive to the middle class public—ugly, dissonant, sexually shocking."[2] Jameson contrasts the "subversive" quality of modernism to the element of "pastiche" that characterizes the postmodern. Emerging in the 1960s as the cultural product of consumer society, postmodern pastiche is characterized by imitation that does not set itself in opposition to a standard or norm of custom or behavior, as did the various forms of modernism. Rather, postmodernism as a cultural phenomenon is typified by the free-floating representation of past representations (one example Jameson provides for this is the wave of nostalgia films of the 1970s and 1980s).

Anthropologist Paul Rabinow sees in Jameson's description an apt application to the current situation within the field of anthropology, which he characterizes as such:

> Interpretive anthropologists work with the problem of representations of others' representations, historians and metacritics of anthropology with the classification, canonization, and "making available" of representations of representations of representations. The historical flattening found in the pastiche of nostalgia films reappears in the meta-ethnographic flattening that makes all the world's cultures practitioners of textuality. (1986, 250)

The contributors to this volume do not all necessarily agree with each specific of the Jameson-Rabinow schema, but all acknowledge that there has occurred within the discipline of anthropology a questioning of its methodology that roughly corresponds to developments in other discursive fields, a kind of meta-practice whose emergence is vitally connected to what Jameson referred to as a "radical break" (1983, 123). Most would agree that the modernism of anthropology historically precedes that break into metaethnography; all share the

[2] Jameson's discussion of postmodernism, in "Postmodernism and Consumer Society," is here quoted from Paul Rabinow, "Representations Are Social Facts: Modernity and Postmodernity in Anthropology," in *Writing Culture: The Poetics and Politics of Ethnography*, ed. James Clifford and George Marcus (University of California Press, 1986), p. 248.

belief that the knowledge of postmodern critiques of form or representation are essential to a contemporary understanding of anthropology preceding the postmodern. What remains highly debated is exactly where and when the break between the modernist and postmodernist occurred, and what specifically constituted it.

In an essay in Clifford and Marcus's *Writing Culture,* Michael Fischer (1986, 194) threatens the legitimacy of even the most generalized conception of modernism as an anthropological period. Fischer adopts Jean-Francois Lyotard's definition of postmodernism as "that moment of modernism that defines itself against an immediate past ('post') and that is skeptically inquisitive about all grounds of authority, assumption, or convention." According to Fischer (1986, 194), this broader definition envisions "cycles of modernism that decay and renew" and as such is liberated from the strictures of chronological periodization (of seeing postmodernism as a mere "unlabeled aftermath of early twentieth-century modernisms") and from what he terms the "unsubstantiated negative political evaluations" of Jameson's theory (194). Fischer and Marcus's own claim for anthropological "modernist texts" illustrates both the notion that the postmodern moment resides within the modernist movement and that modernism itself must be seen, in line with Lyotard, not as a period but as a cyclical cultural manifestation.

Like Jameson, Edward Said (1989, 222) insists that the "negative political evaluations" (as termed by Fischer) are not only applicable but integral to the modernist-postmodernist paradigm. In fact, Said faults Lyotard for failing to hook up the loss of power of the great modernist narratives to the global political and social arena. By saying that "the great narratives just lost their power," Lyotard, according to Said,

> *separates* Western postmodernism from the non-European world, and from the consequences of European modernism—and modernization—in the colonized world. In effect then postmodernism, with its aesthetic of quotation, nostalgia, and indifferentiation, stands free of its history, which is to say that the division of intellectual labor, the circumscription of praxis within clear disciplinary boundaries, and the depolitization of knowledge can proceed more or less at will. (1989, 222)

According to Said (1989, 222), the great narratives lost that power because modernism was "foundered on or was frozen in contemplative irony for various reasons," among them "the disturbing appearance in Europe of various Others, whose provenance was the imperial domain." For Eliot, Conrad, Proust, Woolf, and others, "alterity and difference are systematically associated with strangers," such as natives, who "challenge and resist settled metropolitan histories, forms, modes of thought" (1989, 223). And yet modernism fails at its encounter with other-ness since ultimately the movement answered "with the formal irony of a culture unable either to say yes, we should give up control, or no, we shall hold on regardless: a self-conscious contemplative passivity forms itself, as Georg Lukács noted perspicaciously, into paralyzed gestures of aestheticized powerlessness" (1989, 223).

For Said, modernism's legacy constitutes Western failure "to take the Other seriously" (1989, 223). It is utterly significant that he contains his discussion of modernism within his essay on anthropology's ties to colonialism (a subject discussed later in this Introduction). The implications are clear: the modernist failure to engage the Other and the resulting postmodern trivialization are very much reflected in the failure of modern anthropology as a discipline to recognize its own global implications and thus attempt to free itself from the colonialist ideology that appropriates the Other. Said's "lesson" to anthropologists (expressed as such—and it is important that this piece was first presented as an address at the American Anthropological Association convention) is expressed quite clearly in the conclusion to his discussion of the modernist-postmodernist paradigm: "Thus: think the narratives through together within the context provided by the history of imperialism, a history whose underlying contest between white and non-white has emerged lyrically in the new and more inclusive counternarrative of liberation" (1989, 224).

For Said and Jameson, unlike Lyotard, the significance of the modernist-postmodernist paradigm lies precisely in very real historical, social, political, and economic factors. Lyotard's move to free the modernist-postmodernist relation from mere chronology or periodization becomes, for Said, a mystification of the essentially political *causal* connections between periods. Still, the definitions of Jameson and Said on the one hand and Lyotard on the other do not have to be considered mutually exclusive. Whether occurring once or as one of a number of cycles, for each, modernism represents a rebellion: for Said there was the "challenge" to the metropole that modernist encounters with the Other provoked; for Jameson, modernism was to the middle class "ugly, dissonant, sexually shocking" (1983, 124). And yet, for Lyotard, Jameson, and Said, the modernist rebellion is nonetheless characterized by an assurance that "form" can bring some kind of order to the chaos that is civilization. Said refers to the "formal irony" amounting to an "aestheticized powerlessness" (1989, 223) that constitutes the modernist response to the Other. Lyotard ([1979], 81), in *The Postmodern Condition*, refers to the "solace of good forms" contained in modernism, "the consensus of a taste which would make it possible to share collectively the nostalgia for the unattainable." The postmodern, according to Lyotard, is what "in the modern, puts forward the unpresentable in presentation itself. . . . that which searches for new presentations, not in order to enjoy them but in order to impart a stronger sense of the unpresentable" ([1979], 81).

In a recent unpublished essay, Marilyn Strathern (1987b) attempts to equate current theories on the postmodern with recent developments in anthropology. She perceives just such a "solace of good forms" in the anthropology that preceded the current disillusionment with adequate representation. She borrows Hal Foster's (1983) term "the anti-aesthetic" to characterize the skeptical quality of postmodernism in anthropology. Strathern views most of modern anthropology as roughly parallel to the modernist faith in form, the major difference being only that the "pure aesthetic form" of modernism, represented in literature by the modernist poem or novel, in anthropology becomes " 'society' or 'culture,' which the anthropologists simply represented."

Read in the light of such theories on the anti-aesthetic, the rejection of faith in the monograph (the Anglo-American anthropologist's orthodox form), can be read as the dismissal of the possibility of what Strathern calls "a space beyond representation," that "utopian dream of pure present" (1987b) that characterizes high modernism in both its literary and anthropological forms. But a more complex and perhaps compelling application of the faith in form would be to Lévi-Strauss. While Lévi-Strauss significantly anticipates contemporary attacks on the transparency of anthropological representation, his structural methods put faith in the form of language itself. In the words of Jameson (1981, 61), language functions for Lévi-Straussian structuralism as the "master code or interpretive key" that, although hardly assuming a simple one-to-one correspondence of signifying word to signified cultural object, does function ultimately to explain, interpret, or translate the cultural Other.

A postmodern anthropology, on the other hand, is so acutely aware of its own representational complexes that it openly admits the fallacy of representing the cultural subject in any "real" state. A crucial question arises out of this postmodern awareness: what can anthropology hope to accomplish if it cannot represent its subject? Stephen Tyler (1986a, 123), perhaps the foremost self-identified postmodern anthropologist, follows Lyotard's lead (as stated in *The Postmodern Condition*), arguing that science's dependence upon representation has bankrupted the discipline, especially since representation is an attempt at control. The alternative to representation lies in the ethnography of evocation, defined as follows:

> Evocation is neither presentation nor representation. It presents no objects and represents none, yet it makes available through absence what can be conceived but not presented. It is thus beyond truth and immune to the judgement of performance. It overcomes the separation of the sensible and conceivable, of form and content, of self and other, of language and the world.

Tyler's ethnography of evocation is, as he himself says, eminently "poetic"; it returns to ancient poetry's use of "a performative break with everyday speech" that "evoked memories of the *ethos* of the community and thereby provoked hearers to act ethically" (125–26). Inhering in any ethnography of evocation is "dialogue as opposed to monologue" and "the cooperative and collaborative nature of the ethnographic situation in contrast to the ideology of the transcendental observer" (126). Rather than the teller telling a tale, "there is instead the mutual, dialogical production of a discourse, of a story of sorts" (126). That tale, as a postmodern text, would have not only an especially heightened consciousness toward its own discursive properties, but its very subject would be its own textuality.[3]

Tyler's version of a future postmodern anthropology implements the features of modernist texts as discussed by Fischer. Tyler's is not the only version of a futurist ethnography, but it is probably the most notable attempt to date. Not untypically, there is more talk about the possibilities of a postmodern ethnography than there are attempts to actually practice it. Two texts that are often mentioned as manifestations of postmodern ethnography, however, are Vincent Crapanzano's *Tuhami: Portrait of a Moroccan* and Paul Rabinow's *Reflections on Fieldwork in Morocco*. Both are dialogic in the sense that they involve the Other as participant-collaborator and both are preoccupied with the very communicability of the ethnographic research process.

But, in the main, proponents of postmodern ethnography are more apt to discover strains of the postmodern in the works of a number of present and past anthropological accounts. Indeed, one sees an effort at readjusting anthropology's canon in light of an anthropolo-

[3] The backlash against Tyler within anthropological circles can be illustrated by J. Tim O'Meara's "Anthropology as Empirical Science," *American Anthropologist* 91 (June 1989): 354–69. There O'Meara, focusing on Tyler's work, refers to the "extreme argument that an empirical science of human affairs is impossible or inappropriate, and that interpretation alone is possible" (354). O'Meara's subsequent opinion, "I fear that the pendulum has now swung too far" (354), indicates the reaction of a good number of empirically based anthropologists.

gist's interest in the dialogic and the collaborative: note, for example, Clifford's interest in the French surrealist ethnographers Leiris and Caillois, or Strathern's forced reappraisal of Frazer. In fact, a number of the essays in this book function as revaluations of past texts in the light of current ethnographic aspirations. But, on the other hand, those and other essays also communicate the necessity to critique the adequacy of those theories as *praxis*, to use past texts as a sounding board for future directions in anthropology, and through that assessment to question the applicability of those theories in effecting actual cultural change.

A generation ago an anthology concerning the relation between anthropology and modernism would consist mainly of essays tracing the influence of Frazerian anthropology on the works of American and English modernists such as Eliot, Lawrence, and Yeats. Some of the essays in that hypothetical anthology of a generation ago would have focused on how the literary modernist borrowed certain Frazerian tenets (such as the connection between the ritual killing of the king and vegetation ceremonies) to give artistic form or significance to the literary artifact (Eliot's *The Waste Land*, or Yeats's "The Death of Parnell"); and, more broadly, others would have demonstrated how certain "primitive" beliefs or rites chronicled by Frazerian anthropology (such as "animism" or totem worship) were wholly or partially adopted into the author's set of religious beliefs (for example, Lawrence's notion of "blood consciousness"); and a number of essays from both of the above groups would have enthusiastically assumed that the aesthetic use of the primal and ritualistic profoundly deepened the very spiritual dimension of twentieth-century literature.

Many of the critical assumptions behind those hypothetical essays are oriented around the concept of "mythic consciousness," the notion that cultural productions, in this case literary texts, have access to a mythic condition that represents a return to a more vital, primal, and elemental human state. The myth criticism that emerged in America between the Second World War and the 1960s was profoundly influenced by the work of anthropologists and classicists such as Frazer and the Cambridge Hellenists (Jane Harrison, F. M. Cornford, Gilbert Murray, and others) as well as depth psychologists, especially Carl Jung. The Cambridge Hellenists in particular asserted the primacy of ritual in the formation of art, a view that, although disproved in anthropological circles in the 1920s, persisted in literary criticism for half a century.[4] In "Literary Criticism and Myth: Anglo-American Critics," John Vickery (1980, 210–11) accurately portrays the scene of myth criticism in its heyday:

> Around the 1950s a burgeoning of interest in myth as central to literature and criticism took place. As a result, many bathed in burning fountains while pursuing the quest for myth, in which they might find themselves with an older, more unified, more mythic consciousness. Heroes bore a thousand faces, while gods wore masks to be pierced or at least scrutinized, and both were found to populate more literary works and more unexpected ones than had been dreamt of before.

It was through the channel of the mythic that anthropology was defined as an "interest" to those who studied the relationship of the social sciences to modernism. Literary critics of the midcentury found, for example, Emile Durkheim and Jane Harrison's books rich in imaginative possibilities, and Boas's work limiting in aesthetic application, because the former, unlike the latter, raised the possibility of a primal spiritual or mystical state, harbored in the "primitive," that anthropology gave evidence of, art embodied, and criticism at least ought to chart. The myth critic of the day, although he dutifully mentioned Frazer's ethnocentrism, nonetheless found that the larger ritual patterns performed by the "savage" were more important than the ethnographic accuracy with which the contemporary anthropologist depicted the savage Other.

The contributors to this volume do not represent a wholesale rejection of all anthropologically inspired mythic approaches to the literary text. Nor would they claim that myth has no rôle to play in analyzing anthropology's relationship to its own discourse and others (such as literature): obviously the continuing interest in and influence of Lévi-Strauss and René Girard attest to myth's having a function in current interpretive practices. However, the most recent developments in anthropology's interdisciplinary context have encouraged, in the poststructuralist vein, a turn away from mythic approaches that downplay the discursive and ideological qualities of the text. The new orientation does not announce that myth is disproved; however, it does assume that attaching value to an aesthetic object by plugging it into a deeply resonant *mythoi* is contentious at best and must be viewed as culturally bound and, in part, politically determined.[5]

[4] On the fallacies that originated with the Cambridge Hellenists and were perpetuated in Anglo-American myth criticism, see Richard Hardin's " 'Ritual' in Recent Criticism: The Elusive Sense of Community," *PMLA* 98 (1983): 846–62.

[5] An important work on approaching the mythic qualities of the literary text from a more discursive perspective is Eric Gould's *Mythical Intentions in Modern Literature*

Anglo-American myth criticism broadly conceived culminated in the work of Northrop Frye, whose *Anatomy of Criticism*, in appropriate social scientific fashion, comprehensively classified literature into four "narrative categories"—the comic, tragic, romantic, and ironic—that equated to the four *mythoi*—spring, summer, autumn, winter. Frye's work, as Terry Eagleton (1983, 91) claims, was the answer to the need for a literary criticism that, although "preserving the formalist bent of New Criticism, its dogged attention to literature as an aesthetic object rather than social practice, would make something a good deal more systematic and 'scientific' out of all this."

Clearly Frye was attempting to replicate the methodological strictures of a social science, and yet with the scientific approach came an ideology that was anything but objective. Unlike American New Criticism, whose image-tracing tactics did *not* necessitate a commitment to a Jungian frame of mind (although there were other necessary affiliations), Frye's system assumed a mythically whole universe in which natural seasons and impulses were innately bred into cultural products. Jameson (1981, 69; 71) in *The Political Unconscious* praises Frye's willingness, absent in other myth critics, to "raise the issue of community" but ultimately believes that Frye fails because of his commitment to "religious hermeneutics." Like the other myth critics of the 1950s, Frye appealed to the ethereal goal of clarifying the literary artifact's position in relation to an all-encompassing mythos. Ultimately, neither New Criticism nor Myth Criticism was concerned with anthropological aspirations of acquiring a more accurate picture of tribal custom or mentality: both schools led in quests toward more rarified realities (art, myth), strivings that ultimately drove a decisive wedge between social science and art.

Hayden White, in *Tropics of Discourse* (1978) discusses Frye's distinctions between literature and social science in terms that greatly illuminate midcentury critical assumptions on the relation between anthropology and literature. Frye, White explains, locates the "fictive" in the space between the polarities of the mythic and the historic (here, we can safely read, the social scientific). On the one hand, imbedded in each fiction is a "pre-generic plot structure" or arche-

(Princeton: Princeton University Press, 1981). Gould holds that the notion of the "mythic" must be confined to "semiological fact." The inability to close the "gap" between "event and meaning," between mythic signifier and signified, creates a tension we know as the "mythic" (6). This mythic impulse, however, hardly affirms the existence of the transcendental signified: "The fact that classical and totemistic myths have to refer to some version of translinguistic fact . . . proves not that there are Gods, but that our talents for interpreting our place in the world may be distinctly limited by the nature of language" (7).

typal myth that explains why a story has its distinctive shape. On the other hand, although Frye, according to White, concedes that history can approach the mythic, history in its pure state constitutes something closer to "direct address, or straight discursive writing" and is not literary at all.[6] White (1978, 83) turns the tables on Frye's scheme by maintaining that both history (social science) and myth are contained within the fictive or literary. He refuses the simple opposition of factual to imaginative discourse but sees both social science and literature as characterized by "emplotment." In the case of history, White defines *emplotment* as "the encodation of the facts contained in the chronicle as components of specific *kind* of plot structures," a capability that Frye had reserved for "fictions."

Clearly, when we apply White's textual perspective upon history to anthropological writing, the form of the anthropological work can no longer be seen as a natural or organic extension of content; rather, the writer of anthropology either plugs into preexisting plot structures or creates a new structure out of the amalgam of old forms. For example, James Clifford, George Stocking, James Boon, and Marilyn Strathern have all illustrated how Malinowski's monograph did not spontaneously materialize as the inevitable vessel in which to pour the fieldwork of the ethnographer. Rather, the monograph as fashioned by Malinowski was a carefully premeditated linguistic structure that owed much to Frazerian fieldwork methods, the reports of travelers and explorers, as well as disciplinary politics.[7]

White's contention of the inherent "literariness" of history significantly prefigured the way a number of theorists and historians are now reading anthropology: that is, as text, as writing that is necessarily bound within the parameters of discourse. Clifford Geertz's anthropological writings over the past two decades have similarly affirmed the ultimately discursive nature of anthropology by holding that cultural interplay is itself semiotic, a system of signs that can be interpreted by the culture-reader (his essay on observing a Balinese cockfight has become the classic example of such reading). Geertz's recent book, *Works and Lives: The Anthropologist as Author*, affirms an essentially textual approach to ethnography, claiming that the anthropologists' ability to convince is based primarily not upon the suitability or solidity of fieldwork but upon the very writerly task of convincing us "that what they say is a result of having actually penetrated . . . another form of life, of having, one way or another,

[6] Frye quoted by Hayden White in *Tropics of Discourse* (Baltimore: Johns Hopkins University Press, 1978), p. 83.

[7] See Marcus and Fischer's *Anthropology As Cultural Critique*, p. 24; also, see Mary Louis Pratt's "Fieldwork in Common Places," in *Writing Culture*, pp. 27–50.

truly 'been there' " (1988, 4–5). Furthermore, Geertz holds that anthropology's "family resemblances" to literary discourse come clear when we consider that the Foucaultian "author-function" is "reasonably strong" in anthropological writings: that is, unlike the "hard" sciences, the personal names of modern anthropologists tend to be "attached to books and articles" rather than "findings, properties, or propositions" (1988, 7–8).

The contributions of White and Geertz to anthropology's textual turn cannot be read in a vacuum. Reading anthropology discursively would be impossible if not for the emergence of phenomenology, semiotics, structuralism, and the deconstructionist movement. Well before aestheticians began to pull apart anthropology's text, Lévi-Strauss was importing the anthropological study of structures to the study of the literary text (the foremost example being the structural analysis of Baudelaire's poem "Les Chats" by Lévi-Strauss and Roman Jakobson). But just as crucially, his own anthropological texts, especially *Tristes Tropiques*, announced themselves as "literary." The writerly sense of *Tristes Tropiques*, importantly, arises not only out of a literary style adopted by anthropologist-author, but from the very perspective that the writer takes to his subject.

For one, Lévi-Strauss refutes the simple opposition of the form or vehicle of writing to the subject or content of culture by claiming that they share a common structure: "the material out of which language is built is of the same type as the material out of which the whole culture is built: logical relations, oppositions, and the like."[8] James Boon (1972, 3), in his pioneering *From Symbolism to Structuralism: Lévi-Strauss in a Literary Tradition*, builds from Lévi-Strauss's equation of language to culture an analysis that persuasively demonstrates the strong reciprocal relation between the French Symbolists, as artists of language, and Lévi-Strauss, as a student of culture. Boon's procedure involves showing that both Lévi-Strauss and the symbolists deal with "*texts* (with the work of others as well as their own) and with the bases (their own and others') for *constructing* significance out of the interrelated sensory units comprising those texts."

Lévi-Strauss's work, in other words, centrally concerns not the simple representation of a cultural reality but the very process by which meaning is derived in text. In this respect one could say that the subject of the book is textuality. Geertz (1988, 21) articulates this point by putting the emphasis upon the active role of writing: "*the textualiste* nature of the work, foregrounding its literariness at every

[8] James Boon quoting Lévi-Strauss in *From Symbolism to Structuralism: Lévi-Strauss in a Literary Tradition* (Oxford: Basil Blackwell, 1972), p. 33.

opportunity . . . makes it probably the most emphatically self-referring anthropological text we have, the one that absorbs the world's 'why' most shamelessly into a 'how to write.' " And yet the focus on the process of construction, of writing, is not, according to Boon (1972, 228), an abdication of responsibility or a lapse into solipsism on the part of Lévi-Strauss; rather, the emphasis upon the "how to" versus the "why" or "what" rises from a conviction that the "what" or "why" cannot definitively, finally, be known. From this perspective Lévi-Strauss, according to Boon (1972, 228), precludes "any chance for *final* results, as priority falls to the process of translating 'texts' to 'texts.' "

Tristes Tropiques, in its resistance to the duty of directly rendering the anthropological subject, represents the anthropological text that perhaps most influenced current speculation on the nature of anthropological representation. Geertz (1988, 21), again, points to Lévi-Strauss's contribution when he comments that the book's "relation to 'cultural reality' . . . is oblique, removed, and complexly tenuous"; consequently, the book "puts the established conceptions of the nature of ethnography into useful question" and readers, regardless of their opinions of the book, can hardly "come away from it without feeling at least a little bit deconstructed."

Just as Lévi-Strauss anticipated deconstructive reading, deconstructionism paved the way for White's orientation by reading language itself as ontological first mover. The resuscitation of Nietzsche's writings on metaphor was crucial in this regard. Drawing inspiration from Nietzsche's oft-quoted observation that truth is "a moving army of metaphors, metonymies and anthropomorphisms," deconstructionists sought to circumscribe experience within linguistic structures that are themselves unreliable as simple and direct referents to experience.

Paul de Man's analysis, in *Allegories of Reading*, of Nietzsche's theory of rhetoric highlights Nietzsche as a figure who foresaw the fall of the easy referentiality of language. According to de Man (1979, 106), Nietzsche's early claim that "language is rhetorical rather than representational or expressive of a referential, proper meaning" constitutes "a full reversal of the established priorities which traditionally root the authority of language in its adequation to an extralinguistic referent or meaning, rather than in the intralinguistic resource of figures." According to Nietzsche, the essentially figurative nature of language negates language's capability to mirror reality:

> No such thing as unrhetorical, "natural" language exists that could be used as a point of reference: language is itself the result of purely rhetorical

> tricks and devices. . . . Language is rhetoric, for it intends to convey a *doxa* (opinion), not an *episteme* (truth). . . . Tropes are not something that can be added or subtracted from language at will; they are its truest nature. (DeMan 1979, 105)

The application of Nietzsche's assertions to literary theory are well known; less advertised is the impact that such notions of figurality have recently exercised upon anthropology. Within anthropological circles, the recent claims on the nonrepresentational nature of writing are not *that* widespread and are certainly not widely accepted. That is in part because the current theories on the tropological essence of language have only surfaced in writing about anthropology within the past seven or eight years; indeed, it was not until 1986, with the publication of James Clifford and George Marcus's *Writing Culture,* that a collection of essays emerged to validate that there was a movement underway to question the transparency of anthropology's linguistic medium.

Now, the tropological dimensions of anthropological writing have been an issue to some degree practically since the field's inception; even when the "plain style" of the orthodox monograph was at its height in the 1930s and 1940s, a continual debate within mainstream anthropology persisted between the more literary and the more scientific modes of presentation. Margaret Mead, for example, argued against ethnography as a skill that any graduate student could be taught, and instead viewed the writing of anthropology as something that only the gifted could do: in that respect the writing of social science became equated with the composition of the literary artist. And over the years the heated battles in anthropological journals over acceptable language use (for example, the use of the "I" or the use of the passive voice) certainly served as reminders that anthropologists worked with a linguistic medium that was changeable and changing.

Nonetheless, a great number of anthropologists maintain a strong resistance to the notion that anthropological studies are anything less than reliable transmitters of anthropological data, not because they blithely assume language to be unproblematic, but because they feel that a too-persistent questioning of the medium of language threatens the very status of anthropology as a science. And in a very real sense it does just that. At the heart of anthropology as a discipline is the attempt to understand and convey truths about cultures; if one calls into question the ability to communicate those truths effectively, then the discipline as defined is in trouble. Clifford, in his introduction to *Writing Culture* (1986, 22), quite baldly states that the results of such inquiry represent an attempt "to dislodge the ground from which persons and groups securely represent others." Clifford's statement does not only mean that the vessel of representation is inadequate to hold the cultural truth; rather, Clifford and others echo Nietzsche in questioning the existence of a cultural truth removed from discursive processes.

Clifford labels the conflict over anthropological representation with a sense of urgency (manifest in the book title *The Predicament of Culture*) that is absent from Geertz's more serenely philosophic approach and tone. In his recent book, Geertz (1988, 138) asserts that the awareness of discursive boundaries, and the heavy implication of ethnocentric representation within those walls, ought not and will not cripple the discipline's willingness to persist:

> Once ethnographic texts begin to be looked *at* as well as through, once they are seen to be made, and made to persuade, those who make them have rather more to answer for. Such a situation may initially alarm, producing back-to-the-facts table thumping in the establishment and will-to-power gauntlet throwing in its adversaries. But it can, given tenacity enough and courage, be gotten used to.

The dilemma over anthropological representation has thus far centered upon the rhetorical operations of the monograph, the standard discursive form for anthropology, at least in the English-speaking world, from the early 1920s through the 1960s (indeed, the monograph is still very much in use today, but until the 1960s, its legitimacy went virtually unquestioned). The monograph, as influenced by pioneers such as Boas and Malinowski, is the product of the anthropologist-fieldworker's "writing-up" of the research results garnered while in the "field." The ethnographers constructing monographs work under some self-imposed limitations. For one, they make little use of the previous written accounts of the culture in question (such as the reports of missionaries or earlier fieldworkers), and in that respect clearly distinguish themselves from the armchair anthropologists (such as James Frazer). Also, they confine themselves to a small unit of people and to a distinct local community and take care when broadening their generalizations to a larger constituency.[9]

[9] The writers of monographs did not *always* refuse to consider other sources, such as missionaries, but in general the form tended toward the fieldwork of the anthropologist-author alone. Also, the monograph by definition is fieldwork-based, but the ethnographers considered in this book's second section often *did* compare cultures: see, for example, Mead's *The Coming of Age in Samoa* and Benedict's *Patterns of Culture*. The distinction to be made here is that the comparativism of ethnographers such as Mead and Benedict was based upon the observations of the writers "in the field," as opposed to the armchair variety.

Also, early fieldwork methods at first were tied to the evolutionary framework:

The intended effect of the monograph is that of carefully controlled observation that has led to some hard research results. And yet, at the same time, Clifford and Stocking have shown that the monograph, especially as influenced by Malinowski, depends for its success upon the personality of the ethnographer-fieldworker, whose literal presence in the field, as reflected in the monograph, bolsters the rhetorical or "ethnographic authority" of the ethnographer. That figure becomes, in effect, the hero of a saga that is self-constructed from a field experience. As Clifford points out in the seminal "On Ethnographic Authority," the "feel" that the reader gets of witnessing a fieldwork experience is in fact a carefully constructed fiction, as "the ethnographer transforms the research situation's ambiguities and diversities of meaning into an integrated portrait."[10] The monograph is of especial interest to those who analyze anthropology as text because it is the discursive form that illustrates the tension between the representational and the "fictive" most clearly; or, put another way, the monograph reveals most blatantly the anthropological "fiction" that masquerades as pure representation.

The essays that follow by Strathern, Krupat, Gordon, and Handler all deal, in one way or another, with the representational rhetoric of the monograph, the subject of this book's second section. Strathern's essay views Malinowski's monograph, in contrast to Frazer's comparativist discourse, as textual form that had called into being the modernist epoch of anthropological writing, a form of discourse that framed contexts and thus distanced writer from audience. Krupat's essay, borrowing from Hayden White, sites the anthropological writing of Franz Boas within the "ironic mode," a category of discourse characterized by an "aporitic doubt" that calls into question the ready generalizations of comparativist writing in anthropology.

Gordon in her essay contrasts Margaret Mead and Zora Neale Hurston by treating Mead's text as fundamentally centered in the rhetoric of the monograph; Hurston, on the other hand, severely deviates from the traditional ethnography by creating a consciously ethnic and multivoiced decentered text. And Handler's essay suggests how Ruth Benedict's "quest for self-expression" steered her out of the writing of poetry and into the writing of ethnography. That search for self resulted, in anthropological writing, in a text (*Patterns of Cul-*

Boas's work is a case in point. For detailed discussions of the bridge from early fieldwork to Malinowski, see George Stocking's *Race, Culture, and Evolution*, his essay "The Ethnographer's Magic: Fieldwork in British Anthropology from Tylor to Malinowski," and his recent *Victorian Anthropology*.

[10] *Representations* 1 (1983): 132. This important essay also appears in Clifford's *The Predicament of Culture: Twentieth-Century Ethnography, Literature, and Art* (Cambridge: Harvard University Press, 1988), pp. 21–54.

ture) that, in a characteristically modernist fashion, welded the individual to the whole, as the Boasian diffusionist attention to empirical detail was combined with "the study of cultural wholes." All of the above authors insist upon the essentially writerly nature of ethnography, and, similarly, treat these anthropological texts as participating in a larger aesthetic cultural movement.

The monograph rests its authority upon the actual presence of the ethnographer in the field; the comparative anthropology of Frazer's generation, on the other hand, put a high premium upon the discriminatory powers of the so-called armchair anthropologist, who culled the various field reports submitted by fieldworkers and collected from past accounts by missionaries and other informants. Frazer's text demonstrated a soon-to-be defunct positivist faith in the ability to clearly distinguish the civilized from the primitive and to subdivide that primitive into its constituent parts (those parts might represent different qualities of behavior or actually the various rungs on the evolutionary ladder). The competency to perform such classification was an exercise of the civilized imagination, the property of the learned anthropologist in the study. The very organization of the Frazerian text, into, say, various kinds of behavior or beliefs (each illustrated through scores of examples from scores of tribes and epochs) reflects the anthropologist's own confidence in his ability to integrate and unify, and, more importantly, is reflected in the reader's faith in the organizational capacities of the anthropologist.

That confidence in the armchair anthropologist soon came to be interpreted as naïveté by social scientists intent on narrowing the scope of study (from the comparative to the single culture) and improving the accuracy of fieldwork methods (although it ought to be noted that Frazer himself was quite concerned with fieldwork methods, as Stocking documents). And the criticism leveled at Frazer and his disciples did not emerge anew with Malinowski and his monograph: Andrew Lang, Franz Boas, and others were highly suspicious of Frazer's methods as early as the turn of the century. Curiously, the long decline of Frazer in anthropological circles did not diminish the interest in his methods and results among literary modernists. The obvious reason for the literary community's persistent (and, anthropologists would say, embarrassingly outdated) fascination for the Frazerian lies in the armchair anthropologist's more literary style. Myth-oriented critics of a generation ago, such as Stanley Edgar Hyman, valorized Frazer for the "artistry" that raised him above the common run of social scientists. The implication was that Frazer's work was classically timeless, regardless of the degree to which it deviated from scientific truth or indulged in ethnocentrism. On the one hand, Frazer's theory, propelled by an appropriately majestic manner, transcended the pettiness of scientific accuracy in its approximation to the pure truth of myth; on the other hand, in all-too-typical New Critical fashion, Frazer was crowned as a king of multiple meanings, the fashioner of a mighty verbal icon.[11]

The essays on Frazer that comprise the first section of this volume reflect a revival of interest in him, but for qualitatively different reasons than those that motivated critics of the 1950s and 60s. A textual viewpoint that denies the purely representational aspirations of the monograph looks with renewed curiosity at a text such as Frazer's, which aspires in its language use toward anything but the purely functional. In his Introduction to the 1966 anthology of criticism entitled *Myth and Literature*, John Vickery cites "the critical shift in the last decade or so from rhetoric to myth" (xi). That turn (then exemplified in the shift from New Criticism to Myth Criticism) has now reversed, and this subsequent shift opens up a new perspective from which to view the Frazerian canon. Vickery himself, in the essay that opens this volume, illustrates that textual turn. His essay, in its approach to Frazerian anthropology from the vantage point of genre theory, focuses decidedly on *The Golden Bough*'s textual properties. Vickery considers certain "deep generic traits" that Frazer's text inherited—not from any ur-myth or ritual, but from previous discourses—and passed on in part to modernist literature. In particular, he focuses on the rhetoric of the elegy as it surfaces in the texts of early twentieth-century anthropology and passes into the tone and attitude of modernist literary works in English.

Roth's essay within adopts the textual turn to Frazer by posing *The Golden Bough* as Derridean in its preference for writing over speech. What were interpreted after the rise of Malinowski as Frazerian excesses—in description as well as in the general comparative sweep of Frazer's text—are actually discursive conventions that make sense within an anthropology based upon the written word of the scholar versus the spoken presence of the ethnographer, the "man-in-the-field." The rejection of Frazer by the ethnographer is hardly surprising, then, considering the ethnographer's reliance upon the rhetoric of "presence" rooted in a faith in the primacy of the spoken word.

Like Roth, Strathern considers Frazer's *The Golden Bough* as a type of discourse that stands very much at odds with the later Malinowskian monograph, historical and discursive commonalities notwithstanding. The crucial break between Frazer and Malinowski was generated not so much by the differences in approach to fieldwork

[11] My essay, " 'The Tangled Bank' Revisited: Anthropological Authority in Frazer's *The Golden Bough*," in *Yale Journal of Criticism* 3 (Fall 1989): 107–26, discusses the Frazerian rhetoric that, in one of its turns, privileges literary and mythical resonance and ambiguity over cold and particularizing scientism.

(Strathern and Stocking point to important continuities between the two) but to the distinctions between two very different kinds of writing. To Strathern, the rhetorical effects of Frazer have much to do with the closeness he established between writer and reader and the consequent distance he puts between himself as author and the anthropological subject (the "savage"). Malinowski, on the other hand, typifies an anthropological modernist tendency of "framing off the intellectual exercise" of anthropology and, through this self-conscious act, "creating a distance between writer and reader."

As in Malinowski's monograph, the ethnographic experimentation in France, discussed in several of the essays in the last section of this volume, creates a "frame" that self-consciously distances reader from author and thus, in Strathern's sense, can be called "modernist." However, the differences between Anglo-American and French ethnographic writing are profound. For one, the ethnographic experimentation of 1920s France, unlike the institutionalization of the monograph in Britain, is directly affiliated with the modernist avant-garde (what Lyotard would call the truly "postmodern"). In the fieldwork and writings of Michel Leiris, Georges Bataille, Roger Caillois, and others, discussed later by Richman, we see a coalescence of surrealism and ethnography that James Clifford, in his "On Ethnographic Surrealism," defines as quintessentially modernist. That symbiosis, Clifford (1988, 117–18) states, is based upon the assumption of "the fragmentation and juxtaposition of cultural values. From its disenchanted viewpoint, stable orders of collective meaning appear to be constructed, artificial, and indeed often ideological or repressive." Drawing from Walter Benjamin, Clifford concludes that for that generation, disillusioned by the horrific absurdity of the First World War, "Reality is no longer a given, a natural, familiar environment. The self, cut off from its attachments, must discover meaning where it may" (119).

That meaning was found in the assumption that "for every local custom or truth, there was always an exotic alternative, a possible juxtaposition or incongruity" (Clifford 1988, 120). The ethnographers in question, publishing in surrealist journals, traveling on anthropological missions (such as the famous Mission Dakar-Djibouti), or assisting in the planning of ethnographic museums, were not interested in simply taming the exotic by comparison to the known, or appropriating the savage only as a parable for the modern world; rather, the ethnographic surrealist delighted in the very shock of juxtaposition, exemplified in "that moment in which the possibility of comparison exists in unmediated tension with sheer incongruity" (Clifford 1988, 146). The model for an ethnographic surrealism, then, was and still is the collage:

> Collage brings to the work (here the ethnographic text) elements that continually proclaim their foreignness to the context of presentation. . . . The cuts and sutures of the research process are left visible; there is no smoothing over or blending of the work's raw "data" into a homogeneous representation. To write ethnographies on the order of collage would be to avoid the portrayal of cultures as organic wholes, or as unified realistic worlds subject to a continuous explanatory discourse. (Clifford 1988, 146)

Here Clifford is not so much discussing the accomplishments of ethnographic surrealism, but rather projecting the possibility, first brought to light by those surrealists, of a future surrealist ethnography. In both cases, however, Clifford celebrates the rejection of realism, the jettisoning of an agenda that, in the words of Lyotard ([1979], 74) in *The Postmodern Condition*, seeks to "stabilize the referent" in the interests of perpetuating the Western scientific-industrial complex. Clifford (1988, 144–45) sees the necessary "defamiliarizing" of "cultural reality" in between-the-wars France as ultimately undermined by the growing humanist attitude, in the 1930s, that sought to familiarize and make accessible exotic cultures to the Western (in this case, French) public. The establishment of the Musée de l'Homme, in 1938, represents for Clifford (1988, 145) the victory of the humanists' "consolidation and display of a stable ethnographic knowledge" over the surrealist campaign of assaulting the comfortable, of "provoking the irruption of otherness—the unexpected." The radical ethnography of the 1920s became, in Clifford's words, an "art" that "is displayed and approved by an idealistic, confident good sense" (144).

That "good sense" is the same "communicative rationality" inherited from the Enlightenment that Habermas (1983, 8) celebrates as the hallmark of modernity. Singling out Habermas for attack, Lyotard ([1979], 74) cites that "communicative rationality" (what he calls the "communication code," as a prime vehicle of the Western industrial complex's attempt to wipe out the free play of mind associated with surrealism and other forms of aesthetic experimentation. For this reason, Lyotard posits realism as essentially conformist and thus inimical to the aims of art. Clifford (1988, 138) overtly shares this view in his discussion of French surrealism, and carries that orientation over to the British scene when he compares the ethnography that proceeded from the French Mission Dakar-Djibouti (1931–1933) to Malinowski's monograph: "Little effort is expended on a naturalistic account in the manner, say, of Malinowski's *Argonauts*. Realist effects are seldom attempted; indeed, in the wake of surrealist fragmentation, what would be the point?"

In Clifford's view, the British and American monograph represents, in contrast to French ethnographic surrealism, an overtly realist ethnography. This view is shared by Marcus and Fischer (1986, 23), who identify the monograph with the "ethnographic realism" that "seeks to represent the reality of a whole world or form of life." In fact, Marcus and Fischer see in the twentieth-century social sciences "a persistent oscillation between more realist modes of description and irony," the latter of which is characterized by its "deeply suspicious and critical nature" (14). In one important sense, the monograph and ethnographic surrealism represent the extreme poles of description and irony, respectively. And yet there are several possible hazards to such a labeling. For one, assigning the surrealist to the ironic mode tends to unquestioningly valorize surrealism and fails to point out the possible shortcomings of that movement. Webster's essay in the last section of this volume cites Benjamin and Brecht's suggestions that the surrealist framing-off of the subject tears that very subject out of social context. Webster goes on to claim that postmodern ethnography has inherited the surrealist failure to link to the social (see discussion of this essay in the introduction).

The other hazard of considering the monograph and ethnographic surrealism as descriptive and ironic phases, as described by Marcus and Fischer, is that the gap between the two cannot be seen as an oscillation, since the formations of ethnography in the two countries proceed from two almost entirely different traditions. More to the point is Strathern's assertion that the realism of the monograph is out of sync with "the anti-realism of other forms of Modernism," one of which is clearly the surrealism of which Clifford speaks. The two movements are, in Ardener's words, "out-of-phase."

Strathern's phrase "the anti-realism of other forms of Modernism" implies that there *is* a realist form of the modernist, or that realism need not be seen as simply antimodernist. In the essay within this volume, Strathern makes the significant assertion that what is "modernist" about Malinowski, as opposed to Frazer, is that bracketing of the anthropological exercise and the consequent distancing of writer from reader. Strathern's reader-response orientation enables her to pose Frazer as premodernist in his assumed oneness with his audience; Malinowski, on the other hand, is a modernist in that very distance that he creates, which itself is an admission that, in the eminently modernist sense, "frames are only frames, that concepts are culture-bound."

Strathern's position on Frazer is in response, as she states, to the synchronicity between current experiments in anthropology and the "postmodern condition" that have created a climate in which to perceive Frazer as a postmodernist. For if the monograph is out of sync with the antirealist and nontotalizing aspects of modernism, then the consciously literary and haphazardly organized text that preceded the monograph becomes highly suggestive of recent tendencies.[12] Indeed, the deliberately tropological and seemingly polyvocal prose of Frazer *do* lend themselves to a postmodern textualization. And there is the possibility that it was just such qualities that attracted the literary modernists to Frazer and did not draw them heavily toward Malinowski or Boas.

And yet Strathern hesitates to label Frazer as "postmodern" and indeed claims that the "textualists" who might be tempted to celebrate the postmodern tendencies in Frazer's text are playing a dangerous game by taking Frazer "out of context," ignoring the very real racial and ethnic abuses and misrepresentations emanating from Frazer's text. This caution on Strathern's part to label Frazer "postmodernist" addresses a question at the heart of this volume, one that will be tentatively outlined in the next section: to what extent is the application of contemporary textual theories to older social scientific texts an irresponsible playing with contexts? At what point, if any, does "play" with text cross over into a hazardous ignorance of a writer's very real placement into a power-filled social and historical nexus?

In what one could call the age of Foucault, it is impossible not to recognize that anthropology as a field, like any other, is rife with power relations. Any analysis of the workings of the discipline cannot stay on a discursive level that wholly divorces verbal play from the context of domination. Citing the work of Talal Asad, Edward Said, and others, Rabinow (1986, 251) states that it has only been within the last decade that scholars have addressed in any serious form the power relations, on the one hand, between world power structures and anthropology, and, on the other, between anthropology and its subjects. The result has been that "both the macro- and microrelations of power and discourse between anthropology and its other are at last open to inquiry. We now know some of the questions

[12] Following Hayden White in his use of Frye, several scholars have recently adopted the notion of "strategies of emplotment" in order to help explain the shift from Frazer's comparativist and Malinowski's monographic texts. In contrast to Malinowskian realism, Marcus and Fischer (1986, 13), as well as James Boon, categorize Frazer as a writer of "romance" (as opposed to, say, tragedy and comedy) in that Frazer conceives of his work as a "quest of reason battling through centuries of superstition."

worth asking and have made asking them part of the discipline's agenda."

For one, recent critics have emphasized that anthropology's involvement with issues of power is not due to occasional abuse or to a particular historical factor, such as the rise of Frazerian anthropology, the formation of the monograph, or even the institutionalization of the social science as an academic field. Rather, Johannes Fabian (1983, 1) states, "anthropology's claim to power originated at its roots. It belongs to its essence and is not a matter of accidental misuse." Fabian's important *Time and the Other: How Anthropology Makes Its Object* (1983) asserts anthropology's direct relation to domination, making the claim that within the discipline's discourse space and time, placed in the guise of "natural resources," are in fact appropriated as "ideologically construed instruments of power" (144). Fabian coins the term *chronopolitics* to explain how anthropologists have shaped time "to accommodate the schemes of a one-way history," whose purpose is to defuse the power of the "native subjects" by removing them from the present inhabited by the anthropologist (144–45). Thus, the importance of Fabian's definition of anthropology as "a science of other men in another time" (145).

Recently, a number of scholars have analyzed the relation between colonialism and the rise of anthropology. In *The Conquest of America*, Tzvetan Todorov (1982, 250) has labeled "ethnology," the early manifestation of the field of anthropology, as a direct reflector and reliable gauge of the colonial drive, "at once the child of colonialism and the proof of its death throes." Edward Said (1989, 211–12) has emphasized the field's roots in the colonialist enterprise, claiming that "it is anthropology above all that has been historically constituted and constructed in its point of origin during an ethnographic encounter between a sovereign European observer and a non-European native occupying, so to speak, a lesser status and a distant place." And José Rabasa and Mary Louise Pratt, among others, have brought to light how the discursive practices of the colonialist have carried through, in varying ways, to modern anthropology. Using the writings of a Spanish conquistador, Rabasa claims that conquest narratives constitute the earliest manifestation of anthropological domination. Comparing the Renaissance conquistador's account to modern anthropology, Rabasa holds that "conquest displays forms of colonial encounter . . . that haunts the intended good faith of ethnography."[13]

[13] "Dialogue as Conquest: Mapping Spaces for Counter-Discourse," *Cultural Critique*, p. 133. A comparatively early and important work on the subject is the collection,

Clearly the evolutionary anthropology of the turn of the century was tied to colonialist assumptions and aims. According to Fabian (1983, 147), this anthropology developed a notion of "Naturalized Time" in which primitive cultures were "assigned their slots in evolutionary schemas." This classification thereby distanced the savage from the civilized present and hence assisted in the larger schema of domination. In a more general vein, the positivistic and rationally based presuppositions of Frazer's generation were based upon a conception of the Western white man's superiority and centrality. On the one hand, Frazer eulogized the passing of the primitive as Noble Savage, as Vickery so well describes in the essay in this volume; on the other hand, in a very pragmatic sense Frazer sought ultimately to remove the savage's superstitious ways from our midst. Kurtz's injunction in *The Heart of Darkness*, "Exterminate all the brutes!" indeed is echoed in Frazer's imperative to isolate the characteristics of "primitive mentality" in order to eliminate them from Western European Culture: Frazer is, after all, a salvager of Culture, not "culture." It is in this light that Strathern in the essay within warns against divorcing Frazer's ideology from his text: the valorization of Frazer's textuality tempts one to de-emphasize or forget the ethnocentrism and imperialism that is at the root of his corpus.

With the advent of the monograph, anthropology appeared to have ceased its participation in the ethnocentric colonialist schema. Malinowski, Evans-Pritchard, and others were only too eager to disown the documentation of the biased and untrained participants in colonialism, such as missionaries and government agents of one form or the other. The man-in-the-field largely liberated himself from the evolutionary framework and instead embraced the notion of cultural relativism. His aim, contrary to Frazer's virtually racist program, was not to eliminate but to preserve the record of the native.

Recent critiques of ethnography have emphasized that although the fieldworker's methods have not been as obviously ethnocentric and dominating as those of the evolutionary anthropologist, they still have been integrally tied to Western efforts to subvert and control native populations. Fabian states that even after the fall of evolutionary anthropology, the Other has been kept in another time. According to Fabian (1983, 151–52), modern ethnography's presentation of its "object" as "seen," apprehended not through empathic listening but unidirectional observing, will always deny "coevalness to its Other." Indeed, the visual metaphor is a key vehicle through which

edited by Talal Asad, entitled *Anthropology and the Colonial Encounter* (London: Ithaca Press, 1973).

anthropologists are placed in the "here and now" and the objects of their study in the "there and then," with the result that "the existence of the 'Other'—the 'savage,' the 'primitive,' the 'under-developed' world—in the same time as ours is regularly denied" (Fabian 1983, frontispiece).

Clifford in "On Ethographic Allegory" questions the legitimacy of ethnography's claim, as exemplified especially in the monograph, that it is preserving the record of the vanishing "primitive." Clifford (1981, 112) finds suspicious the "persistent and repetitious 'disappearance' of social forms at the moment of their ethnographic representation" and feels it necessary to regard that "disappearing object" as a trope or allegory he calls "the ethnography of salvage." That allegory perpetuates the notion of ethnography as "a last-chance rescue operation" (113) whose crucial function is to preserve through inscription the values of the vanishing Other. The Other, in this case the perishing tribe, represents what the modernized individual, because of his "sense of pervasive social fragmentation," searches for: a "wholeness" that "by definition becomes a thing of the past (rural, primitive, childlike), accessible only as a fiction, grasped from a stance of incomplete involvement" (114). This is not, however, the healthily recognized fiction at the heart of any piece of inherently tropological discourse. Rather, this quite contrived fiction is wrought at the price of the presence of the Other, as Clifford emphasizes in his quoting from Raymond Williams: "the real step that has been taken is withdrawal from any full response to an existing society. Value is in the past, as a general retrospective condition" (114). The native, as it turns out, is the loser in this game; the winner is the anthropologist, whose text is valorized as the record of our impossible-to-realize pastoral-primitive desires.[14]

In the case of the monograph, that "disappearing object" provided the impetus for the establishment of an institution—that is, anthropology as a career field, becoming solidly legitimated as a social science within academe. The relation between the way anthropologists

[14] The trope of salvage resonates powerfully in ethnography done within one's own culture (the impulse to "preserve" the dying remnant of "folk" culture has been an essential chord in domestic ethnography and folklore studies since the inception of those fields); and yet the recent upsurge in doing ethnography "at home" has brought to many a greater awareness of issues of alterity and power. When the anthropological subject has become not the exotic native or even the quaint Tennessee folk balladeer, but, say, the suburban shopper, the reflexive tendency to construct an allegory that shuttles that person to the exotic margin becomes confounded. And the fact that the ethnographer is of the same culture as the subject may make the ethnographer more aware of the interpersonal liberties that the ethnographer, as a member of a sanctioned discipline, takes for granted when conducting interviews and "writing up" the results.

have written about their subjects and the political establishment of their discipline cannot be overemphasized. George Marcus claims that the rise of ethnography, the textual process resulting from the fieldwork method, must be considered primarily as an institutional phenomenon. The transition from the evolutionary text to the monograph, according to Marcus and Fischer (1986, 17–18),

> should be understood in the broader context of the professionalization of the social sciences and the humanities into specialized disciplines of the university, especially in the United States. Divisions of academic labor, specialization by discipline, the taking on of distinctive methods, analytic languages, and standards, all became the order of the day. Ambitiously generalist fields of the nineteenth century—those well established, like history, and the upstarts, like anthropology—were now mere disciplines among a multitude of others; their grand projects became the specialties of bureaucratized academia.

From this perspective, the monograph can be viewed not only as an abstracted discursive response to Frazerian anthropology but also as a vehicle for career enhancement and, on a larger scale, discipline formation. Lyotard ([1979], xxiii) refers to a science's "discourse of legitimation," through which it validates "the rules of its own game," and makes that construction appear as natural, real, true. Considering the monograph as just such a "discourse of legitimation"—and it is crucial to consider the monograph not as the *only* such discourse but one of a number—we must wonder not only to what extent the monograph was shaped by the imperatives of the desire to gain access to academic power structures, but, conversely, to what extent the formation of anthropology as a field was shaped by the monograph. Marcus and Fischer (1986, 21) believe that the form has played several very important roles in the modern anthropological profession, including as a pedagogical tool, as a writing model, and as "the initiatory activity which has launched careers and established careers and established reputations."

The essays on the monograph that comprise the second section of this volume reflect upon the instititutional ramifications of choosing to write ethnography. Gordon's essay holds that much of the success of Mead is due to the security with which she adopts the institutionally sanctioned monographic text; Hurston, on the other hand, fails to win academic and public support because her decentered text gives "mixed signals" about the institutionalization of the ethnographer's "literary authority." According to Handler, Benedict's decision to move "through biography and poetry to anthropology" was a personally motivated decision that fortunately resulted in professional success. In her case the quest for self-realization, problematic for a woman of her day, was not fulfilled through the composition of poetry. Rather, "she achieved the integral personality that she . . . sought" in the writing of ethnography, where she *could* thrive as a creative woman by achieving distance from her subject and completing a textual closure.

One could say that the recognized newness or modernity of the monograph is what ironically led to its use as a model for an orthodox or standardized form: modernity becoming orthodoxy, freshness becoming reification, the renewal of modernist (albeit realist) innovation decaying into familiar institutionalization. 1922 was a watershed year for literary modernism, but not only because of the publication of poetry and prose of high modernist experimentation (*The Waste Land*; *Ulysses*). According to Michael Levenson, literary modernism came of age in 1922 not with the literary masterworks mentioned but with the founding of Eliot's periodical *The Criterion*. That journal deserves top billing as a shaper of mature modernism, according to Levenson, "because it exemplifies the institutionalization of the movement, the accession to cultural legitimacy."[15] It is not sheer coincidence that in the same year Malinowski's *Argonauts* announced a similar "accession to cultural legitimacy" of modern anthropology, as that volume brought the monograph to its maturation and thus paved the way for anthropology's legitimacy as an academic field.

Levenson also claims that in any avant-garde movement there exists the elements of "provocation" and "consolidation": in literary modernism Levenson cites Pound's role as provocateur and Eliot's as consolidator. Although we cannot exactly refer to the monograph as a product of an avant-garde temperament, certainly both provocation and consolidation play roles in the reader's response to Malinowski's text. Marilyn Strathern's essay in this collection points to ways in which *Argonauts* not only surprised the reader in its novel form but also distanced the reader from the anthropologist-writer (unlike Frazer, who brought the reader into his ken in his distancing from the anthropological subject). As for consolidation, the rapidity with which the monograph came to seem the natural form for anthropological accounts reflects not only the skilled efforts of Malinowski and Boas, and others, to attract disciples and build power structures within the field, but also the accessible textual organization and re-

[15] *A Genealogy of Modernism: A Study of English Literary Doctrine, 1908–1922* (Cambridge: Cambridge University Press, 1984), p. 218. See also in this regard the chapter "Literature and Professionalism" in Louis Menand's *Discovering Modernism: T. S. Eliot and His Context* (Oxford: Oxford University Press, 1987), pp. 97–132.

alist form that would propel itself toward acceptance by the interested social scientist.

Handler applies Levenson's distinction between Eliot as consolidator and Pound as provocateur in his claim that "Pound is to Eliot as [Edward] Sapir is to Benedict." His elaboration upon that equation stresses the oppositional relation, active in both literature and anthropology, between the fragmentariness of provocation and the totalizing effect of consolidation: "the contrast between Pound's iconoclasm and Eliot's Catholicism is similar to that between Sapir's emphasis on the individual and Benedict's championing of culture." According to Handler, whereas "Sapir focused on the individual as a crucial locus for action, and refused to reify culture," Benedict, on the other hand, "emphasized cultural integration and the determination of individuals by culture."

Although not specifically citing Levenson, Krupat also discusses the element of provocation in anthropology. In his discussion of the "aporitic doubt," which calls into question the generalizations of comparative anthropology, Krupat resuscitates the provocation that originally operated in the texts of Franz Boas before the "accession to cultural legitimacy" (Levenson) obscured the freshness of his ethnographic form.

Although current textual approaches do look with interest at the original freshness of ethnographic form (Krupat provides an example, and Clifford's treatment of Malinowski's *Argonauts* figures prominently), those approaches nonetheless have severely challenged the monograph's reification and consolidation of power in the midcentury period. Again, the predilection of the anthropological textualist toward the rejection of faith in "good forms" helps explain that orientation: the monograph's success is harshly critiqued because such a faith flies in the face of textual theories on the unreliability of language as reflective or representative.

That faith, just as importantly, leads to what is from the textual perspective a repellant consolidation of institutional power. The assumption is that power ought to be evenly parceled out: to First and Third World citizen, male and female, anthropologist and subject alike. As in Tyler's ethnography of evocation, Clifford (1988, 51) looks forward to "a utopia of plural authorship" in which the anthropological subject is no longer controlled by the social scientist–writer but, rather, the text's authority is broken down and distributed to a plurality of speaking subjects, including that of the anthropologist. In deliberately Bakhtinian terms, Clifford calls for a finish to the "monologic author" and the promotion of the "polyphonic" text.

Critiques of this critique of power as it resides in the anthropological text were not long in coming. P. Steven Sangren (1988, 407) in

"Rhetoric and the Authority of Ethnography" has made the claim that the "rhetoric" of the textually oriented anthropological theorist (especially Clifford) "reproduces in forms more opaque and 'mystifying' than do many of the older forms it delegitimates the same strivings for hegemony, power, and authority that it attributes to the older forms." Although Edward Said (1989, 225, 210) clearly is including the work of Clifford, Marcus, and others among what he calls "some of the recent anthropological efforts critically to re-examine the notion of culture top to bottom," he also cites "Bakhtinian dialogism and heteroglossia" as one of several "fashionable theoretical correlatives" that fail to engage "the urgent situation of crisis and conflict" inhering in anthropology's relation to colonialism. In fact, Said (1989, 213–14) considers "the fetishization and relentless celebration of 'difference' and 'otherness' " as "an ominous trend" since it obscures, rather than clarifies, the connections between anthropology as a discipline and "the process of empire." Rabinow (1986, 225) in Clifford and Marcus's *Writing Culture* refers to Clifford as one of the "textual radicals" who "seek to work toward establishing relationships, to demonstrate the importance of connection and openness, to advance the possibilities of sharing and mutual understanding, while being fuzzy about power and the realities of socioeconomic constraints." And although he uses Clifford as a support for his assertion, Rabasa's (1987, 139) claim that dialogue "is but one among others of ethnographic authority" undercuts, as does Rabinow's criticism, the assumption that openness, polyvocality, and liberal accomodation of views work toward the equalization of power relations. Indeed, the belief in polyvocality neglects the possibility (as I have stated in my essay on Frazer [1989] that some texts, such as Frazer's, use openness itself as ploy, employing multiple voices in order to bolster the semblance of equality that in turn lends more authority to the author. In other words, polyvocality has to be read in a fuller context of power relations.[16]

[16] Although Renato Rosaldo's most recent book, *Culture and Truth: The Remaking of Social Analysis*, obviously has much in common with the work of Clifford, Marcus, Tyler, and others, its criticism of ethnography's seeming inability to recognize "the cultural force of emotion" (1989, 2) includes recent experimental efforts. Focusing on the actual effects of *grief* upon the subject, Rosaldo notes the failure of ethnographic methodology both past and present:

> My effort to show the force of a simple statement taken literally goes against anthropology's classic norms, which prefer to explicate culture through the gradual thickening of symbolic webs of meaning. By and large, cultural analysts use not *force* but such terms as *thick description, multivocality, polysemy, richness,* and *texture*. The notion of force, among other things, opens to question the common anthropological assumption that the greatest human import resides in the densest forest of symbols and that analytical detail, or "cultural depth," equals enhanced expla-

Rabinow underscores his point on the naïveté of "textual radicals" by contrasting Clifford's stance to Strathern's position on an "anthropological feminism." According to Strathern, the dialogical perspective of the textualists encourages the assimilation of evermore viewpoints, including that of feminism. But, according to Strathern, feminists ought not to be interested in adding to the dimension of a field such as anthropology, whose assumptions radically differ from those of the feminist community. For Strathern, the "mutual interpretation" of varying voices is hardly desirable in this context, for, as Rabinow (1986, 255) explains, "Feminism . . . proceeds from the initial and unassimilable fact of domination. The attempt to incorporate feminist understandings into an improved science of anthropology or a new rhetoric of dialogue is taken as a further act of violence."

Rabinow (1986, 256) praises Strathern for avoiding the pitfalls of the textualists in her "not losing sight of fundamental differences, power relationships, hierarchical domination" and in her avoidance of what he calls "encompassment by a paradigm of love, mutuality, and understanding in which she sees other motives and structures." Clifford (1986, 18) himself is acutely aware of the textualist's dissonant relation to feminist approaches. He feels it necessary, for example, to explain the absence in *Writing Culture* of an essay with a predominantly feminist orientation. He applauds the recognition of supposed cultural "truths" as actually gender-bound assumptions, but ultimately reads the feminist perspective as yet another extended example of "discursive partiality," what he refers to as "the contingency and historical movement of all readings." Clifford is hardly ignorant of the power relations involved—"Culture, and our views of 'it,' " he states, "are produced historically, and are actively contested"—but he does privilege the status of *discourse* over the social and sexual claims of feminists (18). The neglect of women in ethnography, for example, circles back to a universal discursive partiality that reveals itself in men as well: "If women's experience has been significantly excluded from ethnographic accounts, the recognition of this absence, and its correction in many recent studies, now highlights the fact that men's experience . . . is itself largely unstudied" (18–19).

The polemic between an approach, such as Clifford's, that circumscribes anthropological experience within the linguistic circle, and a

nation of culture, or "cultural elaboration." Do people always in fact describe most thickly what matters most to them? (2)

supposedly more political approach, like Strathern's, that emphasizes the very real power relations determining the nature of social scientific study, ought not to be interpreted as the simplistic division between those who ignore social issues and those who reject any notion of anthropology's textuality. Indeed, *The Poetics and Politics of Ethnography,* the subtitle to Clifford and Marcus's *Writing Culture,* testifies to the welding of the literary and the sociopolitical in current writing on anthropological issues. The final section of essays in this volume, entitled Anthropological Modernism: Language, Theory, and Praxis, centers broadly upon the relation between anthropology and social process as inextricably mediated through textual practice. More specifically, the varying essays together comprise a sustained discussion of the characteristically modernist (and, by extension, postmodernist) triadic relation between anthropology, literary aesthetics, and social formation.

The essays here share the contention that no anthropology is apolitical, removed from ideology and hence from the capacity to be affected by or, as crucially, to effect social formations. The question ought not to be if an anthropological text is political, but, rather, what kind of sociopolitical affiliations are tied to particular anthropological texts. Obviously, recognizing the inevitability of anthropology's social involvement does not necessarily translate into a condemnation of the field's practices. Long-overdue concerns with the social reverberations of anthropological representation hardly suggest that anthropological experiment can have no salutary effects. In this respect, Clifford, in his review of *Orientalism,* faults Said's slighting of "a sympathetic, nonreductive Orientalist tradition" and holds that Said's blanket critique does not apply to modern French Orientalist writings.[17] Clifford's departure from Said in this regard is crucial, for Said's axiomatic position that any appropriation of the Orientalist Other is oppressive and ethnocentric denies value to the claim that alternative cultural experience can inform us and that, more broadly, a genuinely fruitful relation can exist between the writings of the anthropologist and the theory and practice of cultural change.

The notion that the anthropological encounter can be used as a positive force in the reformation of the anthropologist's own culture

[17] "On *Orientalism,*" in *The Predicament of Culture,* p. 261. In "Representing the Colonized: Anthropology's Interlocutors," published in 1989, Said is responding in part to Clifford's criticism when he attempts to defend himself against the charge that *Orientalism* "expresses only desperation at the possibility of ever seriously dealing with other cultures" (Clifford 1988, 210). Essentially Said makes the claim that the book's intention was to reveal the deeply woven texture of the Orientalist perspective: a positive critique was not within the compass of the book. The essay ultimately does intimate that some fruitful relations can exist between the discourse of cultures.

is a very important facet of that complex relation between anthropology and social process. Marcus and Fischer (1986, 1) hold that the use of other cultures "as a form of cultural critique for ourselves" represents a fundamental aim of twentieth-century anthropology that has been sadly secondary in the minds of the modern student of culture. For this reason the authors assess this "lightly attended to critical function at home" as largely potential: thus their extensive discussion of anthropology as cultural critique is presented "as an exploration of possibilities for a body of work that does not fully exist yet in anthropology" (4).

The relative dearth of explicit cultural critique in modern anthropology is surprising, given the field's inherently strong attachment to social formation, to making things happen. Anthony Giddens (1984, 354) argues that "seen in terms of being filtered into the world they analyze, the practical contributions of the social sciences have been, and are, very profound indeed." We tend to see the natural sciences as more practical and materially consequential in part because of the clear gap between the materials (and methodologies) natural scientists use and the "world out there" that is affected by their experimentations: the natural scientists "can get on with the job of sifting evidence and formulating theories without interruption from the world to which the evidence and the theories refer" (Giddens 1984, 354). For the social scientists, on the other hand, the gaps between method and practical consequence are "very much less clear." Maurice Godelier believes that the very interpenetration of social scientific inquiry and the material social world results in the great potential for social change, but he isolates anthropology as the field with the greatest potential for making things happen. Godelier (1977, 28) contrasts the anthropologist's involvement with living social process to that of the historian, claiming that "the anthropologist, on the contrary, is inevitably involved and must take part in history; he must justify or criticise his own society which, for the most part, has imposed these changes."

Indeed, the field's potential for actual social change explains one of the attractions that anthropology has in interdisciplinary studies. Loriggio in the essay within comments upon how anthropology's attention to "how and why individuals act" has served as a significant attraction to literary critics seeking a more practical, worldly approach to the study of literature. And of course anthropology's general orientation toward the empirical, functional, "actual" manifestations of social change make sense of the symbiotic relation between Marxist theory and anthropology, from the emergence of those fields to their own parallel postmodern manifestations (discussed in the essay by Sullivan).

Still, involvement with the stuff of social formation does not, in the modern era, necessarily translate into ideological judgments attempting to alter one's own society. A corpus of work in the tradition of cultural critique does not yet exist, but significant strains of that cultural critique do emerge in the modernist era. Those strains become especially evident when we realize that such critiques do not always announce themselves in the form of manifestos or other explicit political statements. Rather, the call for cultural change can be embedded into the text in the form of a trope best described by Clifford as ethnographic allegory, wherein the anthropologist's text functions not only as an account of the Other but also as a parable or lesson for possible cultural change. A notable example of this allegorical dimension is Margaret Mead's "moral, practical lessons For American Society" embedded in her extremely popular *Coming of Age in Samoa*. (Clifford 1986, 103).

Michèle Richman's essay, the first in the section on anthropology and social formation, assesses the evolution of a modernist cultural movement (the Collège de Sociologie) in its own laudatory efforts to apply social scientific observation of the Other to the formation of a new society. Richman, in her treatment of Emile Durkheim's *The Elementary Forms of the Religious Life* as influence upon the College, reads the text as ethnographic allegory, as tropistic comment upon religion as an "antidote to the corrosive effects of excessive social and religious individualism on the foundations of modern social life." According to Richman, Durkheim had a profound influence upon the College's decision to form a radical intellectual community that, based upon a belief in collectivism, would attempt its own anthropological-aesthetic revision of contemporary society.[18]

The College, according to Richman, proves exemplary as a group that, as influenced by aspects of Durkheim's work, avoids the mere eulogizing of archaic cultures but instead "pushed the intellectual exercise to its next stage of critical development," in which "the sociological imagination must generate its own version of collective representations by providing intimations of what the collective life of the future—its feasts and festivals—could possibly be." Significantly, this pronounced use of social science to generate social formation operated within a collective merger of literary-aesthetic and anthropolog-

[18] Jameson in *The Political Unconscious* (1981, 70) speaks of Durkheim's capacity for cultural critique when he states that "the 'illusions' of religion [in *The Elementary Forms of the Religious Life*] were to be read as the complement of a positive social functionality."

ical backgrounds. Although some members of the College emerged from mainly social scientific backgrounds (Leiris, for example), others such as Bataille were more literary in their training; but all worked within the assumption that any fast barriers between the disciplines were inimical to the primary interest in revitalizing society. The primacy of social formation over institutional consistency can perhaps best be seen in the Declaration of the College, which insists, according to Richman, that "the potentially contagious effects of the collective representations it studies not be deflected by sociology's commitment to scientific principles."

The modernist welding of literary and anthropological orientations to effect social change was hardly limited to liberal or left-wing efforts. Ironically, the very same collectivist principles of Durkheim, as articulated in *The Elementary Forms in the Religious Life,* were trotted out in the literary and social criticism of T. S. Eliot, but in this case the contagion of the group was cited in the call for the consolidation of societal institutions. Durkheim's collective representations aided Eliot in his articulation of a model society based upon firm traditions, a group-oriented social structure that was organized around certain leaders: in "primitive" society those who led were the witch doctors and healers; in modern society Eliot's "elites" of course included the poet and the literary critic.

The capacity of Durkheim's text to be read from both leftist and rightist perspectives emphasizes the eminently interpretive nature of much modern anthropological writing on socialization. Clifford's concept of ethnographic allegory applies here in the broadest sense, as the same discursive product, once picked up by different readers, elicits fundamentally opposing responses that roll toward equally opposing efforts toward future social formation. In a quite basic semiotic sense, one could say that the collective group as anthropological concept functions as a Lacanian floating signifier, powerful in its semiotic capacity precisely because of its ability to shift from one ideological signification to another.

Unlike Richman, Francesco Loriggio in his essay focuses explicitly on the reciprocity of anthropology and literary theory, but Loriggio shares with Richman an interest in how the modernist fusion of the literary-aesthetic and the anthropological produces various interpretations of social scientific conceptions that, in turn, can result in practical changes in sociocultural formations. To borrow from Richman's terminology, Loriggio urges "the intellectual exercise to its next stage of critical development" by projecting the complex of anthropology and literary theory beyond the strictly modernist paradigm and theorizing a merger of two critical traditions, the American and the Russian. Loriggio claims that this fusion might provide a valuable approach to integrating anthropology and literary theory in the postmodern era.

Loriggio views the symbiotic relation between modernist anthropology and literary theory as rooted in the central concept of language as social *use*. It is not surprising that he focuses upon Kenneth Burke and Mikhail Bakhtin as critics who recognized the essentially anthropological connections (even origins) between language and material use, and in another sense between the literary and the socially formative. Indeed, the general appeal of anthropology for the literary critic, Loriggio claims, derives from the former's inherently social-pragmatic orientation: as opposed to philosophy, anthropology "deals with the empirical social realm." Again, this essentially materialist tendency explains the close affiliation of anthropological approaches and Marxist theory.

From the point of view of the literary theorist, an especially relevant empirical focus of anthropology is socially manifested behavior, what Loriggio refers to as the "study of ceremonies, of acts that are at once socialized and archaic in nature." Loriggio cites the important collection *The Anthropology of Experience* (Turner & Bruner 1986) as a significant contribution to a resurging, and pan-disciplinary, pragmatism. Loriggio's own emphasis on aspects of "socially manifested behavior" (such as "ritual," "ceremony," and "acts customary") resonates well with Turner and Bruner's (1986, 5) notion of what it is that an anthropology of experience interprets: "expressions," those "representations, performances, objectifications, or texts. . . . that are presented to us by the cultures we study; they are what is given in social life."

Loriggio relates anthropological notions of ritual to Kenneth Burke's conceptions of "communication and symbolic action" within literature, and in particular cites the Cambridge Hellenists as formative influences. Very much indebted to Durkheim's notions of the social origins of religion, the Cambridge Hellenist notion of civilized rituals originating in primitive group expression again illustrates the signifying power of the concept of collectivity, the capacity of the notion to move into quite various theories on social action. For a number of cultural and aesthetic critics from both the left and the right (T. S. Eliot, Northrop Frye, Christopher Caudwell, and George Thomson, to name a few), these essentially anthropological notions of ritual collectivity were fundamental in their statements on the emergence of art as a social formation. And the fact that Durkheim and the Hellenists promoted these theories of ritualized collectivity through exotic cultures was obviously useful to critics seeking Others as vessels for cultural critique.

Loriggio's transition from Burke to Bakhtin signifies an important change of emphasis from dramatic action to actual speech, what in literary terms means a shift from the theatrical to the novelistic. Bakhtin's notion, as stated by Loriggio, that "language exists concretely, as a practice, as socially marked speech" highlights the socially formative role of language and opposes the subjection of it into system. Indeed, Raymond Williams (1977, 31) views the work of Bakhtin and associates as crucial in its resistance to the "projection" of language activity into "essentially idealist and quasi-social forms." In fact, Williams identifies the freezing of language into form, as opposed to its preservation (and celebration) as a social process, as intimately tied to early modern anthropological practice: both early linguistic and anthropological study (and of course the two were often not separated) made necessary "the privileged (scientific) observer of a body of written material." But even when the student of culture encountered speech acts, the "defining situation," of the subordinate position of the colonized in relation to the colonizer-social scientist, "inevitably reduced any sense of language as actively and presently constitutive" (Williams 1977, 26).

As the initiator of the sociological method, Durkheim, in fact, is posed by Williams as partially responsible for the social scientific codification of social phenomenon into systems that can then be abstractly studied. Obviously Durkheim is not alone in this regard: much of evolutionary anthropology was responsible as well for the freezing of social process into system. But Williams finds the "objectivist sociology" of Durkheim in particular as culpable in the obstruction to understanding real communicative social process, as when he correlates Durkheim's systematization of experience to Saussure's notion of language as system versus process.

Loriggio's essay explores the anthropological roots of "socially marked speech," but also projects such notions (Bakhtinian and otherwise) into future anthropological formations: note the example of Victor Turner's anthropology of experience, that implements dialogue and dramatics in an anthropological hermeneutics that refuses "renouncing action." Robert Sullivan's essay, on the concept of the subject in the relation between Marxism and modern anthropology, explores some of the anthropological roots of the Bakhtinian semiology while at the same time anticipating a useful fusion of Marxist views on culture and postmodern anthropological theory on social formation. Just as Loriggio traced the literary interest in anthropology to the latter's essentially empirical and practical foundation, Sullivan delineates the Marxist impulse toward anthropology in the social scientist's essentially materialist conception of culture. The inspiration that Lewis Morgan's anthropological view of the history of ancient societies provided Marx is well known, as is Engel's use of both authors in the explicitly anthropological *The Origin of the Family, Private Property, and the State*. But Sullivan moves beyond early Marxist writings to the early modern anthropology of Frazer, Harrison, Tylor, and the Cambridge School, and sees in their writings on the symbolic import of ritual important correspondences to the essentially semiotic consciousness anticipated in Marx and more fully articulated in Bakhtin.

The semiotic consciousness that Sullivan explores of course includes, but is not limited to, the language as a medium that Loriggio discusses. For both the emphasis is upon the signifying practices, as apprehended by anthropology, that are inhering within a social system. The essays, then, make a simple point that is fundamental to (although contested in) this section of the volume: that anthropology's entry into the social-material realm is dependent upon interpretive practices. In this regard, then, we return to the emphasis of the volume's earlier sections upon an all-encompassing linguistic circle. And yet such a return, again, hardly contradicts the notion of the very material bases of anthropological endeavor, for Bakhtin's notion of language as social utterance precisely weds the linguistic semiotic to the material.[19] Furthermore, according to Williams and Sullivan, the notion of language as "constitutive of" society, as not *only* a simple "response" to the "pre-existent formation" of society, is formulated in the very works of Marx and Engels, as evidenced in this quotation from *The German Ideology*: "Language is as old as consciousness, language is practical consciousness, as it exists for other men, and for that reason is really beginning to exist for me personally as well; for language, like consciousness, only arises from the need, the necessity, of intercourse with other men."[20] Marx's conception of language's inherent socialness and consequent capacity for effecting social formation comes through in the work of Marxist literary critics who worked from anthropological bases. In the writings of Christopher Caudwell and George Thomson in particular we see the pervasive use of anthropological notions of collectivity in Marxist theories on literary art. Significantly, Sullivan's book on Caudwell

[19] Not all the contributors to this section of the volume would readily agree that Bakhtin's notion of language resolves the impasse between the material and the linguistic: Steven Webster's complex genealogy of postmodernist anthropology runs against the grain of a Bakhtinian synthesis.

[20] Quoted in Raymond Williams, *Marxism and Literature*, p. 29.

(1987) treats the impact of anthropological collective theory upon Caudwell's criticism and, among other things, ties Cambridge Hellenist ritualism to Caudwell's thinking on collectivity.

Caudwell's *Illusion and Reality* represents what Maynard Solomon ([1973], 305) calls "the first attempt at creating a whole theory of poetry in the light of Marx": it is hardly coincidental that Caudwell's root ideas on the practical importance of poetry as the projection of primitive group experience draws heavily from Cambridge Hellenist notions of group activity giving rise to ritual formations. According to Caudwell ([1937], 28), through alienation the poet paradoxically brings himself "more closely into communion with humanity," much as the shaman of Durkheim and Harrison's texts enters into a phantasmal that allows him to return to the real world with the power to influence the course of events within the social body.

Caudwell and Thomson's theories on the development of historical societal formations, from the ritualistic to the religious to the secular, derive directly from Cambridge Hellenist conceptions of the evolution of primitive society from ritual to religion to secularization. Solomon speaks of the fundamental sense in which Marxism represents "a search for origins" aligned to the classical evolutionary anthropology of Maine, Morgan, and Frazer, and Marx and Engel's early interest in anthropological writings indicates that orientation. And yet, according to Solomon, Marxism in its materialist orientation came to abandon the evolutionary chase and instead went on the "search for ascertainable causes." Caudwell and his disciple Thomson, according to Solomon, made the crucial turn away from "ascertainable causes" and "plunged into the sources of poetry" ([1973], 343).

This quite clear return to the rather nebulous provinces of evolutionary social science should not be interpreted, however, as a willful disengagement from serious efforts at social formation. Caudwell's ([1937], 307) theory of the nature of poetry, after all, culminates in the insight that the collective dream, the "illusion" that the poet enters into, transforms into pragmatic social change, as poetry ultimately supplies the stimulus for the workers' "need for association." In an important statement, Caudwell ([1937], 194) makes the claim, in *Illusion and Reality*, that poetic fantasy functions "as the inseparable accompaniment of action, which creates it and which it in turn anticipates and calls into being in a richer form." In Caudwell's work we see perhaps the clearest merger of thinking upon modern anthropological concepts of collectivity, theories on literary language, and the impetus toward social change.[21]

[21] Sullivan's book on Caudwell examines the implications of Caudwell's work (es-

Thomson's theories on the evolution of Greek drama, like Caudwell's ideas, are inextricably tied to social formation. Oddly, like the criticism of Eliot, Thomson's writings, most notably *Aeschylus and Athens* (1941), build upon Cambridge Hellenist theories of ancient art and ritual in an ultimate effort toward cultural critique. For example, his theory of catharsis, tied to Cambridge Hellenist beliefs in the efficacy of the collective experience, significantly insists upon not only the conservative effects of art but also the radical: the arts also act subversively, he claims, "because they promote a recurrence of the stresses which they stimulate in order to relieve."[22] Psychologists, according to Thomson, have long complied with the Aristotelian notion that art is conservative in the lulling effects of purgation; through that compliance those same psychologists have actively participated in classed society's efforts to adapt the individual to the established order. In an overt move toward social change, Thomson (1941, 383) insists that psychologists must apply their therapy "to the community as a whole," studying "the laws governing the social environment with a view to adapting it to the patients. The psycho-analyst would become a revolutionary."

Sullivan cites Thomson's writing as exemplary of the historical reciprocity between Marxism and anthropological theory. Thomson's work serves, for Sullivan, as an example of "how a Marxist approach to culture allied with anthropological theory offers a complementary explication of social formations and the subject's positions within them." And yet key to Sullivan's essay is not only that a Marxist-anthropological perspective offers a critique of culture, but that Marxist theory is synonymous with anthropology in that each field has shifted its methodological focus as a *response* to radically altering social and cultural formations. Specifically, Sullivan discusses how ethnography's response to the general postmodern crisis of representation, resulting in a postmodern ethnography, proves to be an illuminating parallel to Marxism's own emergent disciplinary response to contemporary shifts in social and cultural formations. Sullivan then uses these strong lines of similarity to project the possibilities of a new culture critique, stating that "perhaps once again we are at a juncture where the confluence of Marxist analysis and ethnographic investigation could form a fruitful alliance in a theory of cultural materialism, just as it had seemed to Marx and Engels toward the end of the nineteenth century."

pecially its anthropologically oriented stress on ritual collectivity) in the context of such thinkers as Burke, Frye, Williams, and Jameson.

[22] Quoted in Solomon's *Marxism and Art*, p. 347.

Webster's essay within also concerns the interrelation between modern materialist theory and postmodern ethnographic forms. But, unlike Sullivan, Webster finds that postmodern ethnography represents at its roots a severance of text from social theory. Webster concurs with Rabinow that postmodern anthropology is implicated in what Jameson holds to be the larger postmodern cultural tendency toward "pastiche," toward the free-floating representation of representations that, in its participation in consumer culture, ignores history and social process. Webster, alluding to Rabinow's observation on postmodernist "meta-ethnographic flattening," sees postmodern ethnography as enacting a "flattening of theory into practice" that is "characteristic of postmodern art."

Jameson finds in the surrealist avant-garde movement of the 1920s and 30s qualities that significantly anticipate, and implicate, postmodernism. For Jameson, and by extension Webster, the 30s materialist critiques of surrealism, as articulated by Benjamin, Adorno, Brecht, and Bataille, are especially telling in their pointing out of the failures of the surrealist project, shortcomings that reflect, quite importantly, on the nature and success of the postmodern movement. Brecht's claim that the objects of surrealism "do not return again from estrangement" doubles as a critique of both surrealist and postmodern efforts at escaping representation: for both, the attempt to "defamiliarize" worldly objects by recreating them effectively removes them from the practical world that, through alienation, the surrealist artists are attempting to celebrate. Webster's specific application of this materialist insight to postmodern ethnography brings to focus a telling legacy: "this integration of form and text as the simulacrum of practical life, like the historical avantgarde movements, seeks to overcome by fiat the entire material history that led first to a separation of aesthetic form, and now to the separation of social theory, from everyday practice."

Although the modernist surrealist efforts help to frame the problematic relation of postmodern anthropology to social process and materiality in general, Webster holds that the materialist critiques of that surrealism also "may offer a productive critique of these ethnographic forms." His complex reading of the main surrealist critiques leads to certain "cautions" or "lessons to postmodern ethnography," having to do with the avoidance of idealism that puts out of focus the "material constitution" of "historical processes," as well as the "fetishism of commodity form" that "confounds relations between people and the relations between things." In general Webster's lesson is that the effort of ethnographic *form* to be its own theory necessarily removes it from its own material context.

Webster's position represents a significant reversal of a current experimental ethnographic assumption that "rejects all representation as illusory." Webster implies that the postmodernist shunning of "positivist forms of representation" is just as naive and as vulnerable to historical analysis as the traditional ethnographic faith in representation that the postmodernist ethnographers themselves exposed. Indeed, Webster's skepticism toward the postmodernist aspiration that "seek[s] to be integral with, rather than represent, the social practices which are their subject" approximates the charges of naïveté leveled by postmodern ethnography at the practitioners of the orthodox ethnographic form. Perhaps Webster's insistence on the historical placement of the postmodernist enterprise can result in a more even-balanced attitude toward traditional ethnography. It is hardly advisable to posit the reactionary claim that the traditional ethnographers in their various assumptions about representation were "right all along"; and yet Webster's insistence on the naïveté of the postmodernist rejection of all representation could be said to compel a reappraisal of the form that furnished as a kind of whipping boy for those on the cutting edge of the discipline.

Although Sullivan holds that the parallel lines of anthropology and modern Marxist theory point to new hybridic possibilities for cultural critique, Webster more sanguinely points to the genetic problems of postmodern ethnography's effort to effect social formation. Webster holds to the difficulty of collapsing the social theory into the ethnographic form; tracing the lineage of postmodern ethnography again helps reveal its limitations: in this case we find the postmodernist approach to ethnography traceable, in part, to deconstructionist principles, which derive, in part, from Saussurean linguistics. And again we return to Williams's condemnation of Saussure and others who froze materiality into system. The notion, as articulated by Jameson in *The Political Unconscious* (1981, 63), that "the 'discovery' of Language is at one with its structural abstraction from concrete experience" is quite relevant here, for, according to Webster, the mutual roots of aesthetics and anthropology were obscured by Saussure, who "founded 'semiology' as a science of stable language forms distinguishable and methodologically autonomous from the changing historical content of languages."[23]

[23] Saussure, Webster insists, is but one of a number of influences upon postmodernist ethnography; in fact, Webster's analysis emphasizes Bataille and Sapir. According to Webster, "the semiological concept of *culture* entrenched by Kroeber and Kluckhohn in the 1950's" owes much more to "Sapir's linguistic structuralism through Benedict" than to Saussure. I emphasize Saussure here not because I want him represented as the sole or most important influence on postmodernist ethnography, but because I

According to Webster, postmodern ethnography's inheritance of the concept of culture as reified language system makes utterly problematic the entry of that approach into the social sphere. But of course postmodernism's capacity for cultural critique depends very much upon the choice of models articulated, and Webster's selection (which, again, extends well beyond Saussure) would certainly be contested by the postmodern ethnographers and their supporters. Stephen Tyler and James Clifford, like Loriggio, point not so much to Saussure as to Bakhtin, in an effort to articulate an ethnography that evokes voices projecting outward; according to this model, postmodern ethnography is essentially materially constitutive and socially integral.[24]

The choice of models seems a very appropriate subject upon which to end this orientation, for fundamental to this volume is the perspective that a study of modernist texts ought not be confined to synchronic, formal analyses: rather, modernism itself has to be considered diachronically, as a field that integrally relates, socially, culturally, to contemporary society. And in that respect modernist texts, anthropological and literary, function as models. But the relation of modernist text to postmodern condition does not have to be conceived as a smooth continuity; it also can be portrayed, in Jameson's words, as a "radical cultural break" between one epoch and the next. In fact, the nature of the relation is so utterly contentious simply because there are so many modernisms one must consider. After all, the traditional modernism that rebelled against the norms of late Victorian society, as articulated by Jameson, is not quite the same modernism that is founded upon a reification of language into system: the former presupposes a form of cultural critique that could still be of use; the latter practically precludes the possibility of engaging the real.

The versions of modernism in this volume all argue for the eminently interpretive, linguistic nature of anthropological texts, but they often differ radically on the capacity of those writings for positive cultural critique. More broadly, there is no handy consensus reached on the nature of the power, positive or negative, that ema-

---

believe that his example serves as an important, and, I hope illuminating, nexus connecting the essays within this last section.

[24] Webster's analysis suggests that the actual historical significance of Bakhtin upon postmodern ethnography is quite questionable (crucial to Webster's essay is the contention that the postmodern ethnographers have mystified their own origins); it is equally dubious, Webster holds, that Bakhtin would have welcomed the affiliation. I hold significant, however, the postmodern ethnographers' very pronouncement of Bakhtin as a prime influence, and the reasons for that overt gesture of affiliation.

nates from or touches upon the modernist anthropological text. But this lack of agreement hardly signals theoretical failure, for the essays within share similar concerns and often implement the same tools of analysis: those commonalities speak for a broad-based set of interpretive practices that cannot but further the thinking on relations between discourse and culture.

FRAZER: TEXTUAL REEVALUATIONS

Frazer and the Elegiac: The Modernist Connection

JOHN B. VICKERY

MODERNIST LITERATURE has a deserved reputation for being radically experimental in theme, structure, and technique. And yet the more one ponders it and its successors in the century, the more its collective voice appears to speak elegiacally, that is, in accents reflective of one of the most traditional and conventional of literary modes. Recently Peter Sacks (1985, 2) has reminded us that "the myth of the vegetation deity" is one of the elegy's central conventions all of which may be "not only aesthetically interesting forms but also the literary versions of specific social and psychological practices." Both the presence and the particular manifestations of this myth in modernist literature are in substantial measure attributable to *The Golden Bough* and related works. Such a literary impact may be regarded as either a historical accident or a consequence of particular, special, elective affinities between two kinds of texts, literary and nonliterary. Another and a more inclusive explanation—and the one I wish to pursue here—holds that the temper and form of many highly diverse, great modernist works are traceable, although obviously not always directly, as much to the nature, cultural preoccupations, and authorial voice of classical anthropology as to its subject matter and material foci.

Although my argument here is confined to Frazer, I should perhaps say that by the term *classical anthropology*, I cast a very loose net indeed, one that is able to apprehend if not to capture the likes of not only the Cambridge School—Harrison, Murray, Cornford, and Cook—but rivals such as Andrew Lang, Farnell, and Hartland, as well as thinkers of a different stripe such as Lévy-Bruhl, Malinowski, and Freud. In short, the early classical anthropologists, as their contemporaries today such as Clifford Geertz, Victor Turner, and Mary Douglas, sensed that in reading the texts and cultures at their disposal they were responding generically in the manner appropriate to their discipline at that time. As their titles alone suggest, *The Golden*

Bough, Themis, Thucydides Mythistoricus, Argonauts of the Western Pacific, and *Primitive Mentality* have more in common attitudinally, thematically, and perhaps even stylistically, with such contemporary works as *The Interpretation of Culture, Natural Symbols, Dramas, Fields, and Metaphors, The Forest of Symbols,* and *Implicit Meanings* than either group does with historically intervening studies such as *The Religion of the Kwakiutls, The Crow Indians, Culture of the Winnebago,* or *The Material Culture and Archaeology of the Marquesa Islands.*

The critical difference between the generations (and it is a far-reaching one) is that the earlier one stood on one side of a methodological watershed and the latter on the other side. Most of twentieth-century anthropology until quite recently was seriously inhibited by a mission and methodology grounded in a writing model of narrative history aspiring to the condition of empirical science but rooted in actuality in its ideological and philosophical derivatives such as empiricism, positivism (historical and logical), and scientism. The classical encyclopedism, comparative method, intuitive hypothesizing, and generic conceptualizing gave way to limited subject focus, in-depth field work, codified data accumulation, and cautiously restricted inferences. Intellectual rigor was identified with a methodology of quantifiability and terminological rigidity. Only recently has this equation been called into question by countervailing philosophical forces pressing for epistemological scrutiny both of existing disciplinary assumptions and modes of inquiry as well as of the resources and capabilities of language itself. Today, the anthropologists I have mentioned, as well as others, write once again in a humanistic mode more nearly in a manner resembling literary criticism. In doing so, they reflect the age's increasing awareness of the problematic of meaning and interpretation and hence of the duality of intellectual dispositions—toward closure, containment, and communication (predicated on an avoidance of the Cretan paradox made famous for the modern mind by Bertrand Russell) coupled with the skeptical anticipation that openness is at least a probabilistic inevitability.

In short, I would contend that, despite the restrictive model looming before them (Malinowski is the pivotal transitional figure here), the classical anthropologists saw both their immediate subject matter and its implications for their own cultural condition elegiacally. If the history of the elegy from classical to modern times reveals anything, it is the steady expansion of subject matter and diversification of voices with which that matter is expressed. From a lament for the death of a personal friend or public figure to a polyvocal ritual of accommodation and transcendence of loss in all its forms charts the affective and expressive movement from the elegy to the elegiac. In effect, this movement reflects a growing awareness that loss, ruptures in expectancies and responses, and existential discontinuities may be engendered not only by individual persons but by families, relationships, cultures, and historical ages, as well as by philosophical *topoi* such as time, self, war, and religion. One cannot help but sense a steady accrual of objects of loss, lamentation, reflective regret, and disquieted foreboding.

Coupled with this has come a multiplication of attitudinal tonalities or voices ranging from the tragic note of desolation through the pathetic expression of separation and isolation to the satiric or ludic assessment of what remains. Concomitant with these expansions of the resources of the elegy proper there has come a loosening of the formal concept of genre itself so that, as here, a form like the elegy is modulated into a discernible set of voices speaking in and through unlimited or unrestricted kinds of texts on topics possessing family resemblances. So pervasive and powerful has this interactive nexus of loss, sorrow, rage, and recognition become that one is tempted to see the period under discussion as a threnodic age par excellence in which the complexly cadenced elegiac voice speaks not simply to what has occurred but to what is to come. It was this elegiac propensity of attitude, implication, form, and style that forged the modernist connection. With it the concepts of myth, ritual, culture, and the past both historic and prehistoric gave rise to a literature of meditative self-discovery, revelation, and illumination. Modernist literary texts are strikingly, if obliquely, elegiac because their great anthropological pre-texts, such as those of Frazer, were also elegiac in form, attitude, and cultural conditioning.

It has long been understood that the mood of much of Romantic and Victorian poetry is elegiac. It is, as Potts (1967, 235) has argued, "a meditation about death and personal loss, transience, and unfortunate love." Less obvious but certainly worthy of historical consideration, as Fowler (1982, 206) has suggested, is the likelihood that the nineteenth century may have been "the most prolific of all literary periods in experimentation with genre." The term *experimentation* may be too deliberate and overdetermined to apply to Frazer. Nevertheless, his works, their tonalities and attitudes, function as controlled extensions of the modulations, displacements, and transformations of literary genres occuring in the age as a whole. The voice or voices heard in his works both generate elegiac resonances and are the occasion for elegiac reflections by those readers sensitive to textual or cultural reflexivity (or both). Imaginative writers and other individuals aware of history as their emergent immanent destiny could scarcely find the discoveries of classical anthropology other than haunting and saddening evocations of the mutability of culture, history, myth, knowledge, and, ultimately, the self.

This is not the occasion to address exhaustively the whole range of features and intonations that make up a generic elegiac attitude. Nevertheless, it is clear that a modernist form or species of such an attitude is certainly likely to involve a number of traits, which incidentally are far from mutually consistent with one another. Indeed, it would seem very likely that one of the identifying traits of modernism in general is precisely this clash of incompatibles. Out of it emerged both its ironic stance toward unreflective certitudes and its passionate pursuit of new grounds for and modes of conviction. The presence, implicitly and explicitly, of these traits in the texts of and the attitudinal reader responses to the classical anthropologists carries over into the texts and authorial attitudes of the major modernists, as well as of many of their inheritors and successors.

One of most obvious of these traits is the backward look at cultural history perceived as a sequence of receding vistas and superimpositional perspectives. In their several ways, T. S. Eliot, Ezra Pound, William Faulkner, and Ford Madox Ford all testify to the celebratory regret and the unblinking farewell such a look (or looks) arouses in the anthropopoetic mind. For Eliot in particular, as in *The Waste Land*, intertextuality is made to serve not only the ends of an interplay of literary voices sometimes polyphonic and sometimes antiphonal in character. It also functions as cultural and historical indexes of value and attitude united in their subjection to the vicissitudes of human fortune grounded as it is in temporality:

Falling towers
Jerusalem Athens Alexandria
Vienna London
Unreal

(Eliot 1952, 48)

Pound deploys many of the same techniques, but his elegiac focus is less upon the recurring loss of and struggle for religious consciousness than upon the enormous historical, cultural, and educational lacuna between *virtu* and viciousness.

While Eliot and Pound range from prehistory to the contemporary world, Faulkner and Ford foreground the cultural and historical vistas in the relative immediacy of an era and its philosophical values, which are eroding but with integrity. For Faulkner, the locus of loss is the Civil War apprehended bifocally: the Sartorises, Compsons, McCaslins, and Sutpens as they were phenomenologically apprehended by themselves and their contemporaries and as their successors came to read and construe them. The elegy of patrimony deploys myth and antimyth in order to meditate on that mystery of human consciousness that requires both as constituent elements of its sensory awareness of its past. Thus, in *Absalom, Absalom!* Quentin Compson, inheritor of an idealized heroic myth of the Confederacy, and Shrevlin McCaslin, skeptical interrogator of the South's heritage and mores, fuse as narrative explorers of an ethos that is dead but not gone:

> both thinking as one, the voice which happened to be speaking the thought only the thinking become audible, vocal; the two of them creating between them, out of the rag-tag and bob-ends of old tales and talking, people who perhaps had never existed at all anywhere, who, shadows, were shadows not of flesh and blood which had lived and died but shadows in turn of what were (to one of them at least, to Shreve) shades too, quiet as the visible murmur of their vaporizing breath. (Faulkner [1936], 303)

Ultimately this vocative identification with their prime human subjects, Henry Sutpen and Charles Bon, leads them to an ambivalent awareness of the Confederate hegemony reverberant with an elegiac mood of regret, recognition of folly, and the inevitability of both:

> They both bore it as though in deliberate flagellant exaltation of physical misery transmogrified into the spirits' travail of the two young men during that time fifty years ago, or forty-eight rather, then forty-seven and then forty-six, since it was '64 and then '65 and the starved and ragged remnant of an army having retreated across Alabama and Georgia and into Carolina, swept onward not by a victorious army behind it but rather by a mounting tide of the names of lost battles from either side—Chickamauga and Franklin, Vicksburg and Corinth and Atlanta—battles lost not alone because of superior numbers and failing ammunition and stores, but because of generals who should not have been generals, who were generals not through training in contemporary methods or aptitude for learning them, but by the divine right to say "Go there" conferred upon them by an absolute caste system; or because the generals of it never lived long enough to learn how to fight massed cautious accretionary battles, since they were already as obsolete as Richard or Roland or du Guesclin, who wore plumes and cloaks lined with scarlet at twenty-eight and thirty and thirty-two and captured warships with cavalry charges but no grain nor meat nor bullets, who would whip three separate armies in as many days and then tear down their own fences to cook meat robbed from their own smokehouses, who on one night and with a handful of men would gallantly set fire to and destroy a million dollar garrison of enemy supplies

and on the next night be discovered by a neighbor in bed with his wife and be shot to death. (345–46)

In Ford's case, as *Parade's End* persuasively shows, the backward glance is foreshortened dramatically so that the past is in the process of emerging from a dramatic present. Christopher Tietjens is an anachronism becoming aware of itself as such. In the process the world of which he is the recursive consequence is defined at the precise historical moment when it functionally disappears as a social reality. Religion, class, education, region, and political conviction combine and conspire to generate a pathos that arises out of the diminishment and dissolution of a clear moral and intellectual code by a rising tide of cultural barbarism, vulgarity, and hypocrisy that is then projected as the present ever since.

A second trait, closely linked to the first and often mistakenly identified or equated with it, is the identification of a prior time of such diversified cultural or intellectual or moral or aesthetic superiority as to warrant the mythic label of "Golden Age." The prime exemplar of this, of course, is Ezra Pound. He employs the backward glance as a way of locating those civilizations and eras that possess educational and pedagogical potential for the century and culture(s) in which he lived. The greatest concentration of Golden Ages rendered longitudinally through the text is undeniably in the *Cantos*. Yet it is important to note how early and how extensive was Pound's attraction to the ideality of an earlier elsewhere. There are signs of it in *Canzoni* (1911) and *Ripostes* (1912). By *Cathay* (1915) and *Lustra* (1916) it is a fully established geocultural *figura* that functions emblematically as well as heuristically and ironically, that is to say, educatively in Pound's sense of that often misunderstood term. What poems like "The Tree," "Apparuit," and "The River Song" render iconically and imagistically, the *Cantos* develop historically and cross-culturally.

Kung's apothegms on order in Canto XIII ([1948], 63) embody not only useful knowledge and practical wisdom but also an absence of reliance on any human condition entailing futurity:

If a man have not order within him
He can not spread order about him;
And if a man have not order within him
His family will not act with due order;
And if the prince have not order within him
He can not put order in his dominions.
And Kung gave the words "order"
and "brotherly deference"
And said nothing of the "life after death."

In addition, they gain both a plangency and an intensification of their temporal remoteness and cultural unavailability when seen in varied and attitudinally diversified contexts. The apothegms resonate with the futility of desire when read against the scabrous invective concerning his own cultural inheritance leveled in the cantos immediately following as well as the more philosophical judgment on the consequences of usury for civilization rendered in Canto XLV. Pound's furious and persistent ransacking of European, English, and American history to locate nodes of cultural ideality and achievement represents the importation of context into text. With it occurs the generation of a bitter satiric contrast between states of being and nonbeing that forms the structuring carapace without which the elegiac voice would be unable to sustain its stoical threnody. The burden of this oblique lament is developed through the isolate poet's voice affirming the occurrence of achievements of Golden Ages by grammatically negating their functional antithesis, usury, as in Cantos XLV and LI ([1948], 239, 261):

> With usura hath no man a house of good stone
> each block cut smooth and well fitting
> that design might cover their face,
> with usura
> hath no man a painted paradise on his church wall
>
> With usury has no man a good house
> made of stone, no paradise on his church wall
>
> Neither Ambrogio Praedis nor Angelico
> had their skill by usura
> Nor St Trophime its cloisters;
> Nor St Hilaire its proportion.

The greater the geohistorical distance between voice and age and the greater the communicative static, the greater the weight of the loss and the poignancy of the elegiac voice.

A more extended version of this disparity between the ideal harmony between nature and culture occurs with the third trait of the modern elegiac voice. It is the conviction—sometimes an assertion, sometimes merely an obliquely voiced hope—that at some point human society existed in a condition of ideal and archetypal simplicity that was essentially primeval as well as paradigmatic. This represents a secularization of the notion of a prelapsarian ideality and the human struggle to regain it. As such, it is a dominant and shaping factor in the work of D. H. Lawrence, both by virtue of the immediacy of its appeal and the ambiguities of its reality. A striking perspective on this trait is provided by the late Erwin Panofsky's essay on Poussin and the elegiac tradition in which he charts the rationale for the misreading of "et in Arcadia ego" (1957, chapter 7). In a curious but illuminating sense, Lawrence reverses the historical trajectory described by Panofsky. His psychologically initial predisposition is to see man's original state as "a golden age of plenty, innocence and happiness" (1957, 297). Only on closer speculation mixed with examination of other cultures such as the American Indian and the Mexican does this view yield to the apprehension that man's origins represented "an almost subhuman existence full of terrible hardships and devoid of all comforts" (1957, 297).

Works such as *The Plumed Serpent, Mornings in Mexico, Etruscan Places, Sea and Sardinia,* "The Princess," "The Woman Who Rode Away," "St. Mawr," and "The Man Who Died" render in full dialectical complexity this duality of desire and reality. Lawrence's writing aspires to a primitive and basic life that is essentially "civilized life purged of its vices" (Panofsky 1957, 297). But his subsequent experientially-grounded recognition is that such existent approximations as he could examine and such records as he could assess constitute "a civilized life stripped of its virtues" (1957, 297). What gives particular poignancy to novels such as *The Rainbow, Women In Love,* and *Lady Chatterly's Lover* is not simply the precarious and catastrophic interpersonal relationships of the characters. Even more it is the sense, similar in many ways to that of Ford, that the extant civilization that is the ground of dramatic action is profoundly degenerative and disintegrative.

As a result of this basic conviction, Lawrence conceptualizes a desire for a prehistorical cultural ideality so as to root in alterior temporality the possibility of a renaissance of humanity. The quest to regain or restore such an ideality is both imaginative and actual as Quetzacoatl, Rananim, and Taos illustrate. In each instance, however, Lawrence is forced to take the Arcadian harmony of nature and culture projected on the past as a trope of regret for unfulfilled but unquenched desire. The postulate of historical actuality is modulated into one of imaginative potentiality without ever being discarded as actuality. What was becomes what could have been, which then becomes what can be. And in that open-ended pleasure of his texts as the locus of ideality, Lawrence voices his elegiac recognition of fissure as fate. The loss he laments is the gap between ideality and reality, the absence of cultural ideality as historical actuality, not its primeval existence and historical disappearance.

The modernist elegiac attitude is also shaped by another attitude. This one uses both the recent past and the whole historical vista of human culture as an index to its phenomenological difference from the present of the twentieth century. Here, the great modernist exemplar is Joyce, although in their individual ways both Lawrence and Thomas Mann resonate with the same disquiet. All of Joyce's prose works are dominated by the perception that the present is compounded of greater historical mass, sociological density, and empirical detail than any available form or manifestation of the past. In many ways, this perception is modernism's formal inheritance from European and American naturalism / realism, from Zola, Dreiser, and Norris. Where the genius of Joyce, and the modernists in general, comes into play is in the ability to use this perception as the grounds for and condition of generating a greater or lesser measure of spiritual disquiet and uncertainty concerning the individual's specific place and role in such a temporal condition, cosmos, and society.

In *Dubliners,* the focus is on the incertitudes of personal identity and the deceptions and defense mechanisms these arouse when perceived or felt in a present virtually devoid of an experienced past more than generational in scope. *A Portrait of the Artist as a Young Man* and *Ulysses* shift the explicit imbalance between social multiplicity, facticity, and experiential density and the miniscule individual self and its capability for definition. They develop an implicit elegy for the individual through the deployment of narrative memory or recollection, protagonists' historical awareness, and encyclopedic allusions. Stephen and Bloom, for instance, engage in concentrated efforts to learn / establish their identities. Their efforts betray an all-consuming obsessiveness in reaching out to their differing yet overlapping cultural pasts. In so doing, they serve to point up through personal contrast and temporal disparity a transpersonal sense of regret, loss, and memorialization at man's lot in being consigned to forever live in, although not wholly of, the present. When Bloom enters Molly's bed, the fallibility of the conviction of the individual's autonomy and the muted recognition of the tranquility attendant upon "all passion spent" are captured with an economy of power directly related to the prodigality of narrative concern evinced earlier in the novel. There Joyce catechistically presents the elegiac resolution of sexual fidelity in a manner that is not only by but through Bloom:

> If he had smiled, why would he have smiled?
> To reflect that each one who enters imagines himself to be the first to enter whereas he is always the last term of a preceding series even if the first term of a succeeding one, each imagining himself to be first, last, only and

alone, whereas he is neither first nor last nor only nor alone in a series originating in and repeated to infinity. ([1922], 731)

In *Finnegans Wake*, the inundation of the self by an inescapable present compounded of a knowledge explosion (inherited, as many, including Morse Peckham in *Beyond the Tragic Vision*, have indicated, from the nineteenth century) and exponential urban and numerical multiplication is complete. The concept of one text, one language is replaced by multiple languages and multiple subtexts. These, however, are neither variants nor alternative translations of each other because the epistemological ground of interpretation itself has been radically altered. William James's sensory "buzzing, blooming confusion" has been conceptualized as an overload of intellectual storing and processing capabilities. In *Finnegans Wake* this results in the dissolution of the Cartesian subject-object relation and the concomitant self-other dichotomy. Instead of construing the self as an entity either circumscribed or circumscribable, Joyce here regards it as a process of consciousness-of-consciousness. In this process the polarization of past and present is dissolved into a spectrum of phenomenological temporality contingent upon narrativity. In short, Humphrey Chimpden Earwicker is Here Comes Everyone is Human Condition Everywhere. The poignancy of the imperiled self in *Ulysses* is underscored by the inescapable historical myopia that makes the past smaller, simpler, and clearer. This is replaced in *Finnegans Wake* by the poignancy of human consciousness forever committed and limited to itself and its act of awareness, which, however diversified and multiplex, is simply that. Both works subtly tease out the relationships between comedy and elegy—the one, through the ludic dimensions of obsessive identity quests, the other, through the comic prospect of unending and unendable narrativity—in which the arabesques of freedom and triumph are wrought upon the ground or backdrop of necessity and defeat. In so doing, they bracket the very questions of philosophical answers and positions in enacting linguistic attitudes of existential unconditionality.

The history of the elegy, at least in English, calls attention, as Spenser and Wordsworth compellingly demonstrate, to the form's predisposition for philosophical reflection on the products and prospects of human culture. With the knowledge explosion, intensified urbanization, and a deepening preoccupation with the fate of the self, this predisposition assumes a more problematic cast. The elegiac inflection of the modernist consciousness sounds a recognition, half-congratulatory and half-apprehensive, that mankind, at present at least, possesses by whatever means the requisite measure of leisure to allow for reflection and introspection and their imaginative registering. Thus, in *The Years,* Virginia Woolf's characters demonstrate the relevance of leisure to elegiac cultural contemplation. But they also dramatize their and their age's largely unwitting participation in cultural decline and loss. They continue to contemplate and comment on individual and institutional absences and transformations as elegiac witnesses memorializing the drift of both into an imperceptibly but steadily receding past. At the same time, they try to presage an auspicious and emancipatory future that they do not and will not understand and of which they cannot be a part.

The authorial voice alone conveys the full consciousness of both actions in a descriptive and narrative subtext that casts nature as perdurable and culture as transitory in such a manner that the elegists are themselves elegized. The ineluctability of temporality conditions the novel from the opening: "Slowly wheeling, like the rays of a searchlight, the days, the weeks, the years passed one after another across the sky" (Woolf [1937], 2). At its conclusion, all persons have been changed utterly and a terrible beauty born. Its power lies in its engendering in the survivors the deceptive illusion, perceived as such only by the authorial reader, that nothing has altered: "The sun had risen, and the sky above the houses wore an air of extraordinary beauty, simplicity, and peace" ([1937], 469). Yet, as the book's title and subheadings—from "1880" to "Present Day"—recurringly lament, time and temporality are altering, and not for the better, the world human beings inhabit.

Confronted with an imperfect past, an inscrutable and problematic present, and a disappearing self, the modernist sensibility could easily have retreated. It could have withdrawn into a self-pitying cultivation of its tragically historical uniqueness or into a solipsistic imaginative denial of the contemporary realities it had so arduously discovered. To its credit it did neither, although ideologically blinkered successors have on more than one occasion mounted such assertions. Instead, as the later W. H. Auden best demonstrates, it set itself to forge a bifocal vision of man's fate. Collectively, it expressed the vanity of all cultures' achievements in the face of inevitable oblivion but coupled this with the impulse to lament that otherwise unattended "long decay" (the phrase is Spenser's) and necrology of other persons, places, and things. For instance, *The Sea and the Mirror* has Caliban conclude: "it is just here, among the ruins and the bones, that we may rejoice in the perfected Work which is not ours" (Auden 1968, 250). And against that postulated spiritual ideality Ariel replies with the foreknowledge of "what we shall become," namely, "One evaporating sigh" (1968, 252). Clio, the Muse of history, is found to be one who each time "had nothing to say" because engaged in "defending with silence / Some world of [her] beholding" (1966, 309).

Here the elegiac voice of modernism faces human imperfection and the inscrutability of time and history and, in so doing, it deepens from the traditional mourning of the metaphorically elaborated protagonist and the conventional railing against a multifarious but triumphantly antagonistic fate. The focus falls on erring, fallible, mortal creatures who are memorialized and mourned for maintaining their individual human capabilities and their faith, hope, blind conviction, and determination to persist in their work, seen as *the* quintessentially human occupation or task. Thus, Voltaire continues to write because "all over Europe stood the horrible nurses / Itching to boil their children" (Auden 1966, 145). Yeats's silliness does not prevent him from persuading "us to rejoice" or teaching "the free man how to praise" (Auden 1966, 143).

The elegiac voice is given over to quietly celebrating those who, like Freud and Henry James, work within the parameters of human activity as if limits, conditions, and restrictions did not exist either behaviorally or temporally. In tonality and intensity, this voice drops to a minimalism of expectancy couched in a contemporary equivalent of the middle style: "though one cannot always / Remember exactly why one has been happy, / There is no forgetting that one was" (Auden 1966, 341). In the very act of acceptance there still sounds the note of received sorrow. It functions as the ground bass of the elegiac uttered in the primary and essential isolation of the human condition: "The dripping mill-wheel is again turning; / Among the leaves the small birds sing: / *In solitude, for company*" (Auden 1966, 338). Such a *topos* brings the elegiac impulse full circle historically by capturing in a manner both self-aware and self-critical its recapitulation of the late medieval "ubi sunt," Spenser's haunting phrase "the ruins of time," and the Vergilian "lacrimae rerum."

On turning to Frazer, we find that his corpus repeatedly either documents such an attitude or creates the conditions for the attitude's emergence in the minds and reflections of his readers including the contemporary ones. We are all familiar with the opening of *The Golden Bough* and its evocation of the pastoral beauty of Lake Nemi, the ancient religious shrine and sanctuary of the goddess Diana, on the shore of which the isolated priest-killer enacted his bloody ritual of survival. Its nexus of beauty, worship, and death resonates with a powerful thematic interplay of concerns first felt by the Romantics and Aesthetes but which speak even more directly to a post-Freudian audience than it did to Frazer's original readers.

The very power of this nexus may obscure Frazer's equally strong concern to locate this scene of romance—gentle and pious pilgrims disquieted by "that stern and sinister figure," a "belated wayfarer" on a wild autumn night surrounded by thickly falling dead leaves, swirling winds, and a "lowering and stormy sky"—in a reader response context of cultural elegy (Frazer 1911, 1:9). Thus, Nemi is seen explicitly as "an image of what Italy had been in the far-off days," as "a type or miniature of the past" (1911, 1:9). The priesthood of Diana "seems to transport us at once from civilization to savagery," an action that bespeaks simultaneously the stark simplicity of past society and the Golden Age transferred, with conscious overdetermination, to the present where "recent researches into the early history of man have revealed the essential similarity . . . under many superficial differences, [of] the human mind" (1911, 1:8, 10).

In this chapter, as in *The Golden Bough* as a whole, the backward look dominates as a decentered series continually being essayed and refocused. We see the mythic origins of the ritual with Orestes and his flight to Italy, the modification therein of the Tauric Diana's ritual sacrifice of all strangers, the post-Virgilian identification of the sanctuary's tree with Aeneas's Golden Bough, Caligula's short and easy way with the priesthood, and the Catholic Church's conversion of Diana's festival to that of the Assumption of the Blessed Virgin. Such a compressed or micro-backward look is presented with a narrative quasi-discontinuity and serial disruptiveness that adumbrates the modernist contrapuntal mergings and fissurings of the instances of myth and history found in Eliot, Pound, and Joyce.

Similarly, Frazer's ostensible rational conviction of mankind's intellectual progress from magic to science and from superstitious folly to demonstrable truth invests his text with a presumptive aura of being itself a Golden Age product. At the same time, his method and materials undercut any imputation that the human mind's millennium is at hand. The result, as in Lawrence and Woolf, is an ironic incongruity of attainment or achievement and failure or error, which functions as a formal displacement of the traditional elegy's core of untimely loss and bereavement.

His early twentieth-century readers found, particularly in the third edition, two contradictory impulses or insights that could not help but beget an elegiac attitude to match his own. On the one hand, the pages of *The Golden Bough*, like those of the *Cantos* and *Ulysses*, testify remorselessly to the knowledge explosion of the nineteenth century and its increasing density of facticity as well as diversity of forms and kinds of knowledge. Footnotes are peppered with references to classical texts, treatises on comparative religion, classical subjects and authors, records of folklore, reports and memoirs from ethnographers, civil servants, and military personnel, travel accounts, and modern histories, to mention only the most frequent citations. They are also cast in several modern and ancient languages and refer to a welter of civilizations, societies, and ethnic configurations. As a result, they make of this explosion a ceaseless tattoo of documentation that compels assent if only through thwarting refutation by the sheer weight and diversity of authority.

On the other hand, time and again, the presumed knowledge of other eras is found spurious or contradictory. After carefully enumerating them, Frazer concludes that "the stories told to account for Diana's worship at Nemi are unhistorical" or sees the contradictory imputation of the founding of her Nemi worship to Orestes or Hippolytus as "shewing that the true origin was lost in the mists of fabulous antiquity" (1911, 1:21, 22). In these formulations, denials, and admissions of bafflement and inaccessibility lies the paradigm of the stories, rumors, and counterstories that surround such diverse modernist protagonists as HCE, Thomas Sutpen, and Christopher Tietjeans. The thoughtful reader could not help but feel a kind of epistemological claustrophobia emanating from the mass of facts and competing details coupled with a sense of individual diminishment and loss of psychic control or spiritual authority. In a word, the presence of records produced an absence of self as much for the reader of *The Golden Bough* as for the reader of *Ulysses*.

This sense of an enormously complex present with but a highly problematic place for the individual self is intensified even further when Frazer suggests, as he does in the Preface to the third edition, that the entirety of his volumes may ultimately be guilty of "reducing the vast, nay inconceivable complexity of nature and history to a delusive appearance of theoretical simplicity" (1911, 1:x). The same note is sounded on a broader intellectual front in the Introduction to *The Worship of Nature*. There this penchant for reductionism by explanation is held to be endemic to the human condition: "The mind of man refuses to acquiesce in the phenomena of sense. By an instinctive, an irresistible impulse it is driven to seek for something beyond, something which it assumes to be more real and abiding than the shifting phantasmagoria of this sensible world. This search and this assumption are not peculiar to philosophers; they are shared in varying degrees by every man and woman born into the world."[1]

[1] Sir James G. Frazer, *The Worship of Nature* (London: Macmillan, 1926), p. 1. The opening pages of this volume are of great interest to an understanding of Frazer's characteristic rhetorical and logical strategies in situating the elegiac at the point where disappointment and hope fuse. It is no accident that two of his key references should prove to be Bertrand Russell and Tennyson.

Indeed, it is worth noting that Frazer's prefaces, introductions, and opening remarks often work in dual ways to effect a counterpoise of tranquility and disquiet, which is the cornerstone of the elegiac temper. They strive to establish a detached, contemplative view of the *copia* he presents subsequently. At the same time, they implicitly interrogate the material to be presented and the possibilities of its ultimate interpretability with a view to suggesting the inescapable end to individual contemplation to which the material itself testifies. So seen, *The Golden Bough,* like much of Lawrence, controverts the possibility of a present Golden Age in favor of a multiplicity of past ages imaginatively cohering into that paradigmatic age dedicated to celebrating the metamyth of the dying and reviving god. Perfection is found to inhere, so far as it does, in simplicity of structure and process in which the individual self can authenticate its reality and existence through the role of worshiper.

Concomitantly, the differential complexity of the Frazerian present obscures structure and foreshortens process to redundancy while threatening to reduce the self to nothing more than an information receptacle. Thus, although much of *The Golden Bough* endeavors to strike a dominant chord of rationalist confidence in the future eradication of superstition and religious faith, a ground bass of incertitude continually sounds as to the warrant for such a conviction. In short, even to early twentieth-century readers, Frazer already was part of a past to be elegized for its simplicity, certitude, and confidence. Such an elegiac lament for lost security of outlook could only intensify in poignancy when set against the futility and anarchy identified by Eliot as already becoming the present.

The very encyclopedic nature of *The Golden Bough* (as well as of many other works of the classical anthropologists) testified to the existence of leisure for both its author and readers. Yet, in the main, the opportunities for self-reflection and introspection were initially diminished in the face of the narrative impulse to move through the text. But elsewhere, Frazer afforded ample demonstration of and opportunity for self-reflection and introspection. In an essay published shortly after the third edition of *The Golden Bough* began to appear, he provides a stunning instance of how a collection "of examples of two radically different views" of human origins functions both dramatically as a meditative reflection on the very idea of humankind's creation and also narratively as a geocultural comparative redaction of human cosmogonies seen in a bipolar theoretical mode (Frazer 1935, 34).

The first two paragraphs of "Creation and Evolution in Primitive Cosmogonies" develop a richly complex structure of tonalities and attitudinal dispositions, as do certain passages in "Gibbon at Lausanne" and "Condorcet on the Human Mind." These structures are dominated by fond regret for the futility of human labor and knowledge in the face of the transitoriness, mortality, and incertitude that envelops all such efforts. This provides a perspective on the narrative catalog that follows in the essay that is clearly culturally and, by implication, personally elegiac and reflective:

> On a bright day in late autumn a good many years ago I had ascended the hill of Panopeus in Phocis to examine the ancient Greek fortifications which crest its brow. It was the first of November, but the weather was very hot; and when my work among the ruins was done, I was glad to rest under the shade of a clump of fine holly-oaks, to inhale the sweet refreshing perfume of the wild thyme which scented all the air, and to enjoy the distant prospects, rich in natural beauty, rich too in memories of the legendary and historic past. To the South the finely cut peak of Helicon peered over the low intervening hills. In the west loomed the mighty mass of Parnassus, its middle slopes darkened by pinewoods like shadows of clouds brooding on the mountain-side; while at its skirts nestled the ivy-mantled walls of Daulis overhanging the deep glen, whose romantic beauty accords so well with the loves and sorrows of Procne and Philomela, which Greek tradition associated with the spot. Northwards, across the broad plain to which the hill of Panopeus descends, steep and bare, the eye rested on the gap in the hills through which the Cephissus winds his tortuous way to flow under grey willows, at the foot of barren stony hills, till his turbid waters lose themselves, no longer in the vast reedy swamps of the now vanished Copaic Lake, but in the darkness of a cavern in the limestone rock. Eastward, clinging to the slopes of the bleak range of which the hill of Panopeus forms part, were the ruins of Chaeronea, the birthplace of Plutarch; and out there in the plain was fought the disastrous battle which laid Greece at the feet of Macedonia. There, too, in a later age East and West met in deadly conflict, when the Roman armies under Sulla defeated the Asiatic hosts of Mithridates. Such was the landscape spread out before me on one of those farewell autumn days of almost pathetic splendour, when the departing summer seems to linger fondly, as if loth to resign to winter the enchanted mountains of Greece. Next day the scene had changed: summer was gone. A grey November mist hung low on the hills which only yesterday had shone resplendent in the sun, and under its melancholy curtain the dead flat of the Chaeronean plain, a wide treeless expanse shut in by desolate slopes, wore an aspect of chilly sadness befitting the battlefield where a nation's freedom was lost.
>
> But crowded as the prospect from Panopeus is with memories of the past, the place itself, now so still and deserted, was once the scene of an

> event even more ancient and memorable. For here, they say, the sage Prometheus created our first parents by fashioning them, like a potter, out of clay. The very spot where he did so can still be seen. It is a forlorn little glen, or rather hollow, behind the hill of Panopeus, below the ruined but still stately walls and towers which crown the grey rocks of the summit. The glen, when I visited it that hot day after the long drought of summer, was quite dry; no water trickled down its bushy sides, but in the bottom I found a reddish crumbling earth, a relic perhaps of the clay out of which the potter Prometheus moulded the Greek Adam and Eve. In a volume dedicated to the honour of one who has done more than any other in modern times to shape the ideas of mankind as to their origin, it may not be out of place to recall this crude Greek notion of the creation of the human race, and to compare or contrast it with other rudimentary speculations of primitive peoples on the same subject, if only for the sake of marking the interval which divides the childhood from the maturity of science. (Frazer 1935, 35)

First-person narration, scenic focus on a combination of "natural beauty" and elegiac "chilly sadness" of "farewell autumn days of almost pathetic splendour," natural symbols of primeval events and stories, deft invocations of "memories of the legendary and historic past" in which myth (Procne and Philomela, Prometheus, Adam and Eve) and history (Greece versus Macedonia and Rome versus Asia) allusively commingle in the motifs of sorrow and loss. All are utilized to afford an individual vantage point from which to contemplate the persistence, duplicative mirroring, and factual dubiety of human efforts to explain, through narrative, its origins whether unique or developmental.

Even in the relatively brief scope of the essay form, Frazer's account is implicitly redolent with an all-too-mournful sense of misplaced effort, imaginative paucity, and undemonstrability. This sense looks forward to the rendered ironies, shared regrets, and mourning recognitions of modernist, and indeed modern, literature. Both this sense and this attitude are given yet greater depth and pervasiveness in the conclusion. There, Frazer offers his premodernist version of the resolution and consolation of the traditional elegy. He mediates between *Genesis* and *The Origin of Species* in a manner that extends only irresolution, inconclusiveness, and uncertainty as a solace to both partisans and the perplexed alike: "it might perhaps be found, when the scales were finally trimmed, that the balance hung very even between creation and evolution" (1935, 34).

Out of that irresolution, inconclusiveness, and uncertainty stems the attendant pathos that classical anthropology felt for human history and the individual self seeking to comprehend it as the shadows of mortality lengthened. In its richly detailed pages, modernist writers found a polyphonic elegiac voice capable of addressing the losses not only of persons and relationships but of institutions such as the family, whole eras, societies, and cultures, and concepts such as futurity, psychic identity, and religious faith. In doing so, texts as profoundly diverse as Eliot's *La Figlia*, Pound's "Ione, Dead the Long Year," Stevens's "To an Old Philosopher in Rome," Woolf's *The Years*, Hemingway's *The Sun Also Rises*, Fitzgerald's "Babylon Revisited," Ford's *Parade's End*, Sitwell's "Elegy on Dead Fashion," and Auden's memorial poems for Yeats, Toller, Freud, and James left a profound legacy to their successors. That it has been neither squandered nor forgotten is testified to by works such as Olson's "The Death of Europe," Duncan's "An African Elegy," and the elegiac sequences of George Barker, Geoffrey Hill, and John Berryman. Indeed, perhaps the most compelling memorial to *The Golden Bough* and classical anthropology by the atomic and deconstructive era of postmodernism is found in the epigrammatic brevity of W. S. Merwin's single line "Elegy": "Who would I show it to" (1970, 137).

Sir James Frazer's *The Golden Bough*: A Reading Lesson

MARTY ROTH

READING James Frazer's *Golden Bough* as an imaginary construction is made easier by the fact that the *Golden Bough* has long been invalidated as a work of anthropology. Frazer has been made the subject of anthropological "contempt and ridicule . . . abhorrence and denunciation"—his own estimate of the only acknowledgment that a "savage forefather" is likely to get from a modern (Frazer [1922], 307). This intention is further accommodated by the opening of the work itself, which is characterized, first, by particularly "fine" writing—a sudden access of *style*; second, by the display of a work of fine art, a painting that bears an imaginary scene: "Who does not know Turner's picture of the Golden Bough?"; and third, by metaphors of a fictive nature involving sailing or voyaging.

Behind all these signs of the imaginary there is a figured scene, a fiction of blockage or trauma like the opening of that comparable voyage in Dante's *Commedia*. A stunning enigma from the past teases the twelve volumes of the *Golden Bough* into writing, and the detour that it instigates, like Dante's detour, will be as vast as geography itself: a voyage of discovery that "will be long and laborious, but may possess something of the interest and charm of a voyage . . . in which we shall visit many strange foreign lands. . . . The wind is in the shrouds: we shake out our sails to it, and leave the coast of Italy behind us for a time" (Frazer [1922], 10).

As the fiction of the opening, let me suggest that Frazer had already embarked on a contrary venture, a walking trip in Italy, for example. This also was a journey into the past, but a safe and glorious past that supported an exalted sense of the endeavors and accomplishments of "Western culture." Frazer had visited Augustan Rome and basked in the sunlight of its high civilization. A few days later, however, he traveled sixteen miles southeast of Rome to visit a grove consecrated to Diana, and there he caught a glimpse of a "stern and sinister figure" that arrested and paralyzed him: "the sight of him might well seem to darken the fair landscape, as when a cloud suddenly blots the sun on a bright day." This grim figure prowls with a drawn sword in hand peering warily about him. He is "a priest and a murderer; and the man for whom he looked was sooner or later to murder him" ([1922], 2,1).

Sixteen miles of continuous space separate Rome and the grove at Nemi, but the conjunction is an impossible one: the two events cannot be connected or assimilated with each other. Rome is sunlight and high civilization; the grove is darkness, tangle, savagery and murder.[1] Frazer has had an experience of radical absurdity; he has stumbled upon a clue to a shocking crime both within the past and within the construction of culture. The "strange rule of this priesthood has no parallel in classical antiquity and cannot be explained from it" ([1922], 2) and yet it is a part of classical antiquity. When this past emerges in the present, with "a hollow murmur underground" and "a sudden spirt of flame into the air," it "startles" the polite world and takes the form of criminal atrocity: "how a girl has been murdered and chopped up in Russia to make those candles of human tallow by whose light thieves hope to pursue their midnight trade unseen" ([1922], 65).

Returned to England, Frazer must prepare for his second journey. Although he will present it as a world cruise, his title, his structure, and another order of figuration will delineate it as a descent into the classical underworld to find the link between the ritual at Nemi and the daylight lineage ("the classical tradition") that justifies him and his civilization. This double movement is possible because Frazer's world is already folded in regard to space and time: farther and farther outward is farther and farther back,[2] and the farthest out and the farthest back site, the Australian outback, already has that combination written into its name.[3] Frazer's world is also folded in regard to present and past; his quest is instigated by the pressure of "dark-

[1] See James A. Boon "Functionalists Write, Too: Frazer/Malinowski and the Semiotics of the Monograph," *Semiotica* 46, no. 2/4 (1983): 141.

[2] Anthropology thus begins with a dual content, "ancient *things* and savage *customs*." Michel de Certeau, "Writing vs. Time: History and Anthropology in the Works of Lafitau," *Yale French Studies* 59 (1980): 46.

[3] This common language support for Frazer's enterprise is even more appropriate since it identifies the physical site of *The Golden Bough* as well. Among the many charges brought against Frazer is that he took the preponderance of his evidence from studies of the inhabitants of central Australia (see, for example, John Joseph Honigmann, *Development of Anthropological Ideas* [Homewood, Ill.: Dorsey Press, 1976], p. 146). For a general consideration of the function of spatial distance in anthropology, see Johannes Fabian, *Time and the Other: How Anthropology Makes Its Object* (New York: Columbia University Press, 1983), p. 16.

ness" in the present, literally the remnants of the age of magic quoted above, but, more crucially, the "darkness" of Malthus, Marx, and Freud—the "shadows" of poverty and working-class anger and the "shadows" of hysteria and neurosis within middle-class consciousness. To accomplish this voyage of destiny, Frazer, like Aeneas, will need a golden bough.

Frazer begins as he does in order to dramatize his dilemma and his strategy (one might also say his magic); but his beginning is also a textual act, an imitation of the classic works to which he has devoted so much of his life. He *will seek* the vital connection between present and past in the underworld of anthropology, but he *begins to move* by rehearsing once again that moment of the classical epic where a male hero, Odysseus or Aeneas, descends into darkness to meet a shadowy progenitor, a parent, in order to receive a glorious inheritance.[4] The model for investigation that Frazer chooses is the oldest moment of epic, anthropologically speaking, and it has a tremendous part to play in nineteenth- and twentieth-century narrative. In a modified form, it stands behind the historical novel of Scott and Hugo, and behind the movements of the Romantic essay and tale of Irving, Hawthorne and Melville.[5] It is the model of certain massive discourses that are analogous in the force of their desire to the *Golden Bough*: for example, *The Descent of Man* where the pun on "descent" that plays between narrative and discourse is fulfilled by Darwin's descent into the geological museum in order to find an early version of himself on exhibit; and, to some extent, *A General Introduction to Psychoanalysis*—it is no accident that the truths that Frazer finds in the underworld are displacement, condensation, and the mistaken association of ideas. Finally, the underworld journey is also a featured model for the modernist epics of the twentieth century—*The Waste Land*, the *Cantos*, and *Finnegans Wake*. These works not only imitate the descent structure of the classical epic; they also imitate the *Golden Bough*.[6]

Prior to his descent, before trauma inscribes detour, Frazer's first thought will be that culture itself can redeem culture: the golden

[4] Lévi-Strauss will later compare the ethnologist to Lazarus, "returned from the dead to the living, but endowed with a knowledge that is unparalleled and incomprehensible to his contemporaries" (de Certeau 1980, 62).

[5] The question of how you get back to a past for which there are no markers or traces in the present is the instituting problem of *Waverley* and *Notre Dame de Paris*. Both Scott and Hugo answer paradoxically by insisting that you cannot write about the past until all of its signifiers have been erased.

[6] See John B. Vickery's, *The Literary Impact of the Golden Bough* (Princeton: Princeton University Press, 1973).

bough that will unlock the hidden meaning of the past will certainly be a work of high art, since high art traditionally credits itself with an essentialist power that it denies to history and anthropology—the power to know the past directly, without mediation.[7] Accordingly, he holds up before us a painting by J.M.W. Turner: "Who does not know Turner's picture of the Golden Bough?" But the painting, however beautiful, is a lie. Frazer exposes the claims of painting and poetry to represent and instruct and leaves these art forms languishing in the realm of the imaginary signifier. Art, Turner's painting, dispels the terrors of the past by suppressing or sublimating them—converting them into the sublime: "the scene, suffused with the golden glow of imagination in which the divine mind of Turner steeped and transfigured even the fairest natural landscape, is a dream-like vision of the little woodland lake of Nemi" (Frazer [1922], 1).

Like certain other criminal facts of the late nineteenth century—the detective's clue and the psychoanalyst's symptom—the ritual drama at Nemi is the product of repression in culture as well as in art, and there is, consequently, no easy access to it. The fact of the ritual remains in evidence but all of its associations have been buried and forgotten. The "recovery" of classical antiquity was both a recuperation and a loss: Thomas Bulfinch assured his readers that "such stories and parts of stories as are offensive to pure taste and good morals are not given"; Andrew Lang distinguished between "rational myths . . . which represent the gods as beautiful and wise beings," which require no explanation, and irrational and unnatural myths, like that of "Zeus who played Demeter an obscene trick by the aid of a ram," which are in "great need of explanation." The former alone express the true spirit of classical antiquity; the latter are barbarous remnants that need to be allegorized. It is the process of sublimation in another key, and this time identifiably sexual.[8]

Frazer's search involves a repudiation of poetry along with painting, and this is accomplished in movements like the following: "the legends which traced . . . [the] spilt blood [of Hippolytus and other mortal youths] in the purple bloom of the violet, the scarlet stain of the anemone, or the crimson flush of the rose were no idle poetic

[7] This has been asserted by anthropology as well, for example, by J. J. Bachofen: "aroused by direct contact with the ancient remains, the imagination grasps the truth at one stroke, without intermediary links." Elizabeth Fee, "The Sexual Politics of Victorian Social Anthropology," in *Clio's Consciousness Raised,* ed. Mary S. Hartman and Lois Banner (New York: Harper & Row, 1974), p. 90.

[8] Thomas Bulfinch, *Bulfinch's Mythology* (1855; New York: Crowel, n.d.), p. vii; and Andrew Lang, "Mythology," in *The Encyclopaedia Britannica,* 11th ed. (New York: Encyclopaedia Britannica, Inc., 1911), p. 128.

emblems of youth and beauty" ([1922], 8), and in "those days the divinity that hedges a king was no empty form of speech, but the expression of a sober belief" ([1922], 11). Frazer's quest for a proper path and method will eventually involve a repudiation of all aesthetic forms. In the following quotation, what Frazer dismisses is the Renaissance program for art itself: such "representations [the King and Queen of the May, the Whitsun Bridegroom and Bride] were . . . no mere symbolic or allegorical dramas, pastoral plays designed to amuse or instruct a rustic audience" ([1922], 156).

In spite of the falsity of painting and poetry, the truth of the past can still be made out—in the text of art, but more clearly in the text of anthropology: "Thus through the glamour shed round these rites by the poetry and philosophy of later ages there still looms, like a distant landscape through a sunlit haze, a simple rustic festival designed to cover the wide Eleusinian plain with a plenteous harvest" ([1922], 165). Frazer's journey is made possible by a reading lesson—a lesson in the proper reading of myth and ritual drama. His program for recovering the truth of the past is very simple: he will reverse the movement, the drift actually, that made poetry and painting possible in the first place—that arcane fall into modernism, of which Ferdinand de Saussure and his existential interpretors are the prophets, that rupture of the lifeline between signifier and signified, sign and referent, which dooms the word to wander restlessly along the paths of improper association.

Frazer's program will be to read poetry literally or, what is here the same thing, *to read metaphor literally*, to demetaphorize language in readings like the following: in "the flowing tide they see not merely a symbol, but a cause of exuberance, of prosperity, and of life, while in the ebbing tide they discern a real agent as well as a melancholy emblem of failure, of weakness, and of death" ([1922], 39–40). The soul, writes Frazer, is often conceived as a bird ready to take flight and this "conception has probably left traces in most languages, and it lingers as a metaphor in poetry." Malayans, however, try to lure that bird back to its proper place by offering it rice, and the Javanese, when they place a child on the ground for the first time, they "put . . . [it] in a hen-coop and the mother makes a clucking sound, as if she were calling hens" ([1922], 210). The primitive "conception of trees and plants as animated beings naturally results in treating them as male and female, who can be married to each other in a real, and not merely a figurative or poetical, sense of the word" ([1922], 131). Consonant with a split between a naive science and art, Frazer's golden bough is denotative language. Frazer's "primitive man," like

Herman Melville's innocent, Billy Budd, knows only the literal. He has not yet fallen into the postlapsarian world of only metaphor.

If compensation for metaphoric drift guarantees access to the past, the past that one encounters consists of metaphor. Frazer's two kinds of magic, homeopathic and contagious magic, which are based on the principles that "like produces like, or that an effect resembles its cause; and, second, that things which have once been in contact with each other continue to act on each other at a distance after the physical contact has been severed" ([1922], 12) are, in their complementarity, an early version of the opposition between metaphor and metonymy that, for Roman Jakobson, constitutes the self, language and culture.[9] Almost every pair in the Frazerian system turns out to be a version of the metaphor / metonymy distinction: the two poles of anthropology, for example—that classical civilization in whose place we are located as opposed to the present-day frontiers to which we are connected and to which we may travel.

But Frazerian magic is metaphoric throughout, and this shift reproduces the rhetorical dilemma whereby metonymy shuttles between being a trope that is separate but equal to metaphor and a class of metaphor.[10] Whether you kill an enemy by sticking pins into a facsimile (metaphor) or by slowly burning parings from his fingernails (metonymy), the act of staging, of representation, of acting toward a substitute as if it were the person, is a metaphoric relationship.

Frazer's system consists of a Hegelian triad: the thesis is magic, religion is the antithesis, and science is a "true" recovery of magic. But the nagging question provoked by the opening of the book and begged throughout is, what and where is art? What is the place of Turner in all of this? What is the relationship of art to the magic that it resembles so closely? This is a crucial question for Frazer and a crucial question for him to beg since, even in his own time, the place of his work on the line between science and art was a blurred and contended one. This question would be answered by Freud, who in several ways continues the work of Frazer. The answer of an essay such as "The Relation of the Poet to Day-Dreaming" (1908) would be that art is still the aboriginal magic, magic thinking, the doctrine of

[9] Roman Jakobson and Morris Halle, *Fundamentals of Language* (The Hague: Mouton, 1971), p. 95. See also James Fernandez, *Persuasions and Performances: The Play of Tropes in Culture* (Bloomington: Indiana University Press, 1986), p. 201.

[10] See Barbara Johnson, "Metaphor, Metonymy, and Voice in Zora Neale Hurston's *Their Eyes Were Watching God*," in *Textual Analysis*, ed. Mary Ann Caws (New York: Modern Language Association of America, 1986), p. 234; and Christian Metz, *The Imaginary Signifier: Psychoanalysis and the Cinema* (Bloomington: Indiana University Press, 1982), pp. 197–205.

the Omnipotence of Thought that governs the false association of ideas that, for Frazer, is the principle of magic.

In spite of Frazer's opposition to Turner in the name of science, he himself has been reclassified by anthropology as an artist, a worker of magic and not of science. According to Marilyn Strathern, Frazer represents the anthropological Other; "this most literary of figures became of all of them the most completely unreadable" (1987a, 253–54). Like his own primitives, he is someone whose signifiers are mental, all in his head, or, what is just as bad, in his study. Anthropology constituted itself by enacting a separation between a literature—travel literature—and a new science—ethnography—and it has been doomed to repeat that opening act, banishing from its sacred precincts its own one-time Kings of the Wood—James Frazer, Bronislaw Malinowski, Claude Lévi-Strauss—*as literature*. This separation between science and literature is fundamentally the separation of a true speech from a corrupted writing, the speech and writing (and the presence and absence) of Jacques Derrida's deconstructionist project in *On Grammatology*. As a science, anthropology gave itself to a scandalous version of the metaphysics of presence: the unmediated observation and delineation of the cultural other. Ethnography has always allied itself with speech—getting it directly from native informants[11]—and, even in its recent self-reflexive phase, the problem set for it is to defy or circumvent the ethnocentrism of writing more successfully, to transcribe more adequately the scene of plenitude that actually exists at the anthropological site. In order to constitute itself, anthropology had to differentiate itself not only from the writing of literature but also the writing of history: taking as its subject matter only peoples without writing. According to Lévi-Strauss ([1955], 391), for example, the absence of writing is the only trait that one can even wish to retain as a way of differentiating so-called civilized from so-called primitive peoples. What is noticeable, then, in what little attention James Frazer has received from twentieth-century anthropology is how compulsively Frazer is identified with a writing that exists in opposition to speech, not once, say, for its literary style, but over and over in a repeated act of violent repudiation.

For the commentators who would use the exclusion of Frazer to

[11] In his excellent essay "On Ethnographic Authority," *Representations* 1–2 (Spring 1983), James Clifford locates a further binary opposition at the ethnographic site—between seeing and hearing: after Malinowski, anthropology identifies itself with the interpretation that comes from seeing, "a distinct primacy was accorded to the visual" (125, 128, 132). But insofar as this seeing is even more direct and accurate than hearing, it is even closer to Derridean speech than to writing.

reconstitute anthropology, Frazer is not an anthropologist but an artist (or much less of an anthropologist and much more of an artist) because:

1. He is a writer; he is a fine writer; his writing is literary.[12] To that extent he betrays anthropology, which is opposed to literature more or less as content to form. Frazer betrays content to form; he lies.

2. But Frazer lies, betrays content to form, in another way: he writes up his prosaic sources; he "improves" his sources; he falsifies evidence—the cardinal crime in one who pretends to be a scientist.[13] These two forms of lying are the same: the pernicious scientist who distorts evidence does with a guilty conscience what the artist does to his resounding glory.

3. As the *Golden Bough* tells us, Frazer turned to anthropology initially in order to be able to fill lacunae in the Greek and Latin texts he was studying, in order to perfect writing, literature.

4. From another perspective, Frazer marks one of the great pragmatic boundaries in anthropology, for Frazer is a reader of books rather than a listener to speech; he is an "armchair" anthropologist; he never stirred from his library; he did no fieldwork (Honigman 1976, 113; Leach 1965, 25). He got it all from books as opposed to anthropologists who experience the real thing.[14] But, according to Freud in his *Totem and Taboo* (which is also repudiated by anthropology), it is useless to ask the native direct questions about the deep structure of his culture, for, like the psychoanalytic patient, he does not understand it, she has no information to give ([1918], 43).

5. Finally, there is a curious, almost comic version of this opposition in which Frazer cannot speak (he is mute) but can only write. Malinowski is a great teacher, and his influence and inspiration on the coming generation of anthropologists follows from that fact; Frazer cannot teach; he is ner-

[12] There is an irony here in that the anthropological project I have laid out for Frazer in the preceding sections is distinctly antiwriterly. For a presentation of a poststructuralist Frazer, see Marilyn Strathern's essay in this volume.

[13] Edmond Leach, "Frazer and Malinowski: On the Founding Fathers," *Encounter* (November 1965): 26; and see Marc Manganaro, " 'The Tangled Bank' Revisited: Anthropological Authority in Frazer's *The Golden Bough*," *The Yale Journal of Criticism*, 3 (Fall 1989): 107–26.

Derrida accuses Lévi-Strauss of the same crime—of "doctoring" the facts between his thesis and *Tristes Tropiques* in order to present the Nambikwara as a people without writing; *On Grammatology* (Baltimore: The Johns Hopkins University Press, 1974), p. 124.

[14] Ruth Benedict likens Frazer's comparatist method to the construction of a Frankenstein monster—"a right eye from Fiji, a left from Europe, one leg from Tierra del Fuego, and one from Tahiti, and all the fingers and toes from different regions"; *Patterns of Culture* (1934. New York: The New American Library, 1946), p. 45.

vous in large crowds; he is a bad public speaker—and his lack of influence over later anthropologists follows from these facts.[15]

Science and literature aside, the great problem that Frazer poses for anthropology is the extent to which he helped to establish and then threatened to expose its top-secret pornographic agenda. Frazer sexualizes anthropology, or, rather, allows the implicit sexual motive of anthropology to emerge. In Joyce's *A Portrait of the Artist as a Young Man*, Lynch and Daedalus may argue that the difference between the aesthetic contemplation of Venus of Praxiteles and the desire to reach over and pat it on the backside makes all the difference in the world, but the difference between those two motives is generally not marked in either the image of the observer or the written text ([1916], 205). The motives of the anthropological enterprise in Western culture may be various, but my first and most lasting encounter with anthropology was in the pages of *The National Geographic*, and that was mostly an exercise in looking at women's breasts.[16] Michel de Certeau implies the inevitability of anthropology as *primal seeing* when he writes that the anthropological *tableaux* allows us to see our origins "as if through a keyhole." But, in this seeing, there is "something that *should not be seen*: the nudity of the body" (1980, 42).

The oldest strategy of anthropology (and it certainly cannot be unconnected to its appeal) is to look at the "primitive world" and see active sexual practices at the center of everything—"ethnological studies revealed one very vivid fact about primitive societies: they were steeped in sex and sin" (Fee 1974, 92). Simply to write anthropology in the beginning was to produce an erotic or pornographic fiction, like Jacob Bachofen's first stage of civilization, the hetaerist-aphroditic state when marriage was unknown, sexual relationships were unregulated, women were at the mercy of male lust, and promiscuity and sexual exploitation triumphed. And to write anthropology after the beginning was often to unwrite it, as Malinowski does: "this union, monogamous marriage, has always existed in human

[15] See Honigman 1976, 158; Leach 1965, 26; and Bronislau Malinowski, *A Scientific Theory of Culture, and Other Essays* (Chapel Hill: University of North Carolina Press, 1944), p. 182.

[16] In Frank Capra's "It's a Wonderful Life" (1947), the young George Bailey has a copy of *National Geographic* stuck in his back pocket when he comes into the drugstore to go to work. He tells Mary Hatch of his dreams to travel widely and exotically, to have "a couple of harems, and maybe three or four wives." In Gene Saks's "Brighton Beach Memoirs" (1986), Eugene is seen standing by an outside bookstall looking at the bare breasts of native women in *National Geographic*, an adjunct to his reiterated adolescent project to see a naked woman.

societies—so modern anthropology teaches in the face of the older fantastic hypotheses of 'promiscuity' and 'group marriage.' "[17]

Frazer, and Freud after him, look at primitive society and see totemism and incest at the center of everything. Even worse, Frazer almost looks out into the contemporary countryside and sees folks fucking—"at the present day it might perhaps be vain to look in civilized Europe for customs of this sort . . . but ruder races in other parts of the world have consciously employed the intercourse of the sexes as a means to ensure the fruitfulness of the earth; and some rites which are still, or were till lately, kept up in Europe can be reasonably explained only as stunted relics of a similar practice" ([1922], 157)—an occluded view in the present and the historical past. The reputations of the *Golden Bough* and *Totem and Taboo* have been linked to this covert issue of sexual exposure.

Freud's absurdist fact, the clue that stimulates anxious creativity just as Frazer's ritual of Nemi does, is the utter lack of connection between totemism and incest: "This sternly maintained prohibition is very remarkable. There is nothing to account for it in anything that we have hitherto learned from the conception of the totem or from any of its attributes; that is, we do not understand how it happened to enter the system of totemism" ([1918], 7). And one version of anthropology after Freud is driven by the intention to separate them. It is within this context that one must read a remarkable performance, Lévi-Strauss's *Totemism,* which does not even contain the word incest in its index. Incest has been virtually erased from the totemic record, and even when it is alluded to, it is not named nor particularly marked: "from this carnal identification of clan and totem derive both the rule of clan exogamy, on the social level, and the food tabus, on the religious level: like must not be mixed with like, whether by eating or by copulation" (1963, 42). But Lévi-Strauss tells us all this in his opening phrase—"Totemism is like hysteria"—in which he literally invokes another instance of a false system of connections, alludes to the authority of Freud, and puts his work under a comparable ban of sexual repression.

Within the range of complications that wrinkle the anthropological text in *Writing Culture* (1986), voyeurism is not identified. Not until footnote nine do we encounter a critique linking "visually based modes of surveillance and portrayal" to masculine desire, only to

[17] *Science, Magic and Religion* [1916, 1925, and 1926] (1916; Garden City, N.Y.: Doubleday and Company, 1948), p. 41; and see Malinowski, *A Scientific Theory of Culture, and Other Essays.*

find that it is a critique in the act of being excluded, dwelled upon, in fact, as it is being excluded (Clifford & Marcus 1986, 19).

If James Clifford's reading of his own front cover leaves a mother and two children out of the anthropological scenes, his reading of a featured moment in contemporary ethnography leaves out the man who must figure desire. It is an incident in Marjorie Shostak's *Nisa*, "turning on the value of a girl-woman's body," in which Shostak covertly watches a twelve-year-old girl examining her breasts and her body in the side-view mirror of a Land Rover. This is presented as a tender moment between an older and a younger woman (even though a condition of the tenderness, as presented, is that the younger not know that the older woman is looking at her), but there are other faces in that mirror looking at the young girl as she examines her developing breasts—Clifford's and mine at the very least. Rather, the faces are not there: as in the mirror of cinema it is precisely the lookers-on, the subjects for whom the scene figures desire, who are not reflected. Clifford, however, does annotate us; he writes us into the scopic scene, now identified as a generalized, ethical scene of desire: "*Nisa*'s readers follow—and prolong—the play of a desire. They imagine, in the mirror of the other, a guileless self-possession, an uncomplicated feeling of 'attractiveness' " (1986, 108–9).

As if unrelated to anything written above, Edmund Leach—an anthropologist who grows rabid on the subject of Frazer, yet who writes about him obsessively—accuses Frazer of being a pornographer, not because of any bias of anthropology but because of a bias of literature! Frazer's elaborate decorum, Leach writes, "leaves a taste of smut" (1961, 380). Frazer's use of complex periphrasis for genitalia and fucking inevitably leads to polite pornography (1965, 29). And this, rather than any anthropological virtue in Frazer, accounts for his continuing popularity (1961, 383). But Leach goes on and makes Frazer's fame personally dependent on his power as a seducer of women, one young and one old—a young Frenchwoman who became his wife and devoted herself tirelessly to the making of his reputation, and Jane Ellen Harrison. In a complex figure, she almost seems to support the accusation: "we classical deaf adders stopped our ears and closed our eyes. But at the mere sound of the magical words 'Golden Bough'—the scales fell—we heard and understood" (1961, 377).

Out of Context: The Persuasive Fictions of Anthropology[1]

MARILYN STRATHERN

THIS IS the confession of someone brought up to view Sir James Frazer in a particular way who has discovered that the context for that view has shifted. I wish to convey some sense of that shift.

To talk about a scholar is also to talk about his or her ideas. But there is a puzzle in the history of ideas. Ideas seem to have the capacity to appear at all sorts of times and places, to such a degree that we can consider them as being before their time or out of date. One of the things I learned about Frazer was that his ideas were old-fashioned before he wrote them down. But at the same time there were some decidedly modern ideas in fashion. In fact, the experience of turning back to Frazer and his late nineteenth-century contemporaries is to realise how modern they also seem. Yet I am disconcerted by the fact that I simultaneously know that post-Frazerian anthropology is utterly unlike what went before it. There was a quite decisive shift in the subject some sixty to seventy years ago whose result, among others, was a generation of social anthropologists like myself brought up to regard Frazer as unreadable.[2]

The presence or absence of particular ideas does not seem enough to account for such movement. They collapse a sense of history into a sense of *déjà vu*. This is particularly disconcerting for the anthropologist also brought up to imagine that cultural notions "fit to-

[1] This is a version of the Frazer Lecture for 1986, given at the University of Liverpool. The annual lecture, an honour accorded Sir James George Frazer in his lifetime, circulates among four universities: Liverpool, Glasgow, Cambridge, and Oxford. The first given in Liverpool was by Bronislaw Malinowski, the most recent before the present by Marshall Sahlins. I am very grateful to John Peel and to Liverpool University for their invitation, which persuaded me to read Frazer again; this paper is for E. E.

[2] It will be clear that I write from the perspective of British social anthropology, and not from another perspective which would seek to explain this species of anthropology to others. That American as well as British writers become significant in the later discussion of contemporary issues reflects other shifts that have occurred in this perspective.

gether" and that what people think is a "reflection" of their times. Consider, for instance, two examples of ideas about ethnocentrism. Both address the conundrum how to describe the apparently absurd customs of other peoples in such a way as to make them plausible to the reader. One refers to the ancient Israelites, the other to modern savages, topics which Frazer was to bring together in his *Folk-lore in the Old Testament* (1918).

The first is a work published in 1681 by the Abbé Fleury, *The Manners of the Israelites*. An expanded 1805 version was produced by a Manchester cleric, Clarke, in response to public demand following earlier editions. The opening justification of the book is of interest. It is because the customs of God's chosen people are so different from ours that they offend us and that the Old Testament has been neglected; "upon comparing the manners of the Israelites with those of the Romans, Greeks, Egyptians, and other people of the former ages . . . these prejudices soon vanish . . . the Israelites had everything that was valuable in the customs of their contemporaries, without many of the defects" (Clarke 1805, 15). Clarke's intention is to make the Bible readable, to rid the Old Testament of its strangeness, so that his readers can conceive of God's being among the Israelites. He desires (p. 16)

> the reader to divest himself of all prejudice, that he may judge of these customs by good sense and right reason alone; to discard the ideas that are peculiar to his own age and country, and consider the Israelites in the circumstances of time and place wherein they lived; to compare them with their nearest neighbours, and by that means to enter into their spirit and maxims.

These ideas have an uncannily contemporary ring—even to the point of the writer's saying that he aspires not to a panegyric but to "a very plain account" of the people he is describing. But then so, in some respects, do the words of Sir John Lubbock spoken at Hulme Town Hall, Manchester, in 1874. Like Clarke's rendering of Fleury, they are addressed to a large popular audience: a lecture on modern savages in a series, Science Lectures for the People, whose opening address had attracted 3,700 people. (The subsequent attendance is recorded at an average of 675). Lubbock (1875b, 238) starts with the fact of difference:

> The whole mental condition of the savage is, indeed, so dissimilar from ours that it is often very difficult for us to follow what is passing in his mind. . . . Many things appear natural, and almost self-evident to him, which produce a very different effect on us. . . . Thus, though savages

always have a reason, such as it is, for what they do and what they think, these reasons often seem to us irrelevant or absurd.

But by comparing diverse accounts of peoples from all over the world, it is possible to show how widely distributed are those ideas and customs which "seem to us at first inexplicable and fantastic" (1875b, 239). What we—and he means himself and his audience—take as "natural and obvious" will turn out not to be so. Lubbock's special case is a desire to give "a correct idea of man as he existed in ancient times, and of the stages through which our civilisation has been evolved" (1875b, 237).

Like Fleury / Clarke, he argues that to understand people very different from ourselves it is necessary to be aware of their particular premises and values. Lubbock makes his point by substantiating that difference, introducing his witnesses to a disparate range of reasons and customs, examples they would be unlikely to have come across if he had not regaled them with the evidence. The evidence includes such items as belief in the reality of dreams, fondness for ornaments, and marriage ceremonies such as those which reduce women to slaves valued for their services. He sees in this last circumstance an explanation for marriage by capture—still, he says, in some regions a rude reality while elsewhere the mimicry of force alone remains (1875b, 242).[3]

Yet there was also a vast difference between these writers. The Manchester cleric who promoted Fleury in the 1800s held a cyclical model of the world, in which nations rose and fell as they passed through stages of prosperity and decline. Fleury and Clarke bewailed the corruption of their contemporaries which prevented them from appreciating the ancient virtues of the Israelites. It is not to be supposed, they argued, that the further one looks into antiquity, the "more stupid and ignorant" mankind will appear (1805, 18). On the contrary, "Nations have their periods of duration, like men." Consequently we must learn to distinguish "what we do not like, upon account of the distance of times and places, though it be in itself indifferent, from that which, being good in itself, displeases us for no other reason, than because we are corrupt in our manners" (1805, 15). This could not be further from Lubbock and his 1870s implementation of the idea that modern savages were to be understood because they gave an insight into former times: their wretched state measured the distance that civilisation had come. He lived not in a

[3] And proceeds to discover "similar customs" and "traces" of them in both classical and modern Europe, remarking on how "persistent are all customs and ceremonies connected with marriage" (1875b, 242).

cyclical world but in an evolving one. His efforts were directed to substituting one linear view of mankind's progression for another, doing battle with those who saw modern savages as the degenerate descendants of civilised peoples; to see them as examples of a stage since superseded gave hope of progress.

As soon as one set of ideas is put into the context of others, they no longer seem similar at all. In fact, these particular examples could be assigned to radically different paradigms (Stocking 1984).[4]

One could go on. When more than forty years after Lubbock's lecture Frazer came to describe the manners of the ancient Israelites, it was his wide-ranging researches into "the early history of man" which rendered them thoroughly plausible. His aim was to show that the Israelites were no exception to the general law, that their civilisation like others had passed through a stage of barbarism and savagery (1918, 1:Preface). If this was a view similar to Lubbock's, however, it provided a very different context from the ideas about ethnocentrism which Malinowski published four years later. In his famous opening to the work which introduced the Trobriand Islanders of Melanesia, Malinowski ([1922], 25) argues that in "each culture, the values are slightly different; people aspire after different aims, follow different impulses," and that without an understanding of the subjective desires by which people realise their aims, the study of institutions, codes, and customs would be empty.[5] The same aim, to understand other people's values, is differently conceived; for Malinowski the goal is "to grasp the native's point of view." The Trobrianders have become "savage" in a playful sense. Or one could jump to Geertz's ideas expressed in the 1980s. His assertion that anthropology is the first to insist "that the world does not divide into the pious and superstitious" seems a familiar stand. Yet when he adds that "we see the lives of others through lenses of our own grinding and . . . they look back on ours through ones of their own" (1984, 275), this version of a two-way regard in turn makes his meanings a significant departure from Malinowski's.

For a non-historian, the disconcerting point is this: If one looks

[4] Stocking (1984, 136) refers to the early history of anthropology as alternating between two dominant paradigms, both diachronic. Lubbock's writing evinces the progressive-development paradigm and Fleury / Clarke a diffusionary paradigm deriving from biblical assumptions about the genealogy of nations. I invoke this dichotomy not to parody the many styles and strands of thought that contributed to the premises on which Lubbock (and later Frazer) proceeded or to pretend to a history but merely as a sign that there was a history.

[5] A point upon which Marett had also published in his unfortunately chosen terminology of "psychology" (e.g., Marett 1920).

hard enough one can find ideas anticipated long before their time, or one can trace their similarity through time. Yet, when one looks again, and considers other ideas, the sense of similarity vanishes. A model of an evolving world cannot possibly produce the "same" ideas as one in which nations pass through life-cycles. In the same way, Geertz's two-way regard cannot possibly lead to the same kinds of understandings as Malinowski's confidence about grasping the Trobriander's version of the world. In conveying the concept of ethnocentrism, none of these writers appears to intend quite the same thing. This makes it impossible to explain the prevalence of certain ideas simply with reference to other ideas. On what basis is one to foreground some, relegate others to background context? Do we write a history of the idea of ethnocentrism, or a history of its different premises? Or are we not dealing with the "same" idea at all?

These are puzzles intrinsic to cross-cultural comparison. They are familiar anthropological conundrums. The question is, then, what an anthropologist's resolution might look like. The problem is simply that I know that these sets of ideas are different, that the gulf separating Geertz and Malinowski, say, is as wide as the gulf separating Malinowski from Frazer or Frazer and Lubbock from Clarke and Fleury. But how am I to *persuade* myself that I know? If the sequence of ideas is always so ambiguous, from where does our dramatic sense of shifts and gulfs come? It must come from the place those ideas have in our practices. Thus we should look not at whether this or that person could conceive of other cultures in this or that way—whether the idea of ethnocentrism existed or not—but at the effectiveness of the vision, the manner in which an idea was implemented. That is why I mentioned Fleury's popularity and the huge audience for Lubbock's lectures. The point leads into the astonishing phenomenon of Frazer's celebrity.

The phrase is Leach's (1966). Attributing much to the showmanship of Frazer's wife, twenty years ago Leach despatched the idea that this celebrity corresponded to any secure academic reputation, in Frazer's own time, among anthropologists at least. If I return to the same question now, it is because of what has happened to social anthropology in the years since Leach presented his views. I suspend judgement and proceed as if what really is at issue is the grip Frazer had on people's imaginations. This will turn out to be germane to the recent history of anthropological practice, for any survey of the practices of anthropology has to acknowledge the force of Geertz's observation (quoted by Boon 1982, 9): "What does the ethnographer do?—he writes." If we look to practice, we could do worse than look to anthropological writing. I spend some time on the writings of Frazer himself, for the gulf between him and the anthropology which came after tells us much about how we come to imagine that there are gulfs at all, and thus about how we persuade ourselves that there has been a history.

Sir James Frazer

Frazer is widely held to have had a profound effect on the minds of his contemporaries. Downie (1970, 64) repeats Jane Harrison's famous story of a policeman who said to her, "I used to believe everything they told me, but, thank God, I read *The Golden Bough*, and I've been a freethinker ever since." From its first appearance in 1890, remarks Downie, the endeavour was treated generally with respect, and he quotes Malinowski's observation that *The Golden Bough* was "a work known to every cultured man, a work which has exercised paramount influence over several branches of learning" (1970, 57).[6] Indeed, Frazer's *Folk-lore in the Old Testament*, published in 1918, met with ready acclaim in theological as well as literary journals. His work not only appears to have spoken for his times but has exercised a lasting power. Above all, he promoted anthropology. For many non-anthropologists, no one, not even Malinowski, has quite displaced him. Yet what is astonishing about the effect of his writing is astonishing to anthropologists, or rather is astonishing about them, for Frazer has not for many years—some would say never—held a respectable place in the history of the discipline. On the contrary, modern British anthropology knows itself as not just non-Frazerian but quite positively anti-Frazerian. Social anthropologists habitually scoff at Frazer, hold him up to ridicule, and regard his folklore as long superseded.[7]

What, then, was the grip Frazer had on many people's imaginations? And just what was created in turn by those who founded mod-

[6] Malinowski (1962) effusively praises the book as "in many respects the greatest achievement of anthropology." But of course it is by juxtaposition that he also places himself in relation to Frazer—welcoming the abridged edition of *The Golden Bough* as convenient to take into the field! Anthropologists in general had their reservations. Marett's review of the third edition (reprinted in Marett 1920) strongly objects to Frazer's parallelisms; survivals should be treated not as fossils but in a psychological (i.e., sociocultural) context. Some literary reviews of the time were also cool (Leach 1966).

[7] Leach presents a matter-of-fact exposition for a non-anthropological audience: "Frazer's present renown is largely undeserved. Most of what he himself contributed to the study of anthropology and comparative religion has proved worthless" (1983,13). I should make it clear that I do not intend a revision of Leach's views in particular (I read Leach 1966 after the bulk of this paper was written).

ern anthropology? I use the word "modern" advisedly, in a context in which we are informed from all sides that we live in a postmodern age. As will become apparent, this latter-day representation allows a contemporary place for Frazer that was barely conceivable twenty years ago. This most recent shift suggests that anthropologists might after all find parts of Frazer more readable than they thought.

The interesting question is how modern anthropologists came to construct Frazer as demonstrably not of their time, and how indeed the writing which for so many others was eminently readable for them was rendered quite unreadable.[8] My account will inevitably place too much weight for a historian's liking on the significance of this figure, as though he really were central to the shift which took place in the subject. It ignores others, both those who also became unreadable and those to whom anthropologists return from time to time as precursors. It is rare to return to Frazer in this way: this most literary of figures became of all of them the most completely unreadable. Frazer was made visible as a victim of the shift.

In a bitter attack, recently renewed, on modern social anthropology, Jarvie (1964, 1984) deliberately promotes Frazer as victim.[9] He borrows the metaphor of the priest's overthrow: "the first battle-cry of the revolution was 'kill the chief-priest.' " Rather more prosaic, however, is his complaint that "endless doses of the facts of fieldwork are so boring" (1984, 15). Certainly from a postwar perspective, the new anthropology as it developed in the 1920s and 1930s appeared in direct competition with Frazer's, and on the very issue of fieldwork. Looking back, Evans-Pritchard commented on how literary sources had had perforce to stand in for "direct observation" (1951, 10).[10] It was above all through the fieldwork possibilities of direct observation that literary sources could be supplanted and that

[8] Swept along with Frazer were also his contemporary critics such as Marett; a swath of anthropological writing was rendered unreadable. Frazer's work itself came to appear quite dull, not the "glorious and thrilling reading" that Jarvie (1964, 33) finds it.

[9] Jarvie means this literally. Those who do not credit Frazer with much stature take it metaphorically—the real victims are to be found elsewhere. Malinowski's own targets included, for instance, the survey anthropology of Rivers and Seligman (Langham 1981) and the diffusionism of Elliot Smith (Leach 1966). As a comment on the creation of victims, see Urry's (1983) review of Langham's account. Langham is principally concerned not with Frazer and Malinowski but with Rivers and Radcliffe-Brown. Urry points out that Langham accuses Radcliffe-Brown "of practically everything short of murder" in eclipsing Rivers's contribution to British anthropology (401).

[10] Obscured in the dichotomy between direct observation and literary sources is the fact that Frazer's literary sources were to a large extent reports on observations from ethnologists whom he encouraged to correspond with him. The dichotomy thus obscures the literary status of reportage itself.

Malinowski (along with Radcliffe-Brown) assassinated Frazer (the image is Jarvie's [1964, 1]).

Jarvie also promotes Malinowski as the instigator of the revolution, dated to about 1920. In his allegory, "Malinowski plotted and directed the revolution in social anthropology—aiming to overthrow the establishment of Frazer and Tylor and their ideas; but mainly it was against Frazer" (1964, 173). As he sees it, the revolution had three aims: (1) to replace armchair anthropology with field experience; (2) in the domain of religion and magic, to replace Frazer's attention to beliefs with the study of social action (the rite); and (3) to replace false evolutionary sequences with an understanding of contemporary society. Jarvie is far from alone in this view. The received wisdom is that fieldwork observation meant that people's practices could be recorded in their immediate social context. This shifted the kinds of explanations for which anthropologists sought. Malinowski (like Radcliffe-Brown) insisted that practices were to be related to other practices—that exchanges of food and valuables at marriage ceremonies, for instance, were intelligible in the light of local rules of inheritance or land tenure. To account for such ceremonies in the Trobriands, Malinowski turned not to practices found in other cultures but to other aspects of this one culture. The rest is well known—that this led to a view of individual societies as entities to be interpreted in their own terms, so that both practices and beliefs were to be analysed as intrinsic to a specific social context; that societies so identified were seen as organic wholes, later as systems and structures; and that the comparative enterprise which modern anthropologists set themselves thus became the comparison of distinct systems.

Indeed, this view of cross-cultural comparison has become so ingrained within the discipline that it is quite odd to read Frazer's own claim that his was "the comparative method" (1918, 1:viii). Frazer meant not the comparison of social systems but the collecting together of diverse customs in order to throw light on one particular set. Light can be shone from any direction—beliefs and practices from anywhere in the world will illuminate those under study, showing possible antecedents or a tendency for people everywhere to think in the same way. Frazer's comparative procedures included both the proposition that in any piece of behaviour one will find traces of prior habits which help explain current forms and the proposition that practices are to be understood as reflections of beliefs. Thus it was possible to explain widespread practices by widespread beliefs. The revolution was successful to the point that Frazer's comparative method came to seem not simply erroneous but absurd. The new task was the comparison of societies as such. And it required the painstaking attention to those details which make particular societies distinctive and which Jarvie finds so tedious. Yet Frazer was nothing if not attentive to details. As we shall see, it was about their arrangement that Jarvie must have been protesting.

Although there is still some debate over Frazer's own arguments, as frequently as not they are condemned by his style. Rather than addressing the issue of historical residues or the comparability of beliefs, the modern anthropologist tends to object to Frazer's narrative structure. His work is criticised for being *too literary*. It is also criticised for treating events, behaviour, dogma, rites *out of context*. "Frazerian anthropology" is a synonym for undisciplined raids on ethnographic data without respect for their internal integrity, for the way they fit together as parts of a system or have meaning for the actors. In fact, it is very appropriate that it should be his style that upsets the modern anthropologist, for what is above all at issue is the kind of book he wrote.

I take as my example Frazer's *Folk-lore in the Old Testament*, which brought together a classical text and a tradition of biblical historical exegesis with the accumulated results of his comparative method, a vast collection of customs which threw light on ancient Hebrew life.[11] The diversity of his examples is staggering.[12] First, he goes through various episodes of Old Testament history: the creation of man, the fall of man, the mark of Cain, the great flood, the tower of Babel, the covenant of Abraham, the heirship of Jacob or ultimogeniture, Jacob and the kidskins, etc. Second, these are the occasion for disquisitions on origin myths, treatment of homicides, myths about the flood, varieties of sacrifice, inheritance rules, polygamy, etc., each topic treated like a narrative episode. Third, these episodes are made even more episodic by the accompanying discussions. Jacob's marriage is

[11] This work, written on the eve of the Malinowskian revolution, is in direct continuation with the position that Frazer had reached by the third edition of *The Golden Bough*: that he wished a context in which to set forth the information he had been amassing on primitive thought and culture. Indeed, the former may be read as a disquisition on religion, power, and politics (cf. Feeley-Harnik 1985), the latter on kinship, marriage, and—with its passages on inheritance and property relations—economics.

[12] Whereas his predecessor in the field, Robertson Smith, in *The Religion of the Semites* (1956 [1889]), had confined his study to a group of kindred nations (broadly categorised as they were to include Arabs, Hebrews, and Phoenicians, Aramaeans, Babylonians, and Assyrians), Frazer allows himself to roam all over the world. For a comparison between this work and *The Golden Bough*, see Jones (1984). Smith was specifically interested in a contrast *between* Semitic and Aryan religion and thus could not simply assimilate the beliefs and practices of the one to those of the other.

the occasion for a treatise (the term is Marett's) eighteen sections and nearly three hundred pages long: Jacob and his two wives; the marriage of cousins; the marriage of cousins in India, in America, in Africa, in the Indian archipelago, in New Guinea and the Torres Straits islands, in Melanesia; why marriage of cross-cousins is favoured, marriage of ortho-cousins forbidden, including a detailed argument on various theories about cross-cousin marriage; and so on. Finally, the sections are themselves composite: that on marriage in Africa includes references to Herero, Bantu, Nyanja, Awamba, Wagogo, Wahehe, Baganda, Banyoro, Basoga, and others.

Every instance is placed. Frazer faithfully ascribes particular customs to particular people. There is respect for these specific origins, as there would be in establishing the different authorship of classical or biblical manuscripts. But the effect of piling example upon example achieves the opposite. One has long since lost any sense of specificity about the Israelites, let alone distinctiveness about the Torres Straits or Melanesia. In fact, there is a counter-specificity in his demonstration of similarity. Frazer says himself (1918, 2:97), "The story of Jacob's marriage, whether strictly historical or not, reflects the customs which have been observed at marriage by many more or less primitive peoples in many parts of the world; and accordingly we may fairly suppose that at an early stage of their history similar customs were practised by the Israelites." The demonstration of similarity establishes the authenticity of those biblical records as plausible descriptions of real behaviour. One can see the power of this against a background of scholarly work concerned with how true a record it might be. Using (say) Melanesian practices to make Israelite ones seem less strange means, of course, that there can be no sustained internal contrast between Israelite and Melanesian practices. But the strategy is deliberate. Frazer isolates three elements in Jacob's circumstances: cousin marriage, marriage of a man with two sisters in their lifetime, and bride service:

> All three customs I propose to illustrate by examples and afterwards to enquire into their origin and meaning. Although in doing so we shall wander far from our immediate subject, which is the folk-lore of ancient Israel, the excursion may be pardoned if it sheds sober light on the exquisite pictures of the patriarchal age in Genesis, and thereby helps to reveal the depth and solidity of the human background against which the figures of the patriarchs are painted.

His 280 pages of examples "suffice to prove that marriages like that of Jacob have been and still are practised in many different parts of the world. . . . [T]he patriarch conformed to customs which are fully recognised and strictly observed by many races" (1918, 2:371). The biblical account is no "mere fancy picture" but depicts social arrangements "drawn from life."

Yet were the customs ever regarded as mere fancy? He is ambiguous about exactly how his account contributes to debates over the historicity of the Old Testament. Frazer's strategy would make sense in an atmosphere of disbelief about Israelite manners or simply an attitude that regarded many minor features and incidents as narrative embellishments, there for no other reason. His "comparative sociology" would show that within the context of world cultures, the Israelite experience is not so strange. Yet was this really how people of his time regarded the Old Testament? Surely for some of the minds he influenced the Old Testament would have seemed very familiar, its many events an intrinsic part of a story often told. In fact, there is almost a Sunday School ring to the episodes he lists. We cannot really credit Frazer with Fleury's problem of overcoming people's antipathy to the ancient Israelites as an example of a less polite society than their own. It was much more likely that it would be the ethnographic examples which strained credulity.

In setting the Israelites side by side with African or Melanesian cultures, however, Frazer is not just making the Israelites credible. He states that one can assume that the ancient Hebrews, like anyone else, had passed through "a stage of barbarism and even of savagery; and this probability, based on the analogy of other races, is confirmed by an examination of their literature, which contains many references to beliefs and practices that can hardly be explained except on the supposition that they are rudimentary survivals from a far lower level of culture" (1918, 1:vii). He continues: "The instrument for the detection of savagery under civilisation is the comparative method, which, applied to the human mind, enables us to trace man's intellectual and moral evolution" (p. viii). Was it this labelling of contemporary practices as survivals which constituted much of the fascination which Frazer had in his time? Would his readers have applied "the detection of savagery under civilisation" to themselves?

And if Malinowski really did overthrow this priest, was it because he overthrew this central doctrine? Malinowski and his colleagues put forward the same proposition but in reverse: the detection of civilisation under savagery. Perhaps the visibility of Malinowski in modern anthropology partly lies here, for he provided a particularly persuasive context for this proposition by the way he wrote. I follow Boon's observation: Frazerian anthropology was superseded above all by a new kind of book; Malinowski made Frazer's style obsolete (Boon 1982, 13, 18).

It has become very stylish to scrutinise anthropological narratives for their effects, especially in the case of Malinowski, a self-conscious writer with a philosophical background which informed his approach to the art of representation and the concept of a text (e.g., Thornton 1985). I do not touch on the now extensive critical literature. Rather, I take up a narrow question, of the writer's impact on the imagination from the perspective of the kind of relationship that is set up between writer and reader and between writer and subject matter. These are mediated through relationships internal to the text, in the way the writer arranges his ideas. In Malinowski's works appear new juxtapositions, new disjunctions of a kind which enabled the comparative method to proceed in a quite different way. Indeed, to set the scene for a comparison between Frazer's strategies (as evinced especially in *Folk-lore*) and those of modern anthropology, I require a neutral ground, which is why I emphasise their works as literary products. In laying this ground, I shall also attend to the first of the two criticisms frequently thrown at Frazer's writing, that it is *too* literary.

Persuasive Fictions

Marking out a piece of writing as "literary" is like marking out a person as having "personality." Obviously, insofar as any piece of writing aims for a certain effect, it must be a literary production.

Difficulties arise when the apparent facts of a case are altered or distorted for the sake of a particular effect. Frazer is certainly guilty of this charge; he did not strive for a "plain account." Thus he has been accused not simply of creating an atmosphere of romantic savagery but of tampering with his source material to do so (Leach 1966, 564). However, anthropologists have a particular problem of literary production on their hands, and it is this problem which makes Frazer as much an anthropologist as Malinowski.

The problem is a technical one: how to create an awareness of different social worlds when all at one's disposal is terms which belong to one's own.[13] I mean more than simply getting over the flavour of

[13] In part, as I show later, this is a modernist construction (the holistic idea of a culture to which everything belongs). I am grateful to David Lowenthal (personal communication) for the point that the preservation of language allows the otherness of terms (foreign, anachronistic) some life of their own. But in part there is another issue, one which provides the framework for Boon's account: the fact that there is no place outside a culture "except in other cultures or in their fragments and potentialities" (1982, ix). One could regard this as a technical "problem" whose theoretical framework was provided by the perception of a social fact: the presence of social others in the

a particular atmosphere—Frazer and Malinowski both created evocative descriptions, coloured by a sense of locality.[14] I also mean more than the facility to translate from one world view to another. When faced with ideas and concepts from a culture conceived as other, the anthopologist is faced with the task of rendering them within a conceptual universe that has space for them, and thus of creating that universe. If I observe of bridewealth exchanges which accompany a Melanesian marriage that the bride's parents are being paid for their feelings towards her, I am juxtaposing ideas which in the language I am using are normally antithetical. Emotion is not a commodity. Although I might try to wriggle out of the word "paid," it remains clear that I am describing as a transaction what is also an expression of relatedness—one we would normally interpret as a flow of emotions between persons, not something to be transferred to a third party. Space must be cleared before I can convey the unity of an action which an English-language description renders as a composite of disjunct elements.

This is part of a general problem of communication, to "bridge the divide between the reader's experiences and the experiences of the people whom the researcher wishes to describe to him" (Runciman 1983, 249). The effect of a good description is to enlarge the reader's experience. But those very experiences of the reader are themselves a problem—what guarantee is there that the description will not feed prejudice, will not, far from enlarging, merely augment a narrow perspective?[15] We typically think of anthropologists as creating devices by which to understand what other people think or believe. Simultaneously, of course, they are engaged in constructing devices by which to affect what their audience thinks and believes. Preparing a description requires specific literary strategies, the construction of a persuasive fiction: a monograph must be laid out in such a way that

---

world. It led to the kinds of esoteric puzzle-solving techniques that Langham (1981, 19) insists indicate the presence of a mature science.

[14] The writer uses the impressions which the place made on him or her to relay information about that place to the reader. What it is like for a European to live in a tent on the Trobriand Islands thus conveys a picture of a kind about the Trobriands. Thornton (1985, 9) puts this striving for the concrete image in the context of Malinowski's theories of the role of imagination, "founded on a positivistic conception of the real psychological existence of images in the mind that permitted the apprehension of reality to take place."

[15] Goodenough (1970, 105) writes that the problem of ethnography is how to produce a description that satisfactorily represents "what one needs to know to play the game acceptably by the standards of those who already know how to play it." This implies an enormous willingness on the part of the reader to compare standards.

it can convey novel compositions of ideas.[16] This becomes a question of its own internal composition, of the organisation of analysis, the sequence in which the reader is introduced to concepts, the way categories are juxtaposed or dualisms reversed. To confront the problem is to confront the arrangement of text. So whether a writer chooses (say) a "scientific" style or a "literary" one signals the kind of fiction it is; there cannot be a choice to eschew fiction altogether.

I use the term "fiction" to echo Beer's (1983, 3) observation that theory is at its most fictive when it is first advanced. She is referring to Charles Darwin's narrative: "The awkwardness of fit between the natural world as it is currently perceived and as it is hypothetically imagined holds the theory itself for a time within a provisional scope akin to that of fiction." The issue is the new organisation of knowledge. Darwin, she suggests, "was telling a new story, against the grain of the language available to tell it in" (5). How does one "imagine" a natural world not only in a vocabulary but in a syntax created by a social world? Its success is measured in the extent to which the new narrative becomes determining. The question is not simply how to bring certain scenes to life but how to bring life to ideas.

Some tropic release is afforded through imagery. Darwin drew on the metaphor of kinship, among others (see Beer 1986), on the idea of the web of interrelations between kin, to give concrete form to the concept of evolutionary affinity. An image of proximity was extended to the entire living world with specific intent—not just that all the world's creatures could be imagined as under the tutelage of a single law (or deity) but that there were demonstrable degrees of affinity between them. Beer suggests that this demonstration was achieved through more than the promotion of apt images. The idea of an organic whole with diverse parts was conveyed through the organisation of the text itself (Beer 1983, 97):[17]

[16] We may look back on Frazer's arguments about magic and ritual and about the origins of totemism as clearing a conceptual space (in a field otherwise dominated by a dichotomy between religion and science) for, among others, Spencer and Gillen's account of Australian increase ceremonies. Thornton (1985, 10) speaks of Frazer's (and Mach's) influence on Malinowski as creating "a new discursive space for ethnographic argument." On ethnographic space in general, see Marcus and Cushman (1982, 42).

[17] Darwin was not just using "well-understood realities" with which the ill-understood ones "could be brought into the circle of the known" (Geertz 1983, 22). He was altering the sense of well-understood realities themselves. Thus Beer suggests that he played havoc with contemporary class assumptions embedded in the aristocratic connotations of genealogical trees; the history of man became a difficult and extensive family network, always aware of its lowly origins (1983, 63).

> For his theory to work, Darwin needs the sense of free play. . . . In his epistemology argument must emerge out of a plethora of instances because, of its nature, his text must at all costs avoid aligning itself with the procedures of artificial selection. . . . It is essential for Darwin's *theory* that the multitudinousness and variety of the natural world should flood through his language. His theory deconstructs any formulation which interprets the natural world as commensurate with man's understanding of it. It outgoes his powers of observation and is not co-extensive with his reasoning. Yet in the use of metaphor and analogy he found a means of restoring equivalence without false delimitation.

If Frazer also wrote determining fiction, what has to be explained in his case is its astonishingly ready acceptance at large. One reason, I suspect, is that the context for his writing was amply provided by the assumptions of the audience he addressed. Against a background of classical and Hebrew scholarships, whose presence if not the details his readers would have taken for granted, he simply introduced them to a third range of material, the primitive world from which he drew his comparisons. Here was the organising force of his accounts. The effectiveness of this juxtaposition lay in the comparable minutiae of the case he presented. He did not have to create the context in which his ideas could take shape and thus promote as an organising device an image (such as Darwin's metaphor of kinship among living things) drawn from some other domain. Indeed, by the 1900s, many of Frazer's ideas were unremarkable. Finding vestiges of the past in the present, treating the Old Testament as an archive, establishing contemporary parallels to former practices did not of themselves require new conceptualisation.

Frazer dealt with plurality and diversity (as Beer argues was central to Darwin's conception of the profusion of the natural world), but he did not represent this profusion in terms of a novel set of interrelationships. Ideas about the evolution of human thought from savagery to civilisation had been thoroughly aired. Moreover, far from going against the grain of his language, he gloried in the language to hand—the prefaces to both *The Golden Bough* ([1890] 1900) and *Folk-lore in the Old Testament* express his literary kinship with the ancients. The airy music he heard in spirit at Nemi was at one with his ear for the psalmists, prophets, and historians of the Old Testament who lit up the darker side of the ancient story, literary glories "that will live to delight and inspire mankind" (1918, 1:xi). Perhaps, as with the non-existent bells at Nemi, he could take the liberties he did because his language was so secure. One source of Fraser's impact on his general readers, then, must have been the familiarity, not the novelty, of his language and themes. And the *sense* of novelty with which we must also credit him came, as we shall see, from this very closeness to his readers, from what he shared with them, and not, as was to be the case with the anthropology which followed, a deliberate distancing from them.[18]

I want to suggest that self-consciousness about creating a distance between writer and reader, and thus about creating a context for ideas that are themselves novel, reemerged in anthropology as a "modernist" phenomenon. It required that the writer stand in a specific relation to his or her writing. By implication, the observer must stand in a particular relation to the observed, framing off the intellectual exercise as an endeavour of a particular kind.

The books that have become orthodox over the last sixty years are modernist in this sense. Recently, of course, there has been much questioning of the authorial status of the anthropologist. If we are to follow Ardener (1985), this questioning heralds the end of modernism, for it makes explicit the implicit reflexivity of the entire anthropological exercise of that sixty years, the relationship between the anthropologist and the other construed as an object of study (e.g., Crick 1982, 15). The division between observer and observed was always a self-conscious one. What typified the modernism of anthropology was the adoption of this division as a theoretical exercise through the phenomenon of fieldwork. The anthropologist who "entered" another culture carried that self-consciousness of the other with him or her. This was what was invented by the fieldworkers of Malinowski's day. Whatever the nature of their field experiences, it was visibly reinvented in the way monographs came to be organised.

Putting Things in Context

Modernism can mean as much or as little as one wishes. I do not intend a definition of the idea but would simply point to its current appropriation in the definition of a specific anthropological epoch.[19]

[18] Frazer and his predecessors had a clear idea where they stood as moderns in an age which regarded itself as modern. But one does rather get the impression that the savages they present in their pages would, if they could, agree with this arrangement of the world. A different kind of self-consciousness was to follow, which did not even hint at such an agreement. This created a new distance between the ethnographer and his/her readers.

[19] Hence my references to modernism (and postmodernism) are mediated through the writings of a small handful of anthropologists and are weighted towards the commentators on rather than the exponents of the genres.

Ardener is careful to delineate a particular character for modernism in anthropology which is not always in time with modernist forms in other fields. He does, however, associate Malinowski with its creation. Malinowski "completely rearranged social anthropology" (50), giving it a manifesto which above all rested on a perceived change of technique. Fieldwork was the new strategy by which the anthropologist could intervene, as Ardener puts it, at certain points in time and space "in which he or she behaved like an ideal metering device" (57). Historicism was rejected in favour of the discovery of holism and synchrony. The new anthropology rendered previous ways of dealing with cultural diversity quite obsolete, and knew itself as so doing.[20]

Such a genesis for modernism accords with the notion that Malinowski instigated the revolution which overthrew Frazer. At the same time, it is thoroughly tongue-in-cheek to talk of a Malinowskian revolution at all, as though it were an event and as though Malinowski (whatever he claimed himself) single-handedly masterminded it. What we have to explain is how this figure came to *stand for* the idea that there had been a revolution, a shift, in the discipline.

It is important to spell this out, because it is easy to show that what was true of Frazer was also true of Malinowski: his ideas were not particularly novel. Thus, he promoted functionalism, but if functionalist arguments can be traced to Frazer's own work (cf. Lienhardt 1966, Boon 1982) there are more continuities here than the idea of a revolution will allow. It is possible to recall Marett, who in 1912 was pressing for a functionalist interpretation of "the social life as a whole" (Langham 1981, xix–xx; Kuper 1973, 31),[21] or to note that "Jarvie makes it sound as though Malinowski, with no help from anyone else, was reacting directly against the work of Frazer. In fact, Rivers and his colleagues, A. C. Haddon and C. G. Seligman, were decisive in bringing about the change-over from nineteenth-century-style social evolutionism to twentieth-century-style structural-functionalism" (Langham 1981, 59). Or one might prefer to centralise Radcliffe-Brown as the principal instigator of the breakthrough in the oscilla-

[20] This knowing is important. Hence Ardener's claim that the nineteenth century was truly "modern," the twentieth modern only as genre and thus appropriately "modernist." Within anthropology, the modernist phase embodied a displacement of historicism with a deliberate stress on the contemporary.

[21] From the 1912 edition of *Notes and Queries on Anthropology*. Marett recommends an exhaustive and intensive investigation of social organisation, not only statically (cf. structure) but dynamically (cf. process). Moreover, he argues that the only scheme which has scientific value must be framed by the observer himself to suit the social conditions of the specific tribe being studied.

tion of previous diachronic paradigms (Stocking 1984) or to point out the exaggeration in subsequent estimations of Frazer's interest in beliefs rather than rites (Boon 1982, 11). Most ironic of all have been the exaggerated claims made for Malinowski's promotion of fieldwork and the detraction that he did not really invent fieldwork after all.

Firth (1985) points to a tradition of fieldwork well under way before Malinowski's apotheosis of it. He suggests that Malinowski's novelty lay rather in his elevating the method to a theory (cf. Leach 1957, 120). Stocking (1983, 93) has dug up Rivers's prescriptions for fieldwork, which, in 1913, spelled out the programme Malinowski enacted: The worker should live for a year or more in the field, in a community where he comes to know everyone, and, not content with generalised information, study every feature of life in concrete detail. "Long before Malinowski's influence was felt, Rivers was hailed as the apostle of the new approach to fieldwork" (Langham 1981, 50). Was the difference then that Malinowski did it, his fieldwork style a matter of "placing oneself in a situation where one might have a certain type of experience" (Stocking 1983, 112)? Surveying the several anthropologists who left English universities for the field at about that time and noting the intensive nature of their studies, Stocking is forced to argue: "Something more than delayed or institutionally marginal careers would seem to be involved . . . in the lapsed remembrance of these other academic ethnographers of Malinowski's generation . . . [to wit] their early monographs did not present them as self-conscious ethnographic innovators" (84).[22] If Malinowski did not really invent holism, synchrony, intensive fieldwork, and the rest, then was there no invention at all? I have prefigured my answer, that it lay in how he wrote, and specifically in the organisation of text. This implemented the kinds of relationships between writer, reader, and subject matter that were to dominate anthropology, British and beyond, for the next sixty years.

By contrast, his descriptive style as such is retrospective. Indeed, it is for this aspect of his style that Malinowski is often held most closely to imitate Frazer. Leach (1957, 119) refers to his "Frazerian style of fine writing," Firth to Malinowski's romantic mode as opposed to the classical mode of Radcliffe-Brown, and Kaberry (1957, 87) argues that it was the acceptance not of Malinowski's but of Radcliffe-Brown's conceptual distinctions which led to a widespread

[22] See also Leach (1957, 120); interestingly, Stocking (1983, 79) claims a precursor in Spencer and Gillen's *The Native Tribes of Central Australia*, "recognisably 'modern' in its ethnographic style. . . . given focus by a totalising cultural performance." Its subsequent status was compromised, Stocking suggests, by Spencer's failure to leave significant academic progeny.

style of ethnographic writing emphasising definitional precision and plain language. What must be laid at Malinowski's door, rather, is the proclamation of the kinds of spaces that had to be made to convey the "new" analytical ideas. It was because this contextualisation was novel that the ideas themselves came to appear novel and that other scholars who might have been regarded as former exponents of them were rendered invisible. Its power for anthropologists lay in the parallel between the framework of the monograph and the framework of the field experience.

Fieldwork made a new kind of persuasive fiction possible. But I would follow Clifford (1986) in suggesting that this should be considered the other way around: the fieldwork experience *was reconstructed in the monographs* in such a way as to become an organising device for the monograph as such.[23] Malinowski was able to create a context for "new" ideas (such as the perception of society as a functioning whole) by making much of the social and cultural context in which indigenous ideas were found. This indeed was the subject of his Frazer lecture on myth (Malinowski [1925]), a disquisition on the importance of seeing myths in their life-context, that is, the society and culture which the ethnographer describes. Trobriand ideas had functions which could not be grasped otherwise. He acknowledges his debt to Frazer's own insistence on the connection between belief and rite and between tradition, magic, and social power. Yet the importance of setting things in their social context came to be universally underlined in anthropology at large by the disparagement of Frazer's disregard for context, for the new ideas in question had acquired a double identity: the organising analytical ideas of the anthropologists were themselves contextualised by putting into *their* social context the indigenous ideas through which people organised their experiences. Contexts could be compared. This instigated a persuasive literary device in the arrangement of the texts through which societies and cultures were to be described.

It was all very well for Malinowski to expound that Trobriand myths were part and parcel of people's pragmatic experience. How was the distinctive nature of that experience conveyed to a non-Trobriand audience? A juxtaposition was engineered through describing the experience of the central figure of the fieldworker entering a culture (cf. Clifford 1986, 162–63).[24] Trobriand ideas thereby juxtaposed

[23] Clifford (1986, 162): "ethnographic comprehension (a coherent position of sympathy and hermeneutic engagement) is better seen as a creation of ethnographic writing than as a consistent quality of ethnographic *experience*."

[24] Clifford suggests that the insights of fieldwork were constructed less in the field

were contrasted with those of the culture from which the fieldworker came. Thus the Other (Fabian 1983, xi; Marcus and Cushman 1982, 49) was constructed. And however the divide between self and other was constructed in the colonial encounter, in the prejudices of the fieldworker, in the assumptions of his or her audience, it structured the resultant monographs to great creative effect.[25]

The new kind of book which Malinowski wrote was not just the holistic monograph centered on a particular people or the elucidation of the distinctiveness of unique societies that was to be the foundation of subsequent comparative sociology. Leach (1957, 120) points to the significant theoretical assumption that the total field of data under observation must "fit together" and "make sense": "No data outside the immediate subjective-objective present need to be considered." The new kind of book, then, was also premised on a disjunction between observer (subject) and observed (object), a disjunction that made the observer aware of technique and led subsequently to the conceptualisation of anthropological practice as model building. Analytical frameworks became countenanced as deliberate artifice. The contrast between this modernism and Frazer's historicism was embodied in a new version of primitiveness[26]—a version that incorporated a new relationship. The difference between "us" and "them" was conceived not as a different stage in evolutionary progression but as a difference of perspective. "They" did not use the same frames as "we" do through which to visualise the world. Simply as ethnocentricism that was no discovery at all. Rather, ethnocentricism was invented both as a theoretical principle and as an organising framework for writing. And it was displayed in the arrangement and relationship of ideas internal to the monograph. A radical way of presenting the anthropological subject was opened up; its two elements were both creative for the discipline.

The first was the literary implementation of ethnocentrism which has characterised the modernist period throughout: the realisation

(where Malinowski, in his own words, lacked a real character) than in the process of writing *Argonauts*, where he established himself as fieldworker-anthropologist.

[25] It was not just the myth of Malinowski as fieldworker which defined modern anthropology—the fieldworker was a symbolic vehicle for a new kind of literary production. Therefore no amount of demythologising will affect the fact that whatever fieldwork went on before, and however patchy it really was afterwards, the symbol of the fieldworker had a new power in post-Malinowskian writing. This and a number of other points I emphasise are anticipated by Boon (e.g., "The author as fieldworker was always implicitly present; the author as author was always implicitly absent" [1983, 138]). See Beer (1986, 226–27) on Charles Darwin's presentation as the fieldworker.

[26] Captured in Ardener's quip that Malinowski created modern primitivism for modern people (1985, 59).

that frames are only frames, that concepts are culture-bound, that analytical terms are themselves buried in premises and assumptions. From the start the modern ethnographers sought to dislodge the taken-for-granted status of Western concepts—the development of a technical terminology proceeded hand in hand with self-scrutiny. There was always much more to the definitions of terms such as law or family than cultural relativism.

The second was the discovery of the ordinary in the bizarre, civilisation under savagery. The ruling mode of ethnographic presentation became exactly what Jarvie parodies (1984, 15, my emphasis):

> What the fieldwork involves is going to an exotic society and succeeding *in making good sense* to the outsider of its customs and institutions. So each monograph in effect says, "Look here! Pretty bizarre, eh. Just what you expected of benighted, irrational, anarchic primitives. But now look closer. What do you see? They live an ordered, reasonable, perhaps even admirable social life."

"Making sense" was, at least initially, a question of making "commonsense" (Leach 1982, 28–29). Extravagant as he was in his atmospheric writing, Malinowski also insisted on the need to cover seriously and soberly all aspects of tribal culture. What for him was an injunction not to pick out the sensational and singular, to make no difference between the commonplace and the out-of-the-way ([1922], 11), became subsequently a maxim about ordinariness itself. Thus Jarvie dwells on Evans-Pritchard's remark that post-Frazerian anthropology was not searching after strange or colourful appeals to romantic interests but endorsed matter-of-fact enquiries about social institutions (1964, 4, 13, 214). Leach has recently restated the point: "It is always highly desirable that the fieldworker should rid himself of the notion that there is something altogether extraordinary about the situation he is observing" (1982, 29). And how many anthropological courses begin with the adage that the anthropologist's job is to make sense of what is first presented as strange, to render beliefs and acts in terms of their taken-for-granted status in the context of people's lives. Jarvie's complaint is that after the first or second exposure to this revelation, the repetition becomes boring.

For the discipline, both moves were highly productive. They led to the development of various frames by which other societies and cultures could be analysed, and they put the anthropologist in the position of elucidating the bizarre, thus revealing the logic and order in other people's lives. Malinowski himself is sometimes credited with imposing rationality on his subjects. His sense of the ordinariness of Trobriand culture certainly opened up the conceptual space for future investigations into primitive logic and reasoning.[27] At the same time his holism created the context for enquiries into systems, though he did not take this far himself.

In the end it was inevitable that anthropologists should be criticised for treating the people they study as "objects" (cf. Fabian 1983). But that objectification was a product of a positioning of the anthropologist's own ideas (the analytical frames) against those attributed to his other subjects. This remained a structuring framework for the writing of monographs long after Malinowski's functionalism was considered of theoretical interest—the holism that first compelled the subjective-objective relation was no longer required for the endless investigation of that crucial relationship itself. The effect of the observer / observed dichotomy had been to create a sense of alienness or otherness, introducing the reader to the bizarre and simultaneously overcoming it by locating what "we" see as bizarre within a context where for "them" it is familiar and ordinary. The ordinariness was in this sense a technical ordinariness, that is, a product of accounting for ideas or behaviour in terms of the context to which they properly belonged. Foregrounded in the new anthropology (cf. Clifford 1986), "society" or "culture" domestically enclosed such ideas. Strangeness had to lie outside this boundary and was identifiable only in context-crossing.[28] The supreme context-crossing was between observer and observed. Thus was created the central problem of modernist anthropology in whose terms I couched my original question: how to manipulate familiar ideas and concepts to convey alien ones.

The concentration of the new ethnographies on single cultures opened up the possibility of exploiting the dualism of the relation between observer and observed, using one's own language in reversing or turning upside down one's own categories (e.g., we regard payment as antithetical to kin relations, they regard kin relations as based on transactions). Concepts paired in the observer's culture

[27] Stocking (1984, 178) cites with amusement Gregory Bateson's despair at being unable to find a single instance of the word "logic" in the whole of *Coral Gardens and Their Magic*. But functionalism assumed that the anthropologist "could find reason even where it had never in fact presented itself to the individual savage consciousness" (183).

[28] One might recall functionalist examinations of witchcraft and sorcery beliefs here: what was classified as strange or exotic had to be seen to cross some social boundary or other. I would argue that the anthropology of classification and boundaries so prevalent in the 1950s and 1960s spoke to an implicit epistemology which domesticated behaviour (it all "made sense") as the attribute of a particular culture or society and therefore led to a special problem in accounting for people's own concepts of the bizarre and exotic from within those cultures or societies.

could be split apart (e.g., we have a commodity economy, they have a gift economy). Because the other was framed off, it became possible to use terms within the frame for meanings different from those they held outside it (kinship to them is not what we mean by the term). And so on.[29] In these ways, manipulating one's own concepts to conceptualise ones constructed as alien established distances between writer, reader, and the subject of study.[30]

Jarvie berates modern(ist) anthropologists for striving to show that there is nothing exceptional about the lives they describe. The analytical technique, deriving from postulates about the integrity of society and culture, is embedded in literary technique. The imaginative leap becomes between what "we" find ordinary and what "they" find ordinary. Hence the significance of Malinowski's perpetual insistence that "they" were more than projections of Western theories. The burden of his Frazer lecture was that Trobrianders did not treat their myths as armchair theorists speculated they would. Their ideas had to be appreciated in their own terms, not least for the reason that myths could not be treated as some "primitive intellectual armchair occupation" ([1925], 82). There were no armchair theorists on the

[29] Other disjunctions typical of this mode include (1) dividing data into domains, such as kinship or economy, which are then collapsed or seen as versions of one another; (2) defining concepts by negation—the X have (say) no concept of "culture"—in order to introduce discontinuities into what are habitual dichotomies in Western thought (e.g., the contrast between culture and nature); (3) cross-cultural comparison which rests on an elucidation of similarities and differences but always implies the distinctiveness of units so compared; and (4) internal comparison within the analysis between us and them, now and then (the other being presented as a version of oneself or in antithesis to the familiar self).

[30] I hope I have made it clear the extent to which I would defend the Malinowskian disjunctions: artificiality (between "us" and "them") is contained within the construction of a literary product concerned with a question that is far from artificial, making conceptual space for social others. Let me draw on an instance with which I am concerned: the terms "gift" and "commodity" for contrasts between Melanesian and Western exchange systems. The two terms only make sense from the point of view of a commodity economy. At the same time, one can use them to talk about two radically different ways of organising the world. This lays one open to empiricist suggestion that gift was never observed in a pristine state. But objections of this kind leave one serious problem: how otherwise is a writer on Melanesia to present to a largely Western audience the distinctiveness of Melanesian social organisation, of ideas about personhood, of all the subtle and complex, as well as fundamental and crude, ways in which Melanesian concepts do or do not have analogies in the Western world? As a practical literary necessity, how is one to proceed? De Heusch, for instance, shrinks the idea of gift to an economic transaction and puts in its stead the idea of ritual cuisine as "the expression of the social order" (1985, 17). Anthropologists do this all the time; but it makes comparison hard because one needs to know the literary locus of such constructs in the writer's account: what they stand for—not just how they are defined but what part they play in the construction of analysis.

Trobriands! Thus it was necessary to jar his readers / hearers into accepting the distinctiveness of Trobriand passions before expounding on their fitting place within the pragmatics of local life. The audience had to accept the naturalness of Trobriand ideas in their context—once that context had been created in the separation of the culture of those to whom he was speaking from the culture of those about whom he was speaking. The audience was required to connive in its distance from the anthropologist's subject matter. Meanwhile the anthropologist moved between the two. His proximity to the culture he was studying became his distance from the one he was addressing, and vice versa. This, *tout court*, is how the modern(ist) fieldworker has imagined him- or herself ever since.[31]

Out of Context

We are now in a better position to appreciate the persuasion of Frazer's fictions—and his reputation among modernist anthropologists who found them not at all persuasive.

Once the new frameworks for comparison were created—the distinctiveness of different kinds of societies provided a basis for what became in essence a comparison of contexts—Frazer's comparative sociology looked ludicrous. Hence the most common charge against him, that he tore things out of their context.[32] His episodic treatment of the Old Testament and the similarities he shows between Hebrew customs and those from Melanesia, Africa, or wherever seem to entail the worst kind of indiscriminate borrowings, with no regard for historical or social circumstances. Frazer was not manipulating the internal discriminations between writer and subject matter, between observer and observed, that typified the modernists. On the contrary, he depended on a kinship between his own revelations and contemporary interest in the classics, here the Old Testament, and in the early history of man. Far from distancing himself from his audience, he appeared to share much with them.

Certainly he evinced neither of the strategies that were to become

[31] The triad writer/subject/audience was constantly played as a dyad (observer/observed, anthropologist-reporter/reader) (cf. Webster 1982).

[32] Gellner (1985b, 645) uses this phrase of the reaction of Malinowski's functionalism to Frazerian speculation. Frazer assembles a vast array of fragmentary data out of context, whereas Malinowski's fieldwork method, he observes, was an exhaustive exploration of social contexts. Lienhardt (1966, 27) succinctly presents the modernist orthodoxy: Frazer "thought he could understand very foreign beliefs quite out of their real contexts simply by an effort of introspection."

so significant. First, he was not interested in the status of his frames, in perpetually specifying his own ethnocentrism. Hence the ease with which he could comprehend what it was like to be in Nemi or what the ancient Hebrews might be expected to do (e.g., 1918, 3, 80). There was no problem about interpreting people's emotions or motivations. In the course of his disquisition on marriage, Frazer is meticulous in locating the particular sources from which he gleans his innumerable pieces of information. Where possible he quotes such reasons as people are reported giving, but he has no hesitation in supplying them himself. This is a comment on the direct exchange of women in Melanesia (1918, 2, 216):

> No doubt the practice of exchanging women in marriage may be observed from a variety of motives, one of which in certain cases may well be the desire to keep up a sept at full strength by only parting with women on condition of receiving an equal number of women in exchange. But such a motive of public policy seems less simple and primitive than the purely economic motive which I take to be at the base of the custom; for while the economic motive appeals directly to every man in his individual capacity, the public motive appeals to men in their collective capacity as members of a community, and therefore is likely to affect only that enlightened minority who are capable of subordinating their private interest to the public good.

The selection of reasons is governed by what he imputes as likely examples of simple and primitive behaviour. Few modern monographs do not also impute thoughts and feelings to the people being described; the difference is the validating presence of the fieldworker, who uses the self as a metering device (cf. Clifford 1983). In talking of the economic motives of marriage, Frazer had to be guided by the ethnographers who reported to him. Thus, he says carefully that "the natives of the northern coast of Dutch New Guinea are said to regard their marriageable daughters as wares which they can sell without consulting the wishes of the girls themselves" (1918, 2, 217). Yet this leads not to a scrutiny of what the said natives might mean but to a general extrapolation (1918, 220):

> [It] seems probable that the practice of exchanging daughters or sisters in marriage was everywhere at first a simple case of barter, and that it originated in a low state of savagery where women had a high economic value as labourers, but where private property was as yet at so rudimentary a stage that a man had practically no equivalent to give for a wife but another woman. The same economic motive might lead the offspring of such unions, who would be cross cousins, to marry each other. . . .

For a modernist reader, it is not just the economics but the kinship structures which require elucidation. The relationship between these would give an internal authority to the account. Frazer establishes his authority, however, with reference to an extraneous frame, the sense of history which he shares with his readers (1918, 220):

> If the history of the custom could be followed in the many different parts of the world where it has prevailed, it might be possible everywhere to trace it back to this simple origin; for under the surface alike of savagery and of civilisation the economic forces are as constant and uniform in their operation as the forces of nature, of which indeed, they are merely a peculiarly complex manifestation.

Frazer was not particularly interested, then, in framing off his ideas from either those of his audience or those he was describing, and the second point is that consequently he did *not* have to make good sense of the bizarre. True, he sought to show how customs since abandoned and disclaimed as barbaric were not to be dismissed from the Old Testament as fantasy but bore close resemblance to the practice of many cultures. But this is not the same as making sense of them. Rather, it confirms their status as indices of savagery: Frazer's savage was the antique man whose practices of simple and primitive times were still preserved. He established the plausibility of the numerous customs he reported by showing how they occurred again and again, and he supplied motives and reasons from his general understanding of primitive society. But there was no need to justify them in terms of a logical system or tease out their connections with other ideas. His narrative showed example after example of what happened—it could not create an internal context for turning the merely conceivable into a distinctive cultural logic. The customs made sense in only a very limited way. Above all, he had no theoretical motive for rendering the exotic ordinary. On the contrary, the effect of his literary composition was to show, at every point, *the ordinary to be cognate with the extraordinary.*[33]

This perhaps is the power of all those examples out of context. Ap-

[33] Boon (1982, 11) claims that Frazer's prose describes unbelievable rites believably. At the same time, while Malinowski inscribed practices not as exotic specimens but as straightforward human experience, Frazer "represented the culmination of traditional compilations of 'fardles of fashions' and cabinets of curiosities" (1982, 17). Frazer made such curiosities plausible but not logical. Cf. Stocking (1984, 183): "the armchair anthropologist—archetypically, Frazer—could give [irrational beliefs and customs] rational meaning through the in-built rationalistic utilitarianism of the doctrine of survival: what made no rational sense in the present was perfectly understandable as the sheer persistence of the imperfectly rational pursuit of utility in an earlier stage."

ropos the Old Testament, Frazer was taking a story which would have been very familiar to his readers. Whatever was thought about particular incidents, within the framework of the biblical story they had a long-established place.[34] He exposes the story episode by episode, showing the affinities of Hebrew customs to those drawn from savage or patriarchal peoples from all over the world. Incidents which might have been accepted as simply part of the narrative are shown to be remarkable by comparison with exotic customs. Thus the disjunction upon which Frazer plays is between his reader's prior perceptions of biblical customs as ordinary and their far from ordinary cognates. This allows a further disjunction, between the customs the reader takes for granted in his or her own culture and the origins of these same customs under very different, savage, regimes. In short, Frazer has taken his text apart. What coheres, as the biblical tales unfold, is shown to be a palimpsest of reports about events which no longer belong intrinsically to one another but instead have a family resemblance to doings all over the world. They are to be appreciated in the light of social and practical reasons that appear in many times and places: a global culture indeed, differentiated only through the stages of savagery and civilisation.[35]

Frazer's prefatory remarks, dated May 1918, conclude with the observation that "the revelation of the baser elements which underlay the civilization of ancient Israel, as they underlie the civilization of modern Europe, serves rather as a foil to enhance by contrast the glory of a people which, from such dark depths of ignorance and cruelty, could rise to such bright heights" (1918, 1:x). It is not just the multitude of times and places that makes an effect, but that for his parallels Frazer drew on cultures that would already be classified in the general reader's mind as exotic. The revelation was that civilisation so-called should consist of so much former savagery. Was it this juxtaposition of civilisation and savagery that gripped his contem-

[34] Malinowski's own review (reprinted 1962) of the abridged edition of *Folk-lore* comments that Frazer reshapes familiar facts and situations (the "story has been lived through by every one of us") but that though familiar they were always disturbing and incomprehensible, bound up with dreams and fantasies instilled in childhood. Feeley-Harnik (1985) develops the suggestion that *The Golden Bough,* as a treatise on the savage thoughts that compel people to kill in order to prosper, deploys the sacrifice of the priest / king as a metaphor to understand the irrationality and violence underlying, as she puts it, the smooth surface of Christian ideals of progress in Victorian and Edwardian England.

[35] He appears to use this classification from time to time, but it does not organise his arrangement of examples. Nor does he seek historic parallels to his biblical characters. Thus he adduces Papua New Guinea parallels in his discussion of the Patriarchal Age and the Times of Judges and Kings alike.

poraries' minds? In the relationship Frazer enjoyed with his general readers and (through what he read) with those about whom he wrote he presumed a continuity. It was a continuity that embraced the rational and irrational alike, that could be shared on the grounds of *either* savagery or civilisation, neither distinguished in any absolute sense as the attribute of this or that whole society. The "enlightened minority" among his Melanesians foreshadowed a civilised attention to the public good, like the literary light that shone forth from the Hebrew writers. This theme of illumination runs through his narrative in consistent parallel to the unearthing of the "baser elements": "The annals of savagery and superstition unhappily compose a large part of human literature; but in what other volume (than the Old Testament) shall we find, side by side with that melancholy record, psalmists who poured forth their sweet and solemn strains, etc." (1918, vol. 1:xi, my emphasis). Reader and writer share a text: what the writer forces his readers to realise is the unevenness of the text itself, its multivocality, its side-by-side conjunction of savagery and civilisation.

When, fifty years before, Lubbock had lectured at the Royal Institution on "The Origin of Civilization and the Primitive Condition of Man," he had confessed a block to his desire to describe the "social and mental condition of savages" (1875a): he would have to refer to ideas and acts which might be abhorrent to his listeners. Frazer, in command of an astonishing array of materials, much of it collected in the intervening years, gives a vivid discourse on the social and mental condition of savages through the mediating texts of works thoroughly familiar and respectable. The result, I have suggested, is the exoticisation of those familiar and respectable ideas. The world is seen to be plural, composite, full of diverse manners, of echoes from the past. The present, the ordinary, holds all the colourful possibilities of folklore, quite as much as civilisation is revealed as barely concealing a medley of practices which belong to darker, older days.

In fact, one could almost call Frazer an "aesthete with the ability to select references," for whom "the act of invention consists in rereading the past and recombining a selection of its elements" (*The Listener*, March 20, 1986, p. 32), or say that his style "evokes, hints, reminds," in a world of infinite referrals where signs "are not arbitrary because meanings are sedimented in them: signs have 'been around'; they bear the traces of past semantic manoeuvres"; consequently, "instead of analytical steps there is a suggestive use of images, quizzical manoeuvres and numerous asides," so that writing comes to seem a promiscuous dissemination or explosion (Crick 1985, 72–73 and citing Tyler 1984, 329). These remarks are not, of course, made of Frazer but represent two attempts to evoke a postmodern mood. This brings me to my final comments on the nature of Frazer's creativity.

Playing with Context

Whether we are or are not entering a postmodern phase in social anthropology, enough people seem to be speaking as though we were for the idea to be of interest. Crick sees it as among those diverse trends which include reflexive anthropology, critical anthropology, semantic anthropology, semiotic anthropology, and post-structuralism (1985, 71). This, he says (quoting Hastrup 1978), is not a unitary position, but in the aftermath of modernism we are not to be surprised that there appears to be no particular future[36] or that history may be put into reverse. Crick describes as suitably ironic the recent retrieval of Leenhardt, Lévi-Strauss's predecessor in Paris, whose work is ripe for discovery in a post-structuralist era (Clifford 1982, 2; cf. Young 1983, 169). At the same time Ardener (1985) is arguing that although other disciplines may think of structuralism as postmodern, its place in anthropology is as a thoroughly modernist phenomenon. Thus he traces the span of modernism in anthropology from Malinowski (in 1920) to the beginning of the decline of structuralist influence in the mid-'70s. The demise of structuralism / modernism is underlined by the resurrection of Leenhardt, a figure who preceded the chief exponent of structuralism as far as much anthropology is concerned (Crick 1985, 72).

Crick here draws attention to Clifford's biography of Leenhardt. Leenhardt is presented as someone whose work "addresses itself to the present concern with more 'open' cultural theories—modes of understanding capable of accounting for innovative process and historical discontinuity and for reciprocity in ethnographical interpretation" (Clifford 1982, 2). Leenhardt's access to "the native's point of view" was not just through fieldwork empathy but involved a collective work of mutual translation, one that could not be easily domi-

[36] If the modern is a kind of appropriated future, its collapse must be perceived as the collapse of the future (Ardener 1985, 57). However, in the very way current experiments in ethnographic writing bring modernism to consciousness, they may also be seen as part of modernism itself (e.g., Marcus 1986); cf. Foster (1983, ix): "if the modern project is to be saved at all, it must be exceeded." It will be apparent that I use the contrast between modernism and postmodernism to indicate a shift within anthropological writing—one might or might not wish to subsume it all under the term "modern."

nated by a privileged interpretation (Clifford 1980, 526). The context for Clifford's interest is similar reciprocities identifiable in the writing of a new generation of ethnographers concerned with the representation of dialogue—how the fieldwork encounter is itself handled, and thus how ethnography is written.

The historian's championing of Leenhardt also involves something of an assault on Malinowski (Clifford 1983).[37] The time seems ripe to expose the figure of the fieldworker who was the register of the otherness of cultures. Clifford tackles the authority which anthropologists claimed this gave their writings: the fieldworker who came back from another society spoke for it in a determining way which now appears repugnant. Whether or not anthropologists ever did claim such authority is beside the point. It is the kind of book they wrote which is exposed: the monograph presented simply as though it were about a particular people, the author absent because the fieldworker is the authority for the text (and see Marcus and Cushman 1982, 31–32). But "the silence of the ethnographic workshop has been broken—by insistent, heteroglot voices, by the scratching of other pens" (Clifford 1983, 121). For some while now it has become widely accepted that the fieldworker must be written back into the text as also its author and reproduce the conditions of his or her encounter with the other. Reflexive anthropology sees the resultant production as a dialogue between anthropologist and informant so-called: the observer/observed relationship can no longer be assimilated to that between subject and object.[38] The object(ive) is a joint production. Many voices, multiple texts, plural authorship (e.g., Rabinow 1983; Clifford 1980, 1982) suggest a new genre. "Ethnography must hang on in good faith to the myriad contingencies and opaque personali-

[37] "Assault" is too strong a word in the light of his overall appraisal of Malinowski. On subsequently comparing Malinowski as the diarist and as the author of *Argonauts*, Clifford (1986) resurrects him as an original heteroglot, someone capable of trying out different voices, different personae; and he sympathetically describes the "ample, multiperspectival, meandering structure of *Argonauts*" (1986, 156) where modernists have simply seen arguments without structure. The fact that a convincing totalisation always escaped his work, Clifford suggests, aligns Malinowski with latter-day cosmopolitanism. In his earlier article, *Argonauts* had been the archetype for a generation of ethnographies that "successfully established participant-observation's scientific validity" Clifford 1983, 123–24). Clifford's thesis is that what was created in the writing of ethnography was the experience of the fieldworker as a unifying source of authority, dissonant with the fieldwork experience itself. What thus requires assault is the authority embedded in the literary symbol of Malinowski as fieldworker.

[38] Webster (1982, 96) criticises the tradition in anthropology in which the understanding subject and the object understood are grasped as primordial realities. Thinking one can substitute subject for object will not do: we have to know that it is in the course of dialogue that both subjectification and objectification are necessarily created.

ties of reality, and deny itself the illusion of a transparent description" (Webster 1982, 111). Writing has become a question of authorship, even to the point of a new denial of it, insofar as the "negotiated reality" of the text is the social or experiential reality of neither party (Crapanzano 1980).

Over the last decade or two, there has been increasing awareness that the dichotomies which characterised modernism in anthropology will not do, the easiest target being synchrony, the timelessness of descriptions framed not by history but by the distinction between "us" and "them." In fact, there has always been criticism of the ahistoricity of anthropology, in the misleading charge that anthropologists create an idealised break between the pristine society "before contact" and the "social change" since (misleading because, to borrow from Ardener, it reads the dichotomies as a matter of life rather than genre). This has joined with mounting criticism about the audacity of the anthropologist to speak for the other, to treat other persons as objects, not allowing the authors of accounts their own voice, and so on.[39] In short, that powerful modernist frame, the distinction between us and them which created the context for positioning the writer in relation to those he/she was describing, has become thoroughly discredited. The other as literary object, being taken by critics as situating human subjects as objects, can no longer survive as the explicit organising frame of texts. No one set of voices should be denied or privileged—the author must objectify his own position in the ethnography quite as much as he or she strives to render the subjectivity of others.

There is an inherent ambivalence ("ludic" is Crick's word) in certain current exponents of postmodernism. They are deservedly after the event—for their strength lies in exposing the artificial edifice of structuralism, ethnographic authority, or whatever.[40] Structuralist

[39] Marcus and Cushman (1982, 25–26) argue that recent self-reflectiveness in ethnographic writing aims to demystify the process of fieldwork, and thus to confront the objectification of the resultant texts. Geertz [1985] refers to postmodern self-doubt as anxiety about the representation of the other in ethnographic discourse. However, it is interesting to note a parallel between Webster's 1982 criticism of Geertz and Rabinow's criticism of Clifford: both Geertz and Clifford are attuned to multiple texts but proceed to absent themselves from the narrative—i.e., fail to objectify their own participation.

[40] A point also made outside anthropological interest in postmodernism; hence Jameson's comment to the effect that there will be as many different forms of postmodernism as there were established forms of high modernism (1985, 111). If as in anthropology "modernism" is now uncovered in retrospect, there will be considerable ambiguity about what is modernist and what is postmodernist (see n. 36). A simple

and ethnographer alike were playing games too, the difference being that they did not know it. It is that realisation which is crucially postmodern. The appropriate genre is not representation but the "representation of representations" (Rabinow 1986, 250).[41] In the subsequent reappropriation of anthropological history, Leenhardt is particularly interesting as a pre-Malinowskian fieldworker.[42] Perhaps he is attractive because the religious embodiment of his ideas (Clifford 1982, 3) evinces that move away from the separation of the sociological and phenomenological towards signs embedded in human use and intentionality to which Tyler refers (1984, 328). The missionary observer is a good exemplar, since his understandings are purposed. But British anthropology has a prominent figure of its own, so to speak, in Malinowski's supposed predecessor, Frazer. Indeed, in some respects, Frazer's bookish plenitude is highly evocative.

I am not suggesting that Frazer is a postmodern. He could not be, since the mood takes its creativity from modernism (Ardener 1985, 60). But perhaps he is a person whom postmodernism allows us to countenance. It is salutary to think of Frazer because it is salutary to think about what the modernists found so distasteful in him—taking things out of context. The postmodern mood is to make deliberate play with context. It is said to blur boundaries, destroy the dichotomizing frame, juxtapose voices, so that the multiple product, the monograph jointly authored, becomes conceivable. It remains up to the reader to pick his or her way through the differing positions and contexts of the speakers. Mere points of view (cf. Hill 1986), these contexts have ceased in themselves to provide the organising frameworks for the ethnographic narrative. A new relationship between writer, reader, and subject matter is contemplated. Decoding the exotic ("making sense") will no longer do; postmodernism requires the reader to interact with exotica in itself.

However, I want to introduce a note of discord: to raise Frazer both with respect and as a spectre. The discord is between what contemporary anthropologists are doing in toying with labels such as postmodernism and what they continue to do in their writings. Indeed,

---

binarism will not do: insofar as postmodernism recovers the past, it seeks to recover modernism as well and is thus itself a modernist project.

[41] I profited from reading Rabinow's paper in draft form, as I did from Marcus's in the same volume (*Writing Culture*). This and Marcus and Fischer's work on anthropology as cultural critique were published after the lecture was prepared; I do not consider them here, though both are clearly germane to my themes. I am grateful to Paul Rabinow for his comments on the lecture.

[42] Young (1983, 169): "As an ethnographer Leenhardt amply fulfilled the conditions for intensive fieldwork a dozen years before Malinowski, seeking mastery of a native tongue as the key to his research."

as happened in the early programmes for feminist writing, there is more talk about what postmodernism might be than examples of it. I suggest that there is a significant difference between blurring contexts and playing with them, between free play and play, between a composite identity and reciprocity; and that the evocation of postmodernism draws on images not always very appropriate for the anthropology which goes under its name. Such identifiably postmodern anthropologists[43] as there are play with contexts, knowingly; they do not simply scramble them. Crick says (1985, 85) that there is no such thing as free play, that a paradox is impossible without a notion of rules. The problem is that the *representation* of activity as postmodern blurs *that* distinction—dwelling instead on the tropic release afforded by context jumping.[44] This is where the spectre enters. If we really want to scramble contexts, then we have a historical guide in Frazer himself.

At this point, I must make my own account explicit. There is a tension between two styles / frames, neither of which quite encompasses the other. The first might mock itself as following contemporary fashion in stressing the literary rather than the scientific or argumentative aspects of Frazer's work. The very use of the word "fiction" conveys a self-conscious playfulness. This reflects uncertainty on my part as to what the idea of postmodernism is all about. Of course, the answer is that the idea is not "about" (anything other than itself)—it is enacted, performed. The second is a modernist one. I have sought for a certain perspective on Frazer by putting some of his writing into context, and thus have produced a kind of history. Though considering Frazer and Malinowski by reference to their persuasive fictions, I have presented them as though they shared the modernist problem, how to convey alien ideas across cultures.[45] Arguing that Malinowski did this differently from Frazer projects the problem backwards in the very form Malinowski and his colleagues

[43] Or anthropologists who are interested in the questions raised by taking a deliberate postmodern stance but would not necessarily use the label of themselves. This position is exactly analogous to that of anthropologists interested in feminist issues who do not necessarily call themselves feminist anthropologists.

[44] What we might call the misrepresentation of postmodernism comes from the very efforts to represent it. Again, outside anthropology, Foster (1985, xi) takes pains to distinguish postmodernism, a specific conflict of old and new modes, from relativism and pluralism, "the quixotic notion that all positions in culture and politics are now open and equal."

[45] Marcus and Cushman (1982, 46): "Not only must the ethnographer's conceptual and descriptive language make (common) sense to his reader within their own cultural framework, but it must communicate meanings to these same readers which they are persuaded would make (again, common) sense to the ethnographer's subjects."

created. Nevertheless, in setting these approaches side by side, let me suggest both how it is possible to appreciate Frazer in a new light and why we should be cautious about doing so.

A Postmodern Fashion?

If there is one word which summarises the anthropological recognition of a postmodern mood, it is *irony*.[46] And the current rediscovery of irony indicates all the difference between the "free play" which some descriptions of postmodernism hint at and postmodernist "play," if it exists, in anthropological writing. Irony involves not a scrambling but a deliberate juxtaposition of contexts, pastiche perhaps but not jumble.

Those aware of irony find irony in others. I am tempted to suggest that some of Beer's reading of Darwin makes such play. She comments on how rich in contradictory elements Darwin's prose is, how multivalent and full of hermeneutic potential with its "power to yield a great number of significant and various meanings" (1983, 10). He accepts the variability of words, "their tendency to dilate and contract across related senses, to oscillate between significations" (1983, 38). Darwin's profuse metaphors renounce a Cartesian clarity or univocality, she suggests, an echo of the contrast Boon uses in discovering that Frazer's vision as well as his prose may have been touched with irony; Frazer displaced one-dimensional reportage with multidimensional representation (1982, 11).[47] He emphasised the rich array of primitive rite, confronting the paradox (Boon says) that modern anthropologists were to avoid: "how cultures, perfectly commonsensical from within, nevertheless flirt with their own 'alternities,' gain critical self-distance, formulate complex (rather than

[46] I am grateful to Richard Fardon and James Boon for their comments on an earlier draft of this paper, and for pointing out that irony can take many forms. One could construct a virtual typology of ironies. However, it should be clear that I do not intend to discriminate thus between the kinds of distancing mechanism and false recognitions that we may discern in the writings of past anthropologists; rather, my interest is in the fact that "irony" has become a contemporary buzz-word for distance and recognition on the part of contemporary commentators. It is how often the term is now used in contemplation of the writers of the past that intrigues me. Necessarily, therefore, it is the commentators who adopt an ironic stance in its extreme form likened by Jameson to pastiche: "Pastiche is blank parody, parody that has lost its sense of humour: pastiche is to parody what that curious thing, the modern practice of a kind of blank irony, is to the stable and comic ironies of, say, the eighteenth century" (1985, 114, my emphasis).

[47] Compare Downie's remark (1970, 21) that *The Golden Bough* had no single purpose.

simply reactionary) perspectives on others" (1982, 19). By contrast, Boon argues, functionalism after Malinowski became an anthropology without irony.[48]

Beer's concern is with Darwin's problems in precipitating his theory as language (1983, 5). She deals with *The Origin of Species* as an extraordinary example of a work which included more than the maker of it at the time knew, despite all that he knew (1983, 4). We are not required to consider his use of language wholly planned—we are talking about the way a work is registered in the minds of its readers, and thus about its power to persuade. Stocking (1983, 105) writes of Malinowski that while he was aware of ethnography as literary artifice, nevertheless we are left to our own literary critical devices to explicate the method of his artifice. To this one must add: it is *we* then who are interested in the literary devices of others, and in the persuasiveness of their fictions, because in what is also a post-paradigm era, we cannot take their frames as natural boundaries (Marcus 1986).[49] When Beer suggests that Darwin's language fitted his theory, perhaps she means that she must make this true of herself. The same probably applies to any suggestion that Frazer was grappling with the modernist strategies I have imputed to him. Thus the "problem" of conveying alien ideas (ascribed to Frazer) is written (by me) back into his works from my perspective on them. Whether or not this was something he consciously set out to tackle, it appears as an effect of his writing. Yet this appearance in turn must come from the contemporary preoccupation with the representation of representations.

[48] Yet there seems to be no end to the contemporary discovery of irony in others. Thus Thornton (1985, 14), himself juxtaposing contexts (Malinowski and Conrad as writers), presents a portrait of Malinowski as set down in the "self-imposed agony of loneliness at the very juncture of contradiction" (a contradiction between the interaction of imagination and description, civilised and primitive thought, endorsement and doubt). The vision of the ethnographic monograph, of incomparables compared, occasioned a "profound sense of irony": no event was what it seemed to the native by virtue of the universal categories of Western social science. He suggests that by the end of the nineteenth century, ethnographic writing had come to "reflect an ironic vision of people who had to be explained, both to themselves and to the rest of the world" (1983, 516). (Thornton includes Frazer here.) Stocking takes for granted the "gentle irony" of Malinowski's attitude towards his Melanesian subjects as characteristic of much modern ethnography (1983, 108). The ethnographer both shares their vision and knows things about them that they do not (cf. Webster 1982, 93). Clifford (1986, 145) talks of the "ironic stance of participant observation" presupposed in modern anthropology. All I am suggesting is that the discovery of this interplay as ironic seems to characterise 1980s reflection on these topics.

[49] Clifford (1986, 14) talks of the post-cultural, i.e., a syncretic situation not amenable to unidimensional paradigms. The privilege given to natural cultures has dissolved in the contemporary appearance of culture as a fiction.

As far as irony is concerned, I wonder about Frazer. I am not sure that his ironic intentions were the same as those of latter-day ironists and that we can recover him as anticipating our post-functionalist selves. His diversity led to plenitude.[50] He made equivocal contrasts (the two versions of the creation story in Genesis recreate the debate between Darwin and his detractors over evolution and creationism). He decentered his texts (biblical and classical); he restored vestiges of the past; he crammed his books with multiple voices, in a manner of speaking—but only in a manner of speaking. Those numerous juxtapositions, Melanesians and Africans jostling side by side, evincing this or that belief, were not there as "Melanesians" and "Africans." Probably he did think that the way any people thought illuminated other people's beliefs, but since he drew this evidence out of context, *it was not the contexts* (i.e., being Melanesian or African) *which were juxtaposed*. Can this, then, be what post-functionalists understand as irony? Do we not require that contexts be recognised? That irony lie in deliberate play? Beliefs and customs would be juxtaposed not to reveal similarity but to raise questions about it. By contrast with the modernist who "explains" and brings to the surface the grounds for similarity or difference, the postmodernist (I have noted) leaves that work to the reader.[51] He / she is interested in provocation for its own sake. But the legacy of the last sixty years is that the provocation will lie precisely in the juxtaposition of social or cultural contexts. With what meaning, then, do we attribute "ironic comparativism" to Frazer (Thornton 1985, 14)? Is it that we are in the mood to see all comparison as ironic and that without an explicit modernist frame Frazer appears to endorse our own senses of irony?

As one who finds irony in others, Clifford also figures centrally in Rabinow's (1986) account of postmodernism in anthropology and the promulgation of new ethnographic styles. The ethnographic text could conceivably move beyond dialogy (the staged reproduction of an interchange between subjects) to heteroglossia (a utopia of plural endeavour that gives all collaborators the status of authors). Rabinow finds in Clifford's suggestions a mood akin to that described for postmodernism by Jameson (1985) in art: more than a jumble of elements, the pastiche of nostalgia films, for instance, obscures the line between past and present, blurring the specificity of the past. This deliberate historical flattening reappears in the "meta-ethnographic flat-

[50] "Rich, mixed feeding," said Marett (1920, 173). In contrast, Darwin's sense of profusion, of a multivalent world, was controlled by his theory of interrelationships.

[51] Marett again (quoted by Kardiner and Preble 1961, 106): "by the magic of [Dr. Frazer's] pen he has made the myriad facts live, so that they tell their own tale, and we are left free to read their meaning as our several tastes and temperaments dictate."

tening which makes all the world's cultures practitioners of textuality" (Rabinow 1986, 250). A proliferation of references to other representations empties any one of content; the referent of each image is another image.[52] Rabinow voices doubts about this as a recipe—above all that if we attempt to eliminate social referentiality other referents will occupy the voided position (1986, 251)—and doubts whether such discourse strategies in fact fit the intentions of someone like Clifford.[53] If anthropology endorses modernist style in a particular way, so with postmodernism. Its exponents play with different contexts (as in juxtaposing literary and ethnographic productions) rather than blurring them. This play remains self-conscious; hence its capacity for irony.[54]

Reviewing Clifford's biography of Leenhardt, Young notes its plenitude and its open-ended character: "Clifford has thought long and deeply about Maurice Leenhardt, and something of the same complex collaboration between ethnographer and informant, something of the same kind of dialogue which produces an ethnographic text, has in this case ensued between biographer and subject" (1983, 170). The reference to dialogue is also a reference to reciprocity, of recognising relationships (as between ethnographer and informant), not flattening them (cf. Clifford 1980). This is what gives postmodernist anthropology its special flavour—if the relationships involved between writer and subjects are to be negotiated, even fashioned as reciprocity, their cultural contexts after all cannot, as we might speak of Frazer's writing, be scrambled.

In short, there is more talk of jumble than practice of it. Tracing the

[52] Compare Lowenthal's (1985, 382–83) discussion of the reaction to avant-garde amnesia—historical eclecticism in the arts has its architectural counterpart in postmodern classicism (classical motifs are employed with irony, for decorative effect, selected out of context in defiance of their origins and relationships, everything attracting the same degree of interest). Particularly telling is his quotation of a comment on modern Italian architects who salvage not history but their own emotions, nostalgia, and autobiographical incidents in order to escape the tradition of the new.

[53] In distinguishing different sources of postmodemist commentary (he contrasts Lyotard and Jameson), Rabinow detaches pastiche from jumble as Crick detaches play from free play, to create the distance I also perceive as between irony (play with context) and "waddling in" (repudiation of context).

[54] Thus, too, Crick's account of the newer anthropological style which evokes, hints, reminds, is thoroughly recognisable as argument. Its own play is in the deliberate juxtaposition of contexts: a contrast between, for instance, the fieldworker and that figure whom the fieldworker thinks he/she is least like, the tourist. Crick also argues that games require rules. "If 'anything goes,' one has nonsense, not a game" (1985, 85). Boon's attitude towards fieldwork is "playful," because it is a concept of an ideal and action that should be simultaneously debunked and preserved (1982, x). He strives for a discourse that is both interpretive and systematic (1982, 26).

shift which Clifford evinces, Rabinow contrasts him with Geertz, although in the long view Geertz's own self-conscious use of irony (cf. Webster 1982, 92) presaged the shift. Geertz talks about anthropology as an uncentred melange of disparate visions, fieldwork as colloquial, offhand. He talks about recent anthropology within a social context characterised by "a general muddling of vocational (disciplinary) entities" (1983, 23), of anthropology "waddling in" (1985). Yet in the same address as he describes anthropology as seeking to keep the world off balance, pulling out the rug from under complacency (cf. 1984, 275), he also institutes a very deliberate framing. The double negativity of his title, "Anti anti-relativism" (rejecting something without committing oneself to what that something has rejected), is play with frames. Moreover, when Geertz first introduced the idea of irony it was in reference to a moral tension between "anthropologist" and "informant," that is, one embedded in the conduct of a specific social relationship. This makes play with contexts possible but blurring them rather difficult.[55] Why, then, do we entertain a notion of jumble, of scrambled contexts? What is the talk about?

The metaphor of play is a powerful one (as Crick adumbrates). It privileges one context above all: the writer framing off his or her writing with the theatrical message, "Everything within this frame is play." Thus is play imagined as free play. Determining "fictions" appear to turn themselves into fictions, the novel with a new lease of life as an anthropological exercise. One is reminded here of Frazer's admission in the third edition of *The Golden Bough* (1911–1915) that the allegory of the priest/king could be unmasked as a dramatic device for allowing him to talk about primitive thought and society. Of course, it is the unmasking which is the drama—the playfulness is afterthought.[56] But playing with the idea of postmodernism in anthropology raises questions about the kinds of social relationship to which we imagine it speaks. There are problems with the way it is represented, with pastiche interpreted as jumble. Asking whether

[55] Though the phrases "blurred genres" and "genre mixing" are Geertz's. He writes (1983, 23): "The instruments of reasoning are changing and society is less and less represented as an elaborate machine or a quasi-organism and more as a serious game, a sidewalk drama or a behavioral text." Geertz's original elucidation of anthropological irony appeared in 1968, in reference to participant observation as a continuously ironic form of conduct based on the recognition of moral tension between anthropologist and informant.

[56] "Appalled by the luxuriance of the encompassing growths" of the expanding volumes, Marett (1920, 177) notes that there had been a change of design. The unmasking is indeed afterthought, in a book which "must henceforth throw aside the last pretence of dramatic unity, and resolve itself into a series of dissolving views."

we really wish to return to the kinds of thing Frazer wrote is one way of stating them.

Modernist Problems

That there might be problems of representation is suggested from aspects of contemporary feminist scholarship. Much feminist discourse is constructed in a plural way.[57] Arguments are juxtaposed, many voices solicited, in the way that feminists speak about their own scholarship. There are no central texts, no definitive techniques; the deliberate transdisciplinary enterprise plays with context. Perspectives from different disciplines are held to illuminate one another; historical or literary or anthropological insights are juxtaposed by writers at once conscious of the different contexts of these disciplines and refusing to take any single context as an organising frame. If this is recognisably postmodern, then feminist scholarship is akin to the postmodernist mood in anthropology (and see Yeatman 1984)[58] with its conscious play with context.

And if feminist scholarship is successful in this regard, then its success lies firmly in the relationship as it is represented between scholarship (genre) and the feminist movement (life). Play with context is creative because of the expressed continuity of purpose between feminists as scholars and feminists as activists. Purposes may be diversely perceived; yet the scholarship is in the end represented as framed off by a special set of social interests. Feminists argue with one another, in their many voices, because they also know themselves as an interest group. There is certainty about that context. The anthropologist is in a rather different position. There appears no such anthropological interest group. For anthropology, play with internal contexts—with the conventions of scholarship (genre)—*looks like* free play with the social context of anthropology as such (life). In fact the resultant uncertainty is intrinsic to anthropological motivation and the drive to study.

Boon (1982, 21) asks whether we have to choose between anthro-

[57] I have since come across a similar position argued in art criticism. Owens particularly draws attention to the feminist position (in this case voiced by an artist) that there is no single theoretical discourse (1985, 64). What is at stake, he argues, is the status not only of narrative but of representation itself (1985, 66).

[58] Yeatman points to certain analytical strategies within feminist social science as postmodern, e.g., taking apart the art versus nature / public versus domestic paradigm (1984, 47) but is critical of the extent to which feminist social scientists, for all their talk, still subscribe to modern paradigms.

pology according to a lot of would-be Frazers or anthropology according to a lot of would-be Malinowskis:

> [W]hy not a pluralistic system? There are standards of "convincingness" in various cross-cultural styles and genres, just as there are canons of verisimilitude in realist-ethnography. To assess the accuracy of either Malinowski-like or Frazer-like (or Geertz-like or Lévi-Strauss-like) interpretations, we must plumb the complexities of convergent data-theirs and ours—and renounce the Enlightenment faith in analytic "simplicity," assumptions of direct determinacy, and hopes for unmediated communication, cross-cultural or otherwise.

Perceived cultures appear to one another in exaggerated form (as cultures), "each playing to another the *vis-à-vis*" (26). Cross-cultural discourse inevitably deals in such exaggerations. Fieldwork must happen because communication in a common language does not: fieldwork keeps one half of two communicating cultures (*they*) intact while *we* undertake to write what happens. "What could be more extreme or theatrical and less standardized or objective? Ideally all cultures should be *wes* and *theys* to each other in turn. Politics, however, intrudes" (26). There can be play, then, for the sake of communication between "others," as opposed to free play circumscribed only by individual choice. Perhaps it is the consumerist reduction of communication to self-edification, all knowledge to self-knowledge, which also represents communication itself as theatre and cultural life as text. The deliberate pastiches of postmodernist writing at once endorse and expose that view. Texts cannot survive being pluralised.[59]

The justification for pluralism paradoxically runs against the grain of the idea that we view cultures as dramas or texts. What, then, is the power of this latter imagery? It rests on a certain moral appeal: one text has the same claim on our attention as any other. But then the question follows, what model of the social world yields such a morality? Is it the sense of a shrinking world? Here we are side by side, in multicoloured clothes, jostling and elbowing, beaming satellite images to one another—all equally different and thus all equally the same.[60] Echoes of Frazer indeed. This is a world "with too many

[59] They must become (political) discourse. Note that "pluralism" is another of those terms (like "irony" and "pastiche") which can be appropriated either in defence of relativism and free play (see n. 44) *or* in defence of play and context juxtaposition. I wish it to work in the latter sense here.

[60] Geertz labels this as the terror of anti-relativism (1984, 265), a fear that everything is as significant, thus as insignificant, as everything else: "The image of vast numbers of anthropology readers running around in so cosmopolitan a frame of mind as to have

voices speaking all at once, a world where syncretism and parodic invention are becoming the rule, not the exception, an urban, multinational world of institutionalized transience" (Clifford 1986, 147)—one that treats differences like consumer choice, multicultural events as international food, that sees distinctions in the end as cultural creations and not also the workings of social interests against one another—in short, *where all contexts are alike*. All contexts are alike insofar as they give rise to the situated statement, are the frames for people's performances—every reason to adduce example after example simply to show that people's beliefs and practices are all equally bizarre. Is Frazer's compendium, then, our hitchhiker's guide to the global village?

"Global village" is an interesting fiction. Few anthropologists can have actually studied a village that was not riven by conflicting social interests. Indeed, the English village I know best was radically divided between those residents who thought it was a village and those who did not. I do not think anthropologists could take on trust the idea of a global village any more than they really scramble contexts;[61] there is one interest which anthropological writing must continue to endorse, and that is the question of relationships involved in communication. Relationships are specifiable only with reference to contexts.

In considering the disparity between Frazer's popular reputation and his poor anthropological one, I have concentrated on the kind of books he wrote, because it is in people's relations to these artefacts that we see their acclaim or rejection of the author's ideas. Their internal organisation sets up a particular relationship between writer, reader, and subject matter.[62] Frazer shared a text and a language with

---

no view as to what is and isn't true, or good, or beautiful, seems to me largely a fantasy." I am in sympathy with the view that these literary prescriptions may be more preached than practised, but anthropologists were never in the business of dismissing fantasies because they were hard to imagine.

[61] I would echo Crick's conclusion that Dadaism involves anti-Dadaism: "if anything goes, seriousness, better description and more demanding fieldwork are on the cards too" (1985, 86). "All this fiddling around with the properties of composition, inquiry, and explanation represents . . . a radical alteration in the sociological imagination. If the result is not to be elaborate chatter or higher nonsense, a critical consciousness will have to be developed" (Geertz 1983, 23). Geertz (1984) suggests that anthropology ultimately battles against provincialism. Cf. Rabinow's "critical cosmopolitanism," which he sets off from postmodernism. Outside anthropology, pluralism as "a reduction to difference to absolute indifference" (Owens 1985, 58) is also held up as a spectre from which certain types of postmodernism dissociate themselves. Pluralism is suggested, of course, since "postmodern thought is no longer binary thought" (Owens 1985, 62). But on the equivocation of pluralism, see n. 59.

[62] In his analyses of ethnographic fiction, Webster (1982) points to several different

his audience but proceeded to show how heterogeneous that text was, what a mixture of savagery and civilisation, the ordinary cognate with the exotic. Such a relationship affects the fate of the texts themselves. Contemporary anthropology writes its own history with a clear shift held to have occurred in the 1920s. Whatever Malinowski's overt target, it was Frazer whose writings he rendered the most unreadable. Thus it was not really the discovery of new ideas such as synchrony or ethnocentrism which made Frazer old-fashioned: it was their implementation as a fictional device for the framing of a new relationship between the anthropologist and his or her subject matter, one which also invited a new relationship between the writer and the professionals in his audience who identified with him.[63] Anthropologists defined as a professional problem the organising of their writing so as to convey concepts for which their own culture had no ready space. A distance was set up between the society being studied and the society to which the anthropologist's chief audience belonged. In belonging to both, in a manner of speaking, the fieldworker presented him- or herself as a mediator. And what was presented as a mediation between life-styles was of course a mediation produced by the text—the way the society was described and the way the anthropologist came to analyze and theorise about it, self-conscious of the specificity of his or her own. Has that technical problem now gone away?

To some extent it has. Particularly over the last twenty years, certain apparent dichotomies between writer, audience, and subject have folded in on themselves. If anthropologists write now about "other peoples," they are writing for subjects who have become an audience. In describing Melanesian marriage ceremonies, I must bear my Melanesian readers in mind. That in turn makes problematic the previously established distinction between writer and subject: I must know on whose behalf and to what end I write.

Perhaps it is this above all which is captured in the pluralist proclamation of postmodernism, which brings the concerns of anthropology close to those of feminist scholarship, and which makes the pre-

---

constitutions of writer-reader relations; he further brings in the overlooked audiences of those about whom we write.

[63] Jorion (1983) effectively argues that the emic-etic division in anthropological writing, which is held to correspond to different framings of the world, can also be interpreted as a tension internal to the anthropological text. The tension is between commonsense and technical understandings. In commonsense (emic) language, the anthropologist creates certain grounds for a mutual understanding *with his or her readers* which are then denied or distanced in the technical (etic) gloss. Two different relationships with the audience are thus set up.

occupation with fiction a thoroughly proper one. Postmoderns have to take care of their texts in new ways. The new ironic juxtapositions focus on the act of writing itself, and interest in the fictional status of what we write keeps open the question for whom we write. Retrospectively to ask about the persuasive fictions of earlier epochs is to ask about how others (Frazer, Malinowski, and the rest) handled our moral problems of literary construction. In answering the question, we create historic shifts between past writers in terms persuasive to our own ears, thereby participating in a postmodern history, reading back into books the strategies of fictionalisation. To construct past works as quasi-intentional literary games is the new ethnocentrism. There is no evidence, after all, that "we" have stopped attributing our problems to "others."

The 1920s shift between Frazer and modernist anthropology helps interpret the alleged shift from modernism to postmodernism in the 1980s. The phenomenon lies in how anthropologists represent what they do, what they say they are writing, and in the purpose of communication. Ideas cannot in the end be divorced from relationships. One could find precursors of modernism in the ideas of the great generation of the 1870s which preceded Frazer, as one could find a precursor for postmodernist writing in Frazer himself. But there has also been a notable sequence of practices in the evolution of new relationships between writer, reader, and subjects. Frazer is not a postmodern in the contemporary anthropological sense, and the modernism of Malinowski instantiated a different set of relations from those current in the generation which Frazer himself read. There can be only one guide to the present shift. The real question is whether a new fiction will come of all the talk. We shall not be able to return to a pre-fictionalised consciousness, but we might be persuaded that there are still significant relationships to be studied.

Comments

I. C. Jarvie

DEPARTMENT OF PHILOSOPHY, YORK UNIVERSITY

In a recent piece Gellner (1986) lauds social anthropologists for their sensitivity to the difference writing makes to society. He writes, "If men speak to hide their thoughts, they write to hide their society" (referring to the societies studied by anthropologists). The idea is also reflexively true of anthropological writings themselves, which can serve to hide both the narrow society of anthropologists and the wider society to which they belong (Jarvie 1986). Strathern's paper is a case in point.

Strathern's project is to reconceptualise the revolution in anthropology. What was formerly presented as a change in ideas and methods is now to be seen as the invention and diffusion of a new genre of literature. In place of writing in the style of the grand historical speculations of Frazer, the revolution fostered the close-textured, synchronic fieldwork monograph of Malinowski. Each of these genres is a "persuasive fiction." The specific literary strategy of the ethnographic monograph is a reconstruction of fieldwork experience which manipulates "familiar ideas and concepts to convey alien ones." This textual construal of the revolution in anthropology was made possible by another change or turn in anthropology: postmodernism. The traditional functionalist game of scoffing at Frazer's literary genre became vulnerable to the postmodernist *tu quoque*: both Frazerians and functionalists produced persuasive fiction. For Strathern, "the real question is whether a new fiction will come of all the [postmodernist] talk." It is questionable whether this is the *real* question.

While understandably, perhaps, I prefer my own view (Jarvie 1964) of the revolution as a scientific one, involving as it does critical appreciation of past theories and methods combined with their refutation and replacement, I concede that the preference which some anthropologists display for an irrationalist alternative comes as no surprise. The revolution did alter the preferred form of anthropological writings, and the more superficial students of literature have only irrationalist explanations of change. Changes in literary fashion have rendered earlier scientific work (Frazer, Newton) "unreadable" (though not for historians). This is a problem, not an explanation, one that cannot be solved by declaring yesterday's science "persuasive fiction" and then, to avoid entrapment, conceding that today's science is persuasive fiction also, as will be tomorrow's science.

The *real* question in all this is what has happened to truth. Strathern takes over Ardener's phrase "persuasive fiction." The choice of words is pregnant. "Persuasive" has overtones of "appealing" or "attractive" but also of advertising and propaganda. "Fiction" is still richer. Most of literature is fiction, as contrasted to fact. But on behalf of fiction it is often claimed that there is in it poetic, literary, or symbolic truth. Behind the irrationalism lurks the esoteric claim to go deeper, for the "persuasive fiction" of anthropology, we remember, utilises familiar ideas and concepts to convey alien ones. The difference between the familiar and the alien being ethnographic, and ethnography being fiction, one wonders who is to be persuaded of what and how.

There are worse muddles and contradictions in Strathern's paper, but these are for philosophers. More pertinent to readers of *Current Anthropology* is the anthropology of it all, an anthropology summed up in her saying, "Ideas cannot in the end be divorced from relationships." What relationships are married to the ideas in Strathern's text? The list of references displays her affines among postmodernist anthropologists. The auspices under which the paper was prepared—first as a Frazer Lecture and then as an article in *Current Anthropology*—reveal that her ideas are situated within the relationship of a working anthropologist to fellow professionals. These are apparently tolerant enough that one who characterises their work as "persuasive fictions" need not fear anathematisation; rather *Current Anthropology* star treatment!

If first-order ethnographic monographs are "persuasive fictions," meta-anthropological Frazer Lectures, then, are a *fortiori* "persuasive fictions" also. What, then, are such addresses to the profession at large supposed to persuade us of? Can they possibly be aimed at consigning the work of anthropologists to the same rubbish heap on which lie much of modern and postmodern art and all of postmodernist "theory" and philosophy? Are some anthropologists engaged in deconstructing their profession? Will they then ultimately jump into the dustbin themselves? These are not questions I know how to answer. Let me turn instead to one I can handle: what may be being hidden.

A minor theme running through Strathern's present persuasive fiction with which I can claim some familiarity is my own works. Strathern characterises two of my books as "a bitter attack . . . on modern social anthropology." No good my saying that "a critical appreciation of modern social anthropology" would be a better description; father-killing stories make better fiction than critical appreciation. Anyway, the author of the fiction is the sole judge of what is the correct description and of the relationship between the characters that that description entails. Her description is intended to maintain a distance in our relationship, to avoid endorsing either my view of the revolution in anthropology or my sharp critique of its reliance on often boring ethnographic detail. (Assuming that ethnographic monographs are fiction, we may wish them more readable and hence persuasive; for that they would better be modelled on the astringent Trollope, Surtees, or Waugh than, as they so often seem to be, on Melville, Dreiser, and Dos Passos.) For my part also there is great incentive to maintain distance from the irresponsible irrationalists who can label the work of Malinowski, Radcliffe-Brown, Firth, and Evans-Pritchard "persuasive fiction."

But both our efforts at distance are futile: ideas, Strathern informs us, cannot be divorced from relationships. Her rewriting of the revolution in anthropology is partly a critique of my account. This comment on her paper is a countercritique. The social context of this exchange is one in which what counts is truth, not relationships. The profession of anthropology and the discussion section of one of its leading journals exist not as a kind of PEN club but as a collective search for truth. Strong social and historical bonds connect anthropology to the traditions of science and of scholarship. The attempt to forge a connection to fiction hides the connection to science and scholarship, the social context from which anthropology derives and which gives it meaning. In this society "ideas cannot in the end be divorced from relationships" is the opposite of the truth. Such divorce is not only regular, indeed normal, but intrinsic to the social institutions concerned. Newton gets refuted by Einstein, the Old Testament by Darwin without a ramifying collapse of other social institutions and relationships (Gellner 1974, 166–67). Not to understand this is not to have grasped the single most important fact about our society that makes it different from all others: the presence and tradition of science. We should resist fictional accounts of anthropology, however persuasive!

Stephen A. Tyler and George E. Marcus

DEPARTMENT OF ANTHROPOLOGY, RICE UNIVERSITY

What makes Strathern's reading work is what we might call a double chiasmus, signified by the double juxtaposition Frazer / Malinowski and Malinowski / Frazer. If we were formalists, we might write $\langle F \times M \rangle \times \langle M \times F \rangle$. Or, more hieroglyphically, perhaps

$$\begin{array}{c} F \times M \\ \Large\times \\ M \times F. \end{array}$$

Frazer is the *con*-text ("against text") for Malinowski. Frazer is his precursor, dialectic antagonist, and the source of his "anxiety of influence." Because Frazer is the text against which Malinowski writes, Malinowski's is the con-*text* ("with text") for Frazer and the text through which Strathern comes to understand Frazer's unreadability. But, having conned to the fact that Malinowski's holistic *con-text* of custom claims not to be a text and covers up its textualisation, Strathern uncovers the con-text ("trick-text / text-trick")—understands how she was conned by the artifice of the text. This is how the con overcomes the text, and as in Derrida's inversion of the historical relation between Plato and Socrates in the image of Plato dictating to Socrates, we can now speak of Malinowski's influence on Frazer with as much justification as of Frazer's on Malinowski. Since for us there was never a Frazer before Malinowski, what can we make of Strathern's desire to convince herself of the sense of a gap that would make a history? Is this just another piece of structuralist synchrony? Maybe, but why not play with the chiasmi Strathern uses to make the gap, like "savagery in civilisation" / "civilisation in savagery" and "extraordinary to ordinary" / "ordinary to extraordinary," for example? As Strathern says, it makes as much sense for us to read Frazer and Malinowski as if they were writing about our problems as it does to read Frazer after Malinowski, but isn't there something else to play with here? Frazer is the inverse of Malinowski; together they represent the difference between allegory and symbol, hermeneutic and dialectic. Frazer is allegorical and hermeneutical; his is one story told in many ways. Malinowski is symbolical and dialectical; his are many different stories told in the same way. Thus Frazer wrote within a textual tradition that did not call that tradition or its textualisation into question but worked, as Strathern says, to explicate a discourse already known to his audience. He could use the method of sorites, of piling up examples, because the story had already been told. Frazer makes a continuity in a textual tradition that runs from Origen and Philo through Augustine and Aquinas, a tradition whose constant problem was to reconcile the seemingly incoherent jumble of exotic fantasies in the biblical text with Greek skepticism and rhetorical forms, to justify it to an economy of discourse that valued symbol, dialectic, syllogism, dispositio, and episteme—that is to say, form of discourse as form of knowledge over meaning, memory, affect, and ethic—that is to say, content. Perhaps we could say, then, that Frazer wrote because the accommodation between Christian and pagan, barbarism and civilization, Greek and Hebrew, East and West, self and other worked out in the Western tradition had come under renewed attack from such pagan ideas as evolution, which, as Strathern observes, constituted a disruption in textualisation far more severe than the "plain style" of the Cartesians and Baconians because it projected a kind of totalistic emplotment that was both megamyth and metanarrative. Frazer made a new reconciliation. He used the new story of evolution against itself, less in refutation than as a textualising strategy that made the Bible credible in a new way. As we would say, he used its "negative capability." And now we can answer Strathern's question why Frazer's work attracted so much attention in his day. Frazer worked out a new reconciliation between Christian and pagan, using the new pagan story of evolution to retell the old biblical story and telling the new one as if it had been foretold. His was a reassuring tale of reconciliation, continuity, shared discourse, and shared ethos.

Malinowski, on the other hand, wrote with an emerging pseudopagan discourse of science that valued and exemplified disruption and the new—so long as they worked only at the level of content. The form of discourse remained constant, so the many different tales of the other could be told in a form that never varied. The ethnographic genre, whether invented by Malinowski or not, symbolises what Strathern describes as Malinowski's problem—to tell a story about the exotic as if it weren't exotic. The incomprehensible exotic is rendered understandable by an understandable form that must always hide its practices of textualisation lest they undermine its understandability. Textualisation was a problem for Malinowski that he could never acknowledge as a problem except in a manner of surreptitious revelation or in opposition to prior textual practices—notably Frazer's. Malinowski's text was not part of a continuous hermeneutic tradition with a collection of intertextual references; it was projected from the Trobriands as if it had no textual companions. Its gestures toward the tradition of anthropological discourse were defiant and disruptive, those toward the larger discourse of science insinuating and bombastic. Perhaps we can read Malinowski, then, as the quintessential instance of the dialectic that overcomes the resistance of the other by absolute incorporation, even as it seems to have recognized the independence of the other.

But isn't all this easy inversion a little too pat, and far too simplistic? After all, is Frazer free of the symbolic and dialectic? Doesn't the very trope of evolution recapitulate the whole dialectic and its urge to symbolic transcendence? And even though the church fathers used allegories as a major tropic strategy, didn't Augustine and Aquinas come to terms with the Greeks in both rhetoric and logic? And what about the whole thrust of neo-Platonism? And wasn't Malinowski as allegorical as anyone else, rewriting *The Heart of Darkness* and all that? Isn't his notion of "grasping the native's point of view," though amusingly imperialist and redolent of Western metaphors of thought and understanding, a succinct paraphrase of Schleiermacher's hermeneutics? And what about relativism? That doesn't square with incorporating the other, does it? If anyone incorporated, it is more likely to have been Frazer.

Does this mean, then, that Malinowski was already written somehow in Frazer as a kind of subtext and Frazer in Malinowski as a pretext just because neither allegory nor symbol has ever achieved total hegemony, perhaps because they already implicate one another like Christians and pagans so that every pagan insurrection is really only a means to a further transcendence? No, what we have in mind involves neither the transcendence nor the easy irony of modernism. The context is not already there either as a previously structured field of signifiers, as in the "culture" of Frazer, or as a field of structural signifieds, as in the "cultures" of Malinowski. Context is neither a transcendental signifier nor a transcendental signified, for it emerges only within and by means of the contexts it creates as it is created by them. So, the context is neither there already nor not there, and that is why postmodernism is not ironic; irony requires an outside, a place to step back from the context, a *topos* where impartial, objective narrators are not already figured in the ironies that figure them. Except as illusion, no moment of pure freedom enables authors to *de*-scribe as they de-*scribe* or grants texts immunities from communities of readers. Just as there is no place outside the text that does not already implicate the text, there is no text that does not implicate the outside that implicates it implicating it. And so neither texts nor authors break free of the con-texts they can but parody.

In the approximate final third of her essay, Strathern addresses the contemporary reactions to the predicaments posed for anthropology at the moment by the historic chiasmi she has so perceptively explored. Today neither Malinowski's denial of intertextuality nor Frazer's certitude about the textual tradition in which he wrote can hold. Thus, in place of "many different stories told in the same way" or "one story told in many ways" we are faced with "many stories that can be told in many ways" as a problem of postmodern consciousness—"postmodern" having become a term simultaneously disdained as fashion and seductively embraced across the human sciences as a license to unfix canonic readings and reinvent traditions of research practice. Appropriately and remarkably, this part of Strathern's essay parodies the influential "postmodern" documents (mostly those of Clifford) being widely read by anthropologists, which she seems to disdain at times as "all the talk" (as if nothing more were at stake or nothing more substantial were already being produced as ethnography in this mode); the last part of her essay is thus full of hesitations, ambivalences, equivocations, and ironies. There is an unresolved polyphony in her assessment of this postmodern turn that alternates between caution, dismissiveness, and respectful appreciation for the thrust of the critique of anthropology that is being offered. For example, she recognizes with great sophistication the dangers for effective communication in the spiraling inflation of meanings that the multiple and idiosyncratic contemporary uses of the terms "modernism" and "postmodernism" have wrought. Yet, she relies heavily on a particularly idiosyncratic use of these terms in developing her assessment of recent critiques of anthropology. (We believe that anthropology never self-consciously had a "modernist" moment until the present, when the influences of literary and cultural classic modernism of the late nineteenth and early twentieth centuries are finally being brought to bear by bridging scholars such as Clifford, Rabinow, and Crapanzano who are equally schooled in literary theory and in the history of anthropology. The fact that "classic" modernism has worn thin and is being debated and assessed more broadly in the human sciences under the banner of postmodernism is a complicating factor for its explicit and unprecedented introduction as a critique of anthropology at the moment. Strathern is very aware that the present discourse she targets as postmodernist originates essentially in debates that anthropology in its own history has until now ignored, yet she relies heavily on more parochial and odder senses of the terms "modernism" and "postmodernism" derived from recent papers by Ardener and Crick, as if they fit smoothly into the history of anthropology.) To cite another example of equivocation, Strathern denies that Frazer can be considered a postmodernist or even a predecessor for a postmodern style in anthropology, yet she repeatedly evokes the contextless jumble in Frazer's writing to suggest in a cautionary way that this might be where "all the talk" is leading. Here, she parodies the technique of recuperating past figures by finding a current significance for them (e.g., Clifford's treatment of Leenhardt) while denying that this should be done, at least with Frazer. Further, she worries about inattention to cultural contexts and systematic relationships in postmodernist play, but she also acknowledges that those who have recently indulged in this are indeed in control of their strategies of juxtaposition and, at a very sophisticated level, concerned with both context and textualisation of cultural phenomena.

The various ambivalences in the last part of Strathern's essay are fought to a standstill, and she concludes, true to her parody of the postmodern essay, by evoking with a gesture an ideal or a "good" that is undemonstrated and just the other side of those things which have been the subject of her critical gaze; she intimates that after postmodernist talk "there are still significant relationships to be studied." (We would very much be interested in an elaboration of what she has in mind here.)

What distinguishes Strathern's parody of a "postmodern" document most saliently from the real thing is that she is not self-consciously in writerly control of her ambivalences and hesitations as a practicing postmodernist supposedly is, or intends to be. Rather, her equivocations are distinctly those of a reader trying to come to terms with provocations like those perpetrated by Clifford, among others. And the point, we believe, of these provocations for anthropologists is not so much to change writing practices radically, as some fear, as to change the conditions of reception of anthropological work, to create an environment open to many more alternative readings of anthropological work than now occur. Far from "a new fiction" coming "of all the talk," the point of all the talk is to prevent a new fiction from arriving by declining to prescribe what should be but instead characterizing what already is. (The polyphonic ideal of the postmodern essayist in anthropology is just that—an ideal, one among others, that masks a rich body of work that is, at least since the 1970s, both experimental in ethos and, at the same time, more interesting and more sophisticated than but thoroughly in line with preceding ethnographic traditions.)

With a practice such as ethnography, in which writers have not seen themselves self-consciously as *writers*, changes in reception—comment and debate on "research findings"—are far more likely and powerful than suggested changes in writing practices (which do eventually follow in the wake of changes in reading), and it is this focus on reception that the postmodern provocations in contemporary anthropology have developed. Ironically (or parodically?), Strathern's essay both exemplifies this effect of "all the talk" and, on the surface, underemphasises it.

ETHNOGRAPHY AS DISCOURSE: THE ERA OF THE MONOGRAPH

Irony in Anthropology: The Work of Franz Boas

ARNOLD KRUPAT

BORN IN Minden, Westphalia, in 1858, Franz Boas was clearly an extraordinary figure, not only a teacher, but a *maître* in the grand sense, whose students often became disciples, and, in several cases (Kroeber, Mead, Sapir, Benedict, Radin), virtual masters themselves. Boas published extensively on linguistics, on folklore, art, race, and, of course, ethnography, a fabled "five foot shelf," of materials on the Kwakiutl. Yet Boas did not, like his contemporaries Sigmund Freud and Ferdinand de Saussure, found what Foucault refers to as a field of discursivity, a written discourse that gives rise to the endless possibility of further discourse, or a discipline, like psychoanalysis or structural linguistics. The exact nature of Boas's achievement yet remains to be specified.

In 1888, Boas went to Clark University where he taught anthropology until 1892. He held positions with the World's Columbian exposition in Chicago and at the American Museum of Natural History in New York before moving, in 1896, to Columbia University as a lecturer in physical anthropology. He received promotion to a professorship in 1899, a position that he held until his retirement in 1936. Boas died—in the arms of Lévi-Strauss—in 1942. From his academic base at Columbia, Boas's influence was enormous. By 1926, for example, as George Stocking has noted, every academic department of anthropology in the United States was headed by one of Boas's students (1968, 296). That the Winnebago were studied by Paul Radin or the Pawnee much later by Gene Weltfish, that Edward Sapir, and, after, Melville Jacobs gathered Native texts is largely due to Boas.

Both Boas's admirers—who are many—and his detractors—who have been fewer—have agreed only on the issue central to their disagreement, the question of Boas's contribution to a *science* of culture. No one can doubt that Boas did much of worth. But can what he did properly be summed up as serving to found anthropology as a scientific discipline—moving it, as it were, from impressionism to realism, as Alfred Kroeber, Margaret Mead, Ruth Bunzel, and others have insisted?[1] Or is it, rather, as Leslie White and Marvin Harris foremost have claimed, that Boas's practice was, finally, no more "scientific" or "realistic" than that of his predecessors, the accidental "men on the spot," and the so-called "armchair anthropologists," no more "scientific" than his contemporaries, the "museum men," and the fieldworkers of the government bureaus.[2] Moreover, to consider Boas in the context of this volume requires as well that we interrogate his relationship to that curious cultural development broadly called "modernism," as it may or may not be consistent with that "realism" generally taken as consistent with claims to scienticity.

I read Boas, as I do literary modernists, against the backdrop provided by what has been called the epistemological crisis of the later nineteenth century, the shift away from apparently absolute certainties—in religion, linguistics, mathematics, physics, and so on—in the direction of relativity. "In the twenty years between 1895 and 1915 the whole picture of the physical universe, which had appeared not only the most impressive but also the most secure achievement of scientific thought," as Alan Bullock has observed, "was brought into question" (1978, 34). To recall some well-known contextual markers, I note that these are the years of work in the direction of Gödel's

[1] See Ruth Benedict, "Obituary of Franz Boas." *Science* 97 (1943): 61; Ruth Bunzel. *The Golden Age of American Anthropology*, ed. Margaret Mead and Ruth Bunzel (New York: Braziller, 1960), p. 403; and Irving Goldman, "Boas on the Kwakiutl: The Ethnographic Tradition," *Theory and Practice: Essays Presented to Gene Weltfish*, ed. Stanley Diamond (The Hague: Mouton 1980), p. 334. Kroeber says, "I believe there can be no doubt Boas wanted to deal with human rather than inorganic phenomena as soon as he found that it was possible to deal with them *scientifically*." A. L. Kroeber, "Preface" to *The Anthropology of Franz Boas: Essays on the Centenary of His Birth*. ed. Walter Goldschmidt. The American Anthropological Association, vol. 61, memoir no. 89 (October 1959): v (emphasis added).

[2] See *The Ethnography of Franz Boas*, comp. and ed. Ronald Rohner, with an introduction by Ronald Rohner and Evelyn P. Rohner (Chicago: University of Chicago Press, 1969), p. xiii; Leslie White, *The Ethnography and Ethnology of Franz Boas*, Bulletin of the Texas Memorial Museum, no. 6 (1963): 67; and Marvin Harris, *The Rise of Anthropological Theory* (New York: Crowell, 1968), p. 282. One can find an abundance of conflicting testimony in regard to Boas's famed methodological rigor. For all his warnings against the broad conjecturalism of his comparativist predecessors, for example, according to Leslie White, Boas often himself indulged in wild speculation: "His historical constructions are worthless, for the most part, and fantastic in some respects" (White 1963, 65). As for Boas's field methods, Rohner's considered conclusion is that they "were essentially the same as those used by his nineteenth-century predecessors" (1969, xxiii–xxiv). Boas warned against too great reliance on any single informant—but he relied very heavily on George Hunt. He stressed the dispassionate collection of all the facts available, yet seems to have avoided scatological or sexual detail, and managed not to notice Kwakiutl drinking patterns. For all this, it remains possible to quote a great many writers on the superiority and rigor of Boas's methodology.

proof that certain mathematical problems cannot be solved; of the Heisenberg Uncertainty Principle, and finally, of Einstein's relativity equations. These are the years when more than once Freud would speak of psychoanalysis as the third wound to human narcissism, for it demonstrates—after the Copernican and Darwinian wounds—that we are not only not the center of the universe nor descended from the angels, but equally, not masters of our own minds. No wonder that de Saussure could look back upon the nineteenth century's solid accumulation of philological data and conclude only that in language there are no positive quantities but simply differences. This is the period in which Thomas Hardy's sense of the haphazardness of fate would be most fully developed (the last novel dates from 1896, but what is ostensibly Hardy's masterwork, *The Dynasts* was issued from 1903 to 1908). It is the time when Nietzsche's scorn for the unfounded pretenses of religion, logic, or history is felt; the time of fictional experiments with point of view in Conrad, James, and Ford Madox Ford. Consider as a telling[3] image Stephen Crane's "open boat," in his work by the same name (1898), bobbing precariously on an infinity of ocean, its weary passengers trying to survive and to be good, as all the past had told them to do, but as the present made most difficult.

Now, the anglophone writers named were almost surely not direct influences on Boas (if they were at all), as, indeed, Nietszche was probably not. Marvin Harris has traced the German writers, neo-Kantian for the most part, who were directly influential on Boas (1968, 258–82). *Mutatis mutandis,* it looks as though the epistemological and discursive climate in which Boas's work took shape was one with a strong sense of the relative rather than the absolute; of an absence of fixity, of all in flux; of certainty nowhere, uncertainty everywhere. What attitude other than one of skepticism could claim to be appropriate to such a worldview? Irony is the trope identified by the West for the expression of skepticism as a response to uncertainty, and one may imagine either that Boas (1) somehow founded a science entirely against the grain of the ironic temper of his time, (2) that he founded a science in the ironic mode, or (3) that he operated according to an ironic paradigm of a sort that was inconsistent with the establishment of any kind of science whatsoever. These latter two possibilities (I reject the first of these as theoretically improb-

[3] Telling, that is, from the literary and Americanist perspective from which I write—as Marilyn Strathern writes "from the perspective of British social anthropology," this perspectival difference no doubt going far to explain other differences in our approach to some parallel phenomena. See Strathern, this volume, p. 80n.2.

able and in practice untrue) are what I shall explore in the remainder of this paper.

I take irony to be the central trope of modernism. But just as modernism is no monolith—as Marc Manganaro properly notes in his Introduction, there are "many Modernisms to consider"[4]—neither is irony; there are many ironies to consider, as well. Among ironic figures, let me name four: *antiphrasis* or negation, *aporia* or doubt, *oxymoron* or paradox, and *catachresis* or misuse. The figure of aporia (it was not invented by Jacques Derrida, Paul de Man, or J. Hillis Miller, but was well known to classical and Renaissance rhetoricians) is, as I have said, the ironic figure of doubt; the aporitical text, then, is one filled with "doubts and objections" (*OED* 1971, 390). Antiphrasis is the ironic trope of negation, the central trope, for example, of satirical writing in which prior assertions are denied in the interest of promoting opposite or alternative assertions. The figure of the oxymoron presents apparently absurd or incongruous linkages, but oxymoronic figures may be distinguished from catachrestical figures in that the absurdity or incongruity of the oxymoron is only apparent, not real; however paradoxical the statement on the face of it may be, a fully coherent, rational point may be extracted—e.g., in such phrases as "coarse gentleman," or "noble savage." The figure of catachresis is one whose force is particularly difficult to convey. The *OED* (1971, 168) defines it as "misuse with a sense of perversion." According to Henry Peacham in his 1593 *Garden of Eloquence*, "Catachresis in Latine is called Abusio," and Peacham gives as one of his examples of catachresis, the "water runnes," the abuse consisting in attributing animate capacity to something that does not have life (16). For us this figure seems, I believe, purely metaphorical, however. Curiously, the *OED* describes, but does not provide examples of catachresis. Would Milton's "blind mouths," or Dylan Thomas's "the long friends" resonate as indicating perverse or abusive misuse? Or perhaps we need turn to something from popular culture, a phrase such as "jumbo shrimp"—which to me has more catechrestical than oxymoronic force.

The first three of these figures, I suggest, are tropes for the sort of skepticism that founds the modernist work of writers such as Hardy and Crane, of the early Pound and Eliot, of Joyce at least through some of *Ulysses*. And these tropes may also found nonfictional writing of a sort that may generally be considered scientific. The fourth one of these figures I see as the central trope of modernist work of a more radical nature, work such as Nietszche's, perhaps of Henry

[4] See this volume, p. 46

Adams's *Education*, of Henry James's *The Sacred Fount*, probably of *Finnegans Wake*, and of Virginia Woolf's *The Waves*. The catachrestical text cannot be considered scientific according to any of the usual understandings of the term. Merely to note what I shall not have space to develop, it is catachrestical modernism that postmodernism may be taken to continue or extend, while it is aporitic (to choose one of the terms possible here to stand for all others) modernism that postmodernism rejects and rebels against, constituting itself by means of a break.[5]

It is my contention that Boas's work is ironic through and through—but it remains unclear which *type* of irony, the doubtful, paradoxical, and negational, consistent with some sense of realism and of science, or the perverse-absurd, subversive of any sense of science, dominates in it. On the one hand, essay after essay may be cited as instantiating just the sort of hearty skepticism that clears the field for more securely founded hypotheses; on the other hand, the work as a whole either perversely insists upon conditions for scienticity that are in no way attainable, or asserts positions that so thoroughly contradict one another as abusively to cancel each other out, moving beyond the oxymoronic to the catachrestic, and thus subverting the conditions of possibility for any scientific hypotheses whatsoever.

The case for Boasian anthropology, as constituted by the kind of aporitic irony that founds what I will call a modernist realism consistent with science, might focus on the meaning and function of the new relativism in Boas's work. Unlike the nineteenth-century historians who, in Hayden White's account, saw the specter of relativism as serving to "undermine confidence in history's claim to 'objectivity,' 'scienticity,' and 'realism' " (1973, 33), Boas and his students seemed to find the new relativity not the foreclosure but the promise of objectivity, scienticity, and realism. Relativism, for Boas, was understood primarily to mean cultural relativism, and a stance of cultural relativism (which was not taken as implying a general epistemological relativism) as enabling a satiric method by which to expose the abundant undocumented generalizations indulged in by practitioners of "the comparative method in anthropology." In page after page of his writing both early and late, Boas shows a real delight in his ability to expose or deconstruct, as we might now say, generalizations that could not stand up to his aggressive ironic skepticism. In

[5] My understanding of aporia, thus, is rather different from that of de Man, Miller, and the deconstructionists generally; their aporia is what I call catachresis.

its historical moment, this aspect of Boas's intervention most certainly seems to have advanced the project of a scientific anthropology.

But then there is the famous Boasian hostility to theory and to laws. And there are, indeed, many passages in Boas's writing where he warns against the dangers of interposing aprioristic theory between the putatively innocent eye of the observer and the facts or data in themselves[6] (his view of these matters seems positivist in a rather *demodé* manner). Boas also seems to have given many of his students and readers a strong impression that he was implacably opposed not only to theory but to all statements of phenomenal lawfulness, that for him anthropology was the sort of inquiry that best limits its view to the singularity or particularity of cultural phenomena. Nonetheless, as I shall try to show in only a moment more, one can also cite essays in which Boas asserts the statement of general laws as indeed the ultimate aim of anthropology as of any science. Besides the issue of deep self-contradiction, there is the further issue that even in his remarks approving the possibility of scientific generalization, Boas insists again and again on impossible conditions for such generalization, noting that laws will legitimately be discovered only when all the facts are in.

The trajectory of a scientific anthropology, then, was to be the collection of facts in the interest of the discovery of laws. Facts, for Boas, are not conceptual constructs or even choices on the part of the researcher, but simply out there. And laws, for Boas, in the generalization of his understanding of facts, do not either have to be formulated or constructed; rather, once all the facts are in, laws will simply announce or dis-cover themselves to the assiduous observer. Boas would not abandon the goal of stating laws because that would be to abandon the project of a scientific anthropology, but he also would not abandon his adherence to impossible conditions for the actual achievement of a scientific anthropology. Insofar as it is obvious that *all* the facts will never be in, it is not possible ever to satisfy Boas's ironic skepticism, not possible ever to achieve exactly the science he is after. Such a position, I suggest, is not aporitic, but is best figured by the trope of catachresis. But it is surely time for us to do some reading.

In an 1887 text called "The Study of Geography," Boas distinguishes between sciences as they derive from one or the other of two appar-

[6] Cf. Marian W. Smith: "Boas taught his students statistics and phonetics as tools for handling biological series and language, but the greatest lesson we learned was that data had an order of their own" (1959, 51).

ently invariant tendencies in the mind—or at least the Western mind. The natural sciences, such as physics, Boas claims, spring from what he calls the "aesthetic impulse," while those such as "cosmography," or history, what we would term the social sciences, are the expression of what he calls the "affective impulse."[7] The first, a sort of "rage for order," is concerned with stating the general laws governing the phenomena under consideration, while the second is more particularistically concerned with the individual phenomenon itself. For the cosmographer, the historian, or, as Boas spent most of his life insisting, the anthropologist, the "mere occurrence of an event claims the full attention of our mind, because we are affected by it, and it is studied without any regard to its place in a system" (1940, 644). As opposed to the physicist, who seeks to generalize from "mere occurrences," the cosmographer, Boas writes, "holds to the phenomenon which is the object of his study . . . and lovingly tries to penetrate into its secrets until every feature is plain and clear. This occupation with the object of his affection affords him a delight not inferior to that which the physicist enjoys in his systematical arrangement of the world" (1940, 645). It is hard to resist noticing the erotic dimension of Boas's description of the cosmographical romance. But can such a conception be compatible with an anthropological *science*? Boas characteristically answers yes—and no. "Physicists," he writes, "will acknowledge that the study of the history of many phenomena is a work of scientific value" (1940, 642), and, near the end of his essay, Boas pronounces both cosmographical and physical inquiry to be—and it would seem equivalently—"two branches of science" (1940, 646).

What Boas says here of history and cosmography he would say again and again of anthropology: that it was to study its object of affection "without any regard to its place in a system." But he would also say again and again that anthropology, in this regard now quite like physical science ("aesthetic" as distinguished from "affective" science), must indeed search out systematic laws. Only a year after the publication of "The Study of Geography," in an 1888 text called "The Aims of Ethnology," we find Boas writing that "the human mind develops everywhere according to the same laws," and that the "discovery of these [laws] is the greatest aim of our science" (1940, 637). As I have noted, to the end of his life, Boas continued to insist upon the necessity of reducing the multitudinous phenomenal data

[7] Franz Boas, "The Study of Geography," *Race, Language, and Culture* (New York: Macmillan, 1940), pp. 643–44. All citations from Boas are from this work, and further page references will be documented in the text.

of culture to some kind of lawfulness—of finding its "place in a system"—while appending the condition that more and ever more data would first have to be examined before the formulation of explanatory generalizations might legitimately begin. Anthropology must ultimately discover some kind of laws, just as any proper science must, but such laws cannot be discovered until all the evidence is in. Since all the evidence will never be in, the anthropologist, now a kind of "connoisseur of chaos," had best stick to particularities and defer concern for pattern or general lawfulness—although the discovery of laws is, indeed, the goal of ethnology. It is a simple matter to quote Boas on both sides of what seem to me antithetical and—in the form in which they are stated—irreconcilable positions. But further quotation would not be especially helpful, nor, indeed, is it necessary, once we note that Boas himself chose just these two essays—"The Aims of Ethnology" and "The Study of Geography"—with their conflicting positions, to conclude the last major book of his lifetime, *Race, Language, and Culture* published in 1940.

Writing when he was more than eighty years old, Boas announces that these two papers, composed some fifty years earlier, were chosen to conclude his book "because they indicate the general attitude underlying [his] later work" (1940, vi). Boas's attitude is such as to offer firm support for both sides of a great many questions, and such an attitude goes beyond the aporitic ironic skepticism compatible with science to the catachrestical irony that would subvert any pretense to science.

Now, *Race, Language, and Culture* is a volume of six hundred forty-seven pages, comprising sixty-three essays written over a period of forty-nine years. It is a wartime book, and Boas's Preface states his intention that the essays to come may show anthropology's bearing "upon problems that confront us" (1940, v). A section called "Race," consisting of twenty essays, is the first in the book; "Language," with five, is the second; the third section, "Culture," the category of Boas's most substantial contribution, has thirty-five essays.

One might well expect that Boas chose these divisions, representing the three main areas of his work over a long lifetime, and arranged the essays in them in some kind of ascending or progressive order; one might expect, that is, that this large book is organized in such a way as to permit some sort of climactic or at least clear statement of his position. But any such expectation is undercut by the presence of a fourth section, one that, in its structural and thematic effect, is decidedly anticlimactic. For Boas does not end this book, called *Race, Language and Culture,* with the section on "Culture" (or, for that matter, with an Afterword or Conclusion), but instead follows it with something called simply, "Miscellaneous." And it is in "Miscellaneous," that Boas places the texts indicative, as he states in his Preface, of his final position on matters central to his understanding of anthropology. The texts in this final section are not recent work but three nineteenth-century essays that work backward, from 1898 with "Advances in Methods of Teaching," to 1888 and "The Aims of Ethnology" (in which there was a call for the discovery of laws), to "The Study of Geography" of 1887 (a piece that announced that the discovery of laws was not the aim of social science at all).

To conclude his final book this way is to reveal a deeply ironic sense of structure (*which* irony, again, remains to be seen). For what is true of irony thematically, as an "attitude," is true of irony structurally, as a form, as well: ironic structures achieve their effects by frustrating traditional expectations for climax and closure. Ironic texts may seem to work according to the familiar Western patterns of tragedy, comedy, and romance, but in the end they always subvert them. Rather than the revelation and resignation of tragedy, the reconciliation and reintegration of comedy, or the idealistic transcendence of romance, the ironic ending suggests that things just happen as they happen, to no special point, or at least to no clear one. Think of a play such as Samuel Beckett's *Waiting for Godot*, with its last lines, "Well? Shall we go?" "Yes, let's go," and its final stage direction, "They don't move." Nothing moves for the ironist; *plus ça change, plus c'est la même chose*. Even more radically, moving again from aporitic to catachrestic irony, there is the suggestion that the very idea of an ending is an absurdity or paradox; no text can ever *end*. Think of Kafka's *Castle*, or of *Finnegans Wake*, whose final words lead back to its first words. Does the *apparently* contradictory juxtaposition of "The Aims . . ." and "The Study . . ." really have its oxymoronic point? Or is it Boas's ultimate instantiation of perverse misuse, *abusio* having the last word?

For all of this, the scientist reader, if not so hotly the literary reader, may well be asking what, after all, do the essays themselves have to *say*? Speaking from outside the disciplinary borders of anthropology, I would repeat that the essays on race seem ironic only so far as they are skeptical of entirely undocumented, unscientific, and self-serving statements about race. Throughout his long career, Boas insisted on the cultural explanation of cultural differences and profoundly intervened against German racist theories directed against Jews and American racist theories directed against blacks, and these essays lend themselves more readily than usual in his work to focused use and development.

I am not sure what to make of the few (five) essays on language, although it seems difficult to read them without the double sense of, first, Boas's clear insistence on the importance for the ethnographer of learning native languages, and, second, of the uncertainty surrounding his own knowledge of Kwa'kwala, the language of the Kwakiutl: of Helen Codere's statements, for example, that Kwakiutl people she interviewed in 1951 remembered Boas speaking their language (1966, xxiv), and Ronald Rohner's conclusion in 1969 that Boas had learned Chinook jargon but not Kwa'kwala, nor any other "indigenous Northwest Coast language" (xxiv).

The many essays on culture divide into more nearly general, theoretical pieces and specific ethnographic pieces. I will look briefly at the major theoretical piece shortly. As for the ethnographic work, it seems mostly an immense, even celebratory record of randomness: Boas was there when he was there, he saw what he saw, he left us whatever he happened to leave us. Even Helen Codere, for all her enormous respect for Boas, acknowledged that "it is not possible to present a synthesized account of Kwakiutl culture based upon Boas' works" (Harris 1968, 314–15). Whether Boas purposely worked in such a way as to forestall what he would have considered an inevitably *premature* synthesis, or, rather, worked in such a way as to obstruct any synthesis whatsoever remains, I believe, undecidable.

Ronald Rohner, who found his own attempt to work in the field with Boas's Kwakiutl materials beset with difficulties, has noted that even when Boas was aware that some of his texts and ethnographic "materials over time contain[ed] many inaccuracies and inconsistencies . . . he never corrected them in print" (1969, xiii), an observation that reaffirms Alfred Kroeber's statement that Boas knew he was wrong in his account of how the Kwakiutl potlatch functioned "but that he never took the time to re-explain the system" (White 1963, 56). Here, too, it might be that he just "never took the time"; but it also might be that this lack of concern to reconcile conflicting views was a consequence of a radically ironic, catachrestical commitment to sustaining contradiction.

I turn now to the essay Boas placed first in the section on culture, his 1932 presidential address to the American Association for the Advancement of Science, called "The Aims of Anthropological Research." Both the occasion of its original delivery and its placement in this book are such as to suggest that it may fairly be taken as representative of Boas's mature thought. What we find all through this text is irony's ability to doubt and deny; the question for science is whether the doubt and denial are, once again, in the interest of alternative affirmations or go so far as to deny affirmative statements of any kind.

Boas begins with a sketch of anthropology's beginnings from a variety of sources; next, he defines "our objective as the attempt to understand the steps by which man has come to be what he is, biologically, psychologically and culturally" (1940, 244). It appears, Boas says, that "our material must necessarily be historical material, historical in the widest sense of the term" (1940, 244). Having announced the need for historical data, however, Boas then goes on to show how unlikely it is that sufficient data will ever be forthcoming, and then lists the errors and dangers of a variety of positions. He next passes from considerations of race and psychology to those of "cultural anthropology." I will catalog some of his negational figures, without, to be sure, providing sufficient context to understand each of his remarks in itself. My claim is that the sheer number of these figures does the work of establishing Boas's commitment to ironic skepticism. Boas writes: "The material needed for the reconstruction of the biological history of mankind is insufficient on account of the paucity of remains . . ." (1940, 250); "Even this information is insufficient . . ." (1940, 251); "For these reasons it is well nigh impossible . . ." (1940, 252); "This method cannot be generalized . . ." (1940, 252); "It may be admitted that it is exceedingly difficult to give absolutely indisputable proof . . ." (1940, 252); it "hardly admits of the argument that . . ." (1940, 252); "this view is not admissible without proof that . . ." (1940, 253); "It is not a safe method to assume that . . ." (1940, 254); "Even the fullest knowledge of the history of language does not help us to understand . . ." (1940, 255); "The phenomena of our science are so individualized, so exposed to outer accident that no set of laws could explain them . . ." (1940, 257): and so on.[8]

For all that aporia and antiphrasis structure Boas's text, still, the doubts and negations may yet imply some positive recommendations. Nonetheless, even if this first essay on culture is useful for the project of an anthropological science, *Race, Language, and Culture* will still present us, as its conclusion, the "miscellaneously" juxtaposed, contradictory final essays of the book.

And it does indeed seem to me that Boas's writing, taken as a

[8] Just two more of Boas's negative strictures, these quite firmly denying the likelihood of "discovering" laws: "Cultural phenomena are of such complexity that it seems to me doubtful whether valid cultural laws can be found" (1940, 257); "anthropology is . . . one of the sciences the interest of which centers in the attempt to understand the individual phenomena rather than in the establishment of general laws which, on account of the complexity of the material, will be necessarily vague and, we might almost say, so self-evident that they are of little help to a real understanding" (1940, 258).

whole, has a kind of abusive perversity that, as with Nietzsche, undermines the foundations for any claims to scienticity. At the furthest horizon, I believe Boas saw and perhaps rather anxiously was fascinated by cultural and epistemological chaos—that he temperamentally enjoyed an old-fashioned variant of postmodernist free play. If I am at all correct, he partook, therefore, of a kind of *abysmal* ironic vision, which I have tried to link to the figure of catachresis. In this regard, to the extent that he may have become "unreadable" in the present moment, Boas might be recuperated as a sort of precursor of postmodernism. But if I seem here to have conducted Boas to exactly the place Marilyn Strathern brought Frazer,[9] yet I would want to warn even more strongly than she against any attempt actually to reread Boas as postmodernist. No one coming from (say) Stephen Tyler's work will very long be happy with Frazer *or* Boas as a postmodernist *writer*.

Short of the furthest horizon, however, I think Boas was regularly fascinated by the study of phenomena that he probably felt to be more orderly (whatever their order) than chaotic, phenomena that, looked at particularly and carefully, at least were probably coherent in themselves. This sense of cultural things was tropologically figured in varieties of what I have called aporitic irony, the central trope, to repeat, of a sort of realist / scientist modernism: distanced and distancing, skeptical, tough-minded, sensitive to paradox, self-conscious, and so on.

Like a number of writers of the modernist period—and I think this is particularly true of writers of the modernist period and not just of writers in general—Boas's work is difficult to characterize as a whole, the whole not at all comprehensible as the strict sum of its parts. In somewhat similar fashion, the Eliot of the "Preludes" or "Prufrock" is not consistent with the Eliot of the "Four Quartets," or, to cite an author not much considered in these essays as a modernist, the D. H. Lawrence of *The Rainbow* is not fully consistent with the D. H. Lawrence of *Aaron's Rod, The Plumed Serpent*, or even the *Studies in Classic American Literature*. The same, as I have noted, is true of Henry James, whose *Sacred Fount* of 1901 cannot be understood as simply the "mature" work of the author of the *Portrait of a Lady* (1881). In all these authors, as in Boas, any estimate of the whole could not be arrived at simply by adding up the parts.

Yet, I will say that, for all the deep contradictions of his work, Boas today, in our moment as indeed in his own, is much more useful for the residual (in Raymond Williams's sense) project of a scientific

[9] See Strathern, this volume.

anthropology (however modest and circumscribed current claims for scienticity must be) than for either Geertzian semiotic anthropologies or Tylerian postmodern anthropologies. I, at any rate, would like to see him recuperated for such a project, for all that we must allow to his work its catachrestical component.

The Politics of Ethnographic Authority: Race and Writing in the Ethnography of Margaret Mead and Zora Neale Hurston

DEBORAH GORDON

In the 1980s, cultural anthropology in the United States was transformed by a growing body of critical literature that focused on the politics of ethnography. Historians of anthropology, anthropologists themselves, and literary critics have turned their attention toward the writing of fieldwork as a locus of power relations and historical contexts.[1] The text itself, the document that certifies the authenticity of fieldwork, has come under scrutiny from critics who view ethnography not as a transparent window onto another culture but rather as a poetic and rhetorical translation, inevitably partial and contested. This focus on representation as problematic, incomplete, and responsible to specific histories has merged with various analyses of social science as socially constructed practice, situated in global and local politics. Recent critical histories of anthropology and discussions of ethnographic representation merge hermeneutic philosophical trends with an examination of the power dimensions in fieldwork accounts. Knowledge is, thus, understood not as a quasi-transcendental object but constructed and managed in, social and political relations.

Important to the management of anthropology in the United States was its process of becoming a professional vocation undertaken by university-trained experts. In his analysis of the invention of modern ethnographic authority, James Clifford has noted that in the struggle to achieve professional status anthropologists endeavored to shift the social relations between academic practitioners and older workers in the field. The latter group includes colonial administrators, traders,

[1] See Marc Manganaro's Introduction to this volume for a survey of this literature. See also James Clifford and George E. Marcus, eds., *Writing Culture: The Poetics and Politics of Ethnography* (Berkeley: University of California Press, 1986).

missionaries, and members of learned societies—people whom anthropologists such as Franz Boas considered unscientific and too ill-trained to be reporting on "natives," and in positions insufficiently distant from world politics or too explicitly interested in the exotic. These became the "amateurs" over and against whom anthropology, in many ways, constituted itself (Clifford 1983, 121–22). As Clifford notes, in this process of professionalization, modern ethnography took its literary form. Anthropologists of the 1920s and 30s frequently claimed that their practices were distinct from those of earlier field-workers, defining their identity as the privileged persona for interpreting and speaking about non-Western peoples.[2] Because fieldwork has been one of the most important areas of certification of the professional anthropologist, its representation is crucial to the constitution of the discipline. To be a certified anthropologist it is not enough to have a fieldwork experience; it must be authentically conveyed in the writing of ethnography. In the translation of experience into writing, ethnography "enacts a specific strategy of authority" (Clifford 1983, 120). The modern ethnography's claims to authority, thus, are intimately bound to literary conventions of authenticity. In addition to conveying that the fieldworker had a distinctly anthropological experience, the ethnography must also display signs of "scholarship" that are connected to fieldwork but do not necessarily signify a unique fieldwork experience. These textual features signify "professionalism," or the acquisition of academic prestige. For example, most ethnographies claim that the author is university-trained, is connected to other anthropologists who have published ethnographies, has read a certain body of literature, etcetera. Although these do not convey the presence of the ethnographer in the field, they are, nonetheless, important to the authorization of the account. Moreover, in the process of professionalization of anthropology, hierarchies of disciplinary locations are asserted, and, thus, certain questions, issues, and problems bear higher status than others.

With these issues in mind, Margaret Mead's *Coming of Age in Samoa* and Zora Neale Hurston's *Tell My Horse* are two ethnographies from the 1920s and 30s, respectively, that constitute prime examples for examining what could count as professional ethnographic authority during this period. Reading their ethnographies demonstrates that the authority of the discipline was marked by race and gender. Al-

[2] For an account of this in Malinowski's work see George W. Stocking, "The Ethnographer's Magic: The Development of Fieldwork in British Anthropology from Tylor to Malinowski," in George W. Stocking, ed., *Observers Observed: Essays on Ethnographic Fieldwork, History of Anthropology*, Volume 1 (Madison, Wisc: University of Wisconsin Press, 1983), pp. 70–120, and Clifford, "On Ethnographic Authority," 121–22.

though a number of Boas's students were women, they did not, as a group, achieve the academic status that his male students did. And although the late nineteenth century saw the expansion of university education for women, by the interwar period women were attending graduate school but not attaining academic positions (Graham 1978, 759–73). We can see this general trend in the fact that throughout their careers neither Mead nor Hurston ever held a university position. Mead's institutional home remained the Museum of Natural History, while her male peers became associated with the development of anthropology departments at Berkeley, Northwestern, and Chicago. Hurston never completed her Ph.D., and thus practiced fieldwork without one of the most significant symbols of professionalization, and, although her fieldwork was extensive, she did not have an academic career. Both Mead and Hurston, thus, occupy places within the history of the discipline that are unlike those of A. L. Kroeber, Melville Herskovits, Paul Radin, or Ruth Benedict (who was also one of Boas's female graduate students). Benedict and Gladys Reichard, who were perhaps the most successful female academics who studied under Boas, were able to attain academic positions, but did not gain the academic status of their male peers. Benedict had a series of one-year appointments as a lecturer at Columbia, and was slated for the chair of the graduate department in anthropology. Unfortunately, the Dean who had planned on awarding Benedict this position died before he was able to appoint her. Instead, the school appointed Ralph Linton, who held a vendetta against Benedict after he discovered that she had not supported his candidacy. Linton's hostility toward Benedict was so intense, according to Sydney Mintz, that he would occasionally "boast publically that he had killed her."[3]

Reichard was an instructor in anthropology at Barnard, and when her interpretations of Navajo religion conflicted with those of Clyde Kluckhohn and Lee Wyman, she was challenging prominent men in the discipline. They supported each other and countered her with far greater force than she, as a single individual, could assert. Academic debates, of course, are not in theory sexist. Having the institutional resources to put into circulation and impose one's views, however, is linked to structural inequities such as gender. In this case, Kluck-

[3] See Sidney Mintz, "Ruth Benedict," in Sydel Silverman, ed., *Totems and Teachers: Perspectives in the History of Anthropology* (New York: Columbia University Press, 1981), p. 161. Linton's vendetta against Benedict is also noted in Barbara Babcock, "Not in the Absolute Singular: Re-Reading Ruth Benedict," paper prepared for the Wenner-Gren Conference, *Daughters of the Desert: Women Anthropologists and the Native American Southwest,* March 1986, p. 35.

hohn taught at Harvard, where there was a nationally recognized anthropology graduate program and resources to support extensive projects such as the Ramah project and the Comparative Study of Values in Five Cultures project. The Five Cultures project went on for six years and brought many graduate students under Kluckhohn's supervision who disseminated his ideas. He was, thus, able to institute his interpretations in ways Reichard was not. Of those female anthropologists who had Ph.D.s and held positions in academic institutions, many were in small colleges and universities located in the West rather than the East.[4] It is in this kind of institutional disadvantage that female students who trained under Boas found themselves, despite the fact that Boas, himself, claimed that his female students were his best students (Goldfrank 1978, 18). It was, therefore, frequently through popular writing that Boas's female students made their influence felt both in the discipline, and in American society more generally. Benedict's *Patterns of Culture* and Mead's *Coming of Age in Samoa* and *Sex and Temperament in Three Primitive Societies* brought professional anthropology to a public that continues to read these women with passionate interest. If Mead did not achieve the academic status of her male peers, *Coming of Age in Samoa* is, perhaps, the most widely read ethnography of the century in the United States. Contemporary anthropologists may declare *Coming of Age in Samoa* a product of primitive or unscientific fieldwork, but it still remains a reference point for many contestable claims about cultural anthropology.

Although Mead and her white female peers who also studied under Boas have occupied an ambiguous but powerful position within academic anthropology, Hurston has not been recognized as an anthropologist by anthropologists; her status as a folklorist has been claimed by black literary critics such as Robert Hemenway and black feminist writers such as Alice Walker.[5] In addition, *Mules and Men*, her one recognized ethnography, is read increasingly in undergraduate anthropology courses. Despite this interest in her folklore collecting and anthropological work, Hurston has yet to be canonized as an Afro-American anthropologist. Because they completed their

[4] My discussion of Reichard's career and the institutional location of women anthropologists depends heavily on Louise Lamphere, "Gladys Reichard among the Navajo," paper prepared for the Wenner-Gren Conference, *Daughters of the Desert: Women Anthropologists and the Native American Southwest*, March 1986, pp. 30–31.

[5] An exception to this general pattern is John F. Szwed's treatment of Hurston in his article, "An American Anthropological Dilemma: The Politics of Afro-American Culture," *Reinventing Anthropology*, ed. Dell Hymes (New York: Vintage, 1974), pp. 153–81.

degrees and were certified and recognized as anthropologists, Mead and her white female peers had a relationship to academic anthropology of the 1920s and 30s that Hurston had not. Hurston never finished her Ph.D., partly because of tenuous financial support and partly because her writing was situated within different social and political interests, a point to which I will return later. Despite the fact that both Mead and Hurston studied under Boas at Barnard and Columbia, their fieldwork practices and strategies for representing cross-cultural contact were quite distinct. That Mead had a career in anthropology and Hurston one as a literary artist / folklorist was not independent of the textual practices that signaled certain forms of cultural and professional authority. Hurston's marginalization from the center of anthropological activity was also the result of her social location, which was marked by the intertwinings of race and genre during the interwar period. I propose to contrast Mead's ethnographic textual practice with that of Hurston in order to show the connections between disciplinization, style, and race and gender in the making of professional anthropology. Given the recent interest in the relationship between ethnographers as writers and the production of counter- or experimental ethnographic knowledge, I am also arguing that Hurston was an ethnographer who wrote in an unusually experimental style. Her experimentation was not motivated by strictly aesthetic concerns or self-reflexivity for the sake of estrangement, but, rather, was occasioned by intense political and cultural projects. As such, her work demands the kind of recognition and rereading that older ethnographers such as Malinowski have received in the building of an experimental canon.[6]

Coming of Age in Samoa still retains its status as a classic ethnography. The debates surrounding the 1983 publication of Derek Freeman's *Margaret Mead and Samoa: The Making and Unmaking of an Anthropological Myth* confirm the high degree of interest anthropologists still have in this account. Unlike Hurston's ethnographies, which went out of print, and have only recently been reedited and reprinted, Mead's book has gone through numerous reprintings with her updated introductions. It is, thus, worth looking at Mead's writing to discern certain textual practices of the ethnographic monograph.

Mead's text, like much of social science during the period just prior to the Great Depression in the United States, is a self-conscious piece of cultural criticism. Infused with what George E. Marcus and Mi-

[6] This point is also made by Kamala Visweswaran in her article, "Defining Feminist Ethnography," *Inscriptions* 3 / 4 (1988): 39–40.

chael M. J. Fischer note as a sense of "critical mission" (1986, 127), Mead's ethnography uses the heuristic contrast of the "primitive" and the "modern" to create Samoa as a mirror for American self-criticism. The very subtitle of the book, "A Psychological Study of Primitive Youth for Western Civilization," suggests the Western reference point from which the "primitive" is derived. The ideology of the primitive implies a relationship between the West and what it defines as outside of itself; it functions as a place from which to simultaneously affirm and critique its practices. This ambivalence fueled Mead's cultural criticism, and she states in her introduction:

> We know that our subtlest perceptions, our highest values, are all based upon contrast; that light without darkness or beauty without ugliness would lose the qualities which they now appear to us to have. And similarly, if we would appreciate our own civilization, this elaborate pattern of life which we have made for ourselves as a people and which we are at such pains to pass on to our children, we must set our civilization over and against other very different ones. . . . But if we step outside the stream of Indo-European culture, the appreciation which we can accord our civilization is even more enhanced. (1928, 7–8)

In this statement Mead essentializes contrast and culture as oppositionally constructed, signified by the demand in her claim that in order to appreciate our civilization we "must" set it "over and against" others. This metaphysics with its oppositional relationship between the self and other fed "Western civilization's" worries about itself. The self-referential character of primitivism allowed Westerners such as Mead to dispute their own practices and to debate their future. The "debate," however, closed on an "enhanced" appreciation of Indo-European cultures, a subtle ordering of value that affirmed Eurocentrism. This affirmation depended on the setting up of a relationship between self and other in which the other was absorbed within the self, swallowed up by the demand for America's self-scrutiny. Ironically, this absorption threatened the very relationality, itself, between the United States and Samoa, because, by the end of the text, Samoa looks like an "answer" to what Mead perceived as North America's cultural neurosis, "adolescence."

In Mead's conclusion, she represents Samoa as complementary to the perceived chaos and diversity of the West. As she describes Samoa and America at the end of her account, Mead contrasts "a simple, homogeneous primitive civilization, a civilization that changes so slowly that to each generation it appears static, and a motley, diverse, heterogeneous modern civilization" (1928, 114). This contrasting gesture validated the role of the ethnographer as a mouthpiece for the Third World in a very specific way. This "voice" was not a dialogical one, but ambivalently self-absorbed in the pleasure of being "modern" in America. The American desire based in the move to criticize in order to affirm itself established a hermetic, one-way relationship between self and other.

Creating culture as a contrastive object took the narrative form of intertwining two voices, those of the cultural critic and the omniscient observer. They were kept carefully apart—the cultural critic introduced and closed the book while the observer "spoke" the other sections. Written in "free, indirect style," Mead's ethnography seldom utilizes direct quotation and narrated events as if speaking from no particular location or subjectivity. The figuring of authority in such composites as "the Samoans" allowed Mead to speak on behalf of the non-Westerners with whom she interacted and to assume that they existed as a unity to reflect Western concerns. It was this posture of neutral observation that permitted Americans to see themselves as a composite, heterogeneous nation of immigrants.

The creation of Samoa rendered through the omnipresence of the ethnographer can be heard in the beginning of Mead's second chapter, "A Day in Samoa," a description of a "typical" day in Samoa. In it Mead's voice occupies an omnipotent position, overlooking an entire village. Her description suggests that she can see everyone and everything at once:

> The life of the day begins at dawn, or if the moon has shown until daylight, the shouts of the young men may be heard before dawn from the hillside. Uneasy in the night, populous with ghosts, they shout lustily to one another as they hasten with their work. As the dawn begins to fall among the soft brown roofs and the slender palm trees stand out against a colourless, gleaming sea, lovers slip home from trysts beneath the palm trees or in the shadow of beached canoes, that the light may find each sleeper in his appointed place. (1928, 8)

In this scene, Mead establishes her authority to speak as an ethnographer through her monologue. Up in the morning before anyone else, able to read the minds of anonymous young men and to witness the sexual lives of the "natives," Mead's voice claims total vision and knowledge of the "other." Her description signifies that she was present, not with specific Samoans, but figuratively above a "culture" as it revealed its essence. The formal strategy for this is the "typical day" tale. The cementing of Mead's authority based on the representation of herself as omnipotent permits the generalizations that exist throughout the book. Indeed, the chapter that follows the "typical day" vignette begins immediately and assuredly, "Birthdays are of little account in Samoa" (1928, 11). Mead does describe specific Samoans in her text but only as examples of observations she is making and not as active participants in the construction of her account. For example, in discussing the relationship between age groups and friendships, Mead introduces short portraits of different Samoan girls. These portraits occasionally include quotes from particular girls but they are only represented as confirming general arguments rather than acting as any kind of dialogue with Mead.

Besides Mead herself, the only other "presence" in the book is that of Franz Boas, who wrote the book's foreword. Boas's foreword contributes to Mead's authority, as it situates Mead's account within his scholarly patriline, the most powerful in anthropology of this time period. Mead's text also contains "acknowledgments" that refer to her funding sources, including her father's payment of her travel expenses, and other people who aided her in her fieldwork study—museum directors, United States military and medical staff, Samoan chiefs, pastors, teachers, and other leaders of the island, including the Governor of Manu'a and C. F. Pepe, who first instructed Mead in the Samoan language. The labor of these intermediaries is represented solely through the listing of proper names.

This textual practice was based on certain assumptions about fieldwork. First, it assumed that the activity of fieldwork was separate from the forces of colonization that made possible the presence of the anthropologist in regions such as Samoa. Anthropology's very existence as a profession was complexly linked to colonialism, yet the pose of ethnographers was as if they were the first Westerners to encounter the colonies.[7] The representation of fieldwork required *not* the suppression of the collective labor that conditioned anthropological travel, but rather the relegation of certain social relations to the margins of the text, there to signify that the travel was "professional" and "scholarly." American-Samoan colonial relations, with their ambiguous and power-laden exchanges between Westerners and "natives," because they muddied the effect of ethnographic neutrality, found their textual place in a section apart from the "account." By placing signs of colonial relations within the acknowledgments, the reader could recognize colonialism casually, without being troubled or discomforted, so that the total vision of the other could be experienced.

Second, fieldwork was cast during this period as a voyage out, a

[7] On the separation of the fieldworker from the colonial encounter see Johannes Fabian, *Time and the Other: How Anthropology Makes its Object* (New York: Columbia University Press, 1983).

movement into the West's unknown; the field was a separate space in which a single Westerner was to confront a time before the advent of Western society. Colonial personnel were a glaring reminder of the contemporary situation of power in which anthropology was embedded. We shall see in Hurston's account that these markings of social relations took a different form and, in some moments, entered the fieldwork account itself. Hurston's textual practices suggest a different kind of ethnographic knowledge embedded in a different kind of fieldwork, not recognized as professional activity.

If *Coming of Age in Samoa* was one instance in the establishment of a separate literary voice for ethnography, *Tell My Horse,* Hurston's account of fieldwork in Jamaica and Haiti, blurred different forms of travel writing, and thus different modes of ethnographic authority. Its generic complexity went against the very grain of distinctions that were being successfully carved out by fieldworkers such as Mead and Malinowski. The book received a mixed reception in 1938 at the time of its publication, as reviewers expressed genuine confusion about its generic status,[8] and Hurston's biographer, Robert Hemenway, writing in 1977, argues that *Tell My Horse* is Hurston's "poorest book, chiefly because of its form" ([1935], 248). Unlike in Mead's account, there was no stamp of academic legitimacy from Boas or any other professional anthropologist. The 1936 version of the book was dedicated to Carl Van Vechten, the most important white patron of the artistic works associated with the Harlem Renaissance.[9] Simultaneously a travelogue, a piece of journalism and political analysis, a conventional ethnography, part legend and folklore with art criticism and commentary thrown in, Hurston's text voices conflicting visions of what fieldwork involved—a kind of knowledge that enters Mead's letters from the field but not her ethnography.

Because Hurston's account also utilizes textual strategies of travel narratives and journalism, the text includes her conversations with medical personnel, politicians, and other "personalities," as she refers to them, of Haiti. Because Haiti and Jamaica are not represented as complements of the West, but as intimately bound with international events such as the United States Marines' occupation, "fieldwork" is neither an attempt to describe a foreign culture or to reflect

[8] See Harold Courlander, Review of *Tell My Horse, Saturday Review,* 15 October 1938, p. 6; *New Yorker,* 15 October 1938, and Alain Locke, "The Negro: 'New' or Newer," *Opportunity* 17 (February 1939): 38.

[9] Boas did write the preface to Hurston's *Mules and Men,* published in 1935, and his preface gave this book as opposed to *Tell My Horse,* an affect of anthropological legitimacy. *Mules and Men* continues to be cited as Hurston's only ethnography (see Hemenway 1977).

with distance on the United States but, instead, is an activity of ongoing negotiation with specific figures who are situated in distinct positions vis-à-vis the United States and Hurston herself.

At moments the text sounds like a travel brochure offering advice such as, "If you go to Jamaica you are going to want to visit the Maroons of Accompong" ([1938], 34). It is difficult to imagine Mead advising her readers on what to see while in Samoa. Figures of speech found in statements such as "Peeps at personalities in the Black Republic" ([1938], 94), are hardly marks of social science. Neither are the explicit imitations of Haitian sayings (such as "Ah Bo! Bo!") that close some of Hurston's chapters.

At other moments Hurston assumes a stance of ethnographic authority that is similar to Mead's narrative posture. Hurston's style does not eschew the ethnographic monograph, but utilizes the posture of objectivity in order to make counterclaims to previous representations of African-Americans. Because of the complex intermingling of ethnographic poses in the text, there is no unified authority portrayed and no claims to reporting a "culture." It is not unusual for Hurston to strike different, even contradictory, poses within the same scene. At one point in her account, Hurston refers to a colonial's attempt to stage a dance for her. Not wanting to see a dance or ceremony outside of its "natural setting and sequence" ([1938], 36), Hurston declines the offer, not bothering to tell the colonial, but letting the reader know, that she is "too old a hand at collecting to fall for staged-dance affairs" ([1938], 36). Hurston then goes on to claim that she just "sat around and waited" ([1938], 45), for the real Maroon culture to reveal itself. Nevertheless, this self-consciousness of what an anthropologist is supposed to do while in the field is contradicted two paragraphs later. Hurston notes that there are no stoves in Accompong. Horrified by this lack of Western technology, she insists that the colonial purchase one in order to show the natives how to use it. Not content to forget the idea when the colonial tells her that there is no money for a stove, Hurston insists that she will help build one. A curious effect is produced in this juxtaposition of the passive observer waiting for revelation and the rural planner who cannot imagine how the natives can live without a stove. Hurston also claims that she continually "worried" the colonial about having the opportunity to taste jerked pig. Hurston so wants to taste this meat that she insists on being taken on a wild boar hunt. Bothering the colonial, she "kept on talking and begging and coaxing until a hunting party was organized" ([1938], 45). There is nothing "natural" about wheedling the colonial into a dangerous trip into the countryside to encounter a wild boar.

Like Mead, specific scenes of cross-cultural contact are stylized through the portrayal of generalized Others. Hurston, however, tends to interweave generalizations in an objective register with markedly subjective statements. Her style of generalizing is excessive and blatant in its assertions about Jamaica and Haiti. Written into her ethnography are the prejudices, irrationalities, and racism that have been relegated to either the ethnographic diary or fieldnotes.[10] Hurston's ethnography includes scenes of conflict and argument in which she represents herself as antagonistic to particular attitudes she encounters. As Hemenway notes, *Tell My Horse* makes flagrant, ethnocentric generalizations about Haitians, such as: "there is a marked tendency (among Haitians) to refuse responsibility for anything that is unfavorable" (Hurston [1938], 105). In addition, Hurston puts forth her opinion that the American occupation of Haiti aided in the development of the country. By clearly aligning herself with political positions regarding American-Haitian relations, Hurston brings ethnocentrism into the ethnographer's persona. That is, ethnocentrism is not something that the ethnographer simply puts in her / his field diary in order to record more objectively what (s)he observes, but is part of the construction of relations in the field. The anthropologist is not god-like but as caught within the fieldwork situation as the "natives." Working in the field is, thus, represented through myths of disagreement, struggle, and disturbance as well as in images of rapport or friendship. Hurston offers a vision of fieldwork in which the limits as well as possibilities of cross-cultural understanding are explicitly displayed.

In addition to including ways of knowing that are conventionally placed on the margins of the fieldwork narrative, Hurston's account fails to make certain rhetorical moves that signify the authority of the anthropological monograph that Mead wrote so effectively. Unlike other fieldworkers in Haiti, such as Herskovits (who *is* widely recognized as an authority on the Caribbean), Hurston does not critically refer to a unified, past literary tradition that she opposes (Herskovits 1927). Hurston does disagree with what she perceives to be misinterpretations of certain aspects of voodoo practice, but her authority to speak is not based on an opposition to a past set of "distortions." Indeed, at one point in her book she notes that W. B. Seabrook's *Magic Island*, a travel narrative about Haiti, had "fired" her "imagination" and interest in the island, La Gonave. In contrast,

[10] See, for example, Bronislaw Malinowski, A Diary in the Strict Sense of the Term (London: Routledge & Kegan Paul, 1967) and Margaret Mead, *Letters from the Field: 1925–1975* (New York: Harper & Row, 1977).

Mead speaks in *Coming of Age in Samoa* as an anthropologist bringing knowledge of Samoa to a nonacademic audience. In this sense her authority enacts a complementary move in relationship to the constructions of past fieldworkers as amateurs. Both the move to cleanse anthropology of the impurities of the nonscientific past and the move to claim to write without academic "jargon," as Mead refers to it, nonetheless assume a system of classification that separates "popular" knowledge from social science. Hurston's text does not acknowledge that separation.

At its writing, *Tell My Horse* also violated ethnographic codes by virtue of its being an account of visiting two nations, Jamaica and Haiti. Authoritative fieldwork accounts of the period were generally not written about two cultures or two areas, and if they were, it was in a broadly comparative manner.[11] In Hurston's account there is no comparison of Jamaica and Haiti. Jamaica is represented as a kind of stopping-off point in relationship to Haiti. An effect of island-hopping, more "casual" travel is produced in saying relatively less about Jamaica. Jamaica and Haiti are also not interchangeable objects in the text. Jamaica is portrayed as an assimilationist culture, sexist and relatively uninviting, despite Hurston's stay with the Maroons.

To write ethnography in this period was to document a "culture." This abstraction called culture was conceived of as a single, unified whole that could be grasped through one of its parts (Clifford 1983, 125). Hurston could have done this with a voodoo ritual—something like Malinowski's kula ceremony, which organizes his account of the Trobriand Islands or Mead's examination of adolescence in Samoa. Clearly, voodoo is the most easily discernible theme of Hurston's book, but her ethnography does not structure voodoo as representative of some more general abstraction called Haiti. Contemporary critics have read Hurston's book in this manner, that is, as an account of Haiti through the meaning of voodoo. (The book is divided into three sections entitled "Jamaica," "Haiti," and "Voodoo.") These critics have read the final section as the essence of the account, "the heart and secret core of this book" (Callahan 1981, xiii). There is no resolution to this section, however, that would provide the necessary narrative closure to anchor strongly the meaning of voodoo. Hurston's reporting of voodoo rituals and ceremonies harkens back to earlier styles of reporting, in which detailed and extensive listings of folklore and custom are the predominant form.[12] She chooses not

[11] See, for example, Mead's *Sex and Temperament in Three Primitive Societies* (New York: William Morrow and Co., 1935).

[12] See, for example, R. H. Codrington, *The Melanesians: Studies in Their Anthropology*

only to represent her experience of fieldwork but also songs, proverbs, and legends as separate from their function in a particular culture.

Hurston's representation of fieldwork was situated within different institutional frameworks than Mead's ethnography. That a white woman such as Margaret Mead could make anthropology as much a popular myth as a social science goes beyond the obvious and crucial racial discrimination in higher education during this period. Race played an important role in the connections between institutional and textual authority. Here intellectual and social networks, funding and mentoring relations, the framing of the research problems, and disciplinary taxonomies were interconnecting practices in the shaping of Hurston's ethnographies.

Both *Tell My Horse* and *Mules and Men*, Hurston's ethnography of Southern African-American folklore in Florida and Louisiana, are situated within a broad cultural interest in what was referred to as the "New Negro." The beginnings of the articulation of a new cultural and political problematic—how to make citizens and cultured people out of former "savages"—occurred during Reconstruction and continued into the twentieth century. Schematically put, after Reconstruction and the migration of African-Americans from the South into Northern, urban areas, their identity became an object of scientific and popular interest. Anthropology, and social science in general, was not outside this problem, but constituted instead a set of practices that participated in the construction of the "new Negro," to borrow Alain Locke's designation. As John Szwed has noted, Boas was "the chief scientific spokesman on the subject of race and social implications" (1974, 156). In a commencement address at Atlanta University in 1906, Boas argued that Africa could be a pedagogical object for the construction of a new American Negro identity. As Szwed points out, Boas assumed that African-Americans had no distinctive culture because their former African culture had disappeared with slavery. African ethnology was, thus, construed as the material out of which a new Negro identity could be formulated (Stocking 1974, 310–16). Boas even went so far as to request money from Andrew Carnegie for an "African Institute," which was to be a structure for presenting to the public the products of African civilization as well as generating policy regarding African-Americans (Stocking 1974, 316). Although he was not granted the money for the institution, a social scientific discourse on race and a more generally defined process of

and Folk-lore (Oxford: Clarendon Press, 1891), and Frank Hamilton Cushing, *Zuni Folk-Tales* (New York: G. P. Putnam's Sons, 1901).

citizenship for African-Americans allowed this kind of conception of a social problem that anthropology could address. Hurston's interests in African-American materials intersected with Boas's interests in examining folklore "anthropologically." Hurston could not have been doing African-American "anthropology" without African-American "culture."

There was, however, African-American "folklore." Its problems in this period were developed in relationship to the problem of black enculturation. Folklorists throughout the twentieth century have debated whether African-American folktales are European or African in origin. To the extent that African-American folklore could be construed as connected to Africa, it could be a source of knowledge about Negroes. Hurston's work was marked by race, both because she was a black woman in and out of the university at a time when very few ethnic minorities received a college education, and because her work was structured by this new problematic of American social life and its relationship to disciplinary taxonomies.

In addition, Hurston's connections to the intellectual and social milieu of the Harlem Renaissance positioned her work within the race relations of black and white intellectuals in New York City. As critics have noted, white patronage structured the production of black cultural expression at the same time that African-American artists and writers appropriated it.[13] Hurston sat within this complex dynamic of patronage, since a good deal of the funding for her fieldwork collecting came from the white patron, Mrs. Rufus Osgood Mason. The white "imaginary" of the New York literary and artistic industry was based on the desire and fascination with things "exotic," and in the case of Hurston's work this played itself out in significant ways. As a patron, Mrs. Mason legally owned Hurston's folklore materials, and insisted that Hurston's work meet her standards of "primitiveness," as well as her sense of an appropriate timetable for publication. Hurston's folklore collecting between 1927 and 1933, the years of her most intensive gathering of materials, were spent under the apprenticeship of Mason.

Mrs. Mason was a fieldworker of that older generation of ethnographers that became increasingly demoted during the twentieth century. According to Hemenway, Mason had lived among the Plains Indians, financing the fieldwork of Natalie Curtis during the late nineteenth and early twentieth centuries. Mason, thus, had the ex-

[13] For a detailed account of race relations of the literary and artistic movements of the Harlem Renaissance see Nathan Irvin Huggins, *Harlem Renaissance* (London: Oxford University Press, 1971). See also Hemenway's account of the Harlem Renaissance in his previously cited biography on Hurston.

perience of doing fieldwork during a quite different period of cultural reporting. Although there is no evidence that she herself published any fieldwork materials, Curtis did publish a book based on Mason's fieldwork among native Americans. It suggests a different economy of collecting materials than that of Boas, who stresses that folklore should be cast as part of a larger whole called "culture." Curtis's writings on African and native American folklore and songs are dominated by the transcribing of collected materials with no references to a broader cultural meaning. There is a documentary effect produced in the portrayal not of a "culture," but of a collection of diverse materials.

Hurston, in some sense, worked with two "mentors," one, Franz Boas, the other, Mrs. Mason. While Mason clearly did not occupy the teacher status that Boas had she may have exerted as much, if not more, influence on Hurston's style of collecting as well as on the materials gathered. Boas had urged Hurston in her early fieldwork trips to focus on the behavioral or stylistic aspects of the story-telling sessions that she saw in the South. Because Mason had collected folklore materials during an earlier period, she "knew" folklore as a different kind of object than Boas. Folklore for Mason was part of the collecting, amassing, and documenting of African-American exotica for consumption as "art." The push and pull of Mason's interests and Boas's "anthropological" study of folklore was part of the context that made *Tell My Horse* look like a negotiation of these distinctions, a compromise between competing writing styles for the representation of African-Americans—one that was scholarly, objective, and attentive to designating larger meanings, and the other more "popular," laying out of objects as if in an art museum.

Hurston's mentoring situation was even more complex when one considers that Mason's primary advisor was Alain Locke. One of the most influential black male intellectuals of the period, Locke had been a teacher of Hurston's at Howard University in the early 1920s, had played an important role in promoting Hurston's literary career, and probably had introduced her to Mason (Hemenway 1977, 19–20). Locke's interest in Hurston's fieldwork related to his position as an influential editor and arbiter of black literary culture. Locke's promotion of black literary artists was based on his sense of what it meant for African-Americans to have "culture." For him, "race pride" was primarily an aesthetic experience. Black literary publications were conceived as organs for educating what was perceived as a basically inarticulate and uncultured populace as to what was "beautiful." Folklore, for Locke, was to serve as the basis for creating a distinctively "Negro" aesthetic. Although Locke's understanding of aesthetics was, in many ways, contradictory—he promoted an aesthetics that was distinct from social propaganda, and, yet, in actuality edited and promoted work that was not as self-consciously aestheticized as the next generation of African-American artists such as Langston Hughes and Hurston—his interest in racial aesthetics differed clearly from that of Boas.[14] By producing racial "art" African-Americans would be capable of producing "high" culture. Folklore was to be interpreted by black writers through aesthetic mediums and styles. Locke and Mason were able to participate together, albeit in different positions, in the socialization of Hurston as an African-American writer. Hurston's position as an African-American female writer, thus, placed her within the scholarly demands of Boas, Mason, and Locke, a diverse triad of social managers of African-Americans. The consequences of this for her literary style are not necessarily direct or intentional, but suggest that conflicting demands were being met in Hurston's ethnography. This particular predicament created the possibility of multiple rhetorics of authority in ethnographic writing. What Boas, Mason, and Locke shared was a discursive space in which the enculturation of the African-American was defined as a problem for social science, public policy, and popular imagination. Where they differed was in their understanding of folklore and in the purposes of folklore collecting. It is this set of relations that allowed Hurston to work within the discursive space that made African-American identity a "problem," placing her work both tenuously within the field of anthropology and also outside of it because of its style. These relations help situate Hurston's rather striking range of publications, including articles in the *Journal of American Folklore*, the *Journal of Negro History*, *Fire!!* and in Locke's *The New Negro*. *Tell My Horse* was only one example of her "style" that did not readily fit into the literary genres available for producing African-American intellectual life, art, or folklore.

In addition to the question of mentoring and funding, Hurston's immersion in the network of artists and writers surrounding Mason created the conditions in which the boundaries of drama, anthropology, folklore, and art could be merged. Her relationships with these writers made it possible for Hurston to experience fieldwork as simultaneously an "aesthetic" and "social scientific" endeavor, as well as a political activity aimed at changing the consciousness of African-Americans. These social connections allowed her to practice fieldwork as an activity done with other writers such as Langston

[14] On Locke's theory of Afro-American aesthetics see Hemenway, *Zora Neale Hurston*, p. 39.

Hughes. It was Hurston's connections to the literary practices and writers of the Harlem Renaissance that produced unorthodox fieldwork practices and allowed her to write ethnographies that defied the boundaries between "fact" and "fiction." Hurston was literate in what was being defined as Negro dramatic and literary arts, as well as anthropology, although she continually resisted the dominant ideologies of both. Indeed, Hurston mocked the pretentiousness of "avant-gardism," and referred teasingly to other writers and artists of the Harlem Renaissance as the "nigerati."

It would not do justice to Mead to say that Hurston had a rich, racially marked social location and Mead had a simple, privileged one, although clearly Mead's class and racial background had much to do with both the economic resources available to her as well as the knowledge and desire to use the academy in a way that would lead to recognition within social science. The social demands and possibilities Mead existed within, however, permitted a writing style that had a circuitous relationship to the professionalization and disciplinization of anthropology. Mead's ethnographic authority, an effect of both textual and social production, was built on a sense of identity that was not fragmented by the interfacing of racial and literary politics. The authority of Hurston's text was dispersed, fragmented, and excessive rather than whole and tempered by the careful restraining of competing discourses. It, thus, violated one of the most important ideologies of Western history and culture, namely that authorship be neutral, unique, and transcendent. At a time when anthropology's literary authority was being institutionalized, Hurston's work gave mixed signals about its status. Her rather "undisciplined" writing was made possible by the heterogeneity of her social location. Race relations, and the increasing professional disciplinization of fieldwork, never allowed Hurston the status of "anthropologist." What those relations did allow for was a form of ethnographic authority that was polyvocal and conflictual, and, thus, on the margins of professional ethnography.

* I would like to thank Barbara Gottfried for putting me in touch with the editor of this collection and helping make possible this publication. I would also like to thank Donna Haraway at U.C. Santa Cruz for comments on an earlier version of this essay, as well as the American Studies and Afro-American Studies Programs at U.C. Davis for inviting me to present this essay on that campus. A special thanks to Nahum Chandler at the University of Chicago for many stimulating conversations about Hurston and to Harriette Mullen at Cornell University for first introducing me to Hurston's writing and work.

Ruth Benedict and the Modernist Sensibility

RICHARD HANDLER

IN RECENT WORKS, Michael Levenson (1984) and Kathryne Lindberg (1987) have charted the tension within literary modernism between the quest for self-expression and the desire to recover a viable tradition. Both critics, in strikingly different ways, have presented the dialogue and debate between Ezra Pound and T. S. Eliot (among others) as emblematic of the larger opposition of individuality and tradition, or deconstructive originality and cultural constraint. In my work on the literary endeavors of Boasian anthropologists, I have examined a similar tension in the development of a culture theory that could accommodate both cultural holism and human individuality. Using Levenson and Lindberg to reexamine an essay in which I compare the literary and anthropological writings of Edward Sapir to those of Ruth Benedict (Handler 1986), I might now offer the following formula: Pound is to Eliot as Sapir is to Benedict. Put less cryptically, the contrast between Pound's iconoclasm and Eliot's Catholicism is similar to that between Sapir's emphasis on the individual and Benedict's championing of culture. Sapir focused on the individual as a crucial locus of cultural action, and refused to reify culture, whereas Benedict emphasized cultural integration and the determination of individuals by culture.

This theoretical opposition between individual and culture can be located in the work of separate scholars (Sapir versus Benedict), but it can also be traced as a tension in the writings of either one of them. The present paper examines the *interaction* of the quests for individ-

* A brief version of this paper was presented at the Ruth Benedict Centennial held at Vassar College, April 2-3, 1987. I would like to thank Lilo Stern and Judith Goldstein for inviting me to participate. The contributions to the conference of Clifford Geertz and James Boon have provided much stimulation in rewriting the present paper for publication (Geertz's paper is now published in Geertz 1988.) Patricia Wallace, of the English Department at Vassar College, offered insightful commentary on the original paper, particularly with respect to Benedict's feminism; many of Wallace's suggestions have been incorporated into the present paper. Finally, Marc Manganaro has worked with me steadily on various drafts of this paper, and has shared with me his expertise on literary modernism.

uality and tradition in the writings of Ruth Benedict (1887–1948). Although her developed theoretical position within anthropology places her among the champions of culture, I argue that her personal quest for self-expression led her to that position. Linked to this biographical argument is a structural argument, for I suggest that self-expression and cultural holism require each other in any formulation of the modernist sensibility.

My analysis begins with an examination of Benedict's journals, diaries and letters of the years 1912 to 1934, edited and published by Margaret Mead (1959) and exhaustively reviewed in two recent biographies of Benedict (Modell 1983; Caffrey 1989). Benedict's writings document a long period of personal struggle. Graduated from Vassar in 1909 with a major in English literature, Benedict traveled extensively in Europe, worked as a teacher and social worker, married and then watched her childless marriage disintegrate, tried her hand at writing both prose and poetry, and found her way to anthropology. Beginning her studies at the New School for Social Research in 1919, Benedict earned her Ph.D. from Columbia University in 1922. Her early years in anthropology were marked by continuing self-doubt, but she seems to have crossed a threshold to professional maturity during summer field trips among Pueblo Indians in 1924 and 1925. The 1934 publication of her first book, *Patterns of Culture*, can be taken to mark the end, and fulfillment, of Benedict's quest for personality and achievement (Modell 1983, 213).[1]

In Benedict's journals and diaries, we find the almost obsessive concern with self-realization and self-expression that is a hallmark of modernism. I take as characteristic of twentieth-century thought (of which modernism is one variety) the emergence of a fully secularized individualism. In this ethos, still prevalent today, one's highest duty is self-realization or the fullest possible development of one's personality (cf. Lears 1983). True to its Puritan origins, the modern personality proves its existence through work; or, phrased slightly differently, one expresses oneself through one's achievements. In the literary and scientific circles to which Benedict was drawn, work and self-expression meant the production of aesthetic objects, whether poems or scientific studies. The self—"hard," inviolable, unique, authentic—observed the world, experienced the world, mastered the world, proved itself as a locus of ultimate reality against the world (Handler 1986). And from its observations and experiences, the self

[1] Benedict published professional monographs in 1923 and 1931, but *Patterns of Culture* was the first work that she placed with a trade publisher and aimed at a general audience, and, most important, that she herself considered to be a book.

constructed intricate, original, beautifully patterned expressions. The successful products of self-expression could then be consumed by other, lesser selves—the vast public—who were also engaged in the business of self-realization, but vicariously, via contact with the productions of artists whose lives had been deemed 'authentic' (Trilling 1971, 99–100).

The second moment of my argument charts Benedict's progress toward a mature anthropological—and personal—vision, as represented in *Patterns of Culture*. Benedict's private writings do not reveal a personality convinced of its own realization. Such self-assurance would come only with the publication of her first book in 1934, the last year in which Benedict published a poem (Mead 1959, 563). To trace Benedict's scholarly development, I focus on three articles that precede *Patterns of Culture*. The first ("A Brief Sketch of Serrano Culture") is a derivative piece representing Boasian anthropology as Benedict had learned it but before she had contributed to reshaping it. The latter two ("Psychological Types in the Cultures of the Southwest" and "Configurations of Culture in North America") are preliminary versions of portions of *Patterns of Culture*. A third moment of my analysis relates the authorial persona of her greatest works, *Patterns of Culture* and *The Chrysanthemum and the Sword* (1946), to the modernist quest for personality and tradition, and to the transcendence of both.

Experience without Pattern

In a diary entry for December 1915, Benedict describes what she calls the "passionate blank despair" she felt when, as a freshman at Vassar in the winter of 1906, she puzzled over the purpose of life. In that mood, she read the conclusion to Walter Pater's *The Renaissance*:

> And then came Pater. Every instant of that late afternoon is vivid to me. I even know that I had to creep to the windowseat to catch the last dim light in that bare tower room of my Freshman days. The book fell shut in my hands at the end, and it was as if my soul had been given back to me. . . .
>
> Afterwards, I disbelieved. I had much in me to contradict Pater; my early religion which tried so hard to make me a moral being, my pity for others that almost made me an efficient one. But I was not run into either mould. And it is Pater's message that comes back to me as the cry of my deepest necessity: "to burn with this hard gem-like flame"—to gain from experience "this fruit of a quickened, multiplied consciousness," to summon

"the services of philosophy[,] of religion, of culture as well, to startle us into a sharp and eager observation." (in Mead 1959, 134–35)

Benedict's attraction to Pater epitomizes an enduring theme in her private writings: the desire to live intensely, to "have experiences" of an outer reality that prove to oneself the reality of one's personality. As she put it in another journal entry: "Anything to live! To have done with this numbness that will not let me feel" (1915[?], in Mead 1959, 136). The passage concerning Pater, in which she recalls an apparently intense experience of communion with an intensity that matches the initial experience, suggests how early and how profoundly Benedict was committed to—or ensnared by—the modernist sensibility. The desire for experience, as formulated by Pater, leads in two contradictory directions: toward egoism or the cult of personality, and toward a reaction to the meaninglessness or incoherence of a reality defined solely in terms of fragmented personal experiences. In Levenson's genealogy of modernism, mid-Victorians such as Matthew Arnold attempted to ground Christian belief in personal experience instead of dogmatic assertion. But after Arnold, Pater "recognized . . . that to redefine traditional values as phases of the self was to weaken traditional sanctions. . . . [S]ubjectivity was a double-edged sword. In the hands of Pater, it was used not only to cut away the metaphysical, but also the traditionally moral, the traditionally religious, the objective and the permanent" (Levenson 1984, 18–19; cf. Caffrey 1989, 52–59).

The follower of Pater, then, was left alone with the self. Benedict wanted to "realize" or develop that self, but she craved also a source of stability or order beyond the self. On the one hand, her private writings are replete with admonishments to believe in her own personality:

> I have been reading Walt Whitman, and Jeffries' *Story of My Heart*. They are alike in their superb enthusiasm for life[,] . . . their unwavering, ringing belief that the *Me* within them is of untold worth and importance. I read in wonder and admiration—in painful humility. Does this sense of personal worth, this enthusiasm for one's own personality, belong only to great self-expressive souls? or to a mature period of life I have not yet attained? (1912, in Mead 1959, 123)

On the other hand, Benedict describes herself as unfulfilled by episodical epiphanies unconnected to larger patterns of significance: "The trouble is not that we are never happy—it is that happiness is so episodical. . . . I cannot see what holds it all together" (1912, in Mead 1959, 121).

Benedict knew, however, what could *not* hold it all together: conventional culture. In 1912 she described her "real *me*" as hidden behind the "mask" she had donned in choosing the role of schoolteacher (in Mead 1959, 119). Later she described as "distractions" the customary rituals, such as funerals and weddings, that anthropology would teach her to examine more respectfully: "All our ceremonies, our observances, are for the weak who are cowards before the bare thrust of feeling" (1915[?], in Mead 1959, 136). And elsewhere she spoke with mild contempt of the conformity of the masses, "lost and astray unless the tune has been set for them, . . . the spring of their own personalities touched from the outside" (in Mead 1959, 144).

Benedict was also dissatisfied with nonconventional answers to her existential dilemmas, even those formulated by the great creative personalities of history:

> The trouble with life isn't that there is no answer, it's that there are so many answers. There's the answer of Christ and of Buddha, of Thomas à Kempis and of Elbert Hubbard, of Browning, Keats and of Spinoza, of Thoreau and of Walt Whitman, of Kant and of Theodore Roosevelt. By turns their answers fit my needs. And yet, because I am I and not any one of them, they can none of them be completely mine.

Here an "answer," a believable and believed-in moral system, seems of less moment than the need of the personality to appropriate such an answer as "mine." As Benedict's meditation continued, she admitted that moral questions are never solved. "What we call 'answers' are, rather, attitudes taken by different temperaments toward certain characteristic problems—even the interrogation may be an 'answer' " (1913, in Mead 1959, 126). The phrasing is egocentric ("attitudes," "temperaments") and relativistic—a striking prefigurement of the position developed later in *Patterns of Culture*, where authentic cultures are portrayed not as "answers" but as existential attitudes in terms of which both answers and questions are constructed.

In addition to the quest for personality and the rejection of convention—quintessentially modernist themes—Benedict's private writings reveal a painfully explicit consciousness of the dilemmas that the task of self-realization posed for women. She wavered between a belief that woman's "instinctive" vocation is domestic, and a reluctance to sacrifice apparently masculine aspirations to the domestic role. "[N]ature lays a compelling and very distressing hand upon woman," she wrote shortly after her marriage in 1914 to Stanley Benedict. Women might deny "that the one gift in our treasure house is love." However, their quests for fulfillment—"in social work, in laboratories, in schools," with marriage considered merely "a possible factor in our lives"—would end in failure (in Mead 1959, 131, 133). At other times, however, Benedict sensed that the sacrifice of self and self-development to domestic duties could not but lead to frustration, bitterness, and waste. After a year of marriage she felt that she needed a career or mission beyond her marriage: "it is wisdom in motherhood as in wifehood to have one's own individual world of effort and creation" (1915, in Mead 1959, 136). Later she wrote that woman's sacrifice of self to family was both socially wasteful and psychologically harmful. Whatever natural differences there might be between the sexes—another question to be settled by anthropological inquiry!—both men and women had to face up to the "responsibility for achievement of a four-square personality." Yet disparities in culturally constructed gender roles (as we would say today) made the pursuit of self-development more problematic for women than for men: "The issue . . . is fine free living in the spirit world of socialized spiritual values—for men as for women. But owing to artificial actual conditions their problems are strikingly different" (1919–1920[?], in Mead 1959, 146–47). Small wonder that the first anthropology course in which Benedict enrolled was "Sex in Ethnology," taught by Elsie Clews Parsons (Modell 1983, 111; Caffrey 1989, 95–97).

As Benedict struggled to find her way, she sensed that fulfillment was most readily accessible to her in literary endeavor. As a child she had received familial encouragement for her writing, and later, she could record in her journal that "my best, my thing 'that in all my years I tend to do' is surely writing" (in Mead 1959, 144). "I long to prove myself by writing," she wrote in 1917 (Mead 1959, 142), but her problem was to find an appropriate voice and genre. Her first major effort was biography, as she planned a book charting the lives of three famous women. She wrote at least six drafts of an essay on Mary Wollstonecraft, but was unable to finish the project after it was rejected for publication in 1919. As Modell has suggested, Benedict sought in biography to see life whole, to discover her own personal integrity by constructing storied, hence coherent, accounts of women whose lives had been judged by their contemporaries to be out of control. But the biographer could not achieve a satisfactory distance from her subjects: their lives and problems seemed too much her own (Modell 1983, 105–6). We can say the same thing of Benedict's poetry, which she wrote on and off for years: in her poems she could not achieve the "hard," polished self that she desired. Rather, her poems tended to express an unhappy and fragmented self, at times almost hysterically out of control (cf. Modell 1983, 140).

Benedict's search for a literary voice is linked to still another recurrent theme in her private writings, summarized by what she called "detachment." Coupled antithetically to her desire to experience the world with the intensity that Pater advocated is her fear of that intensity. "I dread intense awareness," she wrote in her diary in 1923, on the day that she completed the writing of her doctoral thesis. Yet, having admitted the fear, she went on to express fear of its opposite: "And then it seems to me terrible that life is passing, that my program is to fill the twenty-four hours each day with obliviousness" (in Mead 1959, 67). By contrast, "detachment" seems to have represented a transcendence of both fears:

> I divide the riches of the mind into two kingdoms: the kingdom of knowledge, where the reason gives understanding, and the kingdom of wisdom, where detachment gives understanding. This detachment is the life of the spirit, and its fruit is wisdom. That would cover it fairly well—the life of the artist and the life of the mystic. Its essence is its immediacy—without the distractions of belief or anxiety. It has no dogmas, it has no duties. It is a final synthesis of knowledge, and it is also a laying aside of knowledge. (Mead 1959, 136–37)

Here Benedict envisions an almost utopian solution to the modernist quest. It couples Pater's immediacy to a coherence of perspective that transcends the purely personal. Moreover, transpersonal coherence is not bought at the expense of personal integrity. There will be, Benedict tells us, no "distractions of belief or anxiety," no "dogmas" or "duties." It is almost as if she sought the vision, the voice, the perspective of a god, or of an omniscient narrator.

Drawing together these fragments of Benedict's private writings, we find a neat model of the modernist sensibility. Benedict sought to realize an authentic personality in an individually chosen career or lifework. Although tempted by conventional roles, including domestic duties and female professions, she found herself unable to settle for them. Coupled with her quest for self-realization was the desire to discover an authentic moral order, but such an order had to be acceptable to her personality and temperament. Thus, writing, through which one might create order in a fragmented world, came to represent a solution to her. Anthropology would give her the institutional framework within which to forge an alternative genre.

Mastering Pattern

When Ruth Benedict came to anthropology, the Boasian school was beginning a transition from the study of the distribution of isolated culture "traits" to the study of cultural wholes and the processes whereby traits are assembled to form such wholes (Stocking 1974, 1976). Boas had spent several decades attacking nineteenth-century evolutionary anthropology. He argued that evolutionary schemes of universal history were based upon ethnocentric and unreliable categories, and demonstrated their improbability when confronted with empirical studies of the diffusion and distribution of culture traits. But the ethnographic research that permitted Boas and his students to trace the empirical (as opposed to speculative) origins of culture traits raised new questions. How did such traits come to be amalgamated into living cultures, and what was the nature of the integrative force that held amalgamated traits together? To the latter question, Ruth Benedict's work would provide an important answer.

Like many of Boas's students, Benedict wrote a library dissertation treating not culture wholes but the diffusion of culture traits. (It was entitled *The Concept of the Guardian Spirit in North America.*) The summer before she completed her dissertation, she traveled to Southern California to do "salvage ethnography" on an apparently disappearing Amerindian group, the Serrano. It is unclear whether Benedict lived among the Serrano for any length of time, or stayed mainly with her mother and sister in Los Angeles. Her work consisted in interviewing aging informants about past customs (Modell 1983, 169–71; Caffrey 1989, 104–5, 365–66). In any case, not until her trip to Zuni in the summer of 1924 did Benedict experience what she considered to be her professional initiation, doing fieldwork in a living culture. She returned to the Pueblos the next summer, and made further field trips to the Southwest in 1927 and 1931 (Modell 1983, 171–77; Caffrey 1989, 108).

According to Margaret Mead, "Anthropology made the first 'sense' that any ordered approach to life had ever made to Ruth Benedict." She arrived at Columbia at a time when "Boas was still interested in diffusion and in having his students laboriously trace a trait or a theme from culture to culture" (Mead 1959, 8, 11). Benedict's dissertation on the guardian spirit was just such a tracing, but apparently the work of poring over the technical literature on Amerindian culture did not discourage her: "A good day at relationship [that is, kinship] systems—not Mohave however," is a typical diary entry from 1923 (in Mead 1959, 59). Her field trips to the Pueblos seem to have marked a personal turning point for Benedict. Writing to Mead in 1925 from the Peña Blanca Pueblo, she described her newly won confidence: "three years ago it [a month's isolation] would have been enough to fill me with terror. I was always afraid of depressions getting too much for me. . . . But that's ancient history now" (in Mead 1959, 295).

"A Brief Sketch of Serrano Culture" was Benedict's first publication based on her own field materials (she had already published her dissertation and an article based on it). Modell (1983, 170) points out that Serrano was a culture about which Benedict "had trouble writing . . . partly because data were scant and partly because she did not see a design in the disparate remaining elements of Serrano culture." The article is organized in terms of standard ethnological categories, with major sections on "Social Organization," "Ceremonial Observances," "Shamanism," and "Material Culture." Benedict announces at the outset that she will do little more than report "information . . . [that] is almost entirely exoteric," for "a great deal of the old meaning . . . is undoubtedly lost." From her perspective, the Serrano, like the anthropologist herself, faced the dilemma of a meaningless existence: "It is largely by guess-work that they can give the meaning of any of the ceremonial songs; and any religious connotation in such practices as rock-painting, for instance, is now unknown" (Benedict 1924, 366, 368). However, it is equally possible that the anthropologist's quest for authenticity generated questions that informants could not answer, and thus led Benedict to perceive their situation as meaningless.

Benedict's Serrano article is little more than a listing of traits. Significantly, items that Benedict would bring together in later publications as elements of an internally meaningful ceremonial complex are here reported under different headings (for example, information on the use of hallucinogenics, reported on pages 375, 377, 383). Also significant is the absence in this early work of holistic comparisons, for the placing of whole cultures side by side would become a cornerstone of her later narrative and epistemological method. By contrast, in the Serrano essay, cross-cultural comparison is confined to traits, as it typically is in the work of both evolutionists and diffusionists. For example, Benedict points out that Serrano joking relationships seem congruent with a form of moiety organization well known in the literature, but that kinship terms and joking status do not coincide as they should in the standard moiety system (1924, 373). Benedict's discussion here demonstrates deference to the authority of a technical jargon, but it lacks conviction. The article ends, abruptly and almost surrealistically, with a section on food. Describing Serrano methods for harvesting and preparing mesquite, nuts, and deer, Benedict tells us in the final sentence of the essay that "[t]he bones were pounded in mortars while fresh, and eaten in a sort of paste" (1924, 392).

In the four years between the Serrano article and the first of the papers that resulted from the Pueblo field trips, Benedict reformulated Boasian anthropology into her own approach, in which, as Modell (1983, 171) puts it, "culture wholeness became her disciplinary idea." As suggested, other American anthropologists were moving in the direction that Benedict took. Particularly important was a well-known essay by her close colleague Sapir, entitled "Culture, Genuine and Spurious," one of the first statements in American anthropology concerning what Benedict would call cultural integration (Handler 1983, 224–27). Benedict was also influenced by Jung and by the Gestalt psychologists, as well as by her reading of German philosophers of history such as Spengler and Dilthey (Stocking 1976, 16). In 1928 she presented a paper on "Psychological Types in the Cultures of the Southwest" (published in 1930) and in 1932 published "Configurations of Culture in North America." These papers, and a third on "Anthropology and the Abnormal," published in 1934, together contain most of the central arguments of *Patterns of Culture.*

Benedict's key idea was that cultures are configured or integrated around one or a few dominant drives, themes, or patterns. The obverse of the ongoing diffusion of culture traits is the absorption of borrowed traits into a preexistent culture whole. Benedict argued (in almost unavoidably personifying terms) that each culture selects from material available to be borrowed, as well as from the creative productions of its own members, and reinterprets the materials it chooses to incorporate. Such selection and reinterpretation are to be accounted for by the existence of a "fundamental psychological set" or "configuration" that can be taken to characterize and permeate the culture as a whole.

The 1928 paper on "Psychological Types" confines itself to these points, exemplified in a contrast Benedict draws between the Pueblos and other Native American cultures of the Southwest. She begins where the diffusionists leave off, pointing out that the most striking feature of Pueblo culture—its ceremonialism—hardly distinguishes it from other Native American cultures, since most of them also show "high ritualistic development." The difference, according to Benedict, lies in the spirit of Pueblo ceremonialism: the two groups of cultures differ in their "fundamental psychological sets," which she labels with terms taken from Nietzsche: "Apollonian" and "Dionysian." The Apollonian Pueblos share with their neighbors such religious and ceremonial traits as hallucinogenics, fasting, and the vision quest. However, the Pueblos have purged from these traits all traces of Dionysian ecstasy. Whereas diffusionists were content to plot the distribution of traits and trait complexes, Benedict sought to portray whole cultures by interpreting the inner spirit that knits traits together into a way of life that is meaningful and coherent to those who live it. As she concludes, "It is not only that the understanding of this psychological set is necessary for a descriptive statement of this culture; without it the cultural dynamics of this region are unintelligible" (1930, 261).

A more sophisticated version of these arguments is found in the 1932 essay on North American culture configurations. There, Benedict draws on the interpretive philosophies of history of Dilthey and Spengler in order to develop her notion of a culture's psychological set. She does not abandon psychologistic concepts, but enlarges her notion of culture so that her arguments can no longer be dismissed as psychological reductionism. Moreover, Benedict's comparative hermeneutics of culture is now developed in stunning fashion, setting up a paradoxical resolution to the modernist quest for holism.

Benedict begins by reviewing the "anecdotal" status of most of the ethnological data compiled in the past. These data, she claims, have been presented as "detached objects" with no attention to "their setting or function in the culture from which they came." She then praises Boas's field studies and Malinowski's functionalism as representative of a new anthropology that has begun to study cultures in holistic fashion. But Malinowski's functionalism is inadequate, she argues, because once it has shown that "each trait functions in the total cultural complex," it stops—without considering "in what sort of a whole these traits are functioning" (1932, 1–2). In other words, analysis of a functioning whole differs from that of a meaningful whole, a distinction basic to Boasian anthropology, the roots of which lay deep in German historicism. As Sapir puts it, in his essay on genuine culture (1924, 319), "A magical ritual, for instance, which, when considered psychologically, seems to liberate and give form to powerful emotional aesthetic elements of our nature, is nearly always put in harness to some humdrum utilitarian end—the catching of rabbits or the curing of disease." Not only is the "emotional aesthetic" meaning of culture different from its function, it is, for Sapir and Benedict, more basic. Boas, Sapir, and Benedict all argue that humans rationalize—or invent reasons to justify—those aspects of their culture of which they become conscious. But they remain unconscious of the formal patterns (as in the grammar of one's language) that provide the ultimate ordering in culture. Thus Benedict takes care to distinguish the configurational order that she is trying to describe from the functional order of Malinowski:

> The order that is achieved is not merely the reflection of the fact that each trait has a pragmatic function that it performs—which is much like a great discovery in physiology that the normal eye sees and the normally mus-

cled hand grasps, or . . . the discovery that nothing exists in human life that mankind has not espoused and rationalized. The order is due rather to the circumstance that in these societies a principle has been set up according to which the assembled cultural material is made over into consistent patterns in accordance with certain inner necessities that have developed within the group. (1932, 2)

Benedict's phrasing continues to be evocative and imprecise—"principle," "consistent patterns," "inner necessities." However, her ensuing discussion, drawing on Dilthey and Spengler, makes it clear that culture has become for her a question of the meaning of life, as such meanings are constructed or patterned for the members of each culture. Disparate traits, assembled into a culture from heterogeneous sources, can be understood only in terms of the particular meaningful configuration of that culture; they take their meaning from their place in the pattern, not from their origins or function:

Traits objectively similar and genetically allied may be utilized in different configurations. . . . The relevant facts are the emotional background against which the act takes place in the two cultures. It will illustrate this if we imagine the Pueblo snake dance in the setting of our own society. Among the Western Pueblo, at least, repulsion is hardly felt for the snake. . . . When we identify ourselves with them we are emotionally poles apart, though we put ourselves meticulously into the pattern of their behavior. (1932, 6)

Although Benedict speaks here of emotional attitudes, the issue is, more broadly, one of cultural interpretation. In her example, we are asked to imagine ourselves in the place of the snake dancers. Without an understanding of the meaning of the snake in Pueblo culture, we will impose our own, Western understanding on the ethnographic material, and thus misinterpret the dance, however meticulously we note its external details. Sapir makes a similar argument in a 1927 essay on "The Unconscious Patterning of Behavior in Society," an essay that Benedict must have known. Sapir, like Benedict, concocts a thought "experiment." He asks the reader to imagine "making a painstaking report of the actions of a group of natives engaged in some form of activity, say religious, to which he has not the cultural key." A "skillful writer," Sapir suggests, will get the external details right, but his account of the significance of the activity to the natives "will be guilty of all manner of distortion. . . . It becomes actually possible to interpret as base what is inspired by the noblest and even holiest of motives, and to see altruism or beauty where nothing of the kind is either felt or intended" (1927, 546–47). Sapir goes on to speculate about how it is that natives can regularly reproduce in their behavior cultural patterns of which they have no conscious awareness. By contrast, Benedict's discovery of cultural patterning leads her to issue a programmatic call to her colleagues to reorient field research in order to document the patterns of particular cultures (Benedict 1932, 7). For her, the anthropologist's ability to master pattern was never in doubt. It was the anthropologist's business to stand aside and describe in objective terms the cultural patterns that make life meaningful for the peoples under study.

Yet Benedict's interpretive method is fundamentally comparative and hermeneutic. It thus implies the impossibility of objective descriptions of individual cultures—or, more precisely, of descriptions constructed by an observer occupying neutral ground. In the "Configurations" article, as in *Patterns of Culture* and *The Chrysanthemum and the Sword* (1946), cultures are never described in isolation. Rather, their characteristic configurations or patterns are delineated by way of contrast with the patterns of other cultures. Thus, a Benedictian description of a culture depends as much upon which culture the observer / writer chooses as the relevant point of comparison as it does upon the "facts" of the culture in question. As we have seen, the essay on "Psychological Types" is largely taken up with elaborating on the distinction between the Apollonian Pueblos and their Dionysian neighbors. A similar method is developed to a high art in "Configurations." There Benedict rehearses again the Apollonian / Dionysian distinction. However, not content to stop there, she introduces other, crosscutting contrasts:

> In the face of the evident opposition of these two . . . types of behavior it is at first sight somewhat bizarre to group them together over against another type in contrast to which they are at one. It is true nevertheless. In their different contexts, the Southwest and the Plains [her example of Dionysian cultures] are alike in not capitalizing ideas of pollution and dread. . . . In contrast with the non-Pueblo Southwest, for instance, these two are alike in realistically directing their behavior toward the loss-situation instead of romantically elaborating the danger situation. (1932, 9)

Benedict goes on to elaborate this realist-romantic distinction in a long review of attitudes toward the dead. She is now working with three cultural configurations: Apollonian realists (Pueblo), Dionysian realists (Plains), and Dionysian romantics (non-Pueblo Southwest). However, each discrete type comes into being, as it were, only by way of a contrast deliberately elaborated by the anthropologist. In other words, Pueblo and Plains, distinguished by the Apollonian / Dionysian contrast, turn out to be similar, as realists, when opposed to other cultures that can be characterized as romantics. Finally, Benedict introduces a fourth configuration, that of the "megalomaniacal" Northwest coast cultures. These peoples, too, are Dionysian, but their institutionalization of the "pursuit of personal aggrandizement" represents a new crosscutting of the Dionysian temperament. This yields a configuration that can be contrasted as significantly to the Dionysian realists of the Plains as to the Apollonian Pueblos (1932, 18).

At this point it is worth noting that the cultural configurations that serve as the apparently holistic units in Benedict's comparisons are themselves synthetic, built by the anthropologist from multiple ethnographic sources. Consider, for example, the following sketch of a Dionysian-romantic ritual:

> Years ago in the government warfare against the Apache the inexorable purification ceremonies of the Pima almost canceled their usefulness to the United States troops as allies. Their loyalty and bravery were undoubted, but upon the killing of an enemy each slayer must retire for twenty days of ceremonial purification. He selected a ceremonial father who cared for him and performed the rites. This father had himself taken life and been through the purification ceremonies. He sequestered the slayer in the bush in a small pit where he remained fasting for sixteen days. . . . Among the Papago the father feeds him on the end of a long pole. His wife must observe similar taboos in her own house . . . etc. (1932, 16)

The footnotes to this passage list four sources, including Benedict's field notes, from which the account is constructed. From the mass of details afforded by the sources, she begins with one that emphasizes the practical consequences of an interpretive contrast. The ethnographer, Frank Russell, had noted (1908, 204) that "The bravery of the Pimas was praised by all army officers . . . but Captain Bourke and others have complained of their unreliability, due solely to their rigid observance of this religious law." Just as Americans might read the Western horror of snakes into the Pueblo snake dance, and thus misunderstand it, so American army officers had mistranslated Piman religiosity as "unreliability." It is with this maximal contrast that Benedict chooses to begin her portrait of the rituals.

As Benedict's account develops, she individualizes general information, bringing readers closer to the authentic existence of the natives: "the Pima" (plural) becomes two people acting out a particular ritual: "He selected a ceremonial father. . . . This father had himself taken life. . . ." As the narration takes us through the by now personalized ritual, a "culture trait" from elsewhere is injected: a custom of the Papago that is strikingly illustrative of the Dionysian-romantic horror that Benedict wishes to stress. Note that the narration returns without explicit transition from the Papago father to the Piman wife (cf. Russell 1908, 205). To be sure, the Papago were "closely related" to the Pima. Moreover, the implicit epistemology of Benedict's comparative method justifies her lumping together similar or related groups in order to contrast them, as a holistic culture configuration, to other peoples grouped together as representative of an opposing configuration. Yet the synthetic nature of her culture configurations is belied by much of the rhetoric and organization of *Patterns of Culture*, the first book in which she spoke to the public in the coherent voice of a scientist and professional writer.

The Anthropologist as Modernist Persona

Ruth Benedict's most widely known work, read by several generations of American college students, presents her theory of culture illustrated with three apparently neatly bounded, holistic cultures. It is this image of a world of discrete cultures that undergraduates most easily retain. However, a close reading of *Patterns of Culture* will show that Benedict's comparative hermeneutic is vigorously at work even in a book whose core consists of three separate chapters devoted to three unproblematically separate cultures. This is obvious in chapter four, on "The Pueblos of New Mexico," which is an expanded version of the 1930 and 1932 articles, continuing the presentation of the Pueblos in terms of the Apollonian / Dionysian contrast. Her contrastive method is also apparent in the final two chapters, devoted to the problem of the individual and society. There, Benedict becomes a subtle but pointed critic of American culture, discussing American aggressiveness and competition in the comparative light of Pueblo sobriety and Northwest Coast megalomania ([1934], 244–45, 248, 273–77). In other words, her own culture became an important contrastive focus in her work. Indeed, her final book, the *Chrysanthemum and the Sword*, is more than a study of "Patterns of Japanese Culture," as its subtitle proclaims. Beyond that, it is a sustained contrast between American individualism and Japanese hierarchy in which almost every assertion about Japan is brought home by means of contrastive material on American culture.[2]

But to return to *Patterns of Culture*: the comparative aspects of the

[2] In his essay in this volume, Arnold Krupat links the Boasians' optimistic belief in social reform to their narrative and epistemological use of irony. For Benedict as an ironic social satirist, see Geertz 1988; for Benedict and Sapir as culture critics, see Handler 1986 and 1989.

narrative notwithstanding, the book can easily be read as a description of three distinct cultures. The sixth chapter, "The Northwest Coast of America," elaborates the discussion begun in the 1932 article. However, the mediating configurations of that essay—Dionysian realists and romantics—have been eliminated, as has the argument about crosscutting configurational dimensions. The sixth chapter thus presents the Pueblos' Dionysian opposite, but it does so in such a way that the hermeneutic construction of a contrast is hidden, and cultural differences are made to seem *solely* a function of "objective" differences in two "on-the-ground" cultures. Moreover, chapter five, based on Reo Fortune's Melanesian material from Dobu (Fortune 1932), presents an example drawn from the opposite side of the globe, in place of the mediating North American examples used earlier. Thus is the geographical and configurational gradualism of the "Configurations" article replaced by three apparently well-separated and starkly contrasted culture wholes.

An individualizing vision, then, prevails in *Patterns of Culture*, despite the hermeneutic twist implicit in Benedict's comparative method. The holistic culture sought by alienated modernists is there discovered in portraits of three "collective individuals," to use Louis Dumont's (1970) term. That term is peculiarly apt, given Benedict's characterization of cultures as "individual psychology thrown large upon the screen, given gigantic proportions and a long time span" (1932, 24; cf. [1934], 46). Indeed, I would argue that modern social theory (dating from at least the eighteenth century) swings back and forth between reified conceptions of the individual (as in utilitarianism) and reified conceptions of society and culture (as in most twentieth-century sociology and anthropology). The modernists' quest for what Sapir called "genuine culture" was motivated in part by their perception that an atomistic, rationalistic science had destroyed tradition. But the modernist's genuine culture cannot, in the final analysis, be discovered by a social science that constructs cultural wholes on individualistic principles. Indeed, embodied in governmental policies, modernist social science paradoxically leads away from holism to the routinization of all aspects of social life, bureaucratically fragmented and administered (cf. Handler 1988).[3]

[3] This suggests a new approach to the debate over whether the modernists represent a break with the romantics or are continuous with them. That debate posits individuated historical periods, the historians' equivalent of the "society" and "culture" of social theory. If we deconstruct such absurd "nonentities" (Tyler 1987, 207), the question of continuities and discontinuities can be examined from a semiotic rather than positivistic perspective. We can ask how people reconstruct the past and imagine their relationship to it, rather than search for "true" historical periods (Handler 1984). See

These remarks on the individualistic premises implicit in the theory of cultural integration return us to Benedict's notion of detachment. In *Patterns of Culture* Benedict discovered the authentic, holistic cultures that she sought and from which the modern world excluded her as a participant. The Apollonian, anti-individualistic Pueblos are described with an almost utopian longing, for in them, apparently, the surrender of individuality to society is not even problematic. Here there is no question of conventional ceremonies repressing individual feelings (recall Benedict's rejection of funerals and weddings in her own society). But even in cultures that demanded that individuals assert themselves, as on the Northwest coast, the thorough determination of individual personality by cultural configuration meant that individuals were unself-conscious in their individualism. Sapir, in his essay on genuine culture, writes of cultural authenticity in terms of sincerity, but Benedict objects to the argument: "It seems to me that cultures may be built solidly and harmoniously upon fantasies, fear-constructs, or inferiority complexes and indulge to the limit in hypocrisy and pretensions" (1932, 26). Her rejection of sincerity perhaps reflects the search for that intense yet detached cultural participation that she described in her journal. Sincerity implies self-consciousness, and Benedict sought worlds in which meaningfulness and participation could exist without such an awareness. The Northwest Coast potlatcher could pursue megalomaniacal successes unhindered by modernist self-doubt.

Detachment was also to be found in the persona of the scientist. As an anthropologist-narrator, Benedict wrote into being the holistic, genuine cultures that no longer existed in the modernist's world. At the same time, she preserved her own individuality, controlling and inviolate as a narrative voice (cf. Levenson 1984, 207). It seems clear that the voice of the scientist and the genre of scientific writing worked for Benedict: through them she achieved the "hard" personality that she desired but could not achieve as a writer of poetry and biography. In her anthropological writing she did not eliminate all reference to herself, to the "I." But that "I" was now a scientist, a cultural anthropologist working within an established community of scholars possessed of their own techniques and discourse. For example, in the first chapter of *The Chrysanthemum and the Sword,* the authorial voice identifies itself in a variety of terms, shifting among them gracefully and apparently unproblematically. "In June, 1944, I

Marc Manganaro's essay in this volume for the difficulties of periodizing modernism across disciplines. For a recent critique of individual-versus-society theorizing, see Strathern 1988.

was assigned to the study of Japan. . . . As a cultural anthropologist . . . I had confidence in certain techniques and postulates which could be used. . . . The anthropologist has good proof in his experience that even bizarre behavior does not prevent one's understanding it. . . . The student who is trying to uncover the assumptions upon which Japan builds its way of life has a far harder task than statistical validation" (1946, 3, 6, 10, 17). Thus, in spite of the book's hermeneutic method—Japan and America are each interpreted in terms of what the other is not—the narrative is presided over by an apparently objective persona. Indeed, that persona is more than objective: it is detached, its existence grounded either in its own individuality, or in the universal comprehension of science.[4]

Ruth Benedict's conquest of a voice and a personality as she moved through biography and poetry to anthropology might be summarily described in the words of James Joyce's young artist:

> The personality of the artist, at first a cry or a cadence or a mood and then a fluid and lambent narrative, finally refines itself out of existence, impersonalises itself, so to speak. . . . The artist, like the God of the creation, remains within or behind or beyond or above his handiwork, invisible, refined out of existence, indifferent, paring his fingernails. ([1916], 215)

This is a famous passage, one "indelible in the memory of readers of a certain age," as Lionel Trilling puts it (1971, 7). Ruth Benedict was of that modernist age, and in her anthropological writing she achieved the integral personality that she and so many of her contemporaries sought. The achievement of integrity depended upon writing about—or writing into existence—cultures that could be seen to be whole, holistic, and authentic. That postcolonial, postmodern anthropology has produced a spate of biographies, histories, and literary-critical analyses of our ancestors testifies, perhaps, to an inauthenticity that we perceive in ourselves, and that we try to escape by writing the storied lives of others.

[4] As Stephen Tyler puts it, "The appearance of authorlessness is . . . the aim of all scientific writing" (1987, 42).

ANTHROPOLOGICAL MODERNISM: LANGUAGE, THEORY, AND PRAXIS

Anthropology and Modernism in France: From Durkheim to the *Collège de sociologie*

MICHÈLE RICHMAN

IN 1937, a group of writers, intellectuals, and university professors met as a "Collège de sociologie" to discuss a common interest in what their conveners, Georges Bataille, Roger Caillois, and Michel Leiris termed a "sacred sociology." According to the Declaration issued at the time of their initial reunions, the goals of this essentially intellectual activity were the following: (1) to investigate the nature of social structures in such a way as to complete the overly cautious conclusions of scientific investigations. Usually restricted to the so-called primitive societies, social anthropology tends to be reticent when it comes to transferring its findings to modern social formations; (2) to explore and to encourage the possibility of developing among those engaged in such research a "moral community," in part different from those that ordinarily unite scholars; (3) to found a "sacred sociology" because it looks at manifestations of an "active presence" of the sacred within contemporary social phenomena (Hollier 1979, 10–11). Thus, faced with the dual threats of imminent war and a fascist menace from within as well as without, some of the most brilliant representatives of the interwar generation chose as an intellectual response to examine the status of "myth, power, and the sacred" within modern culture. Although none of the participants ever conceived of the College as a total panacea to the demoralization brought on by the social and political crises, it is nonetheless significant that they should turn to archaic and traditional cultures for insights into their own.

The purpose of this presentation of the College is, then, to explore its exemplary confrontation between French sociology and modernity. From within a historical perspective, I first attempt to answer the query posed by the philosopher Jean Wahl, himself an erstwhile

* I am grateful for the support provided by the John Simon Guggenheim Foundation during the preparation of this study. I also wish to thank M. Michel Leiris for sharing his memories of the College.

College participant, when he noted, "This sociology, of which I was never a fervent adept, now captures young spirits avid for rigor and which hope to find in it an answer to questions they previously sought to answer through surrealism, Revolution, or psychoanalysis." Beyond this observation, he urged "One must try to understand this phenomenon, itself sociological" (Hollier 1979, 102). Wahl's challenge will be met by examining the significance of sociology within the context of the College as a way to appreciate the ramifications of a discipline that, in the broad definition of social and cultural anthropology with which it is associated in France, has been central to the development of contemporary critical thought. But, whereas it may now be commonplace to acknowledge the symbiosis among structural linguistics, anthropology, and psychoanalysis, less attention has been directed to the circumstances conditioning the recourse to sociology, as it is called here. More exactly, since the turn of the century, French intellectual life has been marked by a convergence between the nascent human sciences and cultural avant-gardes. In his account of French sociology in the twentieth century, for instance, Lévi-Strauss admires the "close connection between the French school of sociology and every other tendency having Man at its center" as its distinctive trait (1971, 505). And his foremost illustration of its extension into artistic and intellectual milieus is the College.

I therefore follow Lévi-Strauss's lead by examining the symptomatic value of the College within the important French tradition of what he termed an "anthropological thinking" emanating from Montaigne, where the discourse of social criticism is both prompted and legitimated through a comparative analysis with other cultures. More than emblems of exotic adventure, geographically remote peoples stimulate a reconsideration of issues as varied as political and social organization, child rearing, sexual and social relations, commerce, religion, and war.

Indeed, from the sixteenth century to the present, a distinctive blend of introspection, moral imperative, and social analysis is encountered in essays and novels that regard the other as the basis for self-reflection and criticism. If Montaigne set a precedent for French humanism, it is because his *Essais* record the first self-reflexive mapping of the modern self, an inner voyage whose confrontation with the demonic dualisms of Western consciousness—body and soul, self versus other, intellect over sensibility, contemplation against action and male versus female—were no less formidable than the encounter with the mythic monsters awaiting explorers who trespassed the geographical boundaries of the sixteenth century. The parallel is not merely rhetorical. For the innovation of the author of "Des cannibales" is to have tied the discovery of the modern subject to the exploration of a New World that would irrevocably decenter the Old. Comparison with cultural others was neither invidious nor simply praiseworthy of difference: it was the catalyst for self-scrutiny and reappraisal of the relation of self to society through the standards of an other.

The historical fate of this anthropological discourse in the following centuries until its culmination in the Enlightenment tradition of Montesquieu, Voltaire, Diderot, and the revolutionary impetus of Rousseau is well documented. Not as well appreciated are the reasons for a veritable eclipse during the last century, and only recently has its resurgence in the contemporary period under the aegis of Emile Durkheim been examined. Moreover, although one historian praises the distinctly modernist sensibility reflected in the encounter that forged "ethnographic surrealism,"[1] for instance, the special interaction among disciplines contributing to the discourse to be discussed here has not escaped criticism. For one anthropologist, philosophers who borrow from ethnography bend their references to the needs of a "meta-anthropology," just as tendentious anthropologists orient their research to meet ideological ends (Augé 1977). Durkheim himself has been described as a "*moraliste* led to perceive archaic societies through a superficial type of benign reverse ethnocentrism" (La Capra 1972, 25). Jurgen Habermas has denounced the allegedly conservative political effects of "irrationalism" (that is, the cult of archaic values and the rejection of modernity) fostered by the work of Bataille and his followers, Foucault and Derrida (1981, 3–14). In this country, anthropologists concerned with the blurring of boundaries fear that some ethnographies read, and are read, more like literature than science (Shweder 1986, 1, 38–39). But even if these positions are eschewed as unproductive, one must nonetheless evaluate the recourse to exotic others as a revitalizing mechanism for modern literature and cultural criticism.

Predictably, such strong allegations have generated equally powerful defenses. Most constructive are those discussions where the legacy of the Enlightenment is reevaluated, including the definition of reason under question; the consequences of social rationalization for the diremption of everyday life into discrete cognitive, moral, and aesthetic spheres; the autonomization of art from politics, and the philosophical grounding of the modern subject in rationality. For the

[1] James Clifford, "On Ethnographic Surrealism," in *The Predicament of Culture: Twentieth Century Ethnography, Literature and Art* (Cambridge, Harvard University Press, 1988), pp. 117–51. Clifford's groundbreaking study provides insight into the relation between surrealism and the College that it was not possible to treat here.

purposes of this essay, the important contributions consider anthropology's potential as cultural critique as yet unfulfilled, but inspired by the sort of examples we examine (Marcus & Fischer 1986). Equally relevant is the reappearance of the "anthropological syndrome" Peter Sloterdijk has observed in West Germany, where disaffection from the sociopolitical discourses of the sixties is strikingly documented by the fact that twenty years ago only some five hundred students were enrolled in anthropology courses in contrast with the nearly twelve thousand in 1985 (1986, 114–27)! His appreciation of this fact suggests that the appeal of the other, especially the particular sway held by Asian cultures or those where "erotic reason," trance and ecstasy are encouraged in some form of collective experience, is motivated by the general perception that "God is dead" in Western Europe. Nietzsche's pronouncement has as much relevance to action as to spirituality, especially for the particular conjugation of religion with colonialism in the history of the West: "The historians of the psyche and the writers of the philosophy of history have described the internal drama of modernity as a history of the partially secret, partially declared self-deification of European humanity" (Sloterdijk 1986, 124).

Sloterdijk nonetheless concludes with a caveat. The quest for collective identity within the cultural subgroups and marginal positions resistant to the centripetal forces of homogenization is also the same impetus leading to delusional myths and millenarian movements. If the resurgence of the anthropological syndrome evokes comparisons with the Weimar period (1918–1933), when the cult of neo-antiquity was related to the Dadaist refusal to be subjugated to the clocks and calendars of an industrialized way of life, it also reminds Germans of the distorted use to which myths of a pure "Volk" and invocations of the archaic can be put. A comparable specter haunts intellectual histories of the interwar period in France, especially when they purport to deal with the status of anthropological thinking during that time.

In the essay to follow, the polemics generated by the College are considered in light of the following argument: Whereas cultural critics, historians, and social philosophers are willing to acknowledge the revitalizing effects of an infusion of "primitivism" so that exotic others may challenge cultural assumptions on a host of issues, especially as regards the quality of modern social and affective relations, the atrophy of sensibility and the relation to the natural environment, the turn to developmentally simpler peoples is tolerated and even encouraged. But when the meeting of anthropology and modernity entails a challenge to the superiority of Western science and its more generalized correlative "rationality," in particular the so-called economic rationality responsible for the advancement of bourgeois capitalism, then the same anthropological syndrome is rejected as symptomatic of a regressive turn to unreason, self-indulgent hedonism, and a precipitate of the decline of Western civilization.

Indeed, the resuscitation of the College texts follows this pattern. On the one hand, they promote a critique of modern economic and religious individualism, subsumed under a general lament for the demise of collective experiences and community. On the other, by flirting with the extremes of effervescent encounters, including sacrifice and the relation of the sacred to power, they risked comparisons with the sources of fascism's appeal. Moreover, if specialization within the division of intellectual labor is perceived as progress in the rationalization of knowledge, then the eclecticism and project of totality encouraged by the College make it vulnerable to easy dismissal. The point of view adopted here does not seek to validate the propositions of the College by conventional standards so much as it explores the nature of the collaboration between social anthropology and other intellectual domains in the forging of a "sacred sociology." The historical frame is provided by the career of Durkheim and its posthumous influence. Whereas other studies have emphasized the undeniable importance of Marcel Mauss's teachings for members of the College, I suggest that Durkheim's unusual trajectory offers a frequently neglected but equally convincing illustration of the confluence between social thought and cultural criticism that research in the College wished to emulate.

The heresy of such an assertion stems from the conventional but incomplete portrait of the founder of modern French sociology's "scientific revolution" as the stalwart of Third Republic laicism, rationalism, and moralism. Missing, however, is the pro-Dreyfus activist, the author of a major treatise on socialism who viewed the mission of sociology as social reform and intervention. Most importantly, he is the author of studies of suicide and the division of labor who effected a major shift late in his career by looking to Australian aboriginal religion—the most "elementary" yet "complete" example of religious experience—for a model of collective life in the future. The rituals, feasts, and effervescent experiences of the Arunta offer an antidote to the "mediocre" quality of early twentieth-century social life, as well as demonstrating how the entire symbolic order, including all ideas, even scientific ones, is generated.

The issues just outlined are developed in two parts: the first traces the history of French ethnography and sociology until Durkheim's death in 1917; the second continues with the relations among disciplines until the formation of the College in 1937 and the possibility for a "sacred" sociology.

The specificity of French ethnography is underscored in a 1913 overview by Mauss in which he compares the study of primitive peoples in France and abroad. From its inception in the sixteenth century, when Montaigne drew heavily upon the travel diaries of Jean de Léry in Brazil, French "anthropological thinking" is characterized by a meshing of document, personal memoir, and moral philosophy. Continuing through to the eighteenth-century observations of American Indians by Lafitau and Charlevoix , so "brazenly" pillaged by Chateaubriand, the close tie between observation and commentary led the way for the Enlightenment. Fueled by the early accounts of Jesuit fathers praising the virtues of "noble savages" whose morality evolved without baptism or Bible, the *philosophes* completed the dechristianization process inspired, ironically, by the priestly voyages of the seventeenth century. Along with the better known works of Montesquieu, Diderot, and Voltaire, Mauss mentions the work of the président de Brosses, *Culte des dieux fétiches*, as the first comparative science of religion. By the eighteenth century, observational and comparative studies thus went hand in hand. Unfortunately, this admirable tradition stops in the decades following the Revolution, in sharp contrast with the impressive ethnographic developments throughout the rest of Europe and America that Mauss documents.

The most obvious explanation for the cessation of French ethnography—the lack of exclusively French territories—is challenged by the scholarly preeminence of countries with the fewest colonies. Indeed, the systematic study of indigenous populations under French rule is often conducted by foreign ethnographers, leading Mauss to deplore the relation between French colonialism and ethnography as one of missed opportunities and shirked responsibilities. Neither the French state nor the French intellectual community sought to enlist colonial personnel, those individuals most familiar with local languages and customs. The situation is best dramatized by noting the length of occupation (predating the colonial expansion of the Third Republic) as well as its extent: "France administers more than 60 million natives, 20 million of which are of such a low level of development that they qualify for ethnographic study in the strictest sense" (Mauss 1969, 432). Besides the intellectual scandal, Mauss underscores the moral and political implications by reminding his colleagues that they have scarcely contributed to the knowledge of peoples whom the French occupation has "decimated, decomposed and destroyed" (1969, 409). Without immediate action, it will be difficult to study even those survivors of the colonial ordeal.

How, then, is one to explain the demise of the ethnographic "vogue" in the nineteenth century? Despite the argument presented above, it is true that the earliest French studies dealt with "new France," including Louisiana, Caribbean possessions, and the sea of Mexico, territories lost following the Napoleonic defeat. Mauss concludes that, without indigenous folk to oversee, the French no longer sought to understand them since "both French science and the State have been administered in a more utilitarian fashion than is generally recognized" (1969, 404). A second reason lies in the fact that many of the oldest French explorations were undertaken by Jesuit missionaries cut off by the Holy See in the eighteenth century and replaced by men of inferior quality. The French missions also certainly suffered the effects of the Revolution, but again, these facts point to details without illuminating the larger question. Germany, for instance, had no colonies at all for some time, yet was foremost among early investigators.

Deviating from Mauss's strictly disciplinary approach, it is possible to argue that the national bourgeoisie in the postrevolutionary period, preoccupied with its consolidation of political and economic power within a strong, centralized Jacobin state, was more concerned with containing and subjugating its internal others, (for example regional cultures and urban proleteriat), than it was interested in subsidizing imperial expansion abroad. Well into the latter part of the century, Jules Ferry, responsible for the last major period of French colonialism, had to beg for funds to support his policies. Indeed, until the Third Republic, both expeditions and long-range stays were discouraged. Following the restoration of the colonial empire, neither the State nor individuals made impressive efforts in a scientific direction (and those who did were pushed almost exclusively to explore North Africa). Mauss indicts academics for the greatest inertia. From 1815 on (for political reasons not mentioned), all studies unrelated to the classics or scholastics were virtually banned. In sum, "A sort of generalized, stubborn, reactionary social opposition set itself against the progress of the science of man: ethnography, auxiliary to anthropology, is still, like the mistress science, relegated to the sidelines of the French scientific movement" (Mauss 1969, 405). The educated public, among whom one could count the assiduous readers of the seventeenth and eighteenth centuries, now turned to travel literature, so that only anecdotes and fiction fared well. If, as one critic has noted, the nineteenth century developed its specific form of exoticism, it did so in marked contrast with the social criticism emanating from earlier representations of cultural otherness since "it seldom seems to be directed against the country or continent of origin" (Baudet 1965, 65).

Unlike his bleak assessment of ethnography, Mauss offered a positive tableau of sociology in an article coauthored with Paul Fauconnet as early as 1901. Clearly inspired by Durkheim's ambitions, this picture provides both details of the French school as well as its more global objectives. Reasserting the Durkheimian maxim that social facts are things, that they exist not only in nature but exhibit a nature of their own, Mauss agrees that the object of the discipline is to study such phenomena, their laws, and their movement. Externally observable (Durkheim's second postulate for sociology's scientificity), these *sui generis* forces are responsible for behavior, sentiments, feeling, and thoughts within a group that the individual could neither experience nor possess outside of participation in a collectivity. Moreover, the primacy of the social extends into areas often thought to be safeguarded by the individual as the domain of the personal and the particular: "Even feelings which appear to be completely spontaneous, such as the love of work, of saving, and of luxury, are in reality the product of a social culture, since they are lacking among certain peoples and vary greatly within the same group, according to different social strata" (Mauss 1969, 143). Because collective habits have now become the central object of sociological investigation, the discipline must venture into the realm of opinion and its transmission by means of collective representations. Credited with a causal function, they are viewed as constituting the "intimate basis" of social life. Until the advent of sociology, however, the specificity of a culture was sought within the confines of a national spirit or "Geist." What Durkheim calls the *particulier* of a society will henceforth be investigated at the level of the group, and by means of the representations it produces of itself.

Durkheim's enduring influence stems in part from his mapping of the discipline during its crucial formative period. Not only did he establish the parameters of sociology as an autonomous field of inquiry capable of serving as model for the other social sciences, but he outlined as well a comprehensive scheme of research that culminated in the ambition to subsume all facets of social life, including those of the mind, emotions, and even the body, under one "unifying principle." Social research, he asserts, needs its own "conscience collective": otherwise, it falls prey to the fragmentation found in Anglo-American social anthropology, where "one knows only homo religiousus, ethicus, oeconomicus" (1969, 201). He then proposed "une éthologie collective," or the study of the relations among all social phenomena that would subsume even psychology, albeit of a different order than the science restricted to the individual.

By the time (1933) Mauss updated the survey of French sociology Durkheim had initiated in 1914, the discipline had had considerable success in asserting its independence as a science, and in imposing itself institutionally through courses and degree programs from the baccalaureate to the university. Mauss's tone, however, is overwhelmingly elegaic, mournful of the generation of brilliant young scholars lost to the ravages of World War I. Among them was André Durkheim who was intended to succeed his father and who himself did not survive the devastations of such a massive sacrifice. Following the master's death in 1917, the French school suffered an obvious decline. The survivors' homage was to continue the sweeping research program he had initiated by collecting data to fill any major lacuna. Mauss characterizes the postwar efforts as "less systematic and generalizing, somewhat dispersed and renouncing the terrain of ideas for that of facts" (1969, 438).

By the early thirties, Mauss was the dominant figure of French ethnology and the undisputed heir to his uncle's legacy. Distinguished by a brilliant and erudite style, Mauss's teachings were legendary, and students recount following him from one lecture hall to another. Moving among several institutions, Mauss remained marginal to the university, but was awarded a chair at the prestigious Collège de France (1931–1942), where Durkheim had been denied the same honor. The reversal, claims one historian, is in part explained by the elusiveness of Mauss's positions, less overtly political and moralizing, and therefore less threatening to the intellectual establishment than those of Durkheim (Karady 1972, 33–40). However one interprets the motive for such recognition, it represents a consecration of ethnography as a distinct field, salvaged from marginality as well as from total absorption by sociology.

The tensions within Mauss's position mirror the two directions pulling ethnography in general. On the one hand, he fostered an interest in serious, long-term fieldwork abandoned for nearly a century. This goal was in part realized by the impressive expedition to Africa spanning the entire continent directed by Marcel Griaule between 1931 and 1933. It benefited from the work of a sophisticated interdisciplinary team including the writer and future College sponsor, Michel Leiris. On the other hand, Mauss himself, prototype of the "armchair" anthropologist, drew from the considerable primary sources of others he argued were barely exploited, to author a highly acclaimed field manual that accompanied an entire generation of researchers. Without completing a single major work by conventional standards, his influence rides on a few suggestive rather than systematic essays treating Eskimo life cycles, sacrifice, and gift-exchange. Their presentation is often disorganized and reminiscent of his oral pedagogy, where the esoteric aside or provocative formulation was most effective. Mauss's most important theoretical contribution remains the notion of the "total social fact," an obvious call for the very sort of synthesis he intuited more often than realized.

Mauss's eccentric example cannot account, however, for the lure exerted by ethnography and sociology on some of the most talented minds at a time when university positions were scarce and expeditions rarely funded. Some explanation is provided by the historical impact of Durkheimian sociology on the general configuration of established disciplines. First, Durkheim was able to impose an "epistemological break" with earlier social sciences within the Faculty of Letters. Then there is the sweeping project he had conceived, whose division of labor included investigations into the origin of all social institutions in their "elementary forms" as the means to understand subsequent developments. Finally, relations among disciplines are marked by increasing polarization between the sciences of the unconscious (psychoanalysis) and the "irrational" philosophies (existentialism) on one side, and determinist, materialist ideologies, along with the experimental social sciences, on the other. The good fortune of ethnology was to partake of both camps. Although methodologically closer to the social sciences, it drew insights from other cultures into modes of thought resistant to the definition of logic sanctioned by the West. Most important for subsequent developments in social thought, it provided examples of "the apparent primacy of the symbolic referential over the utilitarian" (Karady 1972, 38).

But, whereas Mauss largely succeeded in extricating ethnography from the imperial grasp of sociology, it is also true that his own idiosyncratic achievements could not outdistance the long shadow of Durkheim. Victor Karady attributes much of sociology's influence in the early years to Durkheim's "anomolous" position as both spiritual guide and intellectual mentor. Spurred by the political debacle of 1870, the perception of lost absolutes fostered by quantum physics, and the revolution in perception advanced by the artistic avant-gardes, Durkheim joined his contemporaries in that "recherche" for a lost social order that sociology was supposed to help reconstruct.[2]

[2] For the sociological perspective on the overlapping of social, cultural, and intellectual milieus at the "birth" of Durkheimian sociology, see Edward Tiryakian, "l'Ecole durkheimienne à la recherche de la sociologie perdue: La sociologie naissante et son milieu culturel," *Cahiers internationaux de sociolgie* 66 (1979): 97–114.

But for the generation of the College, the aura of that formidable figure was less vivid than the extraordinary representations of feasts and rituals awaiting discovery in his last major opus, *Les Formes élémentaires de la vie religieuse* (1912). Because biographers emphasize Durkheim's staid moralism and irreproachable integrity, less interest has been directed at reconciling that profile with the author of powerful descriptions of effervescent encounters, where concentrated energy and intensity are suggested as the cure for the deleterious effects of modern individualism and dispersion. Faced with the enigma of the ostensible break *The Elementary Forms of the Religious Life* marks with Durkheim's preceding works, one scholar posed the question it raises this way: "Why did this highly rational, secular, positivistic Frenchman decide sometime after 1895 to devote nearly fifteen of the most productive years of his life to the exotic cults, dancing, and blood-letting of a primitive people" (Bellah 1973, xliii).

A response limited to the works themselves must focus on the shift that occurs in the analyses of the two types of social organization described in *The Division of Labor in Society* (1893).[3] There, the move from mechanical to organic societies is seen as the result of an evolutionary process, with a clear bias toward emancipation from traditional formations where order must be externally imposed and identity automatic. By contrast, the organic solidarity of highly specialized societies is the outcome of voluntary adhesion, and morality is primarily tied to occupational standards. By the time of *Elementary Forms*, however, the distinction is not presented as developmental, but rather, as occurring within alternating cycles of the same culture, where seasonal changes bring about transformations in the very quality of social life. Just as Mauss had described the regulated oppositions within Eskimo society in 1906, so Durkheim offers a portrait of Australian aboriginal life as oscillating between dispersion and concentration. However, the value attributed to each has been inverted since the *Division* analysis. Durkheim now deplores the state of dispersion and isolation characteristic of summer economic activity "which results in making its life uniform, languishing and dull" ([1912], 246). In contrast, the winter months, when everyone gathers together to consume the food accumulated during the previous season, are charged with concentrations of energy passing through the group and transporting them into a veritable exaltation. The collectivity then witnesses the transmutation of violent cries and gestures into

[3] See W.S.F. Pickering, *Durkheim's Sociology of Religion: Themes and Theories* (London, Boston, Melbourne and Henley: Routledge & Kegan Paul, 1984), for the most elaborate statement of the continuity position.

songs and dances; men engage in transgressions such as incest and wife swapping. Extraordinary activity of this sort, concludes Durkheim, cannot help but foster the conviction "that there really exist two heterogeneous and mutually incomparable worlds. One is where the individual's daily life drags wearily along; but he cannot penetrate into the other without at once entering into relations with extraordinary powers that excite him to the point of frenzy" (Durkheim [1912], 250). The first is the profane domain; the second, the sacred. Moreover, it is from such effervescent gatherings that the idea of religion is born.

Indeed, with this ethnographic reconstruction of the collective origin of religion, Durkheim, known for multi-dimensional notions, forwards an idea which is especially challenging. Religion, he insists, is the most archaic yet complete mode of social life. Responsible for generating sacred and ideal representations, as well as profane and material ones, it is the form from which all others—aesthetic, political, economic—emerge: "religious life is . . . the concentrated form of the expression of the whole of collective life." And because "the idea of society is the soul of religion, religious forces are therefore human forces, moral forces" ([1912], 466). Social, moral, collective, and human, religion so conceived is presented as the most potent antidote to the corrosive effects of excessive social and religious individualism on the foundations of modern social life.

The plausibility of Durkheim's argument hinges on the presuppositions of the continuity / evolution hypothesis, wherein the transition from the archaic to the modern is viewed as taking place within a single process of development. Indeed, this premise becomes fundamental to explaining and justifying the very nature of the sociological enterprise. Thus the opening paragraphs of *Elementary Forms*'s introduction move from delineating the specificity of his field to the general goals of his project:

> Sociology raises other problems than history or ethnography. It does not seek to know the passed forms of civilization with the sole end of knowing them and reconstructing them. But rather, like every positive science, it has as its object the explanation of some actual reality which is near to us, and which consequently is capable of affecting our ideas and our acts: this reality is man, and more precisely, the man of today, for there is nothing which we are more interested in knowing. Then we are not going to study a very archaic religion simply for the pleasure of telling its peculiarities and singularities. If we have taken it as the subject of our research, it is because it has seemed to us better adapted than any other to lead to an understanding of the religious nature of man, that is to say, to show us an essential and permanent aspect of humanity. ([1912], 13)

Durkheim's conviction that the most "elementary" religion is also the most total is reasserted through his refusal to discredit the continuity / evolution hypothesis by installing a hierarchy among religions. Nor does he subscribe to the common perception that science is superior to religion, the outcome of a historical process whereby the profane has displaced the sacred, so that the persistence of religion is dismissed as a vestige of irrationalism. Rather, sociology studies aboriginal religion because the religious nature manifests "an essential and permanent aspect of humanity" ([1912], 13). Science may rightly usurp religion in the study of phenomena amenable to the scientific method, but because it is restricted to the "how" rather than the "why" of things, it can never completely replace religion's willingness to grasp for the "totality."

The parallels between the concentration / dispersion and sacred / profane dualities can now be examined. It was already pointed out that *Elementary Forms* marks a break in Durkheim's thinking because of the change in emphasis given to the articulation of elements within the first pair: instead of conceiving them within a developmental progression, the concentrated / dispersed opposition, following ethnographic evidence, is appreciated as a pattern of alternations within the same culture. It is also possible to approach the sacred / profane duality by means of a comparable analysis, so that the heterogeneous realities are viewed as complementary, each necessary but not sufficient. That the distinct phenomena to which they correspond must coexist, rather than supersede each other, is consistent with Durkheim's opening declaration cited aboved: just as religion responds to permanent needs, so the construction of social reality by the contrastive organization produced by the opposition of the sacred to the profane remains a constant, even in contemporary society.

This reading is corroborated by a revealing passage from *Elementary Forms* in which a quote from Spencer and Gillen, Durkheim's primary source for aboriginal religion, can be compared with his own interpretation. Here is the original account of fire ceremonies: "The smoke, the blazing torches, the showers of sparks falling in all directions and the masses of dancing, yelling men, formed altogether a genuinely wild and savage scene of which it is impossible to convey any adequate idea in words" ([1912], 249). From this rather mediocre and stereotyped depiction, Durkheim extrapolates his explanation for the sacred / profane distinction:

> One can readily explain how, when arrived at this state of exaltation, a man does not recognize himself any longer. Feeling himself dominated and carried away by some sort of an external power which makes him think and act differently than in normal times, he naturally has the im-

> pression of being himself no longer. It seems to him that he has become a new being: . . . And at the same time all his companions feel themselves transformed in the same way and express this sentiment by their cries, their gestures and their general attitude, everything is just as though he really were transported into a special world, entirely different from the one where he ordinarily lives, and into an environment filled with exceptionally intense forces that take hold of him and metamorphose him. How could such experiences as these, especially when they are repeated everyday for weeks, fail to leave in him the conviction that there really exist two heterogeneous and mutually incomparable worlds? . . . the first is the profane world, the second, that of sacred things. ([1912], 249–50)

Durkheim's immediate development of this passage reveals how he understands the connections among the various phenomena. First, effervescent experiences as the source of religion is corroborated by the fact that in Australia "the really religious activity is almost entirely confined to the moments when these assemblies are held" ([1912], 250). Second, the erroneous assumption that the sacred dominates among the most elementary religious forms is reversed by evidence that prayer and ritual occur daily in advanced societies, in contrast with the Australian pattern where "apart from the celebrations of the clan and tribe, the time is nearly all filled with lay and profane occupations" ([1912], 250). Furthermore, the alternations between the sacred and the profane in the religious life of the Australians "demonstrates to them the bond uniting them to one another, but among the peoples called civilized, the relative continuity of the two blurs their relations" ([1912], 250). Although Durkheim deplores the progressive breakdown of the sacred / profane distinction, he also is convinced that it will never completely disappear (even if not always recognized as such), for the important reason that collective gatherings provide the most dramatic realization of the fundamental dualism of human nature. More troubling, then, is the prospect of a complete rationalization of the world through the superior claims of science. In his conclusion, however, Durkheim reasserts his faith in the capacity of religion to perdure because it recognizes the "vital necessities" excluded from a scientific approach.

How are such assertions to be evaluated?[4] What is to be made of the Durkheimian description of religion as essentially social, collec-

[4] For the complex reception to Durkheim's ideas on the relation of science to religion, and the ideological issues raised by the history of this reception, I am indebted to Robin Horton, "Lévy-Bruhl, Durkheim and the Scientific Revolution," in *Modes of Thought*, ed. Robin Horton and Ruth Finnegan (London: Faber & Faber, 1973), pp. 249–305.

tive, human, warm, exalting, intense, concentrated, effervescent, electric, and total? Early reception to *Elementary Forms* was immediately praiseworthy: in 1913 Malinowski recognized the work of "one of the acutest and most brilliant living sociologists" (cited in Pickering 1984, 87). Subsequent evaluations tend to divide between accolades for a theoretical ingenuity expressed by Evans-Pritchard (1965) this way: "Emile Durkheim's thesis is more than just neat; it is brilliant and imaginative, almost poetical" (cited by Pickering 1984, 87), and those who find the theoretical constructs inferior to its superlative use of ethnography. Most revealing is the general sentiment that its contribution has not been superseded by more recent scholarship. As Pickering's extensive study argues, it is one of those rare seminal works to attain the status of a classic precisely because it encourages rereadings. But its special quality was perhaps best expressed by the eminent Durkheim scholar and biographer Steven Lukes's outburst of enthusiasm: "I went and read the *EF* and had my mind blown, and as a result I just became totally immersed in Durkheim" (cited by Pickering 1984, xix).

The present reading is distinguished from the above assessments in its emphasis on those outstanding passages regarding the sacred *quality* of collective life in which Durkheim's iconoclasm becomes most apparent. For it is in such moments of daring that his writing transgresses the norms of scientific prose and reveals his own commitments. Because of them we are able to respond to the question as to the significance of the late shift to the study of Australian aboriginal religion. The answer was provided by the master himself, when he justified his choice of subject matter at the very outset of his presentation. Beginning with his conclusion, Durkheim affirmed the fundamental continuity between the religious past with that of the present and, more controversially, insisted on the debt of contemporary science to its religious origins. Breaking with the propensity of Frazer and Tylor to regard the primitive as "inferior," Durkheim also resists nostalgic projections: he explicitly criticizes Comte for trying to revive "old" gods. But if religion, like society, is to survive in a viable fashion, they must undergo transformations and renewals through "reunions, assemblies and meetings" ([1912], 475):

> If we find a little difficulty today in imagining what these feasts and ceremonies of the future could consist in, it is because we are going through a stage of transition and moral mediocrity. The great things of the past which filled our fathers with enthusiasm do not excite the same ardour in us, either because they have come to common usage to such an extent that

we are unconscious of them, or else because they no longer answer to our actual aspirations; but as yet there is nothing to replace them. ([1912], 475)

Durkheim optimistically reassures the reader that such confusion cannot last indefinitely, so that "A day will come when our societies will know again those hours of creative effervescence, in the course of which new ideas arise and new formulae are found that serve for a while as a guide to humanity" ([1912], 475).

Meanwhile, the role of sociology is to serve the future by opening "a new way to the science of man" (Durkheim 1912, 495). Until now, Durkheim claims, philosophers and moralists confronted with the duality of human nature were caught between elevating one dimension to reconcile it with the other, or vice versa. Science, in its turn, was stalemated by the conviction that the individual was "the ultimate creation of nature," with nothing beyond him for science to reach. Sociology, however, has demonstrated that beyond the individual, society exists. But by defining it as "*a system of active forces*" ([1912], 495, my emphasis), a new manner of explaining becomes imperative as well as possible. Thus, when Spencer and Gillen gauged the intensity of the "wild and savage scene" by declaring it beyond words, they effectively relegated the entire experience to a domain of irreducible cultural alterity. But when Durkheim begins his commentary with "One can readily explain how . . ." the explanation functions at two levels: first, to translate into an eloquent and powerful language the nature of the experience as he imagines it; second, to then insist on presenting a sociological perspective that challenges indigenous as well as philosophical and even anthropological assumptions, all the while recognizing how such errors could occur. By enlisting rhetorical devices that draw the reader into the process of discovery—"How could such experiences as these . . . ," or through simple projections onto the other—"A man does not recognize himself . . . ," Durkheim dramatically reinforces his continuity position. The reader's fantasies are stimulated to identify with an other stripped of any culturally bound details, while he or she is shown that neither cultural nor intellectual distance guarantees a superior understanding of their common experiences.

Because Durkheim does not privilege any explanation other than the sociological, Pickering reiterates the widely held position that *Elementary Forms* does not reflect a significant break within the totality of his work. Other than conceding the obvious fact that it is an ethnographically based monograph, this position is corroborated through examples from earlier writings that indicate an interest in religion in general, and effervescence in particular. Although theoretically consistent with subsequent developments, however, these works do not exhibit the discursive qualities of *The Elementary Forms of the Religious Life*.

In the section to follow, I argue that the research promoted in the context of the Collège de sociologie takes up the special challenges exemplified by *Elementary Forms*. We recall that the initial declaration of the group insisted that the study of archaic cultures be enlisted to appreciate modern social problems, that the potentially contagious effects of the collective representations it studies not be deflected by sociology's commitment to scientific principles, and that the sociologists themselves not fear the results of their own form of collective association, should it lead to action. In calling for a sacred sociology rather than "sociologie religieuse," the College's redefinition was consistent with Durkheim's realization that the real discovery of *Elementary Forms* was the "dynamogenic" quality of religion (Durkheim 1975, 27). By exploring the nature of the forces activated by collective encounters, the College was to remain faithful to Durkheim when he pushed the intellectual exercise to its next stage of critical development: The sociological imagination must generate its own version of collective representations by providing intimations of what the collective life of the future—its feasts and festivals—could possibly be.

The neglect that befell French sociology in the early part of this century was turned about by a revival of interest in the work of Durkheim within British and American anthropology, not sociology. Lévi-Strauss imputes the delay to the long-standing separateness between the two fields. To explain the opposition from which the French school is notably exempt, he cites Kroeber's speculation that the respective disciplines, although historically coeval, must have sprung from differing "impulses"; with sociology attracting individuals committed to integration and anthropology drawing from critics of the social order (1959, 505). Conventional wisdom, however, is challenged by the French example of a social philosophy in which the study of society was prompted by a critical stance. Thus, despite the recent history of modern sociology's role in the moral regeneration of French society following the turmoil of 1789 and the defeat of 1870, the critical thrust of Montaigne, Diderot, and Rousseau continues to be its most enduring model: "In France, sociology will remain the offspring of these first attempts at anthropological thinking" (1959, 505).

The second trait, also inherited from historical precedents, and one to be assumed as common knowledge among College participants, is that "French sociology does not consider itself an isolated discipline, working in its own field, but rather as a method, or as a specific attitude toward human phenomena. Therefore one does not need to be a sociologist in order to do sociology" (1959, 505). Lévi-Strauss's assertion can be enlisted in defense of College participants against attacks of amateurism.

But the distinguishing characteristic of the French school resides in its insistence on the primacy of the collective over the individual. Nowhere is this expressed with less equivocation than in Durkheim's argument that social facts are things, objective representations that follow their own *sui generis* laws and movement. Moreover, social activities are viewed as syntheses, and therefore more complex and even morally "higher" than individual achievements. Lévi-Strauss takes up this claim since it appears to place Durkheim within the reactionary tradition of de Bonald, for whom the collective is both objective and superior to the individual. Such a position is clearly at odds with the fact that Durkheim was known as a democrat, a liberal, and a rationalist. Yet Lévi-Strauss offers his own position with equal assertiveness: "Every moral, social, or intellectual progress made its first appearance as a revolt of the individual against the group" (1959, 530).

Whether the two positions are irreconcilable cannot be further explored within the confines of Lévi-Strauss's historical survey, but the issues raised compel us to reconsider the consequences of Durkheim's legacy for a modernist perspective, especially as regards the conjunction of sociology with anthropology. More precisely, what are the implications of the model stating that the sum is greater than its parts for an analysis of the modern subject in relation to: (1) the growing specialization and differentiation of society, especially due to the effects of technology on the division of labor; (2) a marxist perspective that stresses identity within conflicting groups or classes; (3) the Freudian appreciation of the "divided" subject, split between a conscious mind and an unconscious set of quasi-autonomous desires?

As a response to the general question of the subject, the status of *Elementary Forms* as representative of a break with Durkheim's earlier work will be reconsidered. This time, however, I argue that its final message, as a form of social critique, is complementary to, and even completes, the thrust of his first essays. Evidence for this position is derived from the "Individualism and the Intellectuals" (1898) address, where one consequence of the division of labor is that individuals have left in common only the attributes of a "human person."

The general category comprises "an essential core above the nuances of diversity and natural temperaments" (Bellah 1973, 51). In this classless analysis, there are no intermediary categories nor mediating links between individual opinions and universal humanity except occupational morality. Moreover, because differentiation will only be exacerbated in the future, individualism is not easily overcome. As a sort of ontological affirmation of its inevitability, Durkheim concludes that "each individual consciousness contains something divine and thus finds itself marked with a character that renders it sacred and inviolable to others. Therein lies all individualism; and that is what makes it a necessary doctrine" (Bellah 1973, 52). Consistent with this position is the responsibility that Durkheim burdens the intellectual to assume. Whether as educator or as civil servant, the individual must work harmoniously within a collective effort, as exemplified by the organization Durkheim devised for the program of sociology. The model envisages individuals neither "juxtaposed" nor "entwined," but "coordinated and subordinated to another around some central organ which exercises a moderating action over the rest of the organism" (Bellah 1973, 69). Most importantly, there must exist a social organization to encourage the efflorescence of altruism as the basis for order and not demote it to a mere ornament superimposed upon contractual arrangements, as Spencer had claimed. Society is moral because it exacts sacrifices as a way to consolidate bonds.

More difficult to conceptualize are the alternatives to the "despised" individualism fostered by modern religion and economy. The place of *Elementary Forms* in relation to earlier works becomes clearer since, as Durkheim reiterates in a very late statement, one must reject the "great religions" because they "continue to depict us as tormented and suffering, while only the crude cults of inferior societies breathe forth and inspire a joyful confidence" (Bellah 1973, 156). Seeking to detect examples within contemporary society, Durkheim breaks with his long-standing rejection of class-based analyses in the following remark to citizens gathered for a discussion of the recently published *Elementary Forms*: "All that matters is to feel below the moral cold which reigns on the surface of collective life the sources of warmth that our societies bear in themselves. One may even go further and say with some precision in what region of society these new forces are potentially forming: it is in the popular classes" (Bellah 1973, xlvii).

Significantly, one of the most interesting alternatives to modern individualism is found in the *Elementary Forms* chapter treating social creativity. A description of collective representations condenses all traits that break with a utilitarian, pragmatic, and rationalistic model, in favor of a free-floating effervescence, ultimately crystallized in some object or symbol. The result for society is not an isolated artifact nor emblem, but a comprehensive ensemble of collective representations. Seemingly gratuitous from a practical standpoint, the ideal domain nonetheless generates action: "We say that an object, whether individual or collective, inspires respect when the representation expressing it in the mind is gifted with such a force that it automatically causes or inhibits actions, *without regard for any consideration relative to their useful or injurious effects*" (Durkheim [1912], 237).

Effervescent gatherings can also have political consequences, as when "Under the influence of general exaltation, we see the most mediocre and inoffensive bourgeois become either a hero or a butcher," or when the intensity generated is invested into an individual who is then followed, not necessarily because his opinions seem wise, "but because a certain sort of physical energy is imminent in the idea that we form of this person, which conquers our will and inclines it in the indicated direction" (Durkheim [1912], 237). Religion and politics then risk becoming mystified, precisely because the group no longer perceives their social origin and attributes to them a transcendent cause or being. Similarly, when an individual experiences conflict at having to defer to the demands of the collective, he or she is merely deluded by a false sense of presence or wholeness of an inner world divorced from the social. Whence the need for sociologists, who objectively demonstrate the relation of the individual to the whole, and the place of isolated phenomena within the totality. But it is not only in exceptional circumstances that the stimulating action of society is felt since there is not "a moment when some current of energy does not come to us from without" (Durkheim [1912], 242). Durkheim's resolution of the artificial antinomies of self and other, individual and society, thus leads to a new "economy" of the subject. At the antipodes of the Leibnizian monad, and unlike the Freudian subject torn between libidinal desires and the repressive exigencies of civilization, the Durkheimian subject's consciousness is open to all others. This sociological subject nonetheless remains an individual, but one whose dualism oscillates between the prosaic domain of dispersion and those extraordinary moments of concentrated energy whose collective intensity is greater than the sum of its parts.

The sociological perspective on the individual is reaffirmed and expanded in the work of Marcel Mauss. In his important essay on the "notion of person" (1938), for instance, he asserts the strategic value of sociology as a counter to the idealistic forces within French intellectual life by demonstrating that even subjectivity is amenable to a historical reconstruction. Only with his qualification that it is the exclusive claim of the modern individual to have fully realized the potential for self-reflexivity does he give greater weight to the evolutionary side of Durkheim's continuity premise. A comparable normative judgment also appears in the famous *Gift Essay*, where simpler modes of exchange are seen as giving way to systems at once less complex and more efficient, when they shed the extraneous social obligations encumbering archaic economic forms. While discussing the gift as a "total social fact," Mauss develops the question of the relation of the individual to the group. He takes the opportunity to reassert the Durkheimian methodological principle whereby social facts can only be analyzed by other social phenomena. Thus, the psychological question of a motive for gift-giving, that is, whether it is willed or obligatory, disinterested or egotistic, is settled by showing that it is susceptible only to a holistic appreciation. The gift itself is not an isolatable object since it figures at the nexus of an elaborate system of exchanges in which "all kinds of institutions find simultaneous expression: religious, legal, moral, and economic" (Mauss 1967, 1). Similarly, it is impossible to discuss individual initiative since the self is always already engaged in some phase of the gift-exchange cycle. No matter how delayed in time or space, a seemingly isolated gesture is ultimately appreciated within the global network of reciprocal relations. To the extent that individual vagaries are expressed, it is within the parameters of cultural rules and norms transmitted through a system of highly codified signs.

This last point will not be discussed further since it forms the basis for Lévi-Strauss's structuralist model of culture, although he claims to detect the inspiration for it in Mauss. As I have argued elsewhere (Richman 1982), the elements of Mauss most influential for the formulation of a sacred sociology are those that remain closest to the Durkheim of *Elementary Forms*. In the gift essay, for instance, Mauss underscores the power of the gift as emanating from its ambivalent, labile nature. Like all objects designated as sacred, it is irreducible to the one-dimensionality of signs in a more rationalized economy of exchange. Mauss cannot resolve the undecidability of a phenomenon whose Germanic etymology traces it to both gift and poison. The gift is attributed contradictory properties precisely because it encompasses them all: at once desirable and forbidding, motivated and disinterested, sacrificial and acquisitive, gift giving defies the law of contradiction to which the Western logos is ostensibly held.

We recall that in stressing the total nature of religion, Durkheim pointed out that it subsumed the profane as well as the sacred, the material as well as the ideal, the bad as well as the good. The conclusion among Durkheim's disciples was that the sacred itself must be considered two-dimensional, exhibiting elements they label "right" and "left:" that is, those sanctioned by social conventions in contrast with those deemed dangerous and transgressive of the very rules structuring social existence. This is what accounts for the special atmosphere of gift exchanges, especially the violently destructive potlatch ceremonies among Indians of the Pacific Northwest, since the festivals defy the very norms of economy to which the social whole is otherwise constrained.

Despite his many criticisms of Durkheim, Lévi-Strauss concedes that the future of French sociology depends upon a renewal of the social discourse exemplified in *Elementary Forms*. His own predilections will carry him closer to the work of Mauss, where he finds the basis for a "new humanism" when ethnology is wedded to psychoanalysis and the combinatorial model of structural linguistics. But the consequences of this development are considerable. Whereas Durkheim concluded that the feasts of the past could inspire the communal life of the future, Lévi-Strauss detects in archaic myths the sempiternal conflict between the demands of the collectivity and a nostalgia for that which is denied to social man, "a world in which one might keep to oneself" (Lévi-Strauss [1949], 497).

More pointedly, with the claim that over time the euphoria of archaic gift ceremonies has been lost, Lévi-Strauss expunges the effervescence distinguishing Durkheim's descriptions from his own portrait of exchange and communication. In the general enthusiasm for the global and scientific claims of the structuralist paradigm, with its significant shift from religion to kinship relations as the fundamental organizing principle of social life, the controversial effervescence[5] was not missed. Among French sociologists in the postwar period, Georges Gurvitch stands as an exception. He argued against French sociology's "exaggerated" focus on structure as precluding interest in the effervescent behaviors he qualifies as innovative as well as creative. Gurvitch urges sociologists to resume the role played by Durkheim, in order to demonstrate how certain ideas can only be tested, seized, or affirmed through collective acts. In this way, sociology can again realize its enormous potential as "a negative and critical contribution to philosophy and the works of civilization" (Gurvitch 1963, 1:27).

Marginal to the dominant structuralism, the ideas of Durkheim and Mauss, as reworked by Bataille, were disseminated in the early

[5] See Pickering's discussion (1984) of "effervescent assemblies," pp. 380–417, for one of the rare treatments of the subject.

sixties in the publications of *Critique* and *Tel Quel*. Barthes lauded the particular materialism of the general economy's forces of expenditure and effervescence, as a "third" way out of the static (neo-Kantian) antinomies underlying even the most radical surrealist positions. (See Webster in this collection for more on the Bataille/Breton polemic.) And Kristeva called for a "new rationality" located somewhere else than in the polarization between Marxist infrastructural production and (super) structuralist exchange. In relation to social practice, the notion of expenditure was clearly influential for the May 68 movement. The view of the festival as a mode of social disruption and transgression, the goal of subverting the power implicit in all social relations rather than an attack or takeover of the government, the *groupuscule* as decentralized organization, and so on, are all related to the prescient radicalism that would be rediscovered in the College texts. In the post-'68 conjuncture facilitating their rediscovery, an awareness of critical developments in American anthropology was mediated by the writings of Jean Baudrillard. Drawing parallels between French ethnology and the early essays of Marshall Sahlins, where capitalist as well as Marxist presuppositions regarding the nature of work and accumulation were challenged, Baudrillard facilitated an encounter that was to have considerable repercussions for postmodernist ethnographic developments in this country as well.[6]

From an institutional perspective, the College's exoterism to traditional disciplines, professions, and the usual affiliations, whether universities or museums, is striking. Yet historically, in its very nonconformity, it bears a marked similarity to the mode of production of ideas prevalent within both politics and social criticism during the 1930s (see del Bayle 1969). Motivated by a common disaffection from the dominant political parties, university dogma, and cultural conformity, rightists and leftists, Catholics and free thinkers, banded together in small groups to share ideological perspectives and to generate alternative ways of thinking. They were often allied with a review. In the case of Bataille, the College was the public face of a secret society called *Acéphale*, which nonetheless launched a short-lived journal of four issues.

The specificity imparted to the College by its focus on sociological phenomena is especially evident in its congruence between form and content, where the formation of the group itself was mirrored in its research. Not only was the College dedicated to analyzing collective

[6] See Webster in this collection for further discussion. I am by no means implying a harmonious consensus among these works, only that they drew from Bataille and his sources a repertoire of notions of "collective representations" that provided the discursive infrastructure for subsequent developments in critical thought.

phenomena in the modern world; it was also intended to serve as a model whose collective energies would stimulate a contagious effusion and then lead to action, albeit of unknown outcome. The interest in institutions such as the army was to extend to all human activity, whether science, art, or technology, if it exhibits a "communal" value in the active sense of the word. That all activity leading to unity is deemed sacred, explains the assimilation of the adjective to their definition of sociology. Just as its participants represented a grouping based on elective affinities, so the College would focus on secondary communities, including secret societies, religious and political organizations, outside the purview of academic sociology. These positions are consistent with the College's opening statement, when it claimed that once the intrepid research into the sacred concluded, members of the Durkheimian school tended to dissociate themselves from the "spirit" of their investigations by not indicating that these collective phenomena, although marginalized in the West, could nonetheless provide insight into the affective basis of modern social structures. Myth, death rituals, and festivals are consigned a subordinate status to the allegedly rational foundations of society. Moreover, the College discerns obstacles stronger than the predictable objections raised by scientific criteria in the reticence of their mentors to draw out certain consequences of archaic activity. Bataille, Caillois, and Leiris argue that the real explanation for the self-censorship of their predecessors lies in the "activist" and "contagious" nature of the representations involved, forces that the College sought to encourage. Ideally, the energies activated would encompass the "sociologists" themselves, modify the movement constituting the College, and then lead to the formation of a "moral community, in part different from the one that ordinarily unites scholars: one linked to the virulent character of the realm studied" (Declaration 1938, 10). Besides the dramatic formulation typical of Bataille, with its emphasis gauged in terms of intensity rather than conventional connotations of violence, one also notes the insistence on the moral dimension of the project.

It is relevant to indicate the consequences of the College's interest in groups bypassed by traditional sociology, those initiated or selected by its members. Herein lies the crucial distinction between the College and fascism, which celebrates the "right" side of the sacred, (for example, those institutions sanctioned by official ideology). By turning to the left side, the College drew attention to peripheral areas that reveal how the dominant culture fashions its identity. For instance, it is the difference between the fascist appeal to a "communaute de fait," the eternal "patrie" of "la vieille France," whose mythic solidarity depends on antisemitism, and the College's creation of an intentional secondary community responsive to historical exigencies, that has earned it special consideration in reassessments of the period (Lévy 1981, 25, 205).

In looking at areas shunned by conventional sociology, the College also revealed philosophy's inability to conceptualize the nature of collectivities in the modern world. Taking up the basic approaches provided by Durkheim, Bataille devoted considerable attention to the possible explanatory models derived from the natural sciences. Whence the considerable number of conferences exploring the esoteric notions of "composed beings," or the interrelations between "society," "organism," and "being." In a similar vein, lectures devoted to the reorganization of the State, including possible alternatives to the "devirilization" of modern democracies, speculate on federalism or a new structure of "unity without a head." Underlying these speculations is the moral critique of fragmentation, whose extreme manifestation is found in science. This perspective also highlights the ambiguous politics of the College.

The formation of the Collège de sociologie in 1937 was prompted by the perception of a generalized "moral panic" within a population forced to confront the prospect of imminent war. Characterized by "consternation, resignation, and fear" the disarray of the French only underscored the "absurdity" of available political positions and the failure of a democratic government to foster a united front. The reaction of the College was to eschew the political scene altogether, in order to arrive at an appreciation "devoid of complicity" by studying the collective psychological reactions the spectre of war had evoked. It concluded by condemning the effects of modern individualism, as witnessed among "men who are so alone, so deprived of destiny, that they find themselves absolutely defenseless when faced with the possibility of death" (Declaration 1938, 45).

Generally, the politics of the College are difficult to pin down. In 1938, for instance, the group decried the political sellout of the Munich accords but refused to enlist support for any party. Rather, the purpose of the denunciation of the international crisis was to emphasize the fragmentation analyzed in the following manner: the rationalization of social life according to the laws of the market leads to specialization, isolation, and ultimately, emasculation. The inability to unite spontaneously into collective action fosters the most egregious paralysis of all—the fear of death evoked by the possibility of war. Given the vague nature of the action hoped for, comparisons with Durkheim's descriptions of the sense of power accrued to individuals by collective experience is perhaps most apt, as when the transforming capacity of "contagious effervescence" turns the most timid bourgeois into a fervent revolutionary (or butcher!).

Indeed, Pickering rightly stresses that Durkheim's illustrations of effervescent assemblies are those pivotal historical moments—the eleventh-century Crusades, 1789, 1870, the Dreyfus Affair—when they functioned as precursors to social change. As such, the "rassemblement" must be distinguished from the historically proximate notion of the crowd, represented in the literary naturalism of Zola, prominent in the emergent urban ethnography of Baudelaire and Benjamin, and theorized in the "psychological" analysis of Le Bon. (See Webster for more on this.) Durkheim's assemblies are intentional gatherings, where individual minds are strengthened rather than weakened, where the sacred rather than "evil" emerges, and which Caillois later qualified as "supersocialized" rather than irrational (Le Bon 1895). The latter, unlike Durkheim, "emphasized the terrifying effect crowds had on those who were opposed to them and their goals" (Pickering 1984, 530). Yet such qualifications cannot deter even the most sympathetic reader, such as Evans-Pritchard, whose praise for Durkheim's understanding of religion as an experience of "self-effacement" did not stop him from condemning the effervescent asembly to which it is explicity indebted: "No amount of juggling with words like 'intensity' and 'effervescence' can hide the fact that he derives the totemic religion of the Black Fellows from the emotional excitement of individuals brought together in a small crowd, from what is a sort of crowd hysteria" (cited in Pickering 1984, 396).

The research domain charted by the College—secret societies, religious orders, and political vanguard groups—bypassed by most ethnography, underscores Bataille's contention that "We are whole only outside ourselves, in the human plenitude of an assembly, but we are only whole after having responded (through an assembly) to our most intimate demands" (1946, 45). At stake in the realization of a collective experience is the recovery of a lost wholeness. Yet Bataille also concedes the near impossibility to resort to myth or the favored forms of archaic cultures since "It might be that a whole existence is no longer any more than a simple dream for us, a dream fed by historical descriptions and the secret gleam of our passions" (Declaration 1938, 23).

The totality in question here is distinguished from the "closed" system inherited from Hegel, incapable of accounting for the negativity or force that refuses, subverts, or explodes the recovering effects of the dialectic. As experienced by the Bataillian subject, negativity reveals an individual consciousness suffering the condition of an "open wound," in itself a refutation of Hegel. Refusing the consolation of action defined as productivity, it seeks a sense of completion in a sovereignty differentiated from Hegelian mastery. If Hegel recognizes negativity only when sublimated into work, action, or a project, Bataille characterizes modern negativity as "sans emploi." Immobility sets in not out of fear of action, but "for lack of opportunities." The alternative is the ineffectual "négativité impuissante" of a work of art where, as in the example of traditional religion, negativity is recouped as an "object of contemplation," thus refusing it recognition "at the very moment it enters into the play of existence as a stimulus to major vital reactions" (Declaration 1938, 91). Institutionalized art and religion function to transmute the disruptive violence of negativity into socially sanctioned modes of expression and experience.

The paradigm of conversion from the left to the right sacred is inherited from earlier sociology. With it, Bataille accounts for the movements of "attraction and repulsion" responsible for the sort of collective experiences the College set out to understand. Such an investigation falls under the purview of a sacred sociology since it points to a post-Durkheimian tracing of the subterranean movements of negativity prior to legitimation. Sacred sociology thus overflows the boundaries of the traditional discipline by foregrounding the phenomena of tears, laughter, and sexuality. To appreciate the viewpoint developed here, a comparison with the innovative work of Mauss is instructive.

Whereas Lévi-Strauss balked at the seemingly unlimited capacity of the Durkheimian concept of society to generate collective welfare, he enthusiastically endorsed Mauss's project to relate disparate phenomena at the level of infra or unconscious categories and structures. The outcome is a sociological documentation of the incursion of the social into all areas, including details of the body. In reference to Mauss's "techniques of the body" essay, Lévi-Strauss insists: "It required considerable courage and clairvoyance on the part of a man formed in an intellectual and moral tradition as prudish as that of the neo-Kantian tradition reigning in our universities at the end of the last century, to venture forth . . . in search of the 'lost psychic states of our childhood' " (1950, xi). But if Mauss uncovers the profoundly socialized "obligatory expression of feelings," Bataille seeks a confrontation with those revealing moments when sentiments, poised in their ambivalence, defy socialization into the right side of the sacred. Most intriguing is the "horror" elicited by death, capable of arousing tears as well as laughter or sexual desire.

Although such examples provide insight into the sacred, there remains the issue of sociology. Indeed, it is argued that, in a postsacred society, sociology detects survivals from the past capable of exerting a "constitutive force." But in examining groups and even communities formed through movements of attraction and repulsion, sacred sociology attempts to maintain the polarity of the two extremes. As an alternative to the recuperating effects of the dialectic, Bataille posits a schema of mediation. In the following powerful description he argues the need for a "kernel of violent silence" through which forces otherwise inaccessible or, more likely, intolerable to common states of consciousness must pass: "the fact [is] that union among humans is not immediate union, but is accomplished around a very strange reality, an incomparable and obsessive force; that if human relations stop passing through this middle term, this nucleus of violent silence, they are emptied of their human character" (Declaration 1938, 114). Using the defamiliarizing technique characteristic of ethnographic surrealism, Bataille focuses on the most "banal" center of profane, daily life in a French village—the church and its adjacent courtyard—as a concentration of sacred energy, albeit one whose original force has been defused. The church itself mediates the repulsion elicited by the proximity of the graveyard, with its associations of putrefying flesh, in contrast with the purified skeletal remains of saints within the church itself, which have passed to the right side of religious respect and even become objects worthy of emulation. If Bataille insists on the need for kernels whose active effect or "denaturation" allows for mediated access to the forbidden and forbidding attraction of the horrible and repugnant, it is because he believes "that nothing is more important for us than that we recognize that we are bound and sworn to that which horrifies us most, that which provokes our most intense disgust" (Declaration 1938, 114).

Sociology provides evidence of the institutional equivalent of such ambivalence through the model of taboo and transgression. The possibility to break rules with the approval of those who enforce them, is a challenge to Western logic Mauss had defied his students to consider with his famous quip that prohibitions are made to be violated! Furthermore, because the latent energies associated with the sacred are rarely discerned by other modes of thought and inquiry, sociology's special place is increasingly evident. Its double mission is to detect signs of movement prior to their realization in forms that risk robbing them of their collective potential as creators of unity, and to encourage collective representations in this direction. The two-dimensional process is best exemplified in Caillois's appreciation of the effect of literature on the individual as she or he accedes to the magic circle of a community of readers:

> One can only call religious the subterranean impatience which the novel expresses under so many guises. It marks the moment when these invisible and new forces still remain dispersed, unknown to each other, though linked by a secret element, precisely like the readers of a book. But they are already attracting each other, as so many fine magnetic needles, and risk suddenly revealing themselves soldered and inseparable, manifesting their existence through an unexpected blaze which, only too late, will be perceived as inextinguishable. (1942, 209–10)

The ambivalence retained by means of the taboo / transgression model will exert a comparable impact on subsequent developments within French critical thought. In general, its greatest effect will be to resist liberation movements that argue for the lifting of prohibitions in the cause of freedom from repression. From an ethical standpoint, the sociological model is transposed onto the domain of individual morality by positing the need for a self-regulating mechanism through which a more acute consciousness is attained. As Caillois "recalled" in "The Winter Wind," "a hero is great for having had monsters to do battle with, before being great for having defeated them. There is nothing to hope for from those who have nothing to suppress within themselves" (Declaration 1938, 40). Finally, it is enlisted to displace the Marxist emphasis on a proletarian revolution onto the global need for modes of expenditure so excessive that the only limit is the initial taboo that renders them possible. These various elements merge in the dynamic general economy of expenditure without reserve, to forge a theory of the subject decentered and heterogeneous to the homogenizing principles of bourgeois-capitalist rationality. This model provides a counter to the fragmentation brought about by work and the single-minded action of highly specialized individuals. As an alternative to the passivity connoted by the "negativity without a cause" ("négativité sans emploi") equally deplored by Bataille, one can appreciate the task assigned the sociologist-intellectual responsible for forcing a recognition of such negativity according to the terms designated above. In arguing the "need for loss" and a joyful refusal of the dominant demand for productivity and accumulation, one thus "rediscovers something 'to do' in a world where, from the point of view of actions, nothing is done any more. And what he has 'to do' is to satisfy the portion of existence that is freed from doing" (Declaration 1938, 92). Indeed, Bataille's most severe indictment of modern life is not that it has robbed individuals of pleasure, but rather, of the very means to understand forbidden needs. The one-sided sublimation of energy into work and its complementary consumption of consumer goods occults the fundamental duality he expressed this way: "Being is, in fact, continually drawn in two directions; one leads to the creation of lasting organizations and conquering forces, the other leads, through the intermediary of expenditure of force and increasing excess, to destruction and death" (Declaration 1938, 339).

Bataille's duality is essential to the project of the College and its subsequent impact, precisely because it parallels the Durkheimian opposition of the sacred to the profane. In this equation, the sustaining energies invested into work fill the profane existence antithetical to the sacred festivities and sacrificial banquets in which the accumulated products are consumed. In one of his last lectures, Durkheim again tackled the issue of the sacred's specificity, concluding that it is "radically incompatible" (1975, 115) with the idea of work. In the present study, as well as earlier ones, I have reiterated the importance of this distinction as a way to appreciate the quality of the experience alternately described as effervescent, divine, sacred, or inner, traceable to both Durkheim and Mauss. It was then possible to argue that the examples of Bataille and the College placed them in the curious position of being historical precursors to the poststructuralist positions of Barthes, Foucault, and Derrida (Richman 1988, 79–96). In his turn, Habermas has also insisted on the continuity between the two historical moments, but in relation to what he calls the "incomplete project of modernity" initiated by the Enlightenment. In the nineteenth century, the revolt by the "aesthetic consciousness" against tradition consecrated in the writing of Baudelaire neutralizes the "morality of utility." Habermas sees an "antimodernism" (albeit couched in modernist attitudes) in the decentered subject and emancipation from the criterion of usefulness promoted by Bataille, Foucault, and Derrida. More accurately, they are reproached for taking a step *outside* the modern world since "They remove into the sphere of the far away and the archaic the spontaneous powers of imagination, of self-experience and of emotionality. To instrumental reason, they juxtapose in manichean fashion a principle only accessible through evocation, be it the will to power or sovereignty, Being or the dionysiac force of the poetical" (1981, 13).

Keeping Habermas's characterizations in mind, it is now possible to see why it is imperative to emphasize the College's transference from archaic examples to contemporary social dilemmas. Moreover, recourse to sacred sociology was intended as a counter to the reductionism of an exclusively "aesthetic consciousness," the legacy of the romantic revolt. Indeed, as Caillois lectured to his cohorts, the artist of the twentieth century must redefine his role in relation to society in order to overcome the outdated model of their predecessors in the nineteenth century. As a sign of the modern, the hero as outlaw led to a general denunciation of the family, state, nation, morality, religion, and sometimes even reason and science. But the effects of profaning the [right] sacred, was "illusory," enacted by verbal blasphemy and sarcasm against institutions the capitalist enterprise was already undermining. As Habermas describes it, the avant-garde exhausted itself in the renewed search for objects to defile: "This aesthetic consciousness continuously stages a dialectical play between secrecy and public scandal; it is addicted to a fascination of that horror which accompanies the act of profaning, and is yet always in flight from the trivial results of profanation" (1981, 5).

Against this polemical backdrop, arguably more relevant to the early moments of Dada and surrealism, Caillois's address to the College appears all the more urgent. At the close of the "terrible '30s," he warns that society manifests a "force" directed at breaking down "individual will" so that individuals must constitute themselves into a community of their own. The values uniting such a group, although emanating from a marginal position, must be presented as eventually viable for the "center": a migration from the "Satanic" to a "Luciferian" example (Declaration 1938, 36). Most important, the transformation is described as a move from profanation to *sacralization*.

The resacralization of cultural objects explored in the postwar writings of Bataille and Blanchot announces yet another chapter in the history of relations between French cultural theory and criticism. Whether one chooses to subsume this movement along with its precedents in the College under the label postmodern, is ultimately secondary to the need for a judicious appreciation of the formation of this complex group at an especially challenging moment in history. To those tempted to interpret the demise of the College shortly prior to the war's onset as a sign of weakness, it is relevant that the considerable disagreements and mutual criticisms among Bataille, Caillois, and Leiris did not cause them to disavow their initial adherence. Undoubtedly, the exploration of extreme states of being that flirted with volatile and potentially violent emotions was threatening and disturbing when fascism exerted a fascination for similar reasons. Whatever other pressures were brought to bear upon the group, the criticism by Leiris appears most plausible and relevant to this discussion. For him, the issue was not the attraction of the sacred *per se*, but the almost exclusive concentration by Bataille on its "left" side.[7] Durkheim himself conceded that he could not explain *why* society colors certain objects and representations sacred, only that it always does. Leiris, with the following definition, thus provides the most enduring statement of the goal of a sacred sociology: "If one of the most 'sacred' aims that man can set for himself is to acquire as exact and intense an understanding of himself as possible, it seems desirable that each one, scrutinizing his memories with the greatest possible honesty, examine whether he can discover there some sign permitting him to discern the *color* for him of the very notion of sacred" (Declaration 1938, 31).

[7] Communicated in a personal interview: Paris, 1983. See also Jean Jamin, "Quand le sacré devint gauche," *l'Ire des vents*, no. 3–4 (1981): 98–118.

Anthropology, Literary Theory, and the Traditions of Modernism

FRANCESCO LORIGGIO

THERE IS A PLACE in Richard Rorty's *Philosophy and the Mirror of Nature* that, although indirectly and inadvertently, seems to be setting itself up as a kind of epilogue to the century, an aftermath where finally the relevant tensions crisscross and the whole picture begins to emerge, becomes if not fully explicit at least much clearer. It occurs, very appropriately, toward the last pages of the book.

In the paragraph I am thinking of, Rorty is responding to Jurgen Habermas. He is targeting the claim that the functions knowledge has in universal contexts of practical life can be analyzed only in "the framework of a reformulated transcendental philosophy," and that such philosophy would assume "empirical status" as soon as its "cognitive interests" were deemed to be "the result of natural history" or were to be discussed "in terms of cultural anthropology" (1979, 381). Rorty counters by saying that "cultural anthropology (in a large sense which includes intellectual history) is all we need" (1979, 380). The rejoinder is the book's final push to clinch its long peroration in favor of an "edifying" philosophy. Philosophically, argues Rorty, the twentieth century splits into two separate and often conflicting lineages: it is the work of the epistemologists, those whose goals are knowledge and truth and who are under the constraint to anchor both to some immutable and believable essence, and of the "existentialists," those who are less worried about epistemological or metaphysical grounding than about thinking as such, and whose goal is education, self-formation, finding always new ways of describing human presence in the world. The former are the great "mainstream" philosophers; systematic and constructive, they "build for eternity." The latter are "*intentionally* peripheral" figures: reactive in attitude, they offer "satires, parodies, aphorisms" (Rorty 1979, 369), oppose to the treatise about the accuracy of representation

* I would like to thank two anonymous Princeton University Press readers for their comments on an earlier draft of this paper.

or about correspondence and reflection criteria about how to continue the "conversation of mankind" (1979, 389). The first camp houses the Platos, the Descarteses, the Kants, the Husserls, and the Russells of philosophy; the second the Nietzsches, the Heideggers, and the Deweys.

Most immediately striking about this exercise is, perhaps, the author's ability to do as he says. Rorty defends operations whereby to make "connections between our own culture and some exotic culture or exotic period, or between our own discipline and another discipline which seems to pursue incommensurable aims in an incommensurable vocabulary" (1979, 360), while he is himself weaving, before our very eyes, a complex and enticing network of such "connections." The chapter compares and contrasts the two basic traditions of edification and epistemology. But more than that, it institutes new alliances, points to new tangencies. Along with cultural anthropology, literary criticism and literature also now sit at the head table of the philosophical banquet, sharing full honors: in Rorty's eyes the poet is not unlike the anthropologist, the attempt to edify may well "consist in the 'poetic' activity of thinking up such new words, or new disciplines, followed by, so to speak, the inverse of hermeneutics: the attempt to reinterpret our familiar surroundings in the unfamiliar terms of our new inventions" (1979, 360). Nor is it just this: busy though he is with the sorting of traditions, the reorganizing of disciplines and discourse, Rorty does not forget geography. The view, the history he advocates reinstate the most homegrown brand of American philosophy—pragmatism—within the larger philosophical—and, once we accept Rorty's assumptions, cultural—panorama the current decades have been composing.

Confronted by such a dazzling bit of recapitulatory bricolage, which shows "how things hang together," to adopt a phrase of the Rorty from after *Philosophy and the Mirror of Nature* (1983, xiv), we can quite rightly, here, pop the questions that most readily and most inevitably come to mind. What effect do the affinities revealed, ventilated, or auspicated have on some of the disciplines that are to partake of the *Zeitgeist*? Rorty, it is evident, seeks to trim philosophy down to size, to reduce or abolish altogether the pedestal from which it has legitimized other practices or guaranteed the coherence of knowledge. Declaring it comparable to literature, having it rub elbows with the study of culture, furnishing it with less fastidious and supercilious aspirations does the job perfectly. Should the inverse also be contemplated? Does anthropology's and literature's closeness to philosophy do anything to either of the disciplines? Specifically, does Rorty's recontextualization change our opinion of philosophy's two invitees or, more significantly for us, of the contact postulated between the two of them? And pragmatism, where exactly does it fit? How does it connect with anthropology and literature?

Some of these questions could be answered by a quick glance at the current state of the two disciplines. Both literary criticism and anthropology have witnessed in the eighties, especially here in America, the emergence and rapid flowering of appeals that have favored more fluid, less epistemological, less "scientific" approaches to their material and that somehow pick up on or tie in with the Rortian position. Acknowledgments have perhaps been most overtly voiced in literature: the polemic sparked by the "anti-theory" articles published a few years ago in the journal *Critical Inquiry* has enlisted practically every major critic in North America, and it has been about the "consequences of pragmatism."[1] Even those otherwise occupied and preoccupied and who have not joined the contest have had their say, have not failed to situate themselves. Harold Bloom sums up some of his own concerns and a good portion of the American literary climate when he applauds Rorty for his perspicacity ("he sees that pragmatism and currently advanced literary criticism come to the same cultural enterprise") and then, in the same breath, goes on to out-Americanize him:

> I add only that Emerson, more than Carlyle or Nietzsche, is the largest precursor of this merger. Freud thought that his personal "science" could assert an ascendancy over not only philosophy and religion but literature also. Emerson, a shrewder prophet, could have told Freud that psychoanalysis was another form of the triumph of literary culture over science as well as over religion and philosophy. Usurpation is a high art in Freud, but Emerson formulated the dialectics of that art, and Nietzsche and William James took some crucial lessons from Emerson. (1982, 20)

In anthropology the wrangling is not so concentrated, cannot be easily attributed to any one precise source. Nonetheless, there have been very literal, undisguised exhortations to write histories of the discipline that would include its tangencies with other disciplines, rather than internal histories, histories totally from within.[2] These

[1] See Steven Knapp and Walter Benn Michaels, "Against Theory," *Critical Inquiry* 8 (Summer 1982): 732–42. Replies and comments have come, among others, from Stanley Fish, E. D. Hirsch, Frank Lentricchia, in, respectively, "Consequences," *Critical Inquiry* 11 (March 1985): 433–58, "Against Theory?" *Critical Inquiry* 9 (June 1983): 743–47, and *Criticism and Social Change* (Chicago: University of Chicago Press, 1983), and "The Return of William James," in *The Current in Criticism*, ed. C. Koelb and V. Lokke (West Lafayette: Purdue University Press, 1987), pp. 175–200.

[2] One of the more direct examples is Edward Bruner's "Anthropology and Human Studies," *Cultural Anthropology* 1, no. 1 (1986): 121–24.

pleas are very much in the spirit of that pan-disciplinarism embodied by *Philosophy and the Mirror of Nature*. And they have been delivered—again, in the eighties, especially in the United States—in conjunction, on the one hand, with the theoretical and institutional strengthening of an interpretative, hermeneutic anthropology and the sensibility that accompanies it (a more conscientious, scrupulous mulling over of discursive practices or the philosophies of discourse) and, on the other hand, with concerted efforts to reactualize American pragmatism. In Milton Singer's *Man's Glassy Essence*, a book on the merits of an eventual marriage between semiotics and anthropology, Peirce's "unlimited semiosis," his notion of interpretant (whereby signs are such for someone or something, ergo necessitating interpretation) is a pretext to reactivate some of the less familiar dialogistic components of the American philosopher's thought. The Peircean epigraph that Singer affixes to one of his chapters ("We must not begin by talking of pure ideas—vagabond thoughts that tramp on the public roads without any human habitation—but must begin with men and their conversation" [Singer 1983, 74]) could serve as motto to a lot of what has been happening across the disciplines. The essays of a well-known collection by Edward Bruner and Victor Turner, brought together to lay the groundwork for a possible "anthropology of experience," propose even more emblematic conjugations: while Dilthey and Dewey are the cardinal figures of the anthology's intellectual horizon, those authors who look for other inspiration or longer genealogies end up on the doorsteps of Thoreau's cabin with a fervor or an awe as unrestrained, it seems, as that of the literary critics for whom the *terminus a quo* of any endeavor benefiting from contact with pragmatism cannot but be Emerson's study (Turner & Bruner 1986, 1–30).

I want, however, to move beyond this. I want to suggest that the reassembling of the disciplines postulated by Rorty's reassessment of the tasks of philosophy is of importance for anthropology and literary studies. Not only because it forces us to consider these disciplines in a new light, so that their destiny appears inextricably tied to that of other fields, but because the rearrangement, the updating of their unfolding has repercussions on the premises upon which Rorty's reasoning rests. In other words, the "newness" of the new anthropology or new literary theory consists in the reciprocity that both can now afford or are granted by other disciplines.

A prime corollary of this has to do with the idea of tradition. In evaluating some of the specific proximities and affiliations Rorty speaks of, one is tempted to abide by his precepts strictly and literally. Take the enthusiastic reception of French philosophy and critical discourse on this continent, *the* event in recent American culture, and an event Rorty also celebrates. When accosting it from the perspective of anthropology or of that comparativism which is one of the habits *Philosophy and the Mirror of Nature* recommends *and* a subdivision of literary studies, one could stress its culturalness: it is also another phase—the latest instance—of a set of international or intercultural relations that Americans have, throughout their history, always cultivated. Giving in to temptation further, one might be led to observe that in spite of Rorty's sympathy for Derrida, Heidegger, Nietzsche, etcetera, the end product of the project he embarks on is, as it happens anytime dialogue with another culture is initiated, *inevitably* anthropological, that is, a deeper, more insightful apperception of one's own backdrop. By retracing the history of Western philosophy, Rorty rediscovers philosophical Americanhood. Thus, abandoning finally any and all resistance, one would have to wonder if the revitalizing of the notion of tradition has not been Rorty's real, ultimate aim. This would mean that his project is feedback-like. Pragmatism is resurrected thanks to a heightened awareness of the role of lineage, yet the promoting of this awareness was one of the major contributions of American pragmatism.

The parallels are blatant. Philosophy undergoes its spell of introspection during the very age when self-reflexivity is the order of the day in the social sciences or in literary studies. Anthropology, specifically, has in these same decades begun an epochal repatriation. It has used its experience in the field, outside native grounds, to learn to behave nativistically, to grapple with the (Western) milieu from which it arose, and has returned to the field with that added knowledge, that supplementary burden, to engage the "other" once again. In short, it has defined itself as practice, as the philosophy Rorty envisages is urged to do.

But recognizing that disciplinary reciprocity "produces" self-reflexivity or the recovery of tradition and, in America, of Americanness, enhances the value of an approach routed through anthropology or literature. For a host of discrepancies will then suddenly surface in Rorty's prospectus. The tribute to the conversationalist, edificational impulses of pragmatism has as counterpart the complete neglect of that other idiosyncratic aspect with which pragmatism had hitherto been associated: the glorification of action. Doing is for Peirce, James, and Dewey the dimension in which the remaining issues must converge, the concept on the basis of which to discriminate among philosophies or worldviews.

That the direct descendants of *this* pragmatism may be the philosopher writing about the theory of action or the social scientist à la

Talcott Parsons likewise working on the structure of social action, and thereby the type of company Rorty was trying to free himself from, is a minor complication, and should not bother us very much. It is the duty of the conversationalist to see how "things hang together" in the lineage, the discourses he chooses as models before anywhere else. All the more so since in America tendencies and trends overlap, run into each other. For Peirce the sense of a proposition could best be grasped by analyzing the conduct to which it gave rise.[3] William James's philosophical motto was "rationality, activity, faith" (Burke [1937], 5). The main drawback of Rorty's realignment of the discourses is its failure to deal with this collusion between meaning and action that pragmatism had described in varying but explicit fashion, and, subordinatively, to deal with the overlappings between pragmatism and nonedificational philosophy. In *Philosophy and the Mirror of Nature* a British philosopher, Michael Oakeshott, provides the authoritative quotations for the notion of conversation and its metaphoric congeners. Would the promptings emanating from Paul Grice's lectures on conversational implicatures or speech-act theory—Austin's and Searle's—not deserve some attention, regardless of whether they culminate in disputes about mind and intention? Could not the Searlian conflation of meaning and action be reattached to pragmatism, as the offshoot of that wing most susceptible to contamination by "normal" philosophy? The conversation / action dyad need not be coterminous with the conversation / epistemology dichotomy that *Philosophy and the Mirror of Nature* sees running through twentieth-century thought (and which is one dichotomy its author elsewhere is also able to trace within pragmatism).[4] Certainly some of the heroes of Rorty's book seem to link with both streams of the American philosophical tradition: Wittgenstein's vindication of "use" in language and the study of language bridges very conveniently past and future, Singer's Peirce and the collaborative synthesis of speech and action.

The cultural anthropology Rorty invokes underscores the play of conversation and act. Firstly, by embodying simultaneously the two

[3] One of Peirce's most explicit statements on this is contained in that paragraph of 1932, page 189, in which he explains how an author with "a logical mind" would explain what lithium is by describing what it takes to obtain it chemically. The paragraph ends: "The peculiarity of this definition—or rather this precept that is more serviceable than a definition—is that it tells you what the word lithium denotes by prescribing what you are to do in order to gain a perceptual acquaintance with the object of that word."

[4] Namely in "Pragmatism without Method," in *Sidney Hook: Philosopher of Democracy and Humanism*, ed. P. Kurtz (Buffalo, N.Y.: Prometheus, 1983), pp. 259 ff.

"souls" of the American tradition. The split within the anthropology of the eighties between different versions of pragmatism—which accentuate now the linguistic, dialogical temper of the movement or of single authors (Peirce, Dewey), now their performative, experiential slant, or which pick out now one member or precursor of pragmatism now the other (Thoreau looms large in *The Anthropology of Experience* but is ignored in conversationalist works)—reflects an inherent *disponibilité*, a virtuality dependent on the optic and good will of the interpreter. Conversationalists readily buttress their case with allusions to the "linguistic turn" of the social sciences and philosophy. The experience their adversaries minister to in their theories comprises nonlinguistic moments, and denies the primacy of language. Whereas the ones—conversationalists—will doubt projects that place too much store in the subject and subjectivity, the others—experientialists—end, like speech-act theorists, in the mind (Turner's career, his encounter with neurology just before his death, is exemplary here).[5]

Secondly, anthropology exposes the duality diachronically, with the vicissitudes of its history. During the past decade, in the wake of the "return" of ethnography and the attendant anxieties about anthropology's own textuality, dialogistic-oriented models, inspired primarily by Bakhtin, Gadamer, pragmatism, or a combination of all three, have been highly successful, and perhaps can now be said to prevail in the discipline, even if updated variants of the opposite pole have also survived and, often, thrived. Not so twenty or thirty or forty years ago, when action or action-based conceptions had the larger share of the limelight, even if some kind of dialogical vein often visibly pervaded them.

Of course, the reciprocities and the repercussions I have been alluding to up the ante of the game. If both conversation and action are within pragmatism or the cultural anthropology (and, as we shall see, the literary studies) with which we group it, then we cannot single out any of the disciplines or any of the traditions that endorse or decree disciplinary cohabitation to defend against any other tradition. Once that simultaneity is admitted, the difficulty is no longer how to push back epistemology—the great Western tradition—in the name of local traditions, or of their dialogue. Pragmatism, cultural anthropology, literary studies are themselves at least double. To select, to register preference, is to have already decided that conversation and action are mutually exclusive and to disregard the alternative, to refuse to conceive the possibility that they may be

[5] See "Body, Brain, and Culture," *Zygon* 18, no. 3 (September 1983): 221–45.

compatible, that their synchronous presence is not just a sign of strife, of internal incoherence, but of largesse of spirit, a capaciousness itself to be named and explored. It is to accept the accentuations and omissions history rotates from one period to the next without stopping to inquire about the elements which compose that agonism, about the cumulative effects of their contiguity.

These solicitations constitute, I believe, the frontiers of the contemporary ethos. At this stage, they are as far as one can go. They can neither be avoided nor fully resolved. One can only reiterate them, bear witness to them, or look into their past, subject them to archeological scrutiny. The sections below will be a mixture—part reiteration, part reconstruction. What I plan to do is to examine further anthropology's version of the dichotomy, and particularly those swerves originating in the space between it (the discipline) and literary studies.

The most interesting peculiarities of this reformulation (most interesting to us, at any rate) can be quickly summarized. The anthropologist socializes the two poles of pragmatist thought. Unlike philosophers, he has empirical behavior as his domain; unlike sociologists, he isolates for analysis the behavior commensurate to that of individuals from other societies he has observed or on which he has sufficient data to consult. More precisely, anthropology handles the two models of conversation and action in such a manner that they transmute or can be transmuted into subunits of the much wider category of performance and, finally, of that other very specific but equally capacious genre which is theater.

On the mechanics of this metamorphosis I will have to return. But, to start, as we must, here, with last items first, it might be noted that the "literaturization" of conversation and action that anthropology carries out is neither fortuitous nor capricious. It takes place at a juncture of history when literature has become a compulsory field of study. In *From Ritual to Theatre*, in *The Anthropology of Experience* and the many articles yet uncollected that he wrote in the last years of his life, Turner expatiated at length about the "cross-looping" of social history with the numerous genres of cultural performance, the dialectic whereby the form of social drama is "implicit in aesthetic dramas . . . while the *rhetoric* of social dramas—and hence the shape of argument—is drawn from cultural performances."[6] Just as anthro-

[6] Victor Turner, *From Ritual to Theatre* (New York: Performing Arts Journal Publications, 1982), p. 90. But see also " 'Carnaval' in Rio," in *The Celebration of Society*, ed. Frank Manning (Bowling Green: Bowling Green University Popular Press, 1983), pp. 104–5.

pology as a whole cannot ignore the babelic confusions it encounters abroad and at home, or the many textual "expressions" that record and fix experience but also affect experience's content or form, the study of ceremonies, of ritualistic manifestations, and of social dramas cannot overlook theater. Now that the signs of the West are no less ubiquitous in that distant "elsewhere" that used to be the uncluttered territory of anthropology than the signs of the "elsewhere" in the West (asked about local customs the shaman comes back quoting the latest anthropological monograph on his tribe; Rome and Paris are fast approaching the degree of racial and cultural plurality once typical only of New York or London), defining one's activity as a practice, as a reflexive social science presupposes some basic preliminary compromises. One must be sufficiently in touch with history to willingly concede that one's discipline is also the discipline of the function of texts, that one's business must necessarily also be the analysis of how "written" or otherwise textualized discourses (including anthropology's) interfere or interface with social discourses. Whatever the teleology, the final intellectual destination—pure social science, social science open to dialogue with other disciplines, social science of committed or uncommited politics—the starting line is here, and it cannot be bypassed.[7]

It is these changes, together with or apart from the persuasiveness of literary studies, that have strengthened the prestige of the literary and of literariness within the profession. Commentaries of anthro-

[7] I have kept politics at the edge of my paper not because it is irrelevant to what I am saying but to avoid enlarging further an already lengthy argument and because the problem of how anthropology is or should be political is addressed—excellently—by other contributors to this volume, namely Robert Sullivan and Marc Manganaro. However, the general aspects of the question certainly can be—and recently have been—debated against the specific background I have sketched out. In his *Criticism and Social Change*, Frank Lentricchia accuses Rorty of having desocialized conversation, of having forgotten about the sociocultural rooting of those who engage in it. At the same time he relinquishes the foundational, ontological privileges usually attributed to his Marxist perspective. Marxism is "a rhetoric whose value may be measured by its persuasive means and by its ultimate goal" (1983, 12). Might one not add that if that rhetoric is "revealed to us *textually* . . . and must be grasped (read) and attacked (reread, rewritten) in that dimension" (1983, 24), it is also generic, that is, exposed to the influences not only of texts but of the types of texts a period writes and thinks itself in? And could one not suggest that the choice of genre is always, whatever the perspective, political, and that a reflexive, critical politics of anthropology, or of anything, must also learn to take into account its rhetorical, generic propensities? These questions, I realize, have been already broached and answered by such authors as Hayden White. I would merely point out that White's *Metahistory* (Baltimore: Johns Hopkins Press, 1973) and *Tropics of Discourse* (Baltimore Johns Hopkins Press, 1979), so clearly under the patronage of Kenneth Burke, fall, like Lentricchia's works, within the purview of the lineage being traced here.

pologists about anthropologists today display the same support apparatus once monopolized by literary theorists: the names of Gadamer, Bakhtin, or Derrida are as prominent in the indexes of books currently being written by anthropologists as they are in those of critics of poetry or of fiction. Above all, anthropological works read like literary criticism or, often, literature. And such developments cannot be dismissed by simply ascribing them to the glitter of the bandwagon, to the usual reversal of fortune whereby elegance, richness of vocabulary, or syntax have suddenly become an asset, rather than the impediment or, when remarked, the very perverse kind of compliment they once were in the social sciences. An awareness of form, of the form open to the individual venture or to anthropology in general, is now a basic requisite for anthropological writer and anthropological reader alike: Dan Sperber's stylistic analysis of the passages in which Evans-Pritchard reported, rendered in English prose, his informants' speech (Sperber 1985, 14–16), Stephen Tyler's (1987) recourse to rhetoric as an analytical device in his critical reconnaissance of the foundations of postmodernist anthropological and literary theory are not uncommon, and they are at one with Clifford Geertz's essays (1988) on the anthropologist as author or, more radically still, with anthologies of the creative writings of members of the profession and efforts to theorize an anthropology directly poetic and literary (Prattis, 1985).

But bringing literature fully into the picture that Rorty delineates in his book adds a number of caveats to the perspective on anthropology. The present state of the relations between the two disciplines should not obscure the fact that some affinities have always been there. The writing of earlier anthropologists, even those reputed to be great stylists (a Frazer, for example), does not quite address the basic hazards of the trade, the problems of discourse and discursivity that arise from and impinge on the anthropologist's activities. In this, preceding decades must be separated from the seventies and the eighties. At the same time the distinction reminds us that the seventies and the eighties are the last cogs of a longer history, a history in which the position of the two fields vis-à-vis each other vary: initially the impact of anthropology on literature was broader and more incisive than the impact of literature on anthropology.

Geographically, too, adjustments are in order. When we think concretely about the disciplinary pluralism Rorty would have predominate, and go back to the actual context in which philosophers such as Dewey lived, we discern undergirding and as yet unpublicized continuities. Histories of anthropology will sooner or later have to pay more attention than they have to the hook-ups between the culture-and-personality strivings of the American anthropology of the twenties and thirties and the psychosocial theories of the self of pragmatist sociologists, George Herbert Mead in particular. Literature breaks this unity in one respect and confirms it in another. It is safe enough to say that the anthropology the American writers and critics who were contemporaries of Dewey looked up to was penned not by Boas or Sapir or Ruth Benedict but, essentially, by Frazer and the Cambridge School. With the Eliots, the Pounds, the American interdisciplinary mixture is actually an Anglo-American one.

To a tradition that was to turn action into one of its specialties, which when the thirties came along was ready to develop a philosophy, besides a sociology, of action, Frazerian anthropology contributes an invaluable preliminary twist. The stories of younger kings vying with older ones, the descriptions of seasonal festivals insinuate into the interdisciplinary potlatch more than the study of ceremonies, of acts that are at once socialized and archaic in nature: being institutionalized, repetitive, rituals offer to observation a stretch of behavior that is cut off, segmented from the flow of experience.

It would be possible just from such a scant preamble—even, that is, if one had not read F. M. Cornford on Olympic sports or Jane Harrison on religious festivals or Gilbert Murray on tragedy and if one did not know that Frazer was trained as a philologist and a classicist—to jump to the later Turner, and his writings on social dramas and the mutual interferences between ritual and theatre. Not sufficiently self-conscious, by our standards, to ponder critically their participation in the anthropological enterprise (books are unintrusive interlocutors: the troublesome issues they instigate can be neatly deferred to the textual no-man's-land of the footnotes), Cambridge classicists nevertheless build into anthropology a literary component. By tracing theater back to ritual, to liturgical origins, they established the reversibility that later scholars, who acquired the ethnographical expertise chamber anthropologists lacked, were to investigate with greater aplomb. Frazer and his colleagues unwittingly discovered one of the Copernican laws of the social sciences. Ritual is theatrical in as much as it is transmissible action, action with a beginning and an end, hence action whose quiddities can be treated as a set, can be textualized.

The linearity of the intellectual moves that end in Turner and reflexive ethnography can perhaps be better appreciated if to them we juxtapose the history of sociology. In spite of their very visibly vested interest in theatricality (their vocabulary is replete with references to "actions" and "actors"), sociologists could not explicitly theorize the metaphors intrinsic to their discipline until they were able to devise the notion of frame. Contrary to their confrères in anthropology, who found a good portion of their material ready-made, already well-delimited by society, they were obliged to isolate analytically the routinized, magmatic behavior that was their object of study. Only then, notably with Erving Goffman, did they directly face up to the convergences lurking in the core of their discipline ("roles," "actors," "agents" are the daily grist of sociology). Once that process is initiated, the differences with anthropology are of degree and emphasis more than of substance. Turner first realized that the hermeneutic position of the stage actor is similar to that of the anthropologist and that, therefore, properly executed enactments of non-Western rituals by Western personnel (or "ethnodramatics" as he calls them) can have cognitive value when he helped produce some of Roy Schechner's workshops in experimental theater. He manifested a marked preference for avant-garde plays, for a drama which has by definition license to manipulate, which requires to a heightened degree the kind of interpretative attitudes and aptitudes, or—when the material adapted is foreign or archaic—the procedures, the kind of intellectual and structural translation that lead to a better understanding of other cultures (Turner 1982, 89–101). The long and enlightening chapter on theater and its relevance for the study of social representations contained in Goffman's *Frame Analysis*, the apex of interactionist sociology, is instead about theatrical conventions in their most general aspect (1974, 124–55).

I dwell on this neither to let shine the shared agendas that can be extracted from an appropriate collation of the social sciences of the Anglo-American tradition, nor to stress the differences of the individual disciplines. My point is that major credit for disclosing how decisive, as a topic, the role of texts is for the social sciences or, further, for the idea that the discourse of a whole area of the social sciences may very well depend on their approach and conception of literary genres, should also go to literary criticism. Logically and historically, between Frazer and the anthropology (or the sociology) of the seventies and the eighties, between anthropological criticism and literary anthropology there are the reflexive literati. They inherit or borrow the concepts of ritual and action but hand them back to anthropology or sociology or philosophy in wrapping typically their own.

On this score, as on many others, the epitomizing itinerary is that of Kenneth Burke. Before Turner or Goffman, the author of *Attitudes Towards History, The Philosophy of Literary Form, The Grammar of Motives, Language and Symbolic Action*, and other books he wrote in the thirties, forties, and fifties, touched all the bases in Rorty's disciplinary roster. Of the great patrons of edification, Nietzsche was a significant influence (by Burke's admission, the "perspective by incongruity," one of his trademark tactics, is a variation on a theme by the German philosopher) ([1935], 87–88), as was Dewey. Pragmatism was never far from his mind: together with Dewey, Peirce, William James, and Emerson appear in his essays. Frequent, too, is the mention of George Herbert Mead and Thornstein Veblen. To the classics of American literature (Hawthorne, Melville, Whitman) and to a respectable array of his contemporaries (Hemingway, William Carlos Williams, Djuna Barnes, T. S. Eliot, Marianne Moore, Theodore Roethke) he devoted articles or, again, memorable summarizing asides. As regards cultural anthropology, Burke cites Boas, Sapir, Hymes, and Malinowski's essay on language, and he was obviously familiar with Frazer and the Cambridge School. We know that Burke's work abounds with pages on magic, science, religion, and ritual, which often take their cue from and enlarge upon *The Golden Bough*, that he reviewed Lord Raglan's *The Hero* and alludes to Jane Harrison's *Prolegomena to a Study of Greek Religion* and Gilbert Murray's prefaces to Aeschylus's plays, that he considered George Thompson's *Aeschylus and Athens*, written by a scholar who was not an anthropologist but who availed himself of Cambridge School research, a crucial, "unduly neglected" text.[8]

For Burke, ritual and theater graft on each other symbiotically. In "The Philosophy of Literary Form," the long essay that opens the work by the same name and that was published in the early forties, ritual furnishes the "calculus" by which to retranscribe some of the qualities of the text ([1941], 90). The first step in Burkean methodology consists in sifting through the language and isolating clusters of images, or in identifying the ingredients of a work, the "what goes with what" ([1941], 20). Next we should watch for the "alignment" ([1941], 58) of the items, the "what vs. what" ([1941], 58) and their sequential unraveling, the "from what through what to what" ([1941], 32). In literary criticism, one concentrates either on the "opposition" or the "composition" ([1941], 61). It is a choice that decades later structuralism was to codify for us in more neutral parlance. With Burke, the oppositions are "agons" or "agonistic trials" ([1941], 70). But the analogical nomenclature is not gratuitous. The formal, in-text "equations" ([1941], 63) are historically marked. To guide our

[8] The references to Harrison, Murray, and Thompson are in the Appendix to *Attitudes Towards History* 1937, 365, and in "On Catharsis, On Resolution," *The Kenyon Review* 21, no. 3 (Summer 1959), 343 and 348 respectively. The review of Lord Raglan's work is now in *The Philosophy of Literary Form*, 2d. ed. (New York: Vintage, 1961), pp. 317–18.

observations about the text we need to also account for "the functions the structure serves" ([1941], 86). This calls for an investigation of purposes, of the work's symbolic acts. So we automatically turn to ritual, which, thus, becomes a kind of "Ur-form, the 'hub,' with all other aspects of human action treated as spokes radiating from [it]" ([1941], 87).

Later, the role of model for the analysis of structure is taken over by theater itself. The theories of the more mature Burke, in embracing the whole spectrum of symbolic actions, and not just literature, have their analytical core in dramatism or, more correctly, in the pentad of scene, act, agent, agency, purpose, and the grid of ratios and permutations it permits. As might be expected, the justifying texts are those that initiate the Western tradition in literary criticism. Like Turner, for whom the structure of social dramas corresponds closely to "Aristotle's description of tragedy" (1982, 72), Burke bolsters this part of his work by putting it under the tutelage of the *Poetics* and vicinity (the *Nichomachean Ethics* are also highly praised by him). And like Turner after him, he never disavows the literariness of his ascendancies. When René Wellek chastises him for having concocted a philosophical catchall net, a theory that cannot be of any great incidence on individual fields, on literary criticism, Burke refutes his contention by neatly turning the accusations upside down. Dramatism's extension "beyond criticism," its function as "a logological perspective designed to track down the implications of drama . . . for the study of the humanistic study of man," can hardly be held to diminish its usefulness in literature, if literature is the realm of expression that "served as its model" (1972, 10). In Burke's theory the metaphor that declares the world to be a stage writ large is taken seriously. There are no actions devoid of some degree of theatricality. History can be conceived in the shape of a traditional five-act play, complete with climax and dénouement ([1937], 111–75). Criticism can seesaw between equally theatrical hypotheses: in that period of his life in which stoic resignation was his ideal—the thirties—Burke believed that "whatever literature [was] criticism had better be comic" ([1937], 107); in his more mature years—the fifties and sixties—satire and tragedy were, for him, the touchstone genres of the profession.

As dramatism solidifies into a theory, Burke tends more and more to associate ritual with the ethical and to retain it to throw light on the function, rather than just the structure, of a text. Ritual is the nether side of theater, that which can be explained by the grammar of theater (by the dramatistic pentad) but also that which explains some of the secret whys and wherefores of (literary) theater. A verbal construct, *Attitudes Towards History* tells us in a chapter on the "General Nature of Ritual," is a strategy for seizing a situation. It entails some awareness and positioning with respect to the symbols of authority around which gravitate the public, "forensic" means of communication (and art must communicate to exist, according to Burke). When rejection is uppermost, a counterauthority, with the related tensions and processes, will be erected. Should acceptance be dominant, the writer will "cancel the misfit between himself and the frame by tragic ambiguity" ([1937], 209). He will both "[articulate] his criminality and [exorcise] it through symbolic punishment" ([1937], 209). In either case, some change of identity will have occurred, which is an eminently ritualistic outcome.

Thus, the writer's very humanity, his gist as a symbol-using animal, as the inventor of the negative, will demand of him some sort of ritual stance, will push him into patterns of victimage or purification. Burke expresses it as follows:

> The dramatistic perspective . . . rounds out the pattern in accordance with the notion that insofar as a given order involves sacrifices of some sort, the sacrificial principle is intrinsic to the nature of order. Hence, since substitution is a prime resource available to symbol systems, the sacrificial principle comes to ultimate fulfillment in vicarious sacrifice, which is variously rationalized, and can be viewed accordingly as a way to some kind of ultimate rewards.
>
> By tracing and analyzing such terms, a dramatistic analysis shows how the negativistic principle of guilt implicit in the nature of order combines with the principles of thoroughness (or perfection) and substitution that are characteristic of symbol systems in such a way that the sacrificial principle of victimage (the "scapegoat") is intrinsic to human congregation. The intricate line of exposition might be summed up thus: If order, then guilt; if guilt, then need for redemption; but any such payment is victimage. Or: If action, then drama; if drama, then conflict; if conflict, then victimage. (1968, 450)

In the world depicted by dramatism and its offspring, logology, hierarchy cannot be annulled, and as long as it is not, some fundamental portion of the writer's (and the critic's) fate will be somehow correlated to the goat song and the rhythms it inaugurates. Human language is the instrument of purification but it also taints. Not by chance, Burke in his later works will encourage the comparison of his theory of language and literature to Christian liturgy that one will automatically indulge in by insisting that these parallels actually can and must be hypothesized if we are to comprehend how symbols operate. Dramatism and logology prove, with a logic that would be excitingly relevant for contemporary criticism but that criticism has yet failed to exploit, that any reflection on language must need shade off into theology and that such contaminations are part and parcel of history. What solders words about words, the study of language, to words about the Word, theology, is nothing other than the matters (which Burke duly recounts in *The Rhetoric of Religion*) pertaining to identification or purgation and catharsis ([1961], 7–42).

By its sheer magnitude dramatism, then, refracted back onto the present, puts the entire Anglo-American tradition under the aegis of one genre. Or, to state it more diplomatically, when Burke is the filter of approach the disciplines of Rorty's mosaic reveal themselves to be genre-specific discourses. Suddenly the penchant of such writers as Henry James, E. A. Robinson, Edgar Lee Masters, T. S. Eliot, Ezra Pound, and the William Carlos Williams of *In The American Grain* for the dramatic monologue, and the revival of Elizabethan dramaturgy during the twenties and thirties, or, in criticism, the emergence of such works as R. P. Blackmur's *Language as Gesture*, or as Francis Fergusson's *An Idea of Theatre* and *The Human Image in Dramatic Literature*, all apparently marginal phenomena, can be seen in concurrence with the anthropology or the sociology or the semiotics or the philosophy of the century. And the contiguity holds for the cleavages that traverse each of the disciplines and that seem to govern their internal affairs or the rhythm of their history. Theater, after all, is not just action. It is a performance, and therefore includes the character's words: lexis or diction, to return to the terminology of the *Poetics*, is as much a feature as mythos. If certain writers opt for the monologue and some critics for the plot (Fergusson interprets Dante's *Purgatorio*, a verse epic, through typically Aristotelian and Burkean notions of praxis),[9] and both will remind us of drama, so will conversationalist and action-oriented proposals in the social sciences and philosophy: they send us back to the same implied generic model, of which they also seem to accentuate different aspects.

The very persistence of the duality in the various single disciplines or, often, in the work of individual theorists, favors this analogy. With the exception of perhaps Rorty, all the major figures I have mentioned reiterate in theatrical or paratheatrical coin the pushes and pulls of their tradition. Turner's anthropology has alerted us to

[9] Francis Fergusson deserves special mention among the figures attracted by Burke's work. The author of a valuable commentary on Aristotle's *Poetics*, besides many books of criticism, he overtly tried to use theater as a model for the study of literature. One of his more enticing proposals links the notion of symbolic action to Dante's notion of *moto spiritale*, spiritual motion. See his *Dante's Drama of the Mind* (Princeton: Princeton University Press, 1953), pp. 55–58.

the performanceness of life, to the mixture of language and nonlinguistic experience, but ethnodramatics, in so far as it employs simulated enactments to understand alien cultures, approximates the dialogical relation with the other that has been the cornerstone of hermeneutic theory: it is a dramatization of communication. Goffman's obsession with theatricality took him from the analysis of face-to-face encounters or modes of self-presentation to, in his last works, the analysis of talk.[10] In fact, American social sciences and philosophy have rehearsed views that support both the coexistence and the inversion of the two domains: speech becomes action with speech-act theories and action a form of dialogue in interactionist sociology and psychology.

Burke himself always gives priority to action but without ever negating interaction and interlocution: he knows, like the pragmatists he so much admired, that they are inherent to sign systems and that without them sign systems would make little sense. Language is symbolic behavior because it is persuasive speech, a hortatory "no!" addressed to a listener or a reader. The topic of rhetoric manages to intrude in all of Burke's books, often signaled in the title, as in *The Rhetoric of Motives* or *The Rhetoric of Religion*. The two elements of the dialogic and of the theatrical meet in his definition of literature as "chart, dream and prayer" ([1941], 6) and his portrayal, too vivid perhaps for those accustomed to current critical mores, of the "unending conversation" that for him is criticism (in *The Philosophy of Literary Form* the critic is a person who enters a "parlor," comes upon a heated discussion, catches "the tenor of the argument," "put[s] in [his] oar," elicits answers in defense of or against his opinions, and leaves the discussion "still vigorously in progress" when, the hour being late, he departs) ([1941], 94–95).

It may be objected that, whether or not we maintain some of the tensions, to reformulate the conversation-action duality in this manner, to subsume it under genre, or one particular genre, is to impoverish it. For ethnographers experimenting with form, as well as for many literary critics, the operative notions seem to be those of language or text and textuality, not that of genre, and when the notion of genre is resuscitated, the model is not theater but the novel. Moreover, the proddings to listen to derive not from American criticism but from Bakhtin, the thinker who, in relocating the novel within the genres, has posited a "novelization" of literature, and has introduced

[10] The shift away from the study of self-presentation and face-to-face encounters to the study of dialogue begins, in Goffman, with *Frame Analysis* (which contains a chapter entitled "The Frame Analysis of Talk"), but the work devoted entirely to it is *Forms of Talk* (Philadelphia: University of Pennsylvania Press, 1981).

within literary studies a concept of dialogism that stands for much more than simple theatrical dialogue. On Bakhtinian grounds, the processes typifying this genre lie beyond grammatical, syntactical, or narrative structure (and hence the ken of narratology or the usual stylistic analysis). As the repository of polyglossia, the Bakhtinian novel attests to the plethoric linguistic plurality of everyday life: the societies that foreshadow its advent—Roman Hellenism, the Renaissance—are multi-languaged conglomerates, societies in which languages "interanimate" each other, cross over national or political borders and therefore repudiate or subject to constant tension any homogenizing centralizing forces. As the repository of heteroglossia, the novel resonates with worldviews, those of authorial narration or of any authorial surrogate as well as those voiced by characters. What is "dialogized" are the ideologies sedimented into the text, which respond to each other or to the ideologies in other works. A hodgepodge of discourses, of dialects, and jargons, the novel is thus open-ended. Capable of incorporating any new extraliterary genre and any ideology that the exercise of speech renders available, it achieves "maximal contact with the present (with contemporary reality)" (Bakhtin 1981, 11), and remains oblivious to the great national past—the avatar of closure, of centralization, and of literary monoglot, monologic officiality.

To the extent that it is, with the epic, the literary custodian of this past and of its valences, drama is, in Bakhtin's dialogistic essays, one of the great structural and historical enemies of the novel. In appropriating Anglo-American conversation and action for theater, are we not mistaking intercultural and intergeneric for intracultural and intrageneric relations? Are we not smoothing out and attenuating a bona fide, clear-cut dichotomy, are we not *interpreting* it into something with less bite, less suggestiveness?

Yes and no. It is true that anthropology has also, recently, promoted and defended the "blurring of genres."[11] And one must also grant that Bakhtinian dialogism has reverberations not contemplated by the Anglo-American literary and anthropological theatrical strain. For all his ruminating on words and the verbal, Burke never engages the pluralism, the babelic character of everyday communication: we speak the negative but we do so in different languages, be they of national or societal range. The superordinate, inherent interlocutor in his works is always postulated, faceless, always the group, as if dramatism were a purified Aeschylean type of theatricality, which

[11] The phrase is Clifford Geertz's. See his "The Blurring of Genres," *American Scholar* 49 (Spring 1980): 165–79.

had room only for the protagonist and the chorus, not for any third party. In Turner, too, the communitas so often congenital to the pilgrimages or the rituals he tells about is centered on "I-We," rather than on "I-Thou," solidarities. The Other is never an individualized Other—an other consciousness. It is a class, a series of Others. In spite of Burke's image of criticism as conversation, the American tradition only very recently managed to grasp the possibilities held out by Peirce's unlimited semiosis (which, with its continuous deferral of meaning on to always succeeding, successive interpretants, is the notion closest to dialogism). The escape valve, the *point de fuite* that the necessary, continuous alterity of interpretation installs into the text are never balanced against structure.

But reservations such as these perpetrate perhaps even graver simplifications. By preemptively dissolving all borders, a vocabulary resting too causally on the theoretical priority of language, textuality, or *écriture* trivializes any reference to history. Like oxygen or gravity, the textual or the verbal would be everywhere, abolishing difference, except on a very large scale, between large chunks of time or equally massive epistemic and epistemological features. This is an issue on which Bakhtin, instead of conflicting with Burke or Turner, actually reinforces and radicalizes their position. In his writings, language and textuality manifest themselves as speech and utterance. And, because they are infused with and pervade history, they congregate into "kinds," into more or less stable forms. They are "the short rejoinders of daily dialogue . . . everyday narration, writing, the brief standard military command, the elaborate and detailed order, the fairly variegated repertoire of business documents . . . the diverse world of commentary . . . scientific statements and all literary genres (from the proverb to the multivolume novel)," etc. (Bakhtin 1986, 60–61). The analysis of the relation of the various disciplines to literature is one route by which to resocialize and repoliticize the discourse of these disciplines. The literariness of anthropology, of sociology, of philosophy rebounds back on to them all the discussion about oral genres or about literature's presence in culture and society.

As for the choice of genres, the failure of the Anglo-American literary critics or anthropologists of the modernist period to take cognizance of and to heed Peirce's injunctions, the loose spots in their idea of dialogue do no great damage to the attempt to reformulate the action-conversation polarities in dramaturgical terms. There are within the criticism, which has fastened dialogism too rigidly to the novel, frictions that are difficult to leave alone. To talk about the novel Bakhtin must fall back on a glossary whose referent is theater or the theatrical. He does draw lines between the normal literary varieties of dialogue (the most conspicuous occurrences are the pages in which he defines the version he approves of "internal dialogue" and dramatic dialogue "external dialogue") (1981, 279–85). In describing carnival, laughter, parody, or the grotesque—perennial concomitants of the dialogism the novel condenses best—he does skim over all that involves spectacle.[12] But Bakhtin's epistemology is recapitulated by the remark in which he states that he "hears *voices* in everything" (1986, 169), and his bottom line analogue for the novel and novelized literature remains the conversation between two individuals, which, incongruous as it may be with drama, is an incipient performance. If Burke's dramatism is a theater of action, hence a theater that must find proper ubication for the act (gestural or speech-act), a theater that assigns setting a function, Bakhtin's dialogism is a theater of disembodied words, a phantom theater in which there are only words and silences, a theater played with the lights out. The proximity to the genre nevertheless is not lost upon him and his disciples. On some occasions, it leaves him or the members of his circle open to the slip of the tongue, as when he proclaims the writer "a dramatist (in the sense that he distributes words to the other voices)" (1986, 110), or when Vološinov calls the word "the scenario of an event" (1976a, 106). And the theoretical ambivalence is compounded by many historical oscillations: drama is, with the epic, relegated to the pre-Gutenbergian era, is the literary purveyor of the national past and of centralization, yet Socratic dialogues and comedy are among the forerunners of the novel.[13]

[12] Particularly in *Rabelais and his World*, trans. H. Iwolsky (Cambridge, Mass.: MIT Press, 1968), p. 7.

[13] Curiously, some of the commentators who have equated dialogism most closely with the novel are among those who have remarked the theatrical qualities most lucidly. Here is how, in an early and very influential essay, Julia Kristeva summarizes the whole affair: "The scene of the carnival, where there is no stage, no 'theater' is thus both stage and life, game and dream, discourse and spectacle. . . . [L]anguage escapes linearity (law) to live as drama in three dimensions. At a deeper level, this also signifies the contrary: drama becomes located in language. A major principle thus emerges: all poetic discourse is dramatization, dramatic permutation (in a mathematical sense) of words. Within carnivalesque discourse, we can already adumbrate that 'as to mental condition, it is like the meanderings of drama' (Mallarmé). This scene, whose sympton is carnivalesque discourse, is the only dimension where 'theatre might be the reading of a book,' its writing in operation." ("Word, Dialogue, Roman," now in *Desire in Language*, trans. L. S. Rondiez [New York: Columbia University Press, 1980], p. 79). Here is another illustration, from Katherina Clark and Michael Holquist, *Mikhail Bakhtin* (Cambridge, Mass.: Harvard University Press, 1984), p. 205: "The scenario of any utterance must contain the same three dramatis personae: the speaker, the listener, and the topic. All utterances live and die in the interaction between these participants. In order to emphasize the dramaturgical aspects of these forces, Bakhtin

An anthropology focusing on the diffusion of literary "expressions," on the "literaturization" of the social sciences (and which is, hence, an anthropology of anthropology, an anthropology observing anthropology as it is at that phase of its history when it must concern itself with the presence of texts within the world at large and within itself and its theories), cannot ignore the new debate on the role of genres that dialogism has triggered. No less crucially, anthropology must be careful to weigh these tensions without losing sight of its trump card—the concept of tradition. In Anglo-Americana, the shifts in stress from one figure or one period to the next are deeply rooted in the culture of the place. Turner and Burke appear today to be distillations of the ethos they illuminate and extend so well. The Bakhtin ethnographers or the literary theorists of the eighties champion is, by contrast, divested of all such allegiances. The tensions in his works, the contradictions he visits on his own tradition or the contradictions of his tradition—literary or interdisciplinary—that he personifies have hardly ever had any bearing on the American sympathizers. Since the Soviet cultural milieu is, like the Anglo-American, a milieu in which anthropology and literary theory conspire rather publicly, since comparison is the supreme test of any belief, let us, as they say, contextualize, let us review briefly some of these tensions.

Anyone acquainted with the history of twentieth-century social sciences and literary theory will not be surprised by the fascination of Russian criticism with anthropological disciplines, but the duration and the depth of the commitment catches the eye right away. In the Soviet Union there is contact with astounding regularity, before and after the Revolution. A. N. Veselovsky, the fountainhead of Russian narratology (to him we owe one of the earliest attempts to segment plots in simpler units), straddled philology and folklore. A folklorist by training was Vladimir Propp, whose celebrated study of tales of magic anticipated a large slice of the structuralist research on narration. Obviously steeped in anthropological lore are Bakhtin's notions of the carnivalesque and of dialogism, the first derived from the observation of and reflection upon a folkloric custom (and buttressed with bibliographical references to the specialists of the times, including Frazer and F. M. Cornford), the second amplifying to philosophical proportions an ethnography of speaking. In recent years the Tartu School, which lists mythographers and, again, folklorists among its members, has distinguished itself within semiotics for its

anthropomorphizes the topic, since it is the one element that might otherwise appear to be a nonhuman factor. He calls it the 'hero' of the playlet which unfolds in any utterance" (1980, 205).

single-minded study of culture and cultural typologies (one of its premier exponents, Jurij Lotman, closes the introduction to his latest book with what must be the most direct pronouncement about the anthropological vocation of his discipline and of Russian social sciences: "After having assimilated linguistics, semiotics turns to culturology" [1985, 51]).

Unusually transparent is also the impact of the participation of folklore. The anthropology the Soviet literary theorist adheres to has a local tinge to it. Arduous though it may be, in an age of rampant Westernization, to discriminate between the political and psychocultural position that the Siberian provinces hold in relation to the Muscovite center and the position the Orient or the Pacific islands or Africa have held for Londoners or Parisians, it is still customary to attribute to folklore a specific sphere of action. Technically, the folklorist has no knowledge of colonialism; he accedes to the "primitive," to the archaic in its "weak" intranational, intracultural manifestation. The exoticism he succumbs to comes from places of social as much as geographical distance, from levels of culture rather than from other cultures.

This combination—constant interdisciplinary exchange with anthropology, but via, chiefly, folklore—lends Soviet literary criticism qualities that are unique in the contemporary panorama. No tradition has been more mindful of history and the group at large.

Here the gap with the Anglo-American situation is quite a wide and instructive one. American literary theory not only enjoys contact with anthropology through the auspices of research conducted in the four corners of the Empire; it administers the formalism the century thrusts upon it differently. In the United States, formalism wins. New Criticism starts with very passionate historical and social interests (espousing agrarianism, expressing its stand against the technological, scientific, secularized bias of modernity in the mode of cultural analysis) and later crystallizes into a rigidly literary method: when it achieves institutional success and is the unifying orthodoxy of every English department in Britain and the United States, it is merely a literary ideology, a toolery for the perusal of texts. Which is why a figure such as Burke, who shares the initial cultural and culturalist proclivities of New Criticism and preserves and radicalizes them, continues to appear to some, today, to be the theoretical eccentric, and not, as he is, the critic who exemplifies the theoretical heart of Anglo-Americana.

In the Soviet Union the process goes in the opposite direction. The Shlovskys, the Tynianovs of the twenties, defend the autonomy of literature at the beginning of their career and end by admitting that extraliterary pressures are among the factors determining literary change. In so doing, they merge with a mainstream whose traits are exacerbated by postrevolutionary politics but which was always a vital, pivotal force. Veselovsky's ambition in the 1880s was to lay the foundation—by privileging the study of motifs, of the impersonal, the collective in folkloric or literary creation, by sidestepping the variables of author and biography—of a truly historical poetics. Propp announced back in the twenties, when he was still writing his morphological work, that structural analysis, to be complete, must be able to justify the perdurance, the lasting power of the thematic recurrences, the invariants it finds in the texts. In *The Historical Roots of the Wondertale*, which he published after the Second World War, the plot of the tales records the palimpsest-like superimposition of local material on a story line dating back to ancient rites. For the same reason—because history is a concern that survives in all sorts of weather—a maverick such as Bakhtin is easier to reinstate within the Russian tradition than is Burke within the American. Be they on biography or the chronotopes of narration, Bakhtin's works always present long, panoramic histories of their topic: they are studies in the "historical typology" of a genre or attempts at "historical poetics," as the subtitles of some of the essays indicate (the full titles of the essays on the chronotope and on the *Bildungsroman* are "Forms of Time and of the Chronotope in the Novel: Notes Towards a Historical Poetics" and "The *Bildungsroman* and Its Significance in the History of Realism [Towards a Historical Typology of the Novel]"). One never knows if it is the theoretical wherewithal that occasions the forays into literary history or if it is the inspection of a preexistent corpus that originates the essays and the theories presiding over them.

The attachment to history, to a primitive that is intranational in scope, modifies the internal economy of the anthropology-literary theory trade-off. Far from being a mere fellow traveler, an enlightened intellectual aware of the rumblings in nearby disciplines, the Soviet critic seems rather, not infrequently, to verge on the discipline himself, to be in it. It is a feeling we get on the page, before we separate theory from document and chew over implications. The long chapters on the history of laughter or on the language actually spoken, the passages in which Bakhtin speculates on how the various literary genres or the forms of criticism reflect and reinforce the emergence of the nation-state, of "sociopolitical and cultural centralization" (1981, 270–71) are very simply an anthropology of literature, literature inserted in the web of always different contexts. Bakhtin deploys his analyses in precise, carefully bordered geographies: the upper and lower bodily functions and the body, the marketplace, and the places of authority in the city, Latin and Greek in post-Augustan Rome, language and the structures of a certain society, the novel and serious-comic discourses, etcetera. The universal, the general do not arise from but are the relationships he discusses. For both Bakhtin and the Tartu School criticism and anthropology foster in their own right hybrid, interstitial positionings. Literature (and the novel especially) being the archive of the speech acts and speech forms that come out of social discourse (from the sermon to the diary to the reportage to the private letter), to do criticism is, for Bakhtin, to verify and chronicle the fortune of genres of discourse, to recount how they flow in and out of literature, how literary texts relate to them, which they absorb and which they overlook. Given that language, as speech, keeps the intonations of its speakers, the literary critic studying literature must perforce study the mechanisms and agencies by which voice is silenced or propagated. In Lotman's semiotics, how the culture of a society is classified depends on the kind of texts and the kind of cooperation between the texts it envisions: some cultures are oriented toward expression and conceive themselves as an aggregate of works, others are oriented toward content and conceive themselves as an aggregrate of rules (Lotman & Uspensky 1978, 217–18). Moreover, literature, culture, and society are cybernetically conjoined: methods of textual analysis are influenced by cultural models, typologies of culture cannot be established without some intelligence of the texts. Although the critic does not have to embark, as Bakhtin does, on a "philosophical anthropology" (the terms are his [1986, 146]), he or she is in entangled in anthropological activity by just going about his or her affairs, by just being aware of the function of literary texts within the overall array and/or hierarchy of his or her country's cultural texts.

But what is most pertinent, for us, in the comparison with Anglo-Americana is, first, that in the Soviet Union, the practice of criticism or of literary anthropology underwrites and is underwritten by the choice of two different generic models and, second, that this split echoes the distinctions we have witnessed in the Anglo-American tradition. For the non-Bakhtinian sector of Soviet literary theory, a sector occupied mainly by semioticians and narratologists, the exemplary genre is not the novel, but the tale or narration. And rather than discourse, plot, composition, and action are the relevant theoretical objects of attraction.

As might be expected, in Soviet criticism, too, it is a matter of inflection. The salient individual stances harbor these conflicts no less than the tradition. During the formalist twenties, the orality and rhetoric of tales was an important *topos* of the theory of prose fiction (Eichenbaum 1965, 122). The dialogue/monologue dichotomy also intrigued Russian or Slav non-Bakhtinian semioticians.[14] In a similar vein, while criticism has been ultrareceptive about Bakhtin's essays on dialogism, it has practically ignored those works—a good slice of his opus—in which he writes about the thematic coherence of such genres as biography and the novel of apprenticeship[15] or about how stories are rendered perceptible by the chronotope, by the spatiotemporal coordinates of the representation and without which "even abstract thought is impossible" (Bakhtin 1981, 258). Refuting the image that has been created of him, Bakhtin holds that semantic cohesion is also a necessary condition for the existence of the work of art. Much as societies need linguistic norms (which ensure a "certain maximum of mutual understanding," the unity of the "reigning conversational [everyday] language" [Bakhtin 1981, 270–71]) and are actually held in balance by and evolve thanks to the struggle between centralization and heterogeneity, the text must also "take on the form of a sign" (Bakhtin 1981, 270–71), is constituted by the collision and/or cooperation of centripetal and centrifugal forces.

The symmetry can be pursued still further. As with Anglo-American conversation and action, hovering over the Soviet plot-dialogue duality and hence over both narrative and novel is the uninvited shadow of theater. Drama inhabits the theories of narration in more or less the same guise it does Bakhtin's depictions of the novel: it is a model, inherited historically and harking back to entities and operations logically prior to texts, which somehow guides the critic's perspective on literature, be he sensitive or not to the divergences between the "written" and the oral.

By retaining some of the features of the novel, Bakhtin renders problematic the model's impact, but the novel's distinctiveness in being the only genre to have affirmed itself in the era of the printing

[14] This is a topic still awaiting proper framing, in the light of Bakhtin's dialogism. Some connections are made by Jane E. Knox in her valuable presentation of Lev Jakubinskij's "On Verbal Dialogue," which she translated for *Dispositio* 4, no. 11–12 (1979): 321–36. But a preliminary overview would have to mention at least the articles Jan Mukarovsky wrote in the early forties, now published as "Two Studies of Dialogue," in *The Word and Verbal Art*, trans. J. Burbank and P. Steiner (New Haven, Conn.: Yale University Press, 1977), pp. 81–115 and the many pages on monologue and dialogue in Jiri Veltrusky, *Dramă as Literature*, trans. J. Veltrusky (Lisse: Peter De Ridder Press, 1977), the original of which appeared in 1941.

[15] Together with "The *Bildungsroman* and Its Significance in the History of Realism (Toward a Historical Typology of the Novel)," now in *Speech Genres*, see the long essay entitled "L'auteur et le héros," in *Esthétique de la création verbale*, trans. A. Aucouturier (Paris: Gallimard, 1984), pp. 27–210.

press and the absence of author to reader and reader to author does not stop him from founding his theories on a dialogue-based tropology, or from cataloging classical dialogical forms among the precursors of the novel. The narratologists are only greater purists. They never avail themselves of the results of their analyses, never allow the metaphors that the model offers to blend into, to contaminate the language they use to speak about the tale. One must infer the nexus with theatricality. And the issue of the historical priority of drama is split from the issue of logical antecedence; some theorists will stress the one, some the other.

In the compositional schema Propp obtains from his morphological analyses of folktales, the hero departs from home or travels to another kingdom or gains access to another realm by magical transformation, by changing himself into an animal or by communicating with the dead. He is the fictional homologue of the boy who in *The Historical Roots of the Wondertale* is undergoing initiation and who, in order to learn about the mysteries of death and sex that will make an adult of him, will be separated from his family, will be left alone in a house in the forest for several days, often after being dressed in animal skins or having been given trance-inducing substances. The physical scarring he will be subject to (circumcision, etcetera) is the equivalent of the marks by which the protagonists of the fables analyzed in *The Morphology of the Folktale* are recognized (Propp 1984, 116–17). For Tartu School narratology all texts narrate a *fabula mundi*, a spatialized view of the world, but the largest narrative species—plotted texts—confront that view with a dialectical, oppositional one. They must postulate the existence of at least two topographies or two well-delineated regions. Lotman defines the minimal unit of the plot, the event, as the "shifting of a persona across the borders of a semantic field" (Lotman 1977, 233). The most representative hero of narration, thus, is again he who passes through, who has experience of two realms.

Both instances—Propp's and Lotman's—present us with a narratology the model of which is inherently theatrical. In Propp's theory (1984, 106) the tangencies are genealogical. The wondertale contains many "traces of rituals and customs": its protagonists are camouflaged cognates of the individuals Turner writes about in his essays. In Lotman the links are analogical. Plotted texts are theatrical on several grounds. Because characters acquire their rank, become protagonists by crossing borders, and have been "betwixt and between," they are also willy-nilly acquainted with that psychological state, that state of being, determined by position, that Turner (1982, 24–27) in his writings has dubbed "liminality." They can potentially experience reversal, masking, carnival-type changes of identity, communitas, like the initiands of a performance such as the rites of passage or a social drama such as pilgrimage. Because they are spatially, topographically organized, Lotmanian texts are structurally stage-like (scenographic modes of narrating best exemplified by theater).

In the end we therefore come full circle. Bakhtin specifies some of the problems conversationalism raises for anthropology and literary theory. Against the realism, the ethics of atonement and sacrifice that Burke's responsiveness leaves us with, dialogism gives us a utopian ethics, the ethics of heterogeneity, of voice, laughter, carnival, freedom. And it treats with greater circumspection the controversy about the circulation and function of texts. In Bakhtinian theory Turner's unhindered "looping" of artistic and folk genres, aesthetic drama, and social dramas or performance could not come off without some mediation. It must be filtered by those features that attach to the writtenness of literary narrative. Dialogue is not to the Bakhtinian novel as social drama is to aesthetic drama: like rite for Propp's tales, it is, to repeat, its underlying model.

What neither Bakhtin nor the Soviet critical tradition as a whole do is to alter the perplexities with which we began. Can the vertiginous intertextuality that dialogism insinuates into written works be harnessed back to such things as chronotopes, plots, characters, structure? Is there some conceptual locus where the compositional and the translinguistic in texts intersect? Or are the two twains never to meet, action and discourse each veering off into a theoretical domain irreducible to and irreconcilable with any other? These interrogations do not change.

Bakhtinian dialogism and Burke's dramatism nonetheless do steer our attention toward inklings previously not adequately valorized. As I have intimated at the beginning of this essay, the appeal of the literaturization of conversation and action and the generic, historical model it yields may lie precisely in its capacity to bring together, in non-causal contact, fields of tension, concerns at once compatible and disparate. With theater we have not just (representations of) doings that impose coherence to a set of rejoinders, and not just the chance to convert one into the other (meaningful text that can be seen as action or meaningful action that can be seen as text) but doing plus speech, (the representation of) doings co-present with (the representation of) words.

This literary, holistic arrangement of things, strangely, will widen the range of the interdisciplinary crisscrossings, will take us outside of the humanities more directly than groupings easier to formalize.

"The organization of literary discourse," those who have made the trip admonish, "[can] . . . only be approached through reference to notions of discursive order in general (theories of language and signification), which in turn call into play the most general concepts of disorder and order, and with them, a constellation of disciplines" (Livingston 1984, 6–7). The ideas that have sustained literary criticism, and have gravitated around such crucibles as "norm," "structure," "form," "coherence," "aporia," "determinacy," and "indeterminacy" are not exclusively literary or humanistic. And one could do worse today than to reflect on how the sciences that have discovered or resurrected complexity as a subject of meditation conjugate the centripetal with the centrifugal, propensities for stabilization with propensities for destabilization in their inquiries on organized and self-organizing systems. The lesson that the non-humanistic discourses teaches us is that polarities never abolish each other, that in the order we discern there is a great measure of disorder, and vice versa, even when appearances seem not to be deceiving. It is also the lesson of the models, the heuristic generic heraldries, we get from literature. Presumably, states corresponding to the balance between order and disorder or the dosages producing either strong equilibrium or strong disequilibrium could be identified in the theories we have been surveying. Unbridled dialogistic discursivism would lean toward disorder, emphasis on plot toward order. And perhaps the even overlapping of the two, when it comes down to it, is nothing but undifferentiated, ungeneric textuality or performance, that fluid realm holding both order and disorder as equal virtualities, and on whose precise configuration the jury is—as it perennially seems to be—still out.

Anthropology will no doubt be called upon to amplify its web of comparisons and to investigate such family resemblances, the complicities between the study of texts, the study of society and the study of the *bios* or the *physis* of life, together with their significance for an anthropological theory of practice. But this is another story. For now it is sufficient to know that such a story must begin with the study of how texts circulate among the disciplines, of how anthropology lends and how it borrows.

Marxism and the "Subject" of Anthropology

ROBERT SULLIVAN

I HAVE USED the term "subject" in my title to draw attention to the double meaning of anthropology as a discipline and its association with Marxist theory, and the idea of "subjectivity" as a construct of social forces or formations. When we speak of "social formation" we are confronted with a complex web of interrelationships: the economic foundations of a given society, be it primitive communism or postindustrial capitalism; the social relations pertaining to that particular infrastructure, be they cooperative or highly competitive; and, finally, how the individual is positioned within such a formation, be he or she a member of a tribal community or a denizen of suburbia.

Although the distinction is implied throughout the essay, it will be useful to sketch briefly here the fundamental and ideological differences between the term *subject*, which I have put under scrutiny by placing it within quotation marks in my title, and the more classical and traditionally anthropological usage of *individual*. Essentially, the term *individual* has the ideological weight of an entity that has a coherence, a stability, and a consciousness that transcends—gives meaning to—its cultural environment as a primary active force. Descartes's *cogito* is perhaps the best-known enunciation of this "old stable ego," as D. H. Lawrence put it in another context. By its very nomenclature, the term *subject* denotes an entity that is less in charge of its destiny, but that is constituted *by* various cultural determinations rather than being constitutive *of* them. The subject in this sense is constructed, not only by these "outside" cultural forces or discourses, but also by forces within itself that it also cannot control. I have in mind here the Freudian idea of the unconscious and Lacan's linguistic revision, wherein the individual is subject to the "other's" discourse.

In his book *The Order of Things* (1973, xiv), Michel Foucault summarizes the ideological import of this position when he remarks:

* This essay is a version of a talk given at the *Unit For Criticism and Interpretative Theory*, the University of Illinois at Urbana-Champaign. I would like to thank those people who made comments and offered suggestions.

> If there is one approach [in epistemology] that I do reject, however, it is that . . . which gives absolute priority to the observing subject . . . which places its own point of view at the origin of all historicity—which, in short, leads to a transcendental consciousness. It seems to me that the historical analysis of scientific discourse should, in the last resort, be subject, not to a theory of the knowing subject, but rather to a theory of discursive practice.

These words appear near the beginning of Foucault's book: the argument draws to a close with the reflection that "man is an invention of recent date. And one perhaps nearing its end" (1973, 387). The "discursive practice" of which Foucault speaks (or as he might have it—which speaks him) propounds the notion that discourse manufactures its own referents. "Man," the subject of anthropology, the individual in this case, has been produced by various discourses (by Descartes for instance), and when we cease to speak of him he will disappear, as Foucault puts it in the last sentence of his book, "like a face drawn in sand at the edge of the sea" (1973, 387). Foucault is not speaking here of course about the real flesh and bones, tissue, and mental activity of "man," but our conceptual understanding of him. In this context, a key concept in any theory of the subject is that of discursive construction, a cultural construction whereby the mediation of signifying practices form consciousness and the unconscious.

A fundamental concern arising out of this discursive enterprise is the problem of representation, a problem that can be traced from the concern of Plato and Aristotle with mimesis to contemporary ethnographic enquiry, an enquiry that is hyperconscious of "writing" culture. How do we represent our world? How do we represent those selves, those subjects that help constitute this world, while at the same time they in turn are constituted by socially determined discursive practices?

A recent volume edited by James Clifford and George Marcus highlights cultural anthropology's attempt "to come to terms with the politics and poetics of cultural representation" (1986, viii). Concerned with the ideology underlying "transparent" representation and armed with the post-paradigmatic suspicion of imposing a unity on their own texts, Clifford nevertheless remarks that the essays that follow his introduction find a common ground in the Foucaultian position outlined above. They share the "new space opened up by the disintegration of 'Man' as *telos* for a whole discipline," drawing instead on "recent developments in the fields of textual criticism, cultural history, semiotics, hermeneutic philosophy, and psychoanalysis" (1986, 4). Not only is the Cartesian transcendental subject undermined in such an approach, but so too is the transcendental observer, the authoritative figure who constructs the ethnographic "reality." Such self-reflexive strategies lead to a critique of textual production, questioning monophonic authority—especially the text's silences and absences in its pursuit of a homogeneous totality—in a manner initiated by Pierre Macherey for literary texts. In brief, Macherey's thesis is that the literary work is a complex sign that, when deconstructed, leads to a conflict of meanings, betrays the ideology that permits its production, and effects this not by what it says, but by what it does not say. The ideological desire for a totalizing homogeneity is found, as it were, in the margins (1978).

All the essays in *Writing Culture* are challenging interventions in the contemporary debate concerning the modes of representation, ranging from the problematization of totalizing structures, through the investigation of dialogical modes of production, to a poetics of "evocation."[1] In this interrogation of culture as text, the recognition that "what appears as 'real' in history, the social sciences, the arts, even in common sense, is always analyzable as a restrictive and expressive set of social codes and conventions" (Clifford & Marcus 1986, 10), the contributors to *Writing Culture* contribute to (and elaborate) Foucault's fundamental premise of how the subject is produced and enmeshed within what he calls "the significations of a culture."

A most recent intervention by Paul Smith in this area (the representation of the subject within cultural formations) "identifies a number of different intellectual 'areas' or 'fields'—that is, discursive practices—in which the 'subject' has become either overtly or implicitly a major concern, and attempts to discuss and critique them."[2] I shall have occasion to return to Smith's discussion, but at the outset a brief summary of its intent and its relation to anthropological discourse will be helpful. In vogue with poststructuralism's ludic predilection for etymology, Smith's title utilizes the notions "to cern" and "to cerne." The first sense of the term (*cern*) denotes a "legacy," an in-

[1] See Stephen Tyler's essay in *Writing Culture*, "Post-Modern Ethnography: From Document of the Occult to Occult Document." This is a novel attempt to disarm the critique of origins and "the whole visualist ideology of referential discourse," offering instead a discourse of "evocation," which is less the representation of a "thing" than a discursive process.

[2] Paul Smith, *Discerning the Subject* (Minneapolis: University of Minnesota Press, 1988), p. xxix. Smith's book is a comprehensive rehearsal of many of the theoretical positions—Marxian, Lacanian, Derridean, cultural texualization—taken up in this essay, and it is unfortunate that my essay was virtually complete when Smith's book appeared in print. To engage his book now would be to rethink the whole essay, although I have tried to point to it, either in the body of my text or in footnotes.

heritance, while the second (*cerne*) means to "encircle," or perhaps even more germane to Smith's intention, to "delimit." It is in the conflation of these two meanings that Smith bases his critique of the various discourses in the human sciences, including anthropology: he maintains that such discursive practice shares in the legacy of an outmoded epistemology of the subject, and at the same time (and as a consequence) delimits its potential for resistance to ideological pressure. It is Smith's endeavour, through his various critiques, to "provoke" a reconsideration of the subject, hopefully one that would "dis-cern" it.

Among other things, Smith problematizes the use of the term "individual subject," pointing out its essentially contradictory nature. Given the outline above concerning these two terms, it is evident that we must agree. However, despite its contradictory nature (indeed because of it), I should like to retain the nomenclature since it will help keep in mind that very contradiction—that tension—between the individual (in the humanist sense of the term) and the subject-positions it is compelled to take up. Anthropology is one of the fields into which Smith makes an "incursion," but the essays in *Writing Culture* defuse many (if not all) of his criticisms of, among others, the paradigm of objective narrative in ethnographic representation.[3]

When we, as human beings, enter the world of representation we enter the realm of ideology, be it in the most basic and original sense of the term (how we formulate ideas from sense perception), or in the formation of belief systems as recorded, for example, by the field anthropologists; or in the more modern (but analogous) notion of how we have an imaginary understanding of our "real" social position. In this latter sense, ideology can be understood as a form of "false" representation, a distortion in need of what Foucault calls *dechiffrement*, "an understanding of social practices as having an intelligibility radically different from that available to the actors" (Dreyfus & Rabinow 1983, xxvii). In an analogous manner to textual production as discussed above, ideology could be said to smooth over contradictions within social formations, both providing the illusion of a homogeneous social totality as well as convincing its subjects of their autonomous choice; this, while at the same time helping to perpetuate the "real" divisions within social life.

[3] See Smith's chapter "Paranoia," which concerns itself generally with the epistemological problematic of the observer-observed relation, and more particularly with the "whipping-boy" Clifford Geertz. Smith acknowledges in a note that he had not read *Writing Culture* during the writing of his own book. His remarks need to be interrogated in the light of the essays in Clifford and Marcus, especially Stephen Tyler's essay. See note 1.

Louis Althusser's trope of ideology as being the air we breathe—"the very element and atmosphere indispensable to [a society's] respiration and life"[4]—underscores this concept's crucial importance in any discussion of individual subjects, social formations, and discursive practices. Indeed, ideology is what helps constitute human reality, and it is just this process of signification that forms the intermediary link between the individual subject (itself produced by discourse) and social consciousness. This is ensured (among other ways) by the signifying practice of ritual or mythography (as documented by the field anthropologists), or the metasymbolic system of language emphasized by Marx as "practical consciousness" and given a more modern semiotic turn by someone such as V. N. Vološinov.[5]

Althusser's position on ideology is that it helps formulate the illusion of the unified subject, and that it is a *necessary* component of cohesion for social formations if they are to function at all. In this sense ideology functions as a kind of imaginary bonding similar in a way to myth, or to the way religion functions as a mode of social integration for Durkheim in his *The Elementary Forms of the Religious Life*. This analogous theoretical position between myth and Althusser's brand of ideological bonding points up, perhaps, the latter's weakness as a theory for class society. As Ben Halpern remarks: "The social function of myth is to bind together social groups as wholes or, in other words, to establish a social consensus. The social function of ideology is to segregate and serve special interests within societies in the competition of debate" (1961, 137). This smacks too much of a *conscious* manipulation of one class by another, rather than the working of a system of representations "in men's minds without their being aware of the fact" as Lévi-Strauss remarks of myth.[6] The question, however, is if the Althusserian platform needs modification if it

[4] Louis Althusser, *For Marx*, trans. Ben Brewster (London: New Left Books, 1977), p. 232. The key essay is "Ideology and Ideological State Apparatuses" in *Lenin and Philosophy and Other Essays* (New York: Monthly Review Press, 1971), to which we will have occasion to return.

[5] Vološinov's books *Marxism and the Philosophy of Language* (New York: Seminar Press, 1973) and *Freudianism: A Marxist Critique* (New York: Academic Press, 1976), although "rediscovered" for a time, seem to be overlooked in current theories of the subject and ideology. There is some discussion below of what I feel to be Vološinov's more materialist view of language and consciousness, especially in comparison with Lacan's "metaphysical" position currently in vogue.

[6] Lévi-Strauss, *The Raw and the Cooked*, quoted by David McLellan, *Ideology* (Minneapolis: University of Minnesota Press, 1986) p. 69. McLellan provides a useful, if sometimes cursory, rehearsal of various positions in regard to ideology.

is to account for class positions, if it is not to "expand the concept of ideology to the point where it [is] emptied of political efficacy."[7]

The problematic of change, an allowance for resistance and human agency within such an ideological web, will be taken up in a more concrete setting toward the end of this essay, but before leaving this area between the coincidences of myth and ideology some mention should be made of Roland Barthes's demystification of modern ritual. We have not the space here to go into Barthes's sophisticated theory of signification—for example, how mythical signification is never arbitrary like other signs, but always "motivated"—rather, it is perhaps sufficient to point out here how Barthes's interrogation accentuates the dehistoricizing nature of myth; how, like bourgeois ideology, it attempts to make "contingency appear eternal."[8] Barthes's interrogation of cultural texts as historical contingencies disguised as "natural" forms is akin, as we shall see, to Marx's early use of classical anthropology to denaturalize the seemingly eternal nature of bourgeois norms, and the method finds its contemporary counterpart in anthropology as cultural critique.

This method of defamiliarizing bourgeois culture in the search for a fuller understanding of our situation as social beings is made manifest not only in the ethnographic records of exotic cultures, but is applicable to Western postindustrial society as well. An anthropological semiotics—the interrogation of cultural signification—together with a Marxist cultural critique can help delineate a fuller theory of how the subject individual is constructed within various social formations. If we read the classical anthropologists and the linguistic and symbolic anthropologists of the late nineteenth and early twentieth century—Tylor, Morgan, Frazer, Harrison, Malinowski, Sapir, Cassirer, along with, for example, such modern ethnographers as Pierre Bourdieu and Paul Willis—such a theory of the production of the subject through cultural signification achieves a fuller understanding.

It is such an understanding that is at the center of Paul Smith's agenda. He is dissatisfied with the representation of the subject in contemporary theoretical discourse. The "current conceptions of the 'subject' have tended to produce a purely *theoretical* 'subject,' re-

[7] Terry Eagleton, *Against The Grain* (London: Verso Editions, 1986), p. 3. This is certainly a tempering of Eagleton's earlier enthusiasm. Althusser does distinguish between "ideology" as an ahistorical element, eternally present in social relations, and "ideologies" in their various historical forms.

[8] Roland Barthes, *Mythologies* (St. Albans: Paladin Books, 1973), p. 142. See especially "Myth Today," pp. 109–59. These superlative readings of modern myths as forms of ideology deserve more discussion than given here.

moved almost entirely from the political and ethical realities in which human agents actually live and that a different concept of the 'subject' must be discerned or discovered" (1988, xxix). In one sense this is a very peculiar statement, since all *conceptions* of the subject are "bound," by definition, to be "theoretical." Nevertheless, Smith's concern for specificity is well taken. Conceptual cultural analysis, *theory*, can (and must) be enriched by "going out into the world," either for confirmation or modification. It must be stressed that this is not a question of priority—empiricism in the narrow sense, that "truth" can only be derived from experience—but rather a mutually determining dialectic of theory and evidence. One of the primary goals of this paper is to suggest that just as Marx sought (or *found*) confirmation of his theoretical premises in the work of the field anthropologists, so too can contemporary ethnography as cultural critique supply necessary empirical data for the abstract paradigm of a materialist cultural theory. It need not be an either / or choice between theory and empirical data, but rather a mutual interdependence analogous to Marx's own development, from a critique of Hegel's metaphysics, through his own *theory* of human nature, to a grounding of such theory in political economy.

The Classical Paradigm

It has always been a primary task in any Marxist analysis of society to demonstrate how consciousness and cultural production is reliant upon a theory of objective psychology. Such an analysis must move away from the concept of the individual subject (keeping in mind the inherent contradiction in these terms), certainly a move away from biological principles, toward a social psychology founded upon an intersubjectivity based upon signifying practices. Such a position, implicit in the work of the classical anthropologists—Morgan, Tylor, Frazer, Harrison, Malinowski, and others—is given a more emphatic emphasis in the writings of Marx, Engels, and Plekanov who utilized their findings. If we read these texts selectively, along with those of the linquistically orientated anthropological theorists such as Sapir and the interpreters of symbolic systems such as Cassirer, then it is my belief that we will arrive at a philosophic anthropology comparable (if not compatible) with Marx's own. Far from being idealist, some of these early investigations concerned with the symbolic importance of ritual and myth also stressed (sometimes unintentionally) the economic foundations of such practices. And as we shall see, contemporary ethnography as "cultural critique"—especially as "repatriation"—offers a similar method of scrutinizing modern culture and its products, including ideology.

It is not surprising, then, that Marx saw in the work of Lewis Morgan an independent confirmation of the materialist conception of history and social relations. And it is well known that Engels used Marx's copious notes to write his own anthropologically based treatise, *The Origin of the Family, Private Property and the State*, a work that utilized Marx's anthropological evidence to propagate an historical model of primitive communism, in a similar way to how Freud had sought "historical" origins for his theories in *Totem and Taboo*. Engels remarked that Morgan's *Ancient Society* (1877) had the same importance for primitive society as Darwin had for biology, and that Marx had for the investigation of political economy and the evolution of social structures. There is an interesting ideological parallel here: just as there is a vestigial element of the savage in the modern unconscious so, for Engels at any rate, there is the implicit belief of a socially cooperative being beneath the competitive individual of modern capitalism.

Lawrence Krader has examined in great detail Marx's investigation not only of Morgan's work, but also that of Maine, Phear, and Lubbock.[9] We do not have the space here to rehearse in detail the voluminous and revealing notes Marx recorded from these anthropologists, but a brief synopsis of the classical position is necessary. As Krader reminds us in his "Introduction" to the ethnological notebooks, Marx developed his philosophical anthropology through a series of works, from the critique of Hegel's *Philosophy of Right*, through the *Economic and Philosophic Manuscripts*, *The German Ideology*, and the *Theses on Feuerbach*. Krader notes, quite judiciously, that the transformation of Marx's treatment of anthropology from "a philosophical to an empirical subject" becomes more evident in the citations from ethnological data in the *Grundrisse* and *Capital*—this despite Althusser's notion of an epistemological rupture (1974, 4).

Marx became more consistently—more overtly—interested in anthropological theory from 1880 when he read Morgan's *Ancient Society* until his death in 1883. The earlier philosophic anthropology, the *Critique*, *The Economic and Philosophic Manuscripts*, and other theoretical works, found its *empirical* evidence (its praxis as it were) in Marx's ethnological reading. Although he found weaknesses in Morgan's theoretical edifice (he was less enthusiastic than Engels and modified

[9] Lawrence Krader, *The Ethnological Notebooks of Karl Marx* (Assen, The Netherlands: Van Gorcum & Comp., 1974). This painstaking study of Marx's interaction with anthropology includes Marx's marginilia on Morgan, Phear and Maine and is of crucial importance in any discussion of Marx's thought in this area.

in his Notebooks the chronology of Morgan's schema to emphasize the growth of private property and its relation with the "growth" of the state [Krader 1974, 11]), Marx nevertheless found in Morgan's work a verification of some of his earlier theoretical speculations. The state, for example, was no Hegelian transhistorical, suprasocial institution, but, on the contrary, grew out of the *division* within a communal primitive homogeneity. Indeed, Morgan himself belonged to the tradition of socialist Utopians and although he did not recognize the historical necessity of bourgeois social relations, he welcomed the return to the ancient commune at a higher stage of productive relations: "It will be a revival, in a higher form, of the liberty, equality and fraternity of the ancient gentes" (Krader 1974, 87).

The transformation of Marx's treatment of anthropology from "a philosophical to an empirical subject" (to use Krader's terms) demonstrates a gradual but inexorable movement toward a more sustained engagement with ethnological and ethnographic theory, and this progressive engagement parallels what could be termed a "retrogressive" purpose. Marx wanted to go back beyond feudal society for examples of the evolution of belief systems and their underlying economic foundations and Morgan's evolutionary account was perhaps the most documented explication of its time.

Marx and Engels used these anthropological writings (if we may borrow some structuralist terminology) in both diachronic and synchronic ways. Diachronically they sought to "insert" anthropological evidence in an historical context—to illustrate particular "stages" in preliterate cultures—and, synchronically, they hoped to demonstrate, by juxtaposition or analogy, alternatives to capitalist social structures and by so doing to "de-naturalize" or break down the ideological position that capitalism is some eternal, god-given, structure in human relations rather than a "mere" historical phase. This "synchronic" aspect, or critique by juxtaposition, has its modern analogue in ethnography as "repatriation."[10]

The evolutionary aspect of Marxist anthropology (given more prominence by Engels than Marx), a leaning toward a teleological paradigm in cultural critique, has of course its ideological historical moment. Stanley Hyman, in his book *The Tangled Bank,* reminds us of the broader cultural implications of that historical moment. Hyman remarks that when (in the conclusion to *The Origin of Species*) Darwin had called for an "evolutionary treatment in the sciences of

[10] Maurice Bloch, in his *Marxism and Anthropology* (New York: Oxford University Press, 1983), calls this form of synchronic critique a "rhetorical" strategy. I am indebted to Bloch's thought-provoking survey of Marxism and anthropology.

man . . . he made cultural studies the legitimate heir of evolutionary biology," and that E. B. Tylor's *Primitive Culture* was to a great extent a response to such a call (1962, 6). Tylor's subtitle, "Researches into the Development of Mythology, Philosophy, Religion, Language, Art and Custom" marks the genesis of cultural anthropology, later to blossom into the work of Frazer, Jane Harrison, the ethnographer Malinowski, as well as that of the linguistic anthropologist Sapir and the symbologists such as Ernst Cassirer.

These investigations into the "significations of a culture" (as Foucault has it) are analogous to Marx's emphasis on the "great instrument" language as constitutive of human subjectivity, with its function as a kind of metasymbolic system and its role as "practical consciousness"—its role as mediator between biological being and social existence. Social interaction through signification, the formation of both an individual consciousness and an intersubjective consciousness (the basis for an objective psychology) is reiterated by Marx throughout his writings. The paradigmatic statement is found in the Preface to *A Contribution to the Critique of Political Economy* when Marx states: "It is not the consciousness of men that determines their being, but, on the contrary, their social being that determines their consciousness."[11] The Sixth Thesis on Feuerbach emphasizes what the other theses imply, that "the human essence is no abstraction inherent in each single individual. In its reality it is the ensemble of the social relations." In the *Economic and Philosophic Manuscripts of 1844* (the "Paris Manuscripts") we read: "Not only is the material of my activity given to me as a social product (as is even the language in which the thinker is active): my *own* existence *is* social activity, and therefore that which I make of myself, I make of myself for society and with the consciousness of myself as a social being" (Tucker 1972, 86). Such a stance constitutes, I would contend, an implied semiological understanding of human consciousness—the formation of the human psyche as a result of the *collective* humanization of nature, or, as Marx puts it in the same context: "The *forming* of the five senses is a labour of the entire history of the world down to the present" (Tucker 1972, 89).

It would be redundant to offer further support for this basic premise of Marxist thought, that humankind's adaptation to its environment (and the value systems that arise from this) is not an individual affair, but rather a socially mediated set of circumstances. The indi-

[11] In Robert C. Tucker, ed. *The Marx-Engels Reader* (New York: W. W. Norton, 1972), p. 4. I will use this easily available anthology for the few citations from Marx and Engels.

vidual subject always already finds itself in a world that has been textualized by signifying systems, whether they be mythological texts (and we know that this is not an ancient phenomenon, as the work of Roland Barthes has shown), or the metasymbolic system of language. And although the nomenclature has changed somewhat, the traditional humanist investigators of anthropological structures attest that this is not a singularly Marxist discovery.

Indeed (by way of a brief illustration), one can discern a line of historical correspondences between anthropology and Marxist theory—most particularly the reciprocal interests of how consciousness is produced by particular social relations and how such relations are themselves a product of the material forms of life—from Engels, through Plekanov, to such English theorists as Christopher Caudwell and George Thomson. Engels in the *Origin* (working from Morgan and Bachofen) used anthropological evidence to document the shift in power within gender roles when the "means of production" (the transformation from agriculture to herding and the domestication of animals) led to a radical change in the social formation. For Engels this was the first case of exploitation of one "class" by another, the "*world-historic defeat of the female sex*."[12] The work of George V. Plekanov, influenced by Engels's evolutionary paradigm, forms an important link between the founders of historical materialism and the theorists of the first part of the twentieth century. Plekanov states: "In the sphere of the ideology of primitive society, art has been studied better than any other branch; an abundance of material has been collected, testifying in the most unambiguous and convincing manner to the soundness and, one might say, the inevitability of the materialist explanation of history." He goes on to note over a dozen anthropological references (1969, 60).

I have dealt in detail elsewhere with the importance of anthropological theory on the controversial Marxism of Christopher Caudwell.[13] Plekanov's anthropologically oriented chapter on "Base and Culture" had a profound influence on Caudwell, attempting as it did to explain art in terms of the material conditions of existence. Caudwell, in turn, greatly influenced the English Marxist classicist George Thomson, who remarked that the two important sources for his work were Engels's *Origin of the Family* and Caudwell's *Illusion and Reality*. A survey of Thomson's work—*Aeschylus and Athens: A Study in the*

[12] Ibid., p. 736. Original italics. See Maurice Bloch for a good summary of Engels's position.

[13] See my *Christopher Caudwell* (Beckenham, Kent: Croom Helm Ltd., 1987). A good part of the book attempts to show how Caudwell Marxified his original anthropological base in his revision of *Illusion and Reality*.

Social Origins of Greek Drama (1941), *Marxism and Poetry* (1946), *The Prehistoric Aegean* (1949), and *The First Philosophers* (1955)—would demonstrate how a Marxist approach to culture allied with anthropological theory offers a complementary explication of social formations and the subject's position within them.[14]

Jane Harrison, a member of the Cambridge school, was especially influential. In her books *Themis: A Study of the Social Origins of Greek Religion* (1912) and *Ancient Art and Ritual* (1913) she traces the psychosocial origins of cultural practice; how primitive humans attempted to symbolize their world within the realms of art, magic, and religion. In terms that foreshadow (albeit embryonically) Fredric Jameson's exploration of textualization and historical necessity (1981), Harrison maintains that modern cultural texts should be seen as "a later and more sublimated, more detached form of ritual" (1913, 225). And in at least one place she cites an unlikely source for a material basis: "The two great interests of primitive man are food and children. As Dr. Frazer has well said, if man the individual is to live he must have food; if his race is to persist he must have children" (1913, 49–50). Indeed, Harrison concludes her book with a critique of modern bourgeois art's lack of social consciousness.

It would be impossible to do justice, in such small compass, to the linguistic anthropology of Edward Sapir, especially its contemporary relevance to questions concerning language's role in perception and the structuration of a socialized psyche. His recently reissued *Selected Writings* ([1949] 1985) are a testament to his importance in any search for an objective psychology. Sapir observes (echoing Plekanov) that "primitive peoples have an economic basis of life that, however simple in its operation, is strictly comparable to the economic machinery that so largely orders the life of a modern civilized society" ([1949], 332). And in another essay ([1949], 162) he outlines the importance of language in shaping social formations:

> Language is a guide to "social reality." Though language is not ordinarily thought of as of essential interest to the students of social science, it powerfully conditions all our thinking about social problems and processes. Human beings do not live in the objective world alone, nor alone in the world of social activity as ordinarily understood, but are very much at the mercy of the particular language which has become the medium of expression for their society. It is quite an illusion to imagine that one adjusts to reality essentially without the use of language and that language is merely an incidental means of solving specific problems of communication or re-

[14] See Maynard Solomon, *Marxism and Art* (Detroit: Wayne State University Press, 1979), for a brief but excellent discussion of Thomson and Caudwell.

flection. The fact of the matter is that the "real world" is to a large extent unconsciously built up on the language habits of the group. . . . Even comparatively simple acts of perception are very much more at the mercy of the social patterns called words than we might suppose. . . . From this standpoint we may think of language as the *symbolic guide to culture.*

Bronislaw Malinowski, "supplementing" Ogden's and Richards's theory of symbolism with evidence from the field, moves even more specifically toward a materialist view of language and an anthropologically based objective psychology when his researches lead him to comment: "In its primitive uses, language functions as a link in concerted human activity, as a piece of human behaviour. It is a mode of action and not an instrument of reflection" (1972, 312). Even the "grammatical categories," Malinowski tells us, "are the reflecton of the makeshift, unsympathetic, practical outlook imposed by man's struggle for existence in the widest sense of this word" (1972, 328).

Ernst Cassirer conjoins this materialist view with the function of the symbolic in the structuration of a socially symbolic reality. Cassirer tells us: "For all his immediate needs and practical interests man is dependent on his physical environment. He cannot live without constantly adapting himself to the conditions of the surrounding world" (1944, 17). He defines man as *animal symbolicum* rather than *animal rationale,* remarking in semiological terms not unlike Sapir's:

> No longer in a merely physical universe, man lives in a symbolic universe. Language, myth, art, and religion are parts of this universe. They are the varied threads which weave the symbolic net, the tangled web of human experience. . . . No longer can man confront reality immediately; he cannot see it, as it were, face to face. . . . He has so enveloped himself in linguistic forms, in artisic images, in mythical symbols or religious rites that he cannot see or know anything except by the interposition of this artificial medium. (1944, 43)

Not only does Cassirer suggest a world that is textualized by signifying practice, but there is something peculiarly modern, something Foucaultian or even Lacanian in some of the remarks that he makes in the conclusion to his book, with its very "humanist" title, *An Essay on Man* (1944, 279):

> Here we are under no obligation to prove the substantial unity of man. Man is no longer considered as a simple substance which exists in itself and is to be known by itself. His unity is conceived as a functional unity. Such a unity does not presuppose a homogeneity of the various elements of which it consists. Not merely does it admit of, it even requires, a mul-

tiplicity and multiformity of its constituent parts. For this is a dialectic unity, a coexistence of contraries.

The above not only subscribes to a decentering of the autonomous subject, but it recalls also Marx's Sixth Thesis on Feuerbach, which critiques the idea of an "abstract—isolated—human individual," rather than as the product of the "ensemble of social relations." This emphasis on an intersubjectivity based on the symbolic in social cooperation and adaptation to the environment is given a more modern turn by Lucien Goldmann. Goldmann's anthropological notion of the transindividual subject finds its genesis in a conflation of Marx's emphasis on the essence of the individual as the ensemble of social relations and Piaget's genetic epistemology, an anthropological position that Goldmann saw as compatible with dialectical materialism. Essentially, such a concept of intersubjectivity allows Goldmann to differentiate between a biological being and a social subject, important in any search for an objective psychology, and especially so when compared with more postmodern conceptions of the subject such as that of Jacques Lacan.[15]

It is this form of interactionist epistemology (omnipresent in Marx's own writings), this dialectical interplay between biological existence and social being—mediated in the final analysis by the signifying systems, the symbolic order—that will produce a satisfactory account of the individual subject. Other explications, be they mechanical materialist (the form of materialism for which Marx chastised Feuerbach), or some form of "ideological biologism" as V. N. Vološinov puts it, end up in the final analysis as metaphysics.

The Post-Paradigmatic Situation

The premodernist (or pre-poststructuralist) theoretical paradigm empiricized, as it were, by anthropological findings has reached a crucial historical "moment." The changes in the structure of capitalist, or neocapitalist, modes and relations of production are such that we must ask: are all or any of the classical paradigms still relevant in contemporary theories of social formations and the subject's role within them? Can cultural anthropology or ethnographic enquiry maintain its role as a reciprocal critique? Political economy is no

[15] See especially Goldmann's essay "The Subject of the Cultural Creation," in *Essays on Method in the Sociology of Literature*, trans. and ed. by William Q. Boelhower (St. Louis, Mo.: Telos Press, 1980), pp. 91–110. Lacan's position with regard to a materialist conception of the subject is addressed further on in this discussion.

longer *solely* responsible for hegemonic power structures in the social relations of postindustrial capitalism, mainly due to a less demarcated line between classes and a resultant defusion of class consciousness. This together with a less overt nexus between state and ruling class—indeed state intervention in a once Darwinian laissez-faire economic system—necessitates a refashioning of the classical Marxist paradigm.

It is this hallmark of a post-paradigmatic discursive universe, a "crisis in representation" in the human sciences, that Marcus and Fischer highlight in their recent book (1986). I would like to offer by way of a *paradigm* (which of course in this discursive context is somewhat paradoxical) a text that illustrates emblematically how Marxism is undergoing its own "crisis in representation," and how perhaps in our own historical "moment" we may glimpse the mutual concerns (and difficulties) of both anthropological and Marxist discourse.

In Fredric Jameson's *The Political Unconscious* we bear witness to a type of "meta-allegory" that seeks in its multifarious syntheses to resolve our postparadigmatic dilemma. Marxism can no longer be the monolithic theoretical edifice it once was, even if it offers, in Jameson's parlance, an "untranscendable horizon" in any interpretation of cultural artifacts. Final horizon it may very well be, but in order to reach that geohistorical position we must take on both the baggage and guidance of various structuralist and poststructuralist interpretative strategies along the way. Jameson calls upon the work done by the anthropologists—particularly Lévi-Strauss—the theory of symbolic action as promulgated by Kenneth Burke, the myth criticism of Northrop Frye, a theory of textuality based upon Jacques Lacan's notion of the "real," and (to abbreviate the contributors somewhat) a theory of the subject and ideology based on the work of Lacan's disciple Louis Althusser.

Despite the heavy machinery and the sophisticated explanation of cultural production, Jameson's methodology reveals at *base* a concern with cultural, more particularly symbolic, anthropology. To quote a commentator, Jameson "envisions the first fall out of primitive communism as beginning the process through which the world begins to be drained of its fullness, its vividness, and its color."[16] Just as the

[16] William C. Dowling, *Jameson, Althusser, Marx: An Introduction to the Political Unconscious* (Ithaca, N.Y.: Cornell University Press, 1984), p. 26. In this context of a "fall" into modern alienation, see Michèle Richman's essay in this volume. Richman traces a similar nostalgic impulse in Durkheim and the members of the "Collège de sociologie." John Vickery documents a similar "pre-lapsarian ideality" in modernist literature. See his essay in this volume, "Frazer and the Elegaic: The Modernist Connection."

field anthropologists sought to demonstrate how symbolic acts—what Kenneth Burke would call "strategies"—are attempts to resolve contradictions in social life, so too does Jameson enlist the aid of Lévi-Strauss to show how the primitive through an imaginative act attempts to come to terms with reality, and he links this with Frye's emphasis on the social aspect of desire.

However saturated by modernist and postmodernist strategies, Jameson's essay "On Interpretation" addresses the conflict of collective desire and historical necessity. The texts interrogated later in the book are literary rather than mythical, but anyone who has read the "Introduction" carefully and who has given thought to the subtitle to the book—"Narrative as a Socially Symbolic Act"—will recognize the vestigial elements of an anthropological hermeneutic. When Jameson (1981, 70) invites us to "see literature as a weaker form of myth or a later stage of ritual . . . that all literature must be read as a symbolic meditation on the destiny of community," one is reminded of Jane Harrison and the Cambridge anthropologists (among others) who concerned themselves with such "symbolic meditations," although their findings lent themselves to the concept of a "collective soul" rather than an objective psychology.

Jameson, in his desire to escape the confines of an individual psychobiography—wherein wish fulfillment remains locked within the confines of the individual subject—looks to the work of Jacques Lacan as a possible contribution to a social psychology that would be compatible with historical materialism. There is something attractive in Lacan's replacement of the old autonomous *cogito* with a *process* dependent on the symbolic, a process that finds its roots in the unconscious collectivity systematized by the anthropological work of Lévi-Strauss. However, Lacan's positing of a "true" subject that is alienated when it enters the symbolic order and social relations—when it enters *language*—is essentially a Rousseauesque myth that seems the dialectical opposite of Marxism's insistence on the "ensemble of social relations," which constitutes the "the human essence." Lacan's "true" subject is founded on *biological* being, and what is constitutive of the subject in the Marxist position (and for that matter the earlier anthropologists and mythographers)—the symbolic order, intersubjectivity, language—is for Lacan the very foundation of alienation.

V. N. Vološinov might well afford a more satisfactory account of subjectivity and the groundwork for an objective or social psychology founded on the metasymbolic system of language. In two remarkable books, *Freudianism: A Marxist Critique* (1927) and *Marxism and the Philosophy of Language* (1929) (both of which lay dormant until the 1970s), Vološinov offers a complementary attack on what he sees as the ideological biologism of Freudian theory and provides an alternative semiotic account of consciousness based on the social nature of the sign. In his book *Freudianism*, he is at pains to show how the basic ideological motif of Freudianism is shared by other trends in modern philosophy. After he has outlined the theories of Spengler, Bergson, Driesch, and Georg Simmel (and we might include Jacques Lacan in this list), ideological carriers, as it were, of this motif, Vološinov remarks:

> Thus, we see that the basic ideological motif of Freudianism is by no means its motif alone. The motif chimes in unison with all the basic motifs of contemporary bourgeois philosophy. *A sui generis fear of history, an ambition to locate a world beyond the social and historical, a search for this precisely in the depths of the organic—these are the features that pervade all systems of contemporary philosophy and constitute the symptom of the disintegration and decline of the bourgeois world. . . .*
>
> The abstract biological person, biological individual—that which has become the alpha and omega of modern ideology—does not exist at all. Outside society and, consequently, outside objective socioeconomic conditions, there is no such thing as a human being. . . . After all, "the essence of man is not an abstraction inherent in each separate individual. In its reality it is the aggregate of social relationhips." (1976b, 14–15)

In the transition from biological to social being, our "social birth" as Vološinov puts it—the intersubjective cement that ensures the "aggregate of social relations"—it is signifying practice that is of primary importance. In his later—but in many ways interconnected book—*Marxism and the Philosophy of Language*, Vološinov outlines a dialectical theory of consciousness that is no longer seen as a "realm" but as a *process* whereby inner and outer signs meet and dialectically interpret and modify one another. Such a sociosemiotic position allows Vološinov to offer a less idealistic, or a less mechanical materialist, interpretation of the relation of base / superstructure and the role of ideology. Recognizing the work done by the anthropologists, and its application to modern social structures by such thinkers as Plekanov, Vološinov seeks a more concrete, less metaphysical anthropology of the subject's relation to the social formation.

For Vološinov, *"the inner psyche is not analyzable as a thing but can only be understood and interpreted as a sign."*[17] And since all experience can only be understood, or expressed, via the medium of the sign, even inner experience has to be social. There can be no existentialist, subjective psyche as a unique entity outside of signification. Just as

[17] *Marxism and the Philosophy of Language*, p. 26. Original italics. Vološinov's book—especially the chapter "Philosophy of Language and Objective Psychology"—makes important distinctions between biological entities and social subjects.

for primitive society the universe was one of signs and meanings, so is it as well for modern culture. A sunset is a social event.

Cassirer, whom Vološinov cites approvingly, as well as other anthropologically oriented symbologists and linguists, had stressed the importance of representation, of the symbolic function, in the formation and agency of consciousness. Vološinov's strenuous antibiologism and his negation of the transcendental ego as a reservoir of meaning, both foreshadows contemporary discourse on the subject and refines (and redefines) the earlier anthropological fieldwork that, no matter in how inchoate or unintentional a way, sought to demonstrate the social nature of the psyche through signifying practice.

Vološinov's contribution has not been fully integrated into what Marcus and Fischer have outlined as the various experimental syntheses that modern ethnographic research has taken in its effort to "synthesize Marxist approaches with structuralism, semiotics and other forms of symbolic analysis" (1986, 16). There has been a move within ethnographic discourse toward a semiotic demystification of late Western capitalist society as opposed to the earlier concentration on exotic formations. This enterprise, this "cultural critique of ourselves,"[18] is a modern analogue to Marx's earlier use of primitive society as both a critique of nineteenth-century capitalist economy and as an alternative way of "seeing" social reality. Both critiques have in common the process of demystification, or defamiliarization—indeed demystification through defamiliarization—save that modern ethnography produces its critique within Western industrial society by denaturalizing cultural texts and "reading" their social meaning.

There are still textual exotica of course, particularly in the work of someone like Clifford Geertz, whose symbolic analysis interprets culture as essentially a transaction of signifiers—a modernist version of the traditional hermeneutics of symbol and ritual. As Marcus and Fischer observe, "Geertz is in the tradition of Durkheim," the tradition that emphasizes the fact that "there is no private language; all consciousness is intersubjective, mediated by public communicative forms" (1986, 50). This intersubjective notion of the subject is reflected in his work with the Balinese, particularly the essay "Person, Time and Conduct in Bali." Marcus and Fischer, discussing what they call "personhood," summarize Geertz's findings thus:

> The Balinese act as if persons were impersonal sets of roles, in which all individuality and emotional volatility are systematically repressed. Their notion of personhood and emotional structure is quite different from the European autonomous ego as described by Freud. . . .

[18] See chapter 5 in Marcus and Fischer, "The Repatriation of Anthropology as Cultural Critique." See also Rabinow's remarks in *Writing Culture*, p. 241.

> The most appealing and effective aspect of Geertz's essay is that he does not resort to discussions of psychology, even though he is talking about "the Balinese mind." (1986, 47)

What in fact Geertz is doing is documenting a semiotic notion of consciousness based on ritual and other socially significant practices, offering empirical evidence for the kind of objective psychology that forms the basis of Vološinov's theoretical program. Bradd Shore's ethnographic work in Samoa provides another graphic account of the individual subject as well as offering a documentary gloss on Marx's Sixth Thesis on Feuerbach, which, as we have seen, accentuates the "ensemble of social relations" as constitutive of the human individual. Shore's ethnographic record tells of how the "Samoan language has no terms corresponding to 'personality, self, character'; instead of our Socratic 'know thyself,' Samoans say 'take care of the relationship.' " The greater number of relationships, the more complete the person (Marcus & Fischer 1986, 65).

Apart from offering a critique of Freudian ethnocentricity, this account defamiliarizes our notion of the individual. It is this process of making the familiar strange through the semiotic analyis of cultural texts that is predominant in what Marcus and Fischer call "repatriation as cultural critique." It is especially this cultural critique of ourselves that might offer the kind of "synchronic analysis," or critique by juxtaposition, that Marx had found in anthropology at the end of the nineteenth century, and in our postparadigmatic "moment" might offer a fuller account of cultural materialism.

The authors of *Anthropology as Cultural Critique* suggest that paradigms such as classical Marxism "must be translated by ethnographic inquiry into cultural terms and grounded in everyday life" (1986, 82), and there have been attempts by anthropologists of Marxian persuasion to address this very issue. Indeed, the very title of Stephen K. Levine's essay, "Marxist Anthropology and the Critique of Everyday Life" attempts to address Marcus and Fischer's criticism some years before the publication of their book. At pains to stress the fact that political economy (the "real" foundations of existence) should remain the ultimate causal base, Levine is aware that the individual subject in modern neocapitalist formations is overdetermined by a number of cultural factors. Noting that "the goal is to liberate the subject from the conditions of his alienation" (a program at the heart of Marx's anthropology), Levine remarks that the solution is not to be found solely in political economy, "but rather in those portions of contemporary social science that have attempted to grasp the individual in the context of his society, namely sociology and social psychology" (Diamond 1979, 19). Identity is a construct of social roles, is overdetermined by the everyday acting out of those roles that make us subjects, and to which we willingly subject ourselves: *Homo economicus,* the essential nineteenth century paradigm, gives way to *Homo sociologicus,* to use Ralph Dahrendorf's terms. Levine suggests a viable historicopolitical reason for this revised ideology of the subject: "As the individual entrepreneur in the period of capital accumulation gives way to the corporate employee in a period of capital stabilization, the autonomous ego of the inner-directed man is shattered into a fragmented sense of selfhood dependent upon recognition by others" (Diamond 1979, 21). Of course the autonomous ego was (and is) always an illusion, a fictive construction, but the implication of Levine's position is well-taken: if the subject is constituted by its "internalization of social norms," that is, it depends for its very being on these social positions, how then is it possible to transcend them in the cause of social or revolutionary change? This argument is close—as many will recognize—to the position taken by Althusser, wherein ideology is seen as a necessity if society is to function at all.

Levine's enquiry into "everyday life" reflects a desire (and perhaps a need) to supplement abstract paradigms such as Marxist analysis with more empirical evidence, with microanalyses or ethnographic documentary that would "fill out" the theoretical scaffolding of the paradigm. Such ethnographic evidence could (and in many cases does) substantiate such theoretical concerns as the economic base of ritual; the relativity of bourgeois norms; ideology and its conditioning of the subject; and, as suggested in the work of Geertz and Shore, a denaturalization of the bourgeois individual as autonomous ego.

The kind of program called for here—a modern alliance of Marxism and ethnographic documentary—resembles in many ways the psychosocial program of the Frankfurt School with its emphasis on the family as a microsocial formation and the investigation of how psychical traits can be traced to the social mediacy of peer groups—how subjects can be "called upon" to take up a particular social position. It is no coincidence that Marcus and Fischer should invoke the work of the Frankfurt School in the context of their world of postparadigmatic uncertainty. The Frankfurt School's program had its origin in an antitotalitarianism (surely the ultimate paradigm) and an investigation into the multiple forms of domination, by way of a return to the materialism of Marx, a materialism that allows for the role of human subjectivity.

Whether or not we agree with Marcus and Fischer that the Frankfurt School was too theoretically oriented—that, despite their healthy skepticism of a holistic paradigm, they lacked or were disinterested in empirical evidence (although the School's early concern with ethnographic documentation of anti-Semitism would seem to refute this)—one has to agree with them that ethnographic "microstudies" can (and do) help "fulfill" more abstract macrotheories. We will always need theory, but if theory becomes "impoverished" (as E. P. Thompson would have us believe), then we need to put theory into practice, to enrich it with these ethnographies of everyday life. Paul Willis's *Learning to Labour: How Working Class Kids Get Working Class Jobs* is an excellent example of a microanalysis that both clarifies and substantiates how the working-class subject is positioned (and because of ideological conditioning, is "happily" positioned) within a particular social system, in this case that of the English class structure.

Walter Benjamin (unlike others of the Frankfurt School) had hoped that the advent of mass technological culture would allow particular subcultures to "express" themselves, and through a sense of solidarity and resistance to the dominant culture, achieve a form of liberation from the dominant ideology.[19] Willis's ethnography of working-class schoolboys, however, is a documentary example of how such resistance by a particular peer group ironically aids the workings of this particular state apparatus. It is the members of the "counter-school culture" who, by *opposing* the law of the school, single themselves out for their "calling." The very first sentences of the book accentuate this irony: "The difficult thing to explain about how middle class kids get middle class jobs is why others let them. The difficult thing to explain about how working class kids get working class jobs is why they let themselves" (Willis 1977, 1). Willis's book is divided into two parts, "Ethnography" and "Analysis," the latter offering theories based on the empirical first section. The "theory," especially the section dealing with ideology, is made highly complex because of its "contamination" by the ethnographic research. Those members of the counter-school culture, those *determined* to get factory jobs, are certainly circumscribed by what Willis calls a "hegemony of commonsense"—what we might call the dominant ideology of the school—but it is not as simple as that, as Willis retrospectively attests:

> We have seen in the section on ethnography that many forms of the conventional dominant ideology . . . are minced up, inverted or simply defeated by the counter-school culture. The crucial divisions, distortions and transferences which have been examined arise very often not so much from ideas and values mediated *downward* from the dominant social group,

[19] For a brief history see Tom Bottomore, *The Frankfurt School* (London: Tavistock Publications, 1984). More particularly, for a discussion of the debate between Benjamin and Adorno on the theory of the commodity form, see Stephen Webster's essay in this volume.

> but from internal cultural relationships. Certain aspects of the working class cultural affirmation of manual labour considered here are profoundly important both ideologically and materially, and are, if anything, exported upwards to a largely uncomprehending official ideological apparatus. (1977, 160)

Apart from the specificity of seeing ideology "at work" and the complexity of that working (the most important aspect of Willis's book), the ethnographic section of *Learning to Labour* is replete with contemporary examples of traditional anthropological conceptual analysis. The very opposition to authority is "a *ritualistic* part of the daily fabric of life" (Willis 1977, 12), as is the "*symbolic* importance of drinking as an act of affiliation with adults and opposition to the school" (Willis 1977, 20), especially on the last day when it becomes a *rite of passage*. There are numerous *taboos* in force at Hammertown School, as well as sexual initiation rites and symbolic violence (mock fights), but to document all the cultural significations of this subculture would be to reproduce the whole ethnographic record. Suffice it to say that the "exotic" other is alive and well and living in Hammertown!

Willis takes his epigraph from Marx's *Grundrisse* (his theoretical macro, as it were), from a section that notes the inextricable interdependence of individuality and social interconnection, and Willis's microanalysis fulfills (in every sense of the word) that macrotheoretical premise. Like Geertz (although in a less exotic setting), Willis investigates—through linguistic and symbolic analysis—the transindividuality of a microculture, and he uncovers a "psychology" that is structured by the social group.

One of Willis's goals is to show how the subject is formed "at the cultural and symbolic level as well as at the economic and structural level" (1977, 2) and such an intent returns us not only to a fundamental concern of this essay—how the symbolic helps constitute individual subjects in certain social formations—but also to the vexing question of the possibility of human agency within the confines of ideology. It is perhaps illustrative of what this essay has been attempting to document that Willis's ethnographic study finds itself situated within various contemporary theoretical positions.

In the context of discussing Henry Giroux's *Theory and Resistance in Education*, Paul Smith invokes *Learning to Labour* as a supplement to Giroux's belief that "ideology functions not only to limit human action but also to enable it." In the context of Willis's study, Smith seems right when he asks "whether resistance to ideology can itself be described as ideologically determined, and this is a matter that is clearly tied to the definition of human agency" (1988, 67). It is in the cause of human agency that Anthony Giddens states that "*all social actors, no matter how lowly, have some degree of penetration of the social forms which oppress them*" (1979, 72), and he notes Paul Willis's study as illustrative of such a position. The apparent conflict here—that ideology is impregnable, and yet some breach of the ideological barrier is possible—is more readily understood in the light of the same ethnographic study. Although some of the counter-school culture "penetrates" the "largely uncomprehending official ideological apparatus" (see the above quotation from Willis), it does so only to reaffirm the subordinate's position within the dominant ideology, even if this may be "incomprehensible" to those in control.

Furthermore, it is not much compensation to suggest, as Giddens does, that those who dominate the "conditions of social reproduction" may "in a largely unquestioning way accept certain dominant perspectives [and] may be more imprisoned within them than others are, even though these perspectives help the former [those who dominate] to sustain their position of dominance" (1979, 72). This is only an "imprisonment" in the sense that it is an unconscious fulfillment of what we might call the *laissez faire* nature of cultural capital, a capital accumulated through the workings of ideology. Pierre Bourdieu has remarked that whenever "a system of mechanisms has been constituted capable of objectively ensuring the reproduction of the established order by its own motion . . . the dominant class have only to *let the system they dominate take its own course* in order to exercise their domination" (1977, 190). This certainly seems to be the case with the institutional practices that Willis documents in his ethnography. The subculture's behavior may penetrate upward to an "uncomprehending" elite, but such oppositional gestures only serve to install the working-class schoolboys within what Bourdieu calls the "objective mechanism."

The fact that Willis's study is called upon within these various theoretical contexts is only a contemporary sign of what I have been outlining in an historical manner here. The fusion of ethnographic enquiry as a critique of culture can (and has demonstrated that it can) provide a specificity, not only to a nineteenth-century paradigmatic Marxism, but also to contemporary theories of the subject and subjection such as, for example, that of Louis Althusser. The fact that these working-class teenagers are "interpellated" by virtue of their very rebellion does not refute Althusser's theoretical position, but at the very least it modifies or gives sustenance to it.

Perhaps once again we are at a juncture where the confluence of Marxist analysis and ethnographic investigation could form a fruitful alliance in a theory of cultural materialism, just as it had seemed to Marx and Engels toward the end of the nineteenth century.

The Historical Materialist Critique of Surrealism and Postmodernist Ethnography

STEVEN WEBSTER

FORM HAS become important in some contemporary ethnographic writing. However, the social theory implicit in the writing cannot be easily distinguished from its form. History is obscured in this merger, which is itself historic. In the social sciences, the long-established distinction between aesthetic criticism and social science, although often questioned, seems to have become blurred in practice and problematic in theory since about the 1960s. In aesthetics and literary criticism, on the other hand, the apparent convergence has long been implicit in the conceptual framework of modernism. Since the 1970s the perhaps related processes in some of the social sciences began to be recognized in terms of the textual or formal dimensions of their disciplinary discourses. What was happening in ethnographic practice by 1975, especially in the United States, was tentatively theorized by 1982 in terms of literary forms, first realism and modernism, and then the current notion of postmodernism.

The perception of social science discourse in terms of literary forms is, given the material history of the distinction, necessarily ambivalent. The ambivalence expresses specific histories: in anthropological terms, the new attention to ethnographic form was precipitated by the cultural relativity and skepticism characteristic of the discipline, perhaps further motivated by awareness of professional implication in colonialism and the emergence of new states from old empires. Theorization of the emerging and obviously experimental ethnographic forms was in terms of hermeneutic or interpretive theory. The phenomenological, cultural, and semantic interests of French social philosophy had immediate appeal to many anthropologists. The conceptualization of interpretive reflexivity, originating in phenomenology, offered a sophisticated theorization of the professional anthropological predicament of intensive fieldwork and cultural relativity.

In retrospect, I suggest that at least two major forms of the new ethnography have been developed. While consciously experimental ethnography was being explicated in terms of reflexivity and interpretive theory, another ethnographic form was tacitly taking shape in departures from the previously established theory of anthropological structuralism, rewritten in terms of a semiology of culture history. The experimental form is surveyed and analyzed in Marcus and Cushman (1982) and Clifford and Marcus (1986), and the structuralist form of culture history is tentatively examined in my own essay (1987) and, in different directions, by Hooper and Huntsman (1985), Edmund Leach (1985a,b), and Jonathan Friedman (1987).

Upon closer inspection, the semiotic theory in terms of which the new structuralist culture history was emerging had developed in close association with the interpretive theory that informed experimental ethnography, and more generally with the contemporary deconstructionist theory of the new philosophers of France. In 1985, Edmund Leach, a leading British ethnographic structuralist since the 1950s, realized this common ground and applauded a synthesis between Sahlins's structuralist cultural history, reflexive hermeneutics, and deconstructionism (1985a). Although Ricoeur and the hermeneutic turn in French phenomenology lay behind the implicit theoretical shape of experimental ethnography, Barthes and poststructuralist semiology—and especially the view of history in deconstructionist criticism—lay behind the theoretical shape of the renewed structuralist ethnography. Although Leach seems to have intuited some connections, the history of these implicit theories tends to remain embedded in the writing forms.

What became apparent in literature much earlier has now become apparent in some scientific writing: "the truly social element in literature is the form" (Lukács 1909, in Eagleton 1976, 20). The most significant characteristic of the new ethnographic forms is that their theory, and hence its specific history, is merged indistinguishably with the form. What are the social implications of this? My own theoretical effort pursued here is to regain a critical perspective on these important developments in ethnography by recovering for examination certain aspects of their history. From the point of view of the new ethnographic forms themselves, this is a conservative position, but my own experimental ethnographic practice (1981, 1989) as well as the shortcomings of the emerging forms have driven me back to it.

Perhaps characteristic of the postmodern condition, these ethnographic forms are their own implicit theory. Experimental ethnography tends, for instance, to recapitulate the hermeneutics or reflexivity of fieldwork or a wider social change in the form of the ethnographic text, treating the account itself as part of the same social process (Webster 1987, 1982). Similarly, the form of the text in structuralist culture history (for example, Sahlins 1981; Hanson & Hanson 1982) recapitulates the structuralist or semiological theory that all cultural phenomena are organized in codes; the history of the society is the history of structural transformations within its cultural code. It is significant that in both cases, the traditional theoretical dilemma of anthropology—the cultural relativity of its object—is maintained, either as a problem for hermeneutic reflexivity or as a problem in the translatability and interaction of cultural codes.

But furthermore, in both of these ethnographic forms, the text is implicitly presented as an example or continuation of its subject, not—or not merely—as a representation of it in the conventional sense of a social scientific description or explanation. Deconstructionist theorizations of postmodernist ethnographic forms (for example, Stephen Tyler and Michael Fischer, in Clifford & Marcus 1986) recommend them as textual evocations, performances, or therapy, as distinct from representation, which is problematic in modernism and illusory in the postmodern condition. Thus, the hermeneutic or semiological form of the ethnographic text becomes an implicit theory of the social process described, and this theory furthermore assumes the theoretical problematic of cultural relativism. Or, to put the problem from the point of view of postmodernism, writing practice is no longer estranged from theory; it *is* theory. Indeed, Lyotard (1979) had pointed out that postmodernism is skeptical of metatheories.

These mergers of theory and textual form in ethnography and other social sciences parallel the postmodernist submergence of the modernist predicament of representation in art and literature into pure simulacra, neutral and ahistorical pastiche of re-representations without illusory reference to originals (Jameson 1984). This flattening of theory into practice is characteristic of postmodern art or—to beg with Lyotard the question of a contemporary convergence between art and science—the postmodern condition of all knowledge. Theory and practice, separated by history for Hegel and historically separated for Marx, is no longer a dialectical problem for the ahistorical postmodern condition. Hence the critique of this condition must be an historical critique.

Anthropology and Aesthetic Form

Given further retrospect, the postmodernist programs—including the new ethnographic forms—might appear quixotic or transcendental against the historical momentum of an established discourse tradition and its material conditions, which extend from the Enlightenment. Respect for this momentum has been expressed in various ways. In their 1982 review of experimental ethnography, Marcus and Cushman register cautions in behalf of an established ethnographic genre, which they tentatively treat as a form of literary realism. Following Raymond Williams's discussion of realism, I argue that what the ethnographic genre established might be reification rather than realism, and demand in behalf of scientific objectivity that ethnography be told like it is: a hermeneutic form of political practice (Webster 1986). Rabinow (in Clifford and Marcus 1986) points out that the deconstructionist suspicion of representation is somehow spurious in social science discourse, necessarily subverting itself.

For guidance in the so-called crisis of representation, Rabinow refers to Frederic Jameson (1984), whose analysis of postmodernism as the cultural logic of advanced capitalism both accepts postmodernism as a period of development in material history and (following Habermas) seeks to retain the critical distance characteristic of modernist modes of analysis but collapsed in postmodernism. My specific historical inquiry here pursues Jameson's suggestion that Benjamin's 1930s account of Baudelaire's Paris in the mid-nineteenth century can restore a critical historical perspective to postmodernism (Jameson 1984, 84, 89). Habermas (1983)—following Benjamin and Adorno—suggests that postmodernism, along with a long legacy of other idealist positions, has attempted to close by fiat an historical gap, between subject and object or between practice and theory, within which modernism in its several forms has struggled since the Enlightenment. The merger of theory and textual form in postmodernist ethnography may, upon closer historical examination, prove to be a similarly illusory fiat.

Perhaps more than Rabinow or Jameson knew, their suggestion is indeed promising for anthropology because it fixes on an entwined yet specific history. The debate between Benjamin and Adorno in the 1930s over the representation of Baudelaire's Paris was at the same time an historical materialist critique of contemporary surrealist methods. Furthermore, as participants in the aesthetic avant-garde, they nevertheless sought a surrealist method for their sociological representations. From the contemporary perspective of postmodernism, we could not hope for any more dialectical critique in this significant historical development. The specific situation of surrealist method was, furthermore, anthropological. James Clifford (1981) was the first to examine the common history of French ethnology and surrealism in Paris of the 1920–1930s, and this connection has since become influential in the theoretical conceptualization of experimental ethnographic forms (cf. Marcus and Fischer 1986). Clifford suggests that immediate historical continuities lie through Marcel Mauss and ethnographic surrealism to poststructuralist semiology (1981, 550–53). Below I summarize some that lie through Georges Bataille and deconstructionist social theory. Both members of the Collège de sociologie in Paris, Benjamin and Bataille undertook materialist critiques of surrealism, although in divergent directions.

Although explored in British and European anthropological traditions, experimental ethnography has developed primarily in the United States, and can be traced to the influence of Clifford Geertz, his students, and the advocacies and critiques that followed his introduction of hermeneutic theory to anthropology in the early 1970s. However, the hermeneutic theory that Geertz introduced derived from Paul Ricoeur, a central figure in the development of phenomenology in France. Ricoeur's theory was developed as part of a theory of spiritual alienation that was a critique of both Marx's materialism and Lévi-Strauss's scientism. Diane Austin (1979) also critiques the essentialist or idealist assumptions of semiological theory that inform Geertz's conception of culture. In 1982 I argued that Gadamer's hermeneutics better retained the necessary critical and dialectical ground of an historical objectivity.

Geertz's method struggled ambivalently to retain the objective ground of anthropological method. Nevertheless, the subsequent use of hermeneutic theory in the consciously experimental ethnographic exploration of ethnographic form has, following the phenomenological and essentialist assumptions of Geertz's theory, been dominated by a personal or even subjectivist construal of hermeneutic reflexivity. Marcus and Fischer (1986) have documented experimental ethnographies that have sought to retain a more sociological or political economic interest against the culturalist alternative frequently taken by hermeneutics. Nevertheless, the ambivalent direction that Geertz established has held sway. Furthermore, regardless of superficial hostilities, the semiological interest widespread in anthropology by the mid-1970s was complementary to anthropological structuralism, already established by Lévi-Strauss and Edmund Leach. The anthropological concept of culture was serving as a synthesis of the most diverse social theories.

In French social theory of the 1960–1970s semiological theory led by Roland Barthes and the *Tel Quel* group of scholars rejected structuralism and established poststructuralist theory. Most influential in this movement have been the divergent forms of deconstructionist theory represented by Jacques Derrida, Michel Foucault, Jacques Lacan, Julia Kristeva, Jean-François Lyotard, and Jean Baudrillard. After the 1968 student uprisings, the *Tel Quel* group shifted from militant Maoism to strident anti-Communism (Eagleton 1983, 147), continuing the traditional critique of Marxist materialism that originated in French phenomenology. Marshall Sahlins's structuralist theory of culture history was inspired by this intellectual context. In his *Culture and Practical Reason* (1976) Sahlins took his lead from Jean Baudrillard and rejected the structuralist Marxism of Althusser and Godelier, earlier influences on his work.

In the next section I will briefly outline the antecedents of Baudrillard's and Sahlins's theory, which I have developed elsewhere (Webster 1987, 53–58). However, I will suggest here that the anthropological concept of culture is as crucial to Sahlins's structuralist theory of culture history as it was to Geertz's hermeneutic method and the experimental ethnographic form that developed from it. Addressing Sahlins's theory of culture history, Jonathan Friedman (1987) criticizes his reification of the anthropological concept of culture. This raises one of the central but obscured historical involutions of postmodernist ethnographic forms, both hermeneutic and structuralist.

The apparent convergence of aesthetics and social science in the postmodern condition of knowledge is on a particular historical ground, at least in anthropology. The conceptual residue of this shared historical ground is indicated by the notion of culture: the specialized domain of aesthetics and aesthetic criticism on the one hand, and the increasingly central professional concept of anthropological science on the other. Reflecting the generally divergent history of aesthetics and science since the Enlightenment, the aesthetic and anthropological senses of the notion of culture now appear to be quite different. However, this contemporary appearance needs historical scrutiny. Raymond Williams's sociological and historical exploration of the notion of culture (for example, 1981) has only begun to uncover some of its convolutions. Apparently outside the anthropological mainstream are Herder's and Arnold's usages in German and English romanticism, Lukács's and the Frankfurt School's usages in the revitalization of Marxist critique since the 1930s, T. S. Eliot's sacral blend of the aesthetic and anthropological senses of culture in 1948, and the preoccupation of E. P. Thompson and several other schools of historical research with the concept of culture since the 1960s.

Williams's effort to recover the obscured history of the notion of culture remains to be met from the direction of anthropology, although George Stocking's careful research has begun to close the gap. Kroeber and Kluckhohn's critical historical review of the concepts and definitions of culture in 1952 tended to lose its historical orientation in their conclusion that the contemporary consensus among other United States anthropologists had best identified it. They concluded that anthropologically, culture was best conceived as a "pattern," "style," or "way" of life, a form or whole distinguishable from its content or parts, a "synchronically historical" form in the same sense that language had been found to be constituted by a structure. This emerging preconception of culture on the model of a linguistic or psychological structure had been implicit in anthropological theory since the 1920s, when it was originated by Franz Boas's students, especially Edward Sapir, Ruth Benedict, and Alfred Kroeber. Benedict's influential *Patterns of Culture* in 1934 popularized the anthropological notion of culture as a pattern in the psychological sense of a gestalt. Her approach followed Sapir's, whose influential studies of linguistics and culture in the early 1920s drew in turn on the idealist conceptions of these notions developed in Herder, Arnold, and Croce. In addition to Croce, other influences upon Benedict were Nietzsche and Santayana, and upon Kroeber was Rickert, all leaders in the diversity of idealist philosophical traditions that developed in the romanticist reaction to positivism at the end of the nineteenth century.

Although Stocking was the first to emphasize the continuity between English and German romanticism and the American concept of culture, I think that it can be shown that his understanding of Boas's concept of culture has obscured the crucial role of Boas's students in renewing the romanticist tradition (Webster n.d.). Boas is usually credited with the modern anthropological conception of culture, but he in fact defended a notion of the term that was far less idealist and relativist than that of his students. His European training was strongly influenced by the Berlin *Geisteswissenschaften* school led by Dilthey, but this school was opposed to the neo-Kantian two-worlds theory of the Baden school, led by Windelband and Rickert (Arato 1974). By 1910 the latter school, and especially Rickert, developed the conception of culture as a realm of values and immanent meanings methodologically autonomous from the realm of nature, in which positivist and empirical methodologies were appropriate. The later development of this theory by Heidegger (Roberts 1982, 81) is one of the primary roots of contemporary deconstructionist theory, by way of Alexandre Kojève and Bataille. I will expand on this in the next section.

The later development of the anthropological concept of culture from this and other neo-idealist reactions to nineteenth-century positivism was already compatible with the structuralist theory of Lévi-Strauss. Parallel to the two-worlds conception of culture, in 1916

Saussure founded "semiology" as a science of stable language forms distinguishable and methodologically autonomous from the changing historical content of languages. Subsequently, Saussure's linguistic formalism was extrapolated (against his warnings) into other fields such as literary criticism (Jakobson and the Prague School) and anthropology (Lévi-Strauss and structuralism). Saussure's semiology and structuralism had been consciously antimaterialist, and furthermore developed as a polemic over disciplinary boundaries (Timpanaro 1975).

Later, the developments of structuralism and then semiology in the anthropological sense of culture had lost sight of their own historical origins, and hence of the confrontation between idealist and materialist construals of the world from which they had developed. From different directions and in apparently independent ways, such leaders in anthropological theory as Geertz, Leach, Sahlins, and Pierre Bourdieu reinforced in the 1970s the essentialist conception of culture that was taking shape by the time of Kroeber and Kluckhohn's imprimatur in 1952.

However, it is important to retain material historical bearings on these widespread and influential intellectual developments. These developments themselves must be understood in the specific contexts of new organizations of production in manufacturing and new forms of bureaucratic organization, especially in the centers of industrial growth, by the time of the First World War (cf. Montgomery 1987). Since the Second World War, these revolutions of production have been expanded in the development of information theory and microchip technology. Jameson suggests that "the cultural logic of late capitalism" is the postmodernist expression of these historical processes.

Recent historical and sociological research (Abercrombie et al. 1980) has suggested another important implication in the history of the anthropological notion of culture: its historical correlative in some social theories, including some versions of Marxism, is the misleading notion of a dominant ideology. Emile Durkheim's conception of society appears to be a major source of this implicit theoretical complementarity. Durkheim's concept of a collective or socially transmitted consciousness, ultimately derived from his study of the elementary forms of religious life, has long been the sociological (and British social anthropological) surrogate for the American anthropological concept of culture. In 1958, Kroeber and Talcott Parsons recommended a division of labor between anthropology and sociology that divided up Durkheim's "condensed" concept into its implicit components: culture in the sense of essential meanings and "social system" in the sense of the "relational system" between individuals and collectivities (Austin 1979). This historic arrangement had its history: Parsons's sociological theory derived more directly than Kroeber's from the two-worlds school of the *Geisteswissenschaften* at Baden.

Durkheim's notion of collective consciousness also appears to be a primary historical origin of the idealist misconstrual of Marx's concept of ideology as dominating as well as distorting understanding of historical processes. The assumption of a dominant role for ideology has emerged as an idealist undercurrent in many European left-wing social theories including those of Lukács, the Frankfurt School, Gramsci, Althusser, and the deconstructionists. With regard to the special concern of this essay, Benjamin and Adorno criticized related assumptions in the surrealist movement and in each other's work, and the surrealist theories of the Collège de sociologie were importantly influenced by Durkheim's notion of the collective consciousness (Michèle Richman, in this volume).

One of my main concerns is to trace historically some of the idealist theories that have taken shape in postmodernist ethnographic forms. Still, one may ask, why take recourse to the materialist critique of surrealism in the 1930s to clarify contemporary ethnographic postmodernism? Because, I suggest, the historical aesthetic avant-garde and the contemporary ethnographic avant-garde are sequels in the same general historical development of advanced industrial society. The theoretical developments that obscured the history of the notion of culture obscured a still more general development in the relation between aesthetic form and the practical world. Peter Bürger's *Theory of the Avantgarde* (1984 [1974]) analyzes the material conditions that enabled the avant-garde art movements (for example, dada, constructivism, surrealism) of the interwar years to grasp and react to the implications of aesthetic modernism.

Following Marcuse's critical theory of idealist philosophy, Bürger argues that the historical avant-garde sought—unsuccessfully—to reintegrate in practical life the aesthetic and moral forms that, since the Enlightenment, had increasingly been alienated to an imaginary world. This world paralleled practical life, itself increasingly organized in terms of bourgeois instrumental rationality or pragmatism. Just as the uniformity of this instrumentalist practice and philosophy constituted the material conditions of aestheticism or "art for art's sake" by the end of the nineteenth century, the modernist institutionalization of art as pure form constituted the material conditions of the modernist avant-garde resolution to negate art by transforming practical life in its image.

In this analysis, Bürger extended Marx's reasoning that his revolutionary distinction between the exchange value and use value of labor under capitalism required the material preconditions of the bourgeois ideology of human equality, that is, the institutionalization of abstractly free and equal labor as a commodity. The bourgeois instrumental rationality to which aestheticism formed the historical complement was, in fact, the philosophical expression of the market exchange value of abstract human labor. The consolidation of art as pure alienated form reproduced the ideals of justice and beauty in an imaginary world that paralleled but never touched the world of practical life—except as abstract universals assimilable to this instrumental rationality without changing it. Because the historical avant-garde generally remained bound within the institutional structures of modernism that were the material conditions of its new practices, it too was generally assimilated to these conditions and their instrumental rationality without fundamentally changing their society.

The merger of social theory and textual form in contemporary ethnography can be seen as an historical sequel to the intentions of the aesthetic avant-garde, now attempted in domains of social science rather than art. Given this perspective, it becomes clear that the apparent merger of theory and textual form is actually a separation of theory from practical life, obscured by hermeneutic or structuralist theory, or by the postmodernist claim that the text is a part, performance, or evocation—rather than a representation—of the practical world. This integration of form and text as the simulacrum of practical life, like the historical avant-garde movements, seeks to overcome by fiat the entire material history that led first to a separation of aesthetic form, and now to the separation of social theory, from everyday practice. Necessarily made from this position and these historical conditions, acknowledged or not, these attempts tend merely to reproduce the conditions of their practice. Some of the theoretical critiques of the surrealist movement may, therefore, be relevant to its sequel in avant-garde ethnography.

Surrealist Form and the Benjamin-Adorno Debate

Most members of the surrealist movement were socialist or communist, and committed through the modernist critique of aesthetic autonomy either to express their political theory in surrealist form or to express this form politically. Moreover, Benjamin, Adorno, Brecht, and Bataille were Marxists in the sense that they were students of Marx's writings and explicitly committed to his theory of historical materialism. The value of a closer examination of their positions for a critique of postmodernism lies in their divergent efforts to integrate avant-garde surrealist practice and critical social theory. Each, furthermore, sought to apply, in different ways, key aspects of the social theory of historical materialism: the critique of idealism, the theory of commodity fetishism, and the relative importance of production and consumption in social processes.

I will examine only Benjamin's and Adorno's positions here, and only through one important part of their long intellectual relationship. Although surrealism as a specific historical movement in Paris (Nadeau 1968) did not actually include any of these four Marxists, Bataille and Benjamin were closely associated with it and, through Benjamin, Adorno, and Brecht were thoroughly familiar with the movement, as well as the associated avant-garde theory. Bataille's activities were most closely associated with the movement throughout its course in Paris, and in 1929 he was among the leaders of a confrontation with André Breton, its dominant spokesman. Benjamin began visiting Paris from Frankfurt in 1927, published important essays on surrealism in 1929 and 1936, and took refuge from the Nazis in Paris from 1933 to 1939. Between 1937 and 1939 he participated in the Collège de sociologie, which was founded by Bataille and other dissident surrealists devoted to restoring the sociological ground of surrealism dissipated in Breton's psychologism (Clifford 1981, 559–61; Stoekl 1985, xx–xxi; Richman, this volume). When Benjamin fled from Paris in 1939, he left most of his manuscripts with Bataille, also a librarian at the National Library where Benjamin often worked. The Nazis confiscated the rest and his library in his apartment in Paris. Adorno, a key member of the Frankfurt School of critical theory, which was relocated in New York before the war, specialized in a materialist critique of culture, especially of modern music. He was strongly influenced by Benjamin from their mutual discussions on surrealism in 1929 through to Benjamin's suicide in 1939, and subsequently helped to edit his works.

Susan Buck-Morss (1977, 22; 124) demonstrates the seminal reciprocal influence of Adorno and Benjamins' two months of discussions in Königstein, near Frankfurt in 1929. These included discussions of the surrealist movement, and readings from Benjamin's draft *Passagenarbeit* ("Arcades study" on mid-nineteenth-century Paris), inspired by Louis Aragon's early surrealist novel *Le Paysan de Paris*. An epitome by Aragon on his novel can be seen to invite both the surrealist methodology and Benjamin's Marxist critique of it in terms of the contradictions of commodity fetishism: "Reality is the apparent absence of contradiction. The wondrous is contradiction appearing in the real" (Lunn 1982, 56). A major part of Benjamin's Arcades study later became a long essay on Charles Baudelaire, as a lyric poet in Paris in a mid-nineteenth-century era of high capitalism. The first draft of this was written in 1938. The debate between Benjamin and Adorno that I will examine was primarily over this draft. Benjamin later revised it to satisfy Adorno.

In about 1929–1930 Georges Bataille wrote a counterattack against André Breton, who as leader of the surrealist movement had demanded from him and others confessions of their bourgeois compromises of the rigor demanded of surrealist politics (Nadeau 1968; Stoekl 1985). Bataille's retort was that there were "too many fucking idealists" in the surrealist movement. However, the ambiguity of his own form of materialism is preserved in the epitome of his 1929–1930 essay, quoted from Marx: "In history as in nature, decay is the laboratory of life." The essay developed a conception of "base" materialism against "high" or "Icarian" idealism, claiming that "the old mole" (Marx) would subvert all pretensions to "super-" or "sur-"(realism) by burrowing underneath them (1985, 32–44). As I will note later, Benjamin may have picked up the metaphor of Icarus and idealism.

However, there is no other evidence of an exchange of ideas between them, despite their common interest in the materialist critique of surrealism. Although Bataille rejected any naturalistic conception of "materialism" as idealist (including, with considerable insight, Engels's dialectical materialism [1985, 15; 108]), his psychological and social conception of materialism as "base" or vulgar (for example, 1985, 32, 37) was primarily a reaction to elitism (on which grounds he also criticized Nietzsche as idealist). Bataille also associated materialism with the primitive or "archaic" societies that the ethnologist Marcel Mauss analyzed, and he relied heavily on Mauss's accounts of sacrifice and the potlatch in his sociological theory of expenditure or consumption. Hence, there was a strong romanticist tinge in Bataille's materialist critique of surrealism, ironically reminiscent of Emile Zola's naturalism. In Benjamin's 1929 essay on surrealism, such surrealist "base" materialism had already been identified as the idealist counterpart of bourgeois guilt, expressed in action for its own sake: "Characteristic of this whole left-wing bourgeois position is its irremediable coupling of idealistic morality with political practice. Only in contrast to the helpless compromises of 'sentiment' are certain central features of Surrealism, indeed of the Surrealist tradition, to be understood" ([1929], 234). Also in common with others in the surrealist movement, Bataille similarly appears to reduce Marx's theory of labor and commodity fetishism to the simple bourgeois condemnation of exploitation and greed.

On the other hand, Bataille seriously addresses Marx's dialectical analysis of the relation between production and consumption—and his specific argument in this regard was to be seminal in the social theory of transgression developed in deconstructionism, and in Sahlins's structuralist theory of culture history. Probably because of his fundamental misunderstanding of Marx's value theory of labor, Bataille argues that consumption or nonproductive "expenditure," rather than production and utility, is the defining feature of human nature. He derives his theory of expenditure from Mauss's analysis of the gift in archaic societies, and extends it to modern societies where it is realized, for instance, in class oppression and bloody revolutions of the working class against capitalists (1985, 120–21; 124–26). His model for this theory was Alexandre Kojève's Marxist analysis of Hegel's phenomenology and specifically Hegel's theory of death.

Bataille's social theory of expenditure became central to Baudrillard's theory of consumption and critique of Marx's theory of production (Baudrillard 1972), and subsequently to Sahlins's anthropological critique of Marx and practical reason in general (Sahlins 1976, 148, 155, 166–67, 177; Webster 1987, 53–58; n.d.). However, these subsequent refinements of Bataille's thesis continue to rely on his fundamental assumptions regarding materialism and idealism, labor, production, and consumption. In retrospect, it is clear that these assumptions were themselves reifications derived, through misunderstanding of Marx, from the contradictions of the surrealist movement itself. Bataille's critique of surrealist form had only retained the radical posture of historical materialism, while in practice subverting its key principles.

The value of Benjamin and Adorno's critique of surrealist form is their prolonged effort to interpret closely the theory of historical materialism, while at the same time recognizing that the practice of this theory had to come to terms with a new historical context—an important expression of which was avant-garde modernism. Benjamin, Brecht, and Adorno were more on the periphery of the surrealist movement than Bataille, but had the intellectual advantage of firsthand familiarity with the revitalization of historical materialism, taking place especially in Germany. Unlike their Parisian colleagues, their social milieu had benefited especially from the confluence of avant-garde aesthetics and socialist theory in Berlin in the 1920s, the publication of Georg Lukács's *History and Class Consciousness* in 1923, and the publication of Marx's early writings and draft outline of *Capital* in the early 1930s.

As I will briefly describe, it was Lukács who had laid the theoretical basis for a renewal of Marxist theory in a practice that was integral to the new historical conditions of advanced capitalism. He had also seen that modernism was a central expression of these new conditions. While benefiting from Lukács's theory, Benjamin, Brecht, and Adorno were able to go beyond him in the recognition that modernism was integral to the production processes of advanced capitalism, and not merely their ideological expression. The material conditions of a critique of modernism included modernist forms themselves. Consequently, they were committed to an immanent critique of surrealist form, that is, a critique that developed its theory dialectically, through surrealist practice. The value of their insights for a critique of postmodernist ethnographic forms lies in this specific project, and in the historical continuity that it demonstrates between avant-garde modernist theory and postmodernist theory.

As I will show, central to the Benjamin-Adorno debate was the question of "constructions," the appropriate textual form to be taken by critical representations of social objects. In their hands, the synthesis of historical materialist and surrealist methods approached what was also, by the 1930s, becoming the methodology of modern ethnography: intimate participant observation of specific social situations or objects, rendering the familiar unfamiliar, or the unfamiliar familiar, through resolute doubt and penetration of given social appearances. As Clifford (1981) shows, the artifacts and cultural exotica of high colonialism preoccupied the radical social analysis of both the surrealist movement and nascent ethnography in Paris. Surrealist practice of the 1920–1930s sought radically to defamiliarize taken-for-granted objects of the postwar world of declining imperialism—including the conventions of their own literary or visual representations—and evoke radical new grounds of refamiliarization.

However, the results of this pan-ethnological surrealism were, as Bataille's example illustrates, often abstruse, mystifying, or theological, even in their conscious materialist attempt to escape idealism. Brecht commented in 1935 that the objects of surrealism "do not come back again from estrangement" but remain a merely magical reflection of the objective world. In 1936 Benjamin criticized the cult "aura" that a surrealist rendition of cultural or historical exotica retained, insofar as its mode of empiricism nostalgically fetishized the uniqueness of these objects rather than established their historical relation to present social practice (1969). Earlier, and echoing Bataille's position, Benjamin and Adorno resolved in 1929 to turn surrealist method from a potentially religious form of "illumination" to a profane or insistently materialist form (Buck-Morss 1977, 124–28).

The commitment of these theorists to modernism and surrealist method nevertheless sought, through an immanent critique, to sensitize the French surrealists to the subtleties of fascist aesthetics. As Benjamin forcefully put it in the second version of his essay on Baudelaire, the basis of reactionary modernist ideology was the "phantasmagoria of 'culture history,' in which the bourgeois relishes its false consciousness" (in Roberts 1982, 193). This comment foresees the historical connections I have outlined above, from the ethnographic surrealism of 1930s Paris to both the postmodernist forms of structuralist culture history and deconstructionist experimental ethnography. However, before returning to these connections, I want to analyze the Benjamin-Adorno debate on its own specific historical grounds.

The focus of Benjamin and Adorno's debate was the representation of Baudelaire's participation, observation, and poetic representation of Paris in the nineteenth-century era of high capitalism. An appropriate analysis of Baudelaire's predicament could epitomize the historical development of modernism and its crisis in avant-garde theory. Baudelaire's image of the *flâneur* (stroller, loafer, lounger) was at the same time a critique of the crowd—the new phenomena of urban masses appearing in Paris's era of high capitalism. The representational form that Baudelaire's theory of the Parisian crowd took manifested a contradiction between his own participation in and representation of the crowd, and his implicit understanding of it. Benjamin's unfinished analysis of this contradiction is in terms of Marx's fetishism of commodities, extended from industrial production to poetic reproduction, and—as his and Adorno's surrealist theory demanded—into his own essay form.

Benjamin and Adorno's debate concerned successive drafts of portions of Benjamin's Arcades study (*Passagenarbeit*) of Baudelaire's predicament and mid-nineteenth-century Paris. The debate is partly reproduced in *Aesthetics and Politics* (Livingstone et al. 1977, 100–41) and is analyzed by Susan Buck-Morss (1977, 136–84). In my assessment, the most penetrating commentaries are by Buck-Morss, R. L. Kaufmann (1981), and the editors of *Aesthetics and Politics*. My own interpretation is based on a re-analysis in the light of the original correspondence published in *Aesthetics and Politics* and the original Baudelaire essay published as "The Paris of the Second Empire . . ." in *Charles Baudelaire: A Lyric Poet in the Era of High Capitalism* (Benjamin [1938a], 9–106). The general assumption, most compellingly presented by Buck-Morss, is that, although Adorno remained intellectually in debt to Benjamin, throughout his exile in Paris Benjamin was forced to accede to Adorno's critical demands for the sake of the continued support of the Institute for Social Research, by then resituated from Frankfurt to New York.

However, building upon the insights of these commentators, I have been better able than they to identify the strength and stubbornness of Benjamin's position relative to Adorno's. The primary shortcoming of these and other commentators is, I think, not to have appreciated the affinity between Benjamin's rabbinical philosophy and historical materialism, and thus to have exaggerated the disparity between his "theological" or "philological" interests and his Marxism. This misunderstanding appears to have followed Adorno's own criticism of Benjamin. But, as I hope to show, Adorno's criticism in this regard actually masked his real opposition, which was to the particular textual form that Benjamin demanded as appropriate to an historical materialist critique of surrealism. Given this perspective, it is Adorno's textual form that turns out to have more affinity with the idealist shortcomings of surrealism, which they both sought to counter.

On the other hand, other Marxist commentators on the debate have missed all of these implications, concluding for instance that Benjamin's materialism was compromised by guilty self-castigation as well as idealist Messianism (Eagleton 1981, 114–15), and that his dialectical method was impotent and submissive under Adorno's severe criticism of the Arcades study (Lunn 1982, 149, 172). Julian Roberts's brief assessment of the relationship of Benjamin to Adorno (1982, 172–74) and more generally of Benjamin's theoretical intentions in textual form, reinforces my own, while expanding primarily upon important historical influences on Benjamin.

Benjamin and Adorno's critiques of surrealism were based on Marx's theory of the commodity form, and its seminal reinterpretation by Lukács in 1923. In 1867 in the first chapter of *Capital* Marx demonstrated the fundamental principle of the fetishism of commodities: through the general historical displacement of social use value by abstract exchange value, which characterizes the production of commodities in capitalism, social relations between people (as producers of commodities, including their labor itself) take on the misleadingly natural appearance of things, specifically the exchange relations between commodities. Conversely, relations between things take on the appearance of the social relations between their producers, the latter having been made misleadingly natural through displacement of social use value by the exchange value of commodities. These fetishized appearances of people or things, as natural and ahistorical, obscured an objectively dialectical process and a specific historical development of contradictions that was focused in the commodity form. The example of this analysis, which I will examine below, is Benjamin's application of Marx's theory of commodity fetishism to Baudelaire's critique of the Parisian crowd.

Marx's own elaboration of this fundamental thesis remained largely within a circumscribed economic domain of the processes of capital, conceived as the groundwork for any further materialist social and historical analysis. However, in 1923 Lukács ([1922], 83–84) argued that

> we must be quite clear in our minds that commodity fetishism is a *specific* problem of our age, the age of modern capitalism. Commodity exchange and the corresponding subjective and objective commodity relations existed, as we know, when society was still very primitive. What is at issue *here*, however, is the question: how far is commodity exchange together with its structural consequences able to influence the *total* outer and inner life of society?

Lukács proceeded to show that key dilemmas in European philosophy remained dilemmas because they themselves were implicated in the contradictory structure of the commodity form. Far from being irrelevant, philosophy was implicated as the ideology of modern capitalism. The resulting contradictions were obscured by "reifications" of the fetishized appearance of the commodity form not only in economic phenomena but throughout "the *total* outer and inner life of society." Against the current Marxist dogma of economic base and ideological superstructure, Lukács argued that " 'ideological' and 'economic' problems lose their mutual exclusiveness and merge into one another," and that "the essence of the dialectical method lies in the fact that in every aspect [of society] correctly grasped the dialectic of the whole totality is comprehended and that the whole method can be unraveled from every single aspect" ([1922], 34, 170, pointed out by Buck-Morss 1977, 26).

The significance of Benjamin's and Adorno's critiques of surrealism is that they sought to extend this method of materialist analysis into the form of the surrealist work itself, and ultimately into the form of its critique: their own text. "Constructions" within their texts of social objects and situations were to reveal the social process of the commodity form in its dialectical terms of mystification, contradiction, and revolution. The surrealist preoccupation with experience of the familiar and unfamiliar, closely associated with what was also being established as the methodology of ethnography—participant observation—was in this particular way also Benjamin and Adorno's starting point.

In 1935 Benjamin drafted an outline for his Arcades study of mid-nineteenth-century Paris. Whereas his and Adorno's earlier plan was to decipher the Parisian street phantasmagoria as a figure of hell, by 1935 he had rejected this abstract and evocative theme for a more concrete level of analysis in his opinion closer to both the surrealist and the historical materialist methods. He sought a "panorama of dialectical images" in textual constructions counterpoising such characters as a collector of refuse, prostitute, *flâneur* (stroller), conspirator, and gambler, with historical fragments on taxation, fashion, photography, architecture, and drawing rooms. Such images would portray an "epoch in the sense of an ur-history [history of origins] of modernity." By starkly juxtaposing the immediate images of Paris with these concurrent historical fragments, Benjamin sought both to present a realization of surrealist method and critically sublate it in a "profane illumination" (Benjamin [1938a], 155–70; Buck-Morss 1977, 106–7; 146). However, Adorno detected in Benjamin's concrete imagery an idealist misconstrual of the commodity form in psychological terms, and a romanticist presentation of history that subverted the specificity and precision that the materialist method demanded (Adorno [1935–1938], 110–20; Livingstone et al. 1977, 102–3).

There is in Lukács' theory of the commodity form an idealist potential to fetishize Marx's critique itself. Following Adorno, Althusser was later to criticize this as the evocation of society as an "expressive totality." From Adorno's point of view, the commodity form cannot be taken in isolation from the material conditions emerging from the dialectical contradiction between the forces of production and the social relations of production in a *specific* historical context. In this regard, Adorno's criticism of Benjamin's method was an important materialist corrective to the latter's social theory. However, it failed to grasp Benjamin's point with regard to textual form, and in this regard betrayed Adorno's own inconsistency, which was rooted in his hostility to the influence of Bertolt Brecht on Benjamin.

Along with romanticist history, Adorno also rejected Brecht's confidence in the revolutionary potential of the modern proletariat, implicit in Benjamin's draft. Like that of Benjamin and Adorno, Brecht's theory was built into his dramatic form (Benjamin [1939], 147–54). His criticism that the objects of surrealist method "do not return again from estrangement" reflects his criticism of traditional drama, which seeks an emotional catharsis and sense of harmony in an imaginary realm estranged from everyday life. Against both the traditional stage and the idealist version of surrealist method, Brecht sought to reproduce on the stage concrete images of the real fragmentation of ordinary life. Through the experience of shock, rather than an illusory catharsis and reconciliation, this reproduction of mutual estrangement among dramatic elements, actors, and audience demanded action in real life.

This was Brecht's equivalent of the surrealist textual "construction" that Adorno and Benjamin also seek to develop in different ways. Adorno rejects Benjamin's version of it as a form of "replica realism" (Adorno 1977, 111) that reproduces in the imagination the dogma of a revolutionary proletariat. However, what Adorno was really rejecting was Benjamin's conception of the textual construction as a form of social and historical praxis, stigmatizing it with a logically spurious association with orthodox Marxist theory of a revolutionary proletariat. Adorno's charge of "replica realism" consequently reveals his own idealist assumptions about a text as much as it does Benjamin's about the abstract nature of the commodity form.

An exchange in 1934 between Adorno and Benjamin over the latter's essay on Kafka clarifies this basic divergence of expository method. Benjamin's criticizes Kafka's parables for unfolding in a rabbinical sense of relic, precursor, or prophecy, but lacking the necessary reference to a "doctrine" ([1936], 122). Adorno urges that Benjamin's own textual form of criticism should "unfold" in a more Hegelian and less Judaic way: Benjamin's revelation in textual form of the contradictory structure of objects relies on a mystifying juxtaposition of the fragments constituting it (relic, precursor), rather than prompting an unfolding of the intrinsic conceptual contradiction that is its actual material constitution (Buck-Morss 1977, 142–43). However, Benjamin's metaphor is actually as telling against Adorno's conception of textual constructions as it is against Kafka:

> The word "unfolding" has a double meaning. A bud unfolds into a blossom, but the boat which one teaches children to make by folding paper unfolds into a flat sheet of paper. This second kind of "unfolding" is really appropriate to the [social role of the] parable; it is the reader's pleasure to smooth it out so that he has the meaning in the palm of his hand. Kafka's parables, however, unfold in the first sense the way a bud turns into a blossom.

This text (Benjamin [1936], 122) is both a description of Benjamin's own method of constructions and, in textual form, an example of it. Both Adorno and Buck-Morss miss his point, finding Benjamin's juxtaposition of Kafka and rabbinical method merely mystifying. However, the method to which Benjamin refers is more straightforwardly materialist than they appreciate: as is made clear on the same page; all that Benjamin means by a foundation "doctrine" here is the concrete social and historical context of the text and its readership, a basic rabbinical principle. What clarifies a text in a person's practice, like unfolding a parable "in the palm of his hand. . . . [is] in every case . . . a question of how life and work are organized in human society. This question increasingly occupied Kafka as it became impenetrable to him." *Replica* realism is not the issue. Kafka's—and implicitly Adorno's—textual form of critique presents itself as passively *continuous* with "how life and work are organised in human society," but not as actively *participant* in this organization. Benjamin's method for textual form is an extension of Marx's insistence on a theory integral with concrete social practice. Like that of Marx, it is also a critique of an Hegelian and idealist form of "unfolding" that is estranged from social practice.

In 1938 Benjamin drafted his first essay on Baudelaire, intended as a major part of the Arcades study ([1938a], 9–106). Similar to his criticism of the Kafka essay, Adorno's central charge is that Benjamin "ascetically" juxtaposes concrete modes of behavior (the "pragmatic contents" of Baudelaire's poetic images) with "materialistic excursions" into the social history of Baudelaire's times. Juxtaposed images of economic base and ideological superstructure invoke "a realm where history and magic oscillate. . . . at the crossroads of magic and positivism. That spot is bewitched" (Adorno [1935–1938], 128–29). Instead, Adorno urges the "mediation" of these juxtaposed images by an immanent "theoretical interpretation" through "the total social process" of "the commodity form in Baudelaire's epoch."

> Materialist determination of cultural traits is only possible if it is mediated through the *total social process*. . . . The direct inference from the duty on wine [drawn from Marx's contemporary comment] to *L'Ame du Vin* [Baudelaire's poem] imputes to phenomena precisely that kind of spontaneity, palpability, and density which they have lost in capitalism. In this sort of immediate—I would say again, anthropological [that is, ahistorical]—materialism, there is a profoundly romantic element, and the more crassly and roughly you confront the Baudelairean world of forms with the necessities of life, the more clearly I detect it. (Adorno [1935–1938], 129)

Adorno's conception of the theoretical mediation needed within these textual constructions is, in his own way, insistently materialist. In Hegelian fashion, he contends that the mediation is an "objective historico-philosophical category" immanent in the material object itself—if apprehended not in a naturalistic or fetishized sense but as it was in fact under capitalism: a dialectical subjective and objective process of the commodity form. Hence the immediate spontaneity, palpability, and density imputed to phenomena was a positivist illusion that obscured its objective historicophilosophical category. A piece of music, a block of theater seats, horoscopes, a bourgeois drawing room, could be analyzed to the point of intrinsic conceptual contradictions and a dialectical reversal of understanding without the intervention of extrinsic or abstract dogma. Somewhat as in the methods of Benjamin and Brecht, the resulting contradictions were left unresolved, just as they are in real life (Buck-Morss 1977, 96–101).

However, the debate between Benjamin and Adorno over the Arcades work unavoidably implies that for Adorno this textual structure was a passive extension of practical life rather than an active participation in it. The difference was, I think, as basic as the difference between a materialist theory based on production and one based on consumption—the crucial contemporary inversion of Marxist theory that emerged first with Bataille. There are grounds to believe that a similar theoretical divergence was developing between Benjamin and Adorno, expressed by Benjamin in terms of "the fruitful tension between your theory about the consumption of exchange value and my theory about empathy with the soul of the commodity" (Livingstone et al. 1977, 135).

In the remainder of this commentary, I will examine the active or participatory structure of Benjamin's textual constructions at three levels of his discourse, and Adorno's opposition at each level: (1) Benjamin's representation of the ragpicker image in Baudelaire; (2) Benjamin's intended construction at the level of the overall development of the Arcades text; (3) and the implications of the "fruitful tension" between Benjamin and Adorno's theories of the commodity form.

The materialist and dialectical yet passive form of Adorno's textual constructions can be clarified through his comments on Benjamin's analysis of the ragpicker image in Baudelaire. Similarly here, Benjamin fails "to close the gap," although I hope to clarify why:

> It seems to me that his destiny as the figure of the lower limits of poverty is certainly not brought out by the way the word ragpicker appears in your study. It contains none of the dog-like cringing. . . . [N]othing in it of the comet's tail of jeering children behind the old man. . . . [T]he figure . . . should have been decoded theoretically. . . . [T]he capitalist function of the ragpicker—namely to subject even rubbish to exchange value—is not articulated. (Adorno [1935–1938], 130)

It is important to appreciate that the theoretical "decoding" that Adorno demands is materialist in the sense that it is on the order of further description: dog-like cringing, jeering children—the observable manifestations of "the total social process" that have rendered the ragpicker what he materially is as a cultural phenomenon. It is also important to note that the theoretical articulation is to arise not as an aside, but in the form of the ragpicker text itself: in "the way the word ragpicker appears in your study." This is Adorno's materialist way to reveal the historicophilosophical category immanent in the figure of the ragpicker—a category that, I will suggest, Adorno encapsulates in his theory of "the consumption of exchange value."

Adorno and Benjamin's ("empathy with the soul of the commodity") theories are theories of textual construction as well as of society. In Benjamin's case, this becomes clear in his intended method of construction of the whole Arcades text. The point, in the overall form of the Baudelaire essay, at which Benjamin introduces the ragpicker, he insists on limiting his analysis to the conceptualizations participants employed in the specific historical context he was examining. Here Benjamin limits himself to an elaboration much more restrained than Adorno's: "when the new industrial processes have given refuse a certain value, ragpickers appeared in the cities in larger numbers . . . a sort of cottage industry located in the streets" ([1938a], 19). In a footnote he adduces further contemporary detail, and allows himself an assessment: just as the ragpickers' cottage industry worked over "the vomit of surfeited Paris," a careful contemporary account of the expenditures of a ragpicker family (published in Baudelaire's time) attempted "to make abject misery appear less objectionable by neatly arranging it under rubrics."

Reflecting his rabbinical or linguistic materialism, he calls this textual method the "true philological attitude," and replies to Adorno's demand for theoretical articulation, explaining that

> the problem is one of construction. I believe that speculation can start its necessarily bold flight with some prospect of success only if, instead of putting on the waxen wings of the esoteric [the Icarus metaphor for idealism perhaps derived from Bataille], it seeks its source of strength in construction alone. It is because of the needs of construction that the second part of my book [the first Baudelaire essay was to be this second part] consists primarily of philological material. What is involved there is less an "ascetic discipline" than a methodological precaution. . . . When you speak of a "wide-eyed presentation of mere facts" [Adorno's criticism of Benjamin's mode of construction], you characterize the true philological attitude. This attitude is necessary not only for its results, but had to be built into the construction for its own sake. (Livingstone et al. 1977, 136)

The "source of strength" that lies in Benjamin's version of construction is its initial representation of the object "with complete naturalness at the empirical level" of what he calls the "specific gravity" of its particular social and historical context (Livingstone et al. 1977, 135, 137). The textual beginning of the necessarily bold flight of historical materialist critique had to be strictly limited to the appearances of "second nature," the reified world of commodity forms that, through fetishism, are taken by its participants as natural.

Just as in life, the construction must be "obstructed" from a clear view of its truth in "an artificially darkened chamber" (Livingstone et al. 1977, 135). Before he wrote the second Baudelaire essay to the satisfaction of Adorno, Benjamin attempted to circumvent his criticism with a methodological introduction to the first essay. Significantly, the opening words of this aborted effort are: "Sundering truth from falsehood is the goal of the materialist method, not its point of departure. In other words, the point of departure is the object riddled with error. . . . [I]f it is claimed to approach the object the way it is 'in truth,' it would only greatly reduce its chances. . . . It is, to be sure, tempting to pursue the 'matter in itself' " (Benjamin [1938a], 103). Although Adorno accuses Benjamin of a mystifying materialism of immediacy to the cultural and historical fragments of Baudelaire's time, Benjamin sees in Adorno's textual method the more telling form of idealism: placing the "matter in itself" methodologically before the matter as it socially and historically appears to be—a "second nature" lived by its participants. Adorno's is the fatal estrangement of theory from practice—tantamount to the arrogant "illusion of vulgar Marxism that the social function of a material or intellectual product can be determined without reference to the circumstances and bearers of its tradition" (Benjamin [1938a], 104). Adorno's conception of the total social process that mediated the commodity form lacks a dialectical empiricism, which was "necessary not only for its [social] results, but had to be built into the construction for its own sake," that is, as a specific social part of the history that could lead to these results.

Benjamin's method, however, is social and historical, not remedial. Although restricted "philologically" to the "specific gravity" of his subject, Benjamin nevertheless constructs "traces" of his theory earlier in the text. In terms of his criticism of Kafka, although his initial construction "with complete naturalness at the empirical level" serves as the "doctrine" of "how life and work are organised in human society," these traces serve as the prophecy of a later theoretical unfolding. Although "the philosophic foundations of the book cannot be perceived from the vantage point of the second part . . . the treatment of traces in this second part must remain at this level, precisely in order later to receive in the decisive contexts its sudden illumination" (Livingstone et al. 1977, 135). The first draft of the Baudelaire essay was intended to be the second part of the Arcades work. Traces of the final construction, then, appear in material form throughout the text. Benjamin points out that he has allowed a trace of his own theory, "unobstructed," to emerge at the culmination of his discussion of the *flâneur* (stroller), the second of three sections in the second part of the book. Nevertheless, Benjamin's theory appears here only in the terms of Baudelaire's own theory of the Parisian crowd as seen through the eyes of the *flâneur*. This ray, "broken down prismatically, suffices to give an idea of the nature of the light whose focus lies in the third part of the book," which was never written.

Can the "philosophic foundations" of the Arcades work nevertheless be deduced from the construction of traces in the text as far as they go? I think they can and, furthermore, I suggest that these foundations are Benjamin's theory of "empathy with the commodity," here underlying Baudelaire's theory of the Parisian crowd as articulated through the perceptions of the *flâneur*.

The culmination of the second section to which Benjamin directs Adorno's attention recapitulates Baudelaire's perception (as a *flâneur*) of the big-city crowd as an amorphous "spectacle of nature" or a "crystallised social aura." Following Baudelaire's perceptions, Benjamin suggests that this amorphously natural or social spectacle variously takes on the atmosphere of an heroic refuge (for Baudelaire himself), of the general popular will (for Victor Hugo, as socialist demagogue), and of racial "fate" (for the National Socialists). Although the crowd of individuals subjectively appears in these concrete manifestations, earlier in the section Benjamin points out that

> socially they remain abstract—namely, in their isolated private interests. Their models are the customers who, each in his private interest, gather at the market around their "common cause." In many cases, such gatherings have only a statistical existence. This existence conceals the really monstrous thing about them: the concentration of private persons as such by the accident of their private interests. . . . [and] the market economy which brings them together in this way. (Benjamin [1938a], 62–63)

The amorphous potency of the urban crowd rested upon its objective abstractness—which in turn concealed its real and specific social history. In Baudelaire's own time, Marx had similarly described the industrial marketplace, pointing out that it was not, as in the economists' influential ideology, structured naturally and universally by private interests expressing the general interest of society; "The real point. . . . is rather that private interest is already a socially determined interest" historically specific to capitalism. "The dissolution of all fixed personal (historic) relations of dependence in production" of earlier eras had been transformed under the social processes of capitalism into

> the reciprocal and all-sided dependence of individuals who are indifferent to one another. . . . This social bond is expressed in *exchange value*, by means of which alone each individual's own activity or his product becomes an activity or product for him; he must produce a general product—exchange value, or, the latter isolated for itself and individualised, *money*. ([1857], 156–57)

I suggest that Benjamin characterizes the results of this historical process as "empathy with the soul of the commodity." It can be shown that traces of this implicit social theory are built up throughout the three sections of the first Baudelaire essay, extending from the conditions of Baudelaire's daily life as poet, *flâneur*, and urban refugee to the constitution of his poetry.

The opening paragraph of the essay juxtaposes Marx's comments on *la bohème* of Paris, as lumpenproletariat conspirators, with Baudelaire's own abrupt and fragile politics of opportunism. At the end of the first section this construction is augmented by the image of Baudelaire's ambiguous exploration of the "bottomless bonhomie" of the Parisian arcades: "Baudelaire knew what the true position of the man of letters was: he goes to the marketplace as a *flâneur*, supposedly to take a look at it, but in reality to find a buyer" ([1938a], 34). In the final section of the essay ("Modernism"), Benjamin begins to show that modernism—even restricted to Baudelaire's use of the term—was the material extension of this ambiguously crystallized perception of the *flâneur* from the poet's living conditions into his poetic production itself. The crowd comprised of private interests, the precariousness of Baudelaire's own daily life, and "the continuous series of tiny improvisations" with which he constituted his poems in the conscious image of *fencing*, each exemplify the general "empathy with the soul of the commodity" that already characterized Paris in the era of high capitalism. "The necessity that is here disguised is not only a material one; it concerns poetic production" ([1938a], 70–71). This was modernism in Baudelaire's own time.

Benjamin points out that Baudelaire's commentary on the ragpicker as collator of the "annals of intemperance," stockpiling "like a miser guarding a treasure, the refuse which will assume the shape of useful and gratifying objects between the jaws of the godess of Industry" is an "extended metaphor for the procedure of the poet in Baudelaire's spirit" ([1938a], 79–80). The ragpicker / poet construction seems to illustrate the "tension" between Benjamin's theory of "empathy with the soul of the commodity" and Adorno's theory of "the consumption of exchange value." Adorno's insistence that Benjamin's construction be decoded theoretically to reveal "the capitalist function of the ragpicker—namely to subject even rubbish to exchange value" reflects his fascination with the abstract processes of consumption through which a means of production is transformed into new exchange values. Benjamin's primary concern, however (like Marx's in the passage quoted above), remained with the production of exchange values, in the process of which social relations come to be confounded with relations between commodities. In this way, "empathy with the soul of the commodity" was also produced at all levels of production—necessarily including the structure of Benjamin's text itself.

The difference from Adorno is fundamental: from Marx's point of view, the specific *productive* processes of labor in the forces of production—including that which is appropriated as surplus value and the "dead labour" of previous generations now constituting capital (even in the form of the ragpicker's hoard)—are the motive forces that burst specific oppressive relations of production and constitute historical revolution. For Benjamin, even "Baudelaire was a secret agent—an agent of the secret discontent of his class with its own rule" (1973, 104n). He traces the changes in Baudelaire's successively more sociological revisions of his poem "The Ragpicker's Wine" from 1852, when he almost piously attributed wine's delusions to God, to 1857, when his far more rebellious attribution of these delusions was to humankind ([1938a], 18–20). Baudelaire's attitude toward the ragpicker and the working class was by then reflected ominously in his words: ". . . this sickly population which swallows the dust of factories. . . . this languishing and pining population to whom *the earth owes its wonder;* who feel *a purple and impetuous blood coursing through their veins* . . ." (in Benjamin [1938a], 74).

In the last analysis, "empathy with the soul of the commodity" was this historical force—which included Baudelaire's poetic production. This understanding of productive forces as they have been throughout the history of capitalism would have probably been the "philosophical foundations" to take fuller shape in the third part of Benjamin's Arcades work. It was through a study of art nouveau that he intended to elucidate "a dialectics of the new and the unchanging" (Livingstone et al. 1977, 135–36).

Conclusion

Jameson suggests that Benjamin's account of Baudelaire, despite the specificity of its historical context (Benjamin's 1930s analysis of Baudelaire's 1850s), might offer a critical perspective on postmodernism as the cultural logic of late capitalism. My interpretation above confirms his intuition and, I hope, in a more concretely historical way than Jameson himself would have sought. For Benjamin, Baudelaire's account had revealed "baselines" that "converge in our own historical experience" (Livingstone et al. 1977, 137). With regard to postmodernist ethnographic forms, there is a significant historical discontinuity between Baudelaire's and Marx's time and postmodernism, which I will describe later. However, the historical continuities I have discussed between Benjamin's time and postmodernist ethnographic forms should be reviewed.

In addition to the specific effect of surrealist sociology through Georges Bataille upon poststructuralist semiology and deconstructionist theory (see also Clifford 1981, 546n1; Habermas 1983, 14), there were several more general intellectual continuities that I have emphasized: following Clifford, the common beginnings of French ethnology and the surrealist movement in Paris, and the continuity of theory between Mauss's ethnology and poststructuralist semiology; the historical affinities between these developments and the culturalist theories developed in American anthropology by Boas's students; the historical affinities of the semiological construal of culture emerging in the 1950s from Sapir and Benedict and the European development of semiology from Saussure to Barthes; the more general division of labor between the anthropological notion of culture and the dominant ideology thesis; and the theory of the aesthetic avant-garde and its historical sequel in postmodernist ethnography.

I will recapitulate some of the aspects of postmodernist ethnographic forms that I describe at the outset. Experimental ethnographic form has taken shape in ethnographic accounts that reproduce in textual form the hermeneutic or reflexive theory of fieldwork or of social change. This form may follow a mutual definition of meanings in the ethnographer's emerging understanding of a problem, in the personal experiences of ethnographer and hosts, or in the social or historical changes that constitute the host community. In any case, the hermeneutic position of the ethnographer or the society that he or she represents is integral to the development of the textual form, in purposeful contrast to earlier ethnographic forms. Structuralist culture history, on the other hand, has taken ethnographic shape in accounts that rewrite ethnographic or historical materials in terms of a semiological theory of structural forms. Events are shown to constitute historical change in the sense of transformations among the established forms of a semiological code, which is the culture of the society being transformed. Either in the account of specific events or in its overall structure, the formal development of the text exemplifies both the theory and the history.

Whereas the ethnographer or the ethnographer's society is the primary reference point in the textual form of experimental ethnography (even in "representations of the Other"), the primary reference point in the textual form of structuralist culture history is the cultural code and its transformations, objectively a characteristic of the host culture and its history. However, Leach (1985a; 1985b) suggests that the epistemological principle of hermeneutic reflexivity necessarily underlies any knowledge between cultures, and consequently the historical transformations of any culture code. He also suggests, in this connection, that the structuralist rewriting of cultural histories in accord with native codes was a "deconstruction" of received history, distorted by European codes.

Leach's theoretical excursion brings to the surface of both ethnographic forms a common history in French social theory. Sahlins's structuralist cultural history is based on a theory derived from deconstructionist writers and ultimately from the surrealist movement, as well as from Lévi-Strauss. Experimental ethnographic form derives from phenomenological hermeneutics in France, augmented by Ricoeur's semiological interests. Following Geertz, anthropological hermeneutics took this semiological turn toward the reading of cultures as texts (Austin-Broos 1987). The adaptation of this variety of essentialist theories to ethnography has tended to be raised to a higher power through the anthropological principles of culture and cultural relativism, which in turn are often separated from their own history by their expression as textual form.

Whereas aesthetic modernist works struggle with the antinomies of representation, postmodernist works avoid representation as a positivist metaphysics, treating their subject as pure simulacra or images without originals. The postmodernist aspects of these ethnographic forms, then, extend from the hermeneutic representation that, through reflexivity, simply avoids positivist forms of representation, to the deconstructionist evocation, performance, or therapeutic exercise that rejects all representation as illusory. In one way or another, postmodernist ethnographic forms thereby seek to integrate with, rather than represent, the social practices that are their object. This integral relationship with practice is, at the same time, their form and their theory.

The dialectical questions that stubbornly remain, however, are with *what* social practice does their form integrate, and about *what* social practice is their social theory. The questions remain because a material history is not overcome by theory, or by theory in the form of textual form. They are dialectical because they arise from these material conditions and are an immanent critique of it. Once the social theory is pried apart from the textual form, and the history of the theory is made more explicit, these are the questions to which the materialist critique of surrealism can suggest answers.

I suggested earlier that the ethnographic avant-garde was in some ways a sequel to the aesthetic avant-garde of the interwar years, with shortcomings parallel to those that Bürger analyzes for the earlier historical movement. Whereas the aesthetic avant-garde sought vainly to reintegrate form with practical life through the medium of art, the ethnographic avant-garde now seeks to reintegrate form with practical life through the medium of social theory. The expression of this form is the scholarly text—not surprisingly, given the material conditions of the ethnographic discipline. I also suggest, however, that the apparent merger of social theory and textual form is actually a separation of theory from practical life, obscured by the theory itself—in its hermeneutic, structuralist, or deconstructionist variations. This separation is not, of course, out of this world, if only because it sincerely intends to be an integration with practical life rather than a separation from it. Which social practice the form is integral with, and which social practice the theory is about, remain specific empirical issues and consequently of interest to social science itself.

With regard to surrealism, in 1929 Benjamin had already concluded that the movement was stillborn through "an irremediable coupling of idealistic morality with political practice." Benjamin has in mind here the sort of socialist radicalism exemplified by Bataille, whose "base" materialism was actually an idealist morality, and whose sociology of transgression only postured as a political practice. Following Benjamin's early work on German tragic drama, Adorno later characterizes parallel sorts of "radical" idealist separations of theory and practice as a "collapse of subjectivity into objectivity." The Hegelian and Marxist problem of reintegrating theory and practice cannot be resolved by ignoring the specific history of their separation nor, like the aesthetic avant-garde, by simply flattening theory into practice by an act of will.

The parallels with the postmodernist turn in modernism are striking. In 1980, receiving the Theodor W. Adorno prize from the city of Frankfurt, Jurgen Habermas suggested that the Left Wing *Tel Quel* deconstructionists deriving from Bataille continued to juxtapose to instrumental reason (the supposed dominant ideology) "in Manichean fashion a principle only accessible through evocation, be it the will to power or sovereignty, Being or the Dionysiac force of the poetical (1983, 14). But the Manichean universal war between Good and

Evil is a theology. Among the surrealists, this Manichean Marxism had had two primary effects: the modernist illusion of autonomy in the domain of art was destroyed, but only *as* an illusion; the socially objective boundaries to the domain were actually reinforced by an abortive effort that, even if successful, would have been only a partial revolution—that is, none at all.

> These experiments have served to bring back to life, and to illuminate all the more glaringly, exactly those structures of art which they were meant to dissolve. They gave new legitimacy, as ends in themselves, to appearance as the medium of fiction, to the transcendence of the artwork over society, to the concentrated and planned character of artistic production as well as to the special cognitive status of judgements of taste. . . . First, when the containers of an autonomously developed cultural sphere are shattered, the contents get dispersed. Nothing remains from a desublimated meaning or a destructured form; an emancipatory effect does not follow. . . . The second mistake [of surrealism] has more important consequences. . . . breaking open a single cultural sphere—art—[provides] access to just one of the specialized knowledge complexes. The surrealist revolt would have replaced only one abstraction. (Habermas 1983, 11)

Habermas goes on to say that "in the spheres of theoretical knowledge and morality, there are parallels to this failed attempt of what we might call the false negation of culture," although less pronounced. I suggest that the collapse, in postmodernist ethnographic forms, of the parameters of theoretical critique between social theory, textual form, ethnographic object, and ethnographer subject is an example of a false negation of knowledge.

Benjamin and Adorno's efforts came closer to achieving the surrealist goal in a manner that was not confined to one sphere, moving in immanent critique from within the social totality as a material historical process. Nevertheless, their struggles expose the irreducible difficulties of transforming a specific, material, and historical social totality through texts—for the very reason that texts are part of that totality. The ethnographic avant-garde falls short of their efforts, partly because the specific history of these forms diverge from that of Benjamin and Adorno, and follow instead Mauss, Bataille, Jakobson, Sapir and Benedict, and others. The result has been a form of textual radicalism: the reintegration of postmodernist ethnographic forms with practical life, but often in an abstract and ahistorical sense, obscuring both the actual separation of these forms from practical lives in any specific historical sense, and their actual integration with specific practices that are not so heroic.

Whereas there was this important historical divergence of social theorists, these contingencies in turn must be explained by a more significant and general historical development of the forces of production and associated scientific theory. Here a significant historical difference arises between the predicament of Baudelaire's modernism and the aesthetic avant-garde that was not yet clear to Benjamin and Adorno; in this particular respect Jameson's cautions about the historical comparability of Benjamin's critique and postmodernism may be drawn against my view that the ethnographic avant-garde are a sequel to the aesthetic avant-garde.

The problem can be approached through the empirical issues I raise above: what are the actual social practices of the postmodernist ethnographic forms? I suggest that the specific social practice with which their forms are most integral is the composing of ethnographies as texts. Rabinow approaches this point when he proposes an examination of the social and institutional context of writing ethnography (1986). However, there is a more important empirical question: what practice is their theory actually about? In general terms, the social practice that their theory is implicitly concerned with is, as Benjamin would say, "empathy with the soul of the commodity." I will conclude the essay with an attempt to trace this preoccupation more specifically.

In postmodernist ethnographic forms, this historical and material empathy with the soul of the commodity is manifested most directly in variations of semiotic theory. Experimental ethnography has derived this influence especially from Geertz and hence Ricoeur's semiotic phenomenology; structuralist culture history has derived it especially from Barthes and deconstructionists such as Baudrillard. The general result has been the analysis not of social—hence specific and historical—totalities, but of cultural totalities conceived semiotically as systems of essential meaning, abstract and ahistoric, although sometimes approached in terms of specific meanings. Asad emphasizes the central *a priori* assumption of *authenticity* that is built up with regard to such a cultural system of essential meanings, either in a particular culture or in the ethnographic description of it (1979). The social and historical questions of what specifically maintains or undermines such a semiotic system as authoritative are often subordinated or absorbed in the system itself.

Both the historical continuity and the significant discontinuity between the aesthetic and ethnographic avant-gardes can be outlined with regard to the role of the marketplace in the total social process. I point out the continuity that Benjamin was developing in the terms of "modernism" between Baudelaire's understanding of the Parisian crowds and his own critique of surrealism. In Baudelaire's time, Marx had emphasized that the apparent private interests comprising the chaotic "magic hand" of the marketplace were in fact socially and historically determined expressions of exchange value, through which commodities and their producers not only became exchangeable but also became interchangeable. In *Capital*, a decade later, this process was analyzed in terms of the fetishism of commodities. In this work Marx develops his analysis of the marketplace in terms that can, I think, accommodate the historical change since his time that underlies postmodernist ethnographic forms.

> This sphere [of the marketplace], within whose boundaries the sale and purchase of labour-power goes on, is in fact a very Eden of the innate rights of man. There alone rule Freedom, Equality, Property and Bentham. Freedom, because both buyer and seller of a commodity, say of labour-power, are constrained only by their own free will. They contract as free agents, and the agreement they come to, is but the form in which they give legal expression to their common will. Equality, because each enters into relation with the other, as with a simple owner of commodities, and they exchange equivalent for equivalent. Property, because each disposed only of what is his own. And Bentham, because each looks only to himself. The only force which brings them together and puts them in relation with each other, is the selfishness, the gain and the private interests of each. Each looks to himself only, and no one troubles himself about the rest, and just because they do so, do they all, in accordance with the pre-established harmony of things, or under the auspices of an all-shrewd providence, work together to their mutual advantage, for the common weal and in the interest of all. ([1867], 172)

In 1857 Marx had emphasized that the historical condition that underlay this social process was not the imagined dominant ideology of the general will or magic hand of the marketplace, but the social objectivity or "second nature" of exchange value. In 1867 he emphasized that this social objectivity obviated moralization in terms either of an imagined dominant ideology, or of greed and brutality. Marx makes it clear that this method of determining the value of labor power "is prescribed by the very nature of the case"—that is, by the historical conditions of capitalism—not by such ideas or motives ([1867], 166, 169). On the other hand, here he suggests how the fundamental values of the Enlightenment—freedom, equality, justice, private property, individualism—had come to be reproduced in intimate association at the center of commodity exchange: the buying and selling of labor as a commodity to produce commodities. Just as social-use values, which are the origin of capital, subsisted at the heart of commodity production in contradiction with the commodity's exchange value, so were these values both confirmed and contradicted in the buying and selling of labor in the marketplace.

The history of the semiological sciences since Saussure and formalism has sometimes developed in an explicit dialogue with this market process, perhaps reflecting a certain empathy with the soul of the commodity. Saussure's theory of linguistic signs was an escape from materialist theories, but nonetheless developed by analogy with economic exchange values. Semiology was the science of sign values on the model of exchange values, and signs were characterized by the arbitrariness of the semantically determined relationship between the signifier and signified, and the abstract equality of signs as interlocked in a system of signs. (Significantly, Sahlins explicitly founds his structuralist cultural history on this analogy—1981, 6.) Key aspects of Saussure's theory can be read as a theory of language, but also as an expression of the reproduction of the fundamental capitalist values of freedom, equality, property, and justice in the buying and selling of labor power.

Similar dialogues within this analogy can be identified in Jakobson and Lévi-Strauss as linguistic formalism was extended into literary and anthropological structuralism. Saussure's semiology by economic analogy is implicit throughout Barthes's *Elements of Semiology,* but has been most explicitly developed in Baudrillard's *For a Critique of the Political Economy of Signs,* a deconstruction of Marx's theory of production. Derrida, avatar of deconstructionism, discards Saussure's duality of the sign in favor of the "materiality" of the play between signifiers at the "letteral" level of language; thus he appeared, misleadingly, to return to Bakhtin's materialist concerns with discourse (Eagleton 1983, 146). On the other hand, one could say that at this point the analogy with the exchange value of labor had become reified in another world quite apart from discourse.

The empathy of the central values of capitalism with the soul of the commodity appears to have gone through a major historical modification with the advent of new processes of production and production science, information processing, cybernetic technology, and semiological theory. This is only dimly foreseen by Marx in his analysis of abstract labor and exchange value, and identified in a preliminary way by Lukács, Benjamin, and Adorno. Bürger's analysis of the theory of the avant-garde suggests that "postmodernism" is primarily the emergence of an awareness of these historical conditions, arising from the conditions themselves. These developments have had their effects throughout the arts and social sciences as well as the technological sciences.

In anthropology the concern of theories with meaning, classification, social structures, or rules was well established in the 1920s, although a qualitative break has sometimes been claimed for the New Anthropology, explicitly based on one or another model of language since the 1950s (Asad 1979, 608). These developments are likely to be found in the general historical and material conditions of postmodernist ethnographic forms. That is to say, these forms are integral, not with social practice in general but with the specific social practice of composing ethnographic texts, and the theories implicit in these forms are not theories of society, but theories that through assumed linguistic models, empathize with the soul of the commodity. Nevertheless, these conditions of postmodernist ethnographic forms are also the conditions of its recognition and critique.

Afterword

VINCENT CRAPANZANO

THERE IS AN AUTHORITY vested in an Afterword that I would *authoritatively* like to disclaim. It is one thing to write an Afterword after one's own words and quite another to write one after the words of others. The first is a continuation of one's words after a chiasmus, which marks a stock taking and adds authority to these words and its own. The second has imperial possibility. It possesses, it organizes, the others' words—even in the guise of a continuation or a dialogue. Here I will continue—no doubt entering into implicit dialogue with the essays in this collection, with the collection as a whole, but without commenting on any one of the essays, hoping, thereby, to preserve the illusion of their independence, *as I see it*.

Whose words are these others' words? Those of the authors of the texts that precede the Afterword? Those of the authors of the texts—here Frazer, Bataille, Benedict, etcetera—they claim to represent (note the ambiguity of the term!), paraphrase, comment on, elucidate, situate, or explain? Or are they the paraphrastic words of understanding?

The author of an Afterword is in a position not unlike the author of an ethnography. His problematic, his problem, like the ethnographer's problematic, his problem, is one of vantage point. Traditionally, convention—literary convention—determined critically his vantage point the way (with less success perhaps) convention—literary convention—determined the ethnographer's vantage point. (I include in my understanding of vantage point its ambiguity, its illusory stability, its vulnerability.) What is surprising to any reader of classical or modernist anthropology is how resistant these conventions were—are—to potential subversion by their subject matter. Or, put another way, how powerful their framing (I pun) of that subject matter was—and is. It was, it is, of course, supported by an "important" theoretical armamentarium, whose independence from these literary and other conventions is altogether questionable. The writer of an Afterword does not possess such a mighty arsenal or at least he must conceal it—tactfully—for, otherwise, his Afterword would become a reductive appropriation of the words that precede his own. He must maintain the pretense, as the ethnographer must maintain the pretense, that he is open, hermeneutically open to the cultural and historical determinants of his understanding—open-minded, as we used to say. The pretense is a moral affectation, a deception that denies its deceit, in short an absurdity; for, who can withstand a subversive onslaught, particularly of the conventions with which one frames (again, I pun) the subversive material?

The vision is a bit paranoid. I do want to stress, however, the masochistic dimension to any opening up—the interpreter as victim sacrificed (dare I say?) to truth—and the restorative, indeed the therapeutic, deflections (call them "defenses," call them "artifice") that inevitably ensue. A passion tale, one of descent and return, of illumination, lies behind every act of interpretation. The ethnographer enacts the tale twice—in the field and in the study. An ancient, an archetypal tale, it is given a peculiarly subjective cast during the romantic era—one that is incorporated into modernist expression and resisted (and thereby negatively confirmed) in the postmodernist. (Frazer's researches share this formulation with those of Malinowski and the other field anthropologists.) The anthropologist can assume neither the Orphic lyre nor the crown of thorns, although I confess to hear salvationist echoes in his desire to protect *his* people. The field site is not—cannot be taken as—a place of elemental darkness, where primitive impulse is embodied in the savage, the cannibal, or the headhunter and played out in barbarous, cruel, and erotic, ritual. No—the reality principle intervenes. The field site is not a *place* for promiscuous projection. It has to be taken as it *really* is or, as we say in this epistemologically sensitive age, in conformity with the tenets of realism. Yet, when we look at "modernist" ethnography deeply, including the photographs that accompany it, we discover that elemental darkness and primitive impulse is often poorly repressed and that the "real" is a little less than real. Field sites are less than paradise; the people studied, less than noble. Projections may be positive or negative. The reality principle is in fact less a succumbing to *reality* than the assumption of a moral stance. We have, however, learned to identify the real with the ordinary and, thereby, protect ourselves *empirically,* as it were, from the consequences of our moral positioning. We should situate the social categories, "ordinary," "commonplace," "everyday," "banal," and "mediocre" in the play—the morality play—of desire and (desired) reality. It is the ideologically and axiologically sanctioned scene for modernist enactment and presentation—the field and the ethnography.

"La modernité, c'est le transitoire, le fugitif, le contingent," Baudelaire

(n.d.) wrote in 1860, *"la moitié de l'art, dont l'autre moitié est l'éternel et l'immuable."* Unlike the *flâneur,* whose aim is immediate sensation, the artist, that solitary figure blessed with an active imagination, whom Baudelaire incarnates in the initials M.C.G. (M. Constantin Guy), traveling across "the great desert of mankind" has to draw the poetic from the historic, the eternal from the transitory. He is like the ethnographer, the modernist one, who has to draw the general from the particular, the rule from the seemingly unruly, without giving up the particular, the unruly—the fleeting and the transitory—in his cultural portraits, for they provide the textured background for his rules and generalizations. The tension is enormous, and it is exacerbated by all sorts of institutional factors, by hierarchies of knowledge and social rewards. Certainly in the twentieth century, the rule and the generalization, however banal, have been in the ascendent. In this respect, Frazer and at least the Malinowski of *The Argonauts of the Western Pacific* have more in common than Malinowski and contemporary ethnographic technocrats and Theorists.

Theory (with a capital *T*) is the rage today. Despite its professed concern for the subversive, it is potential deflection from precisely that which subverts. I am not taking an antitheoretical position here. I am calling attention to the historically contingent ascendency of a peculiar style of discourse—a metadiscourse—whose very focus on reflexivity seems paradoxically to bar the self-critical appreciation of the contingency of its own determinants. Although the authors of the essays in this collection participate in their several ways in this metadiscourse, they are united, perhaps, in their discontent with its self-framing—a discontent that cannot be equated, I believe, with the indulgent, at times playful, epistemological anguish that tones, for the lack of a better term, the metamodern sensibility. They are forced to accept the challenge to (traditional) authoritative, totalizing narrative and theoretical formulations that textualist—deconstructive and postmodern—critics pose without succumbing to the textualists' own promiscuously incorporative, displacedly authoritative formulations. Whether they succeed or fail in offering another perspective or revitalizing an existent one (few claim to do either), they do point to the limits of currently popular metadiscourse. They struggle with the problem of contingency—more important with the problem of discovering and defining determining contingency.

The postmodernist proclamation that master narratives are dead does not prevent the taking of an "extra-textual" stance, although there are some who, *pour se jouir,* would maintain it does. It does put into question the taking of (and the justifying of the taking of) an extratextual position—of accepting a narrative. It demands a thinking, a *continual morally sensitive thinking*, about what it means to take a position. In this thinking—I would argue, although I cannot pursue the argument here—pragmatic and utilitarian justifications of the accepting of a position, of a narrative, would be as out of place as the absurdist justifications of the existentialists. There is great pathos in the Marxist and Freudian confrontation with the postmodernist position . . .

What we do observe in the move to the meta level is the deflection, indeed, the suppression, the repression, perhaps even the foreclusion, the *Verdrängung*, of the purported subject matter of the commentary. In the seemingly endless chain of commentaries, of arguments and counterarguments, of responses, the original—the originary—subject matter is (to use the jargon) metaphrased. It quickly becomes an empty signifier that serves a pragmatic function—the preservation of the metaframe or, in the now fashionable questioning of that frame, the metametaframe.

But perhaps I am mistaken. Perhaps the empty signifier's singular function is phatic: the maintenance of contact among the commentators who have lost *vital* contact with the original, the originary subject matter—the subversive subject matter.

There has been much talk and writing about the writing of ethnography, about different styles of ethnography—classical, modernist, and now postmodernist ethnography—but the talk and the writing have tended to be in sweeping terms about movements and genres and fabulation rather than about specific texts. (The essays in this collection are an exception.) I am not certain what these movements are. I am not certain what an ethnography is. I do know that of the thousands of works, written in many languages, that have been called ethnographic, the writing school of ethnography has chosen to discuss only a few and repetitively so. They have, thereby, created, or confirmed, a canon. I do know that when I read ethnography, even the canonical works, I find them to be stylistically contradictory. Realism is coupled with exoticism. Descriptive constraint with loose speculation. Scientism with at least a dim recognition of allegorical possibility. Theoretical abstraction with concrete particularism. Discipline-internal intertextuality with often crudely self-proclaiming discipline-external intertextuality. Pretenses of authorial omniscience, of control, with confessions of authorial blindness, and intimations of failed control. From a literary perspective these contradictions are fascinating, and, I like to think that when ethnography, as we know it, is dead, they will reveal its true relational character—its invention. But, for the moment, we have to recognize that the chain of commentary, the talk and the writing about movements and genres and fabulation tend to a mystification that, insofar as its original and originary subject matter is lost, cannot be corrected through any vital (!) engagement with that subject matter.

I am reminded of a marvelous travel essay, *Reise im nordlichen Afrika,* by one of the great modernist writers, Hugo von Hofmannsthal (1969). I remember Hofmannsthal's musings about the French language, as he sits with some of Lyautey's officers on the roof of the Salé *madersa,* looking across the Bou Ragreg at Rabat. I remember the incongruity—and the incongruity of my own thoughts, so personal, so removed from where I was, as I sat on that same roof more than forty years after Hofmansthal did. I re-read the *Reise.* It is in two parts. The first describes Fez. Hofmannsthal reports no conversation. He can have none in this "delicately threatening" city. He likens the entanglement of markets, mosques, houses, and work places to ornaments of entangled script, which seem to repeat entangled Fasi life lines. The second part is in fact written from Salé. It is about language. A French captain describes how he was able to subdue the Sleuh because he had learned their language from a grammar written by a German who happened to meet a Berber dancer in Leipzig and became fascinated by the dancer's language. Hofmannsthal falls into revery. He watches a large bird fly across the river and perch on a tree at Chellah, an ancient pilgrimage site on the outskirts of Rabat. He remembers visiting Chellah as he listens to the captain and his companions talking. He tells them what a rich source of sociability the French language is. . . . His fantasy of Chellah, its deep exotic past, merges with his musings about language. He senses their unity. His revery, his *Traumerei,* is interrupted by one of the Frenchmen, who tells him how wonderful the German language is. The Frenchman recalls a Christmas night in the trenches during World War I. The shooting had stopped. From the distance the Marseillaise could be heard. Suddenly from the German trenches a wonderful tenor sings Bach. . . . A great language like German isolates more than it unites, the Frenchman observed. "But greatness always isolates, the poetic isolates, genius is always alone." Hofmannsthal is moved by the Frenchman's use of the word "*weltlos*"—worldless—"so tender, as mirrored, something ghostly." In the light of the setting sun everything seemed mirrored, in harmony, spiritualized.

Isolation, tension between isolating languages, feelings of unity, the anxiety of the individual, loneliness, delicate sensualism, intense subjectivism, epiphanous insights, exoticism, deep historicism, the sense of the primal, the spiritualization, the *Vergeistigung,* of the world, of nature, an appropriating impressionism, the confusion of reality and imagination, personalization, idiosyncratic and collective symbolism, mythic evocation, irony, nationalism, illusionism, mirroring—I could go on. These are some of the features—modernist features that are still deeply infused with romantic preoccupations—that one finds in Hofmannsthal's essay. You (no doubt) and I are overwhelmed by it—in thirteen pages! We feel the impoverishment of modernist ethnography—and some relief in its evasion of cloying subjectivism. There is courage in the ethnographer's commitment to objectivity.

There is also a determined naïveté in that commitment—one that the writing school ethnographers have pointed out many times—but there is an even more troubling naïveté in the commentators who articulate the problem of objectivity in terms of fiction and nonfiction. They take *fiction* and *nonfiction* as universal categories, or at least ahistorically, aculturally, when they are in fact culturally and historically specific categories that entail a very particular philosophical outlook, a notion of creativity, and an attitude toward narration, language, and representation. The application of these categories is certainly culturally and historically specific. I am not denying that the fiction-nonfiction distinction has influenced anthropologists' writing in this century. I am simply observing that it is one thing to discuss the influence of certain social and cultural categories on a specific work and quite another to write as if these categories were somehow transcultural, transhistorical, universal. This naïveté—and we find it also in discussions of narrative, discourse, text, drama, dialogue, and representation—seems entirely alien to the spirit of ethnographic investigation. It is as though in all this "literary talk" the ethnographer has lost his footing and sense of precisely what he as an ethnographer can contribute to such talk. Ethnography is not simply the description of manners and customs or the elucidation of social and cultural regularities. It is inherently comparative insofar as the ethnographer treats the social and cultural world he is investigating as distinct from his own, and as such, at least in its classical and modernist versions, it has a critically creative epistemological effect, if not explicit aim. It calls attention to the limits of one's own social and cultural outlook. It may be eminently creative in this respect, as were the works of Frazer (despite his aloof, hegemonic, Edwardian, and Victorian stance) or it may, in conservative times such as the one in which I am writing, spur crude backlash.

The field anthropologist, that is, the good field anthropologist, experiences this epistemological challenge intensely over a symbolically important span of his life, and it is probably safe to say that, despite all his efforts, he is never able to return fully to his culture and society. We have ample—conventionalized—accounts of this. The ethnographer straddles worlds—partialized worlds—and he is marginalized in all of them. I have likened him to a trickster—here, I would stress a *reluctant* trickster, for I find little irony (although many contradictions) in the ethnographer's relation to his field research, his writing, and his discipline. It is all serious, morally serious, and irony can have no part in that seriousness—certainly not in public displays of the ethnographer's métier. In this respect, ethnography differs dramatically from literary modernism, which incorporates irony in its own seriousness. There is more play in the modernist's stance than in the ethnographer's because the literary modernist's assumption is less deeply challenged. The split, the alienated, the isolated, the self-ironizing self is the (literary) conventional self. Hofmannsthal remains finally untouched by Fez, Salé, Chellah—the Moroccan and his languages.

The ideologically constituted position of the ethnographer is not his position in the texts he writes, although they are often read as if they were. Ideological readings, like those that simply accept stated intention—they are institutionally affirmed in the Abstract—fix the ethnographer's position in the text. They preclude (possible) changes of position in the text and the radical reevalution of ethnography—of that which it reports—that a reading sensitive to changes of position demands. Such changes are symptomatic of the relationship the ethnographer has to his data and they become important to any understanding of social and cultural description that sees the social and cultural as the work—the invention—of the mutually, although asymmetrically, engaged anthropologist and informant(s). Recognition of positional changes subverts ethnographic authority where authority is evaluated, as it has been in the social sciences, in terms of consistency. It can of course be evaluated in other terms—such as heteroglossic play—that seek to encompass the positional changes within some ironically transcending purview.

As with any documentary writer, any writer for that matter, the ethnographer has to establish his authority to make his work credible, and this he does rhetorically, mustering not only intra- but inter- and extratextual support for that authority (Clifford 1983). It would seem that a text-internal approach to understanding the constitution of authority is severely limited, for, I would suggest, one of the distinguishing features of the documentary, the "nonfictional," the ethnographic is its blatant appeal to extratextual authority (for example, institutional affiliation, time in the field, being there). The appeal is doubly authoritative for, not only does it reveal the author's credential, but, by appealing to "extra-textual factors," it breaks out of (or, as the deconstructionists would probably put it, it gives the illusion of breaking out of) the text itself and thereby confirms (the possibility of) the *extratextual reality* of the author's representation. He who trespasses domains (like the ethnographer) always has a certain—call it criminal—cachet. In fact that extratextual reality is, for lack of a better word, precipitated (although not created) through the ethnographer's appeal to authorized frames of understanding and conventions of representation. The experimental quality of those "experimental" ethnographies that abandon—more accurately, give the illusion of abandoning—authorial authority is in fact authoritative. It has its own appeal. It precipitates (its) reality. Text and reality are always implicated in each other.

Whether the sudden concern for ethnographic authority in anthropological circles relates to fundamental changes in the distribution of power in the postcolonial world or to the narrative dislocations of the postmodern world, it certainly oversimplifies the complex indexical—the context-calling—play in even the most monotonous ethnographies. The ethnographer is both in—implicated in—the reality he describes and out of that reality. His position in the text is perhaps isomorphic with his position in the field. It is moralized. An appropriate distance must be maintained—in the field (no sex, no leading questions, no arguments, no condescension) and in the text (no exoticizing, no eroticizing, no irony, no contestations, no constructions). And yet . . .

The authoritative assertion by whatever rhetorical means of an objective (credible) representation, interpretation, or explanation of social and cultural reality may well cover other rhetorical strategies that subvert that objectivity, that credibility, that authority. It has sometimes been said that the work of anthropology is translation, and etymologically as a carrying across, a *transferens,* it can be taken as such. This understanding of anthropology's work highlights, if it does not produce, the asymptotic divide, the rupture, so dear to modernist sensibility, that characterizes any frontier. What the ethnographer carries across has always to be taken in quotation marks—as coming from and yet removed from those across the divide. Here, perhaps, is one of the sources of that peculiarly contradictory attitude so apparent among modernist anthropologists: a sense of loss—nostalgia, the elegiac—coupled with the excitement of discovery, of presence.

The quotation marks not only proclaim the decontextualized—the abstracted—voice of the other but they challenge the ethnographer's (his readers') social and cultural assumption, his philosophical outlook, his language. They demand that that which ought to be written in quotation marks in its entirety ought also to be written *sous rature,* under erasure, as necessarily distorting, wholly problematic. No wonder ethnography is never enclosed in quotation marks. No wonder it is subject to such a severe—a serious—discipline. No wonder it has resisted irony, even in its modernist formulations, for irony always calls attention to artifice.

"In the fields with which we are concerned," Walter Benjamin (1983–1984) wrote, "knowledge comes only in flashes. The text is the thunder rolling long afterward."

Notes on Contributors

Vincent Crapanzano is Professor of Anthropology and Comparative Literature at CUNY Graduate Center. His interests include theories of interpretation, ethnopsychiatry, and literary anthropology. He has published, among other works, *The Hamadsha: A Study in Moroccan Ethnopsychiatry* (1973), *Tuhami: Portrait of a Moroccan* (1980), and *Waiting: The Whites of South Africa* (1985).

Deborah Gordon teaches in the Program in Culture, Ideas, and Values at Stanford University. She has published articles on feminism, gender, and ethnographic authority. She is completing her Ph.D. thesis, "Ethnographic Authorities: Gender, Race, and Practices of the Self in Contemporary Anthropology," in the History of Consciousness Program at the University of California, Santa Cruz.

Richard Handler is Assistant Professor of Anthropology at the University of Virginia. He is the author of *Nationalism and the Politics of Culture in Quebec*, published in 1988. Another book, *The Fiction of Culture: Jane Austen and the Narration of Social Realities*, co-authored with Daniel Segal, is forthcoming. He has published extensively on American anthropology and modernism.

Arnold Krupat is a member of the Literature faculty at Sarah Lawrence College. With Brian Swann he has co-edited two books, *Recovering the Word: Essays on Native American Literature*, and *I Tell You Now: Autobiographical Essays by Native American Writers*. His book *The Voice in the Margin: Native American Literature and the Canon* is forthcoming from the University of California Press.

Francesco Loriggio teaches Comparative Literature and Italian at Carleton University, Canada. He has written primarily on the relation between the social sciences and literature, Italian literature, and literary semiotics. He also has edited a collection of essays on the reception of turn-of-the-century Italian literature.

Marc Manganaro is Assistant Professor of English at Rutgers University (New Brunswick). He has published essays on T. S. Eliot, James Frazer, and modernism. His forthcoming book, *A Modernist Will to Power: The Rhetoric of Anthropological Authority*, concerns a rhetorical authority behind the writings of Frazer, Eliot, Northrop Frye, and Joseph Campbell.

Michèle Richman teaches French literature and culture at the University of Pennsylvania. She has written on anthropology and intellectual movements in the twentieth century. Her first book, *Reading Georges Bataille: Beyond the Gift,* was published by Johns Hopkins University Press in 1982. She is currently completing a study of the Collège de sociologie and preparing another on French notions of otherness since the sixteenth century.

Marty Roth is Professor of English at the University of Minnesota (Minneapolis), where he teaches American literature, popular culture, and film. He has published largely on Washington Irving, Poe, and Melville, and has a book circulating on mystery and detective fiction.

Marilyn Strathern is Professor of Social Anthropology at Manchester University, England. The titles of her books indicate some of her interests: *Women in Between* (1972) and the edited collections *Nature, Culture, and Gender* (1980) and *Dealing with Inequality* (1987). A general critique of Melanesian anthropology appeared in 1988 under the title, *The Gender of the Gift,* and she has used the 1989 Morgan Lectures (*After Nature*) for a disquisition on the present cultural revolution.

Robert Sullivan is Assistant Professor of English at the University of Illinois, Urbana-Champaign. He has written a study of Christopher Caudwell, the young communist theoretician who was killed in the Spanish Civil War, as well as other essays and reviews on modern literature.

John Vickery is Vice-Chancellor for Faculty Relations and Academic Support and Professor of English at the University of California, Riverside. He has written a number of books on the relation between literature, myth, and anthropology, including *The Literary Impact of "The Golden Bough," Robert Graves and the White Goddess,* and *Myths and Texts: Strategies of Incorporation and Displacement.* He also edited the collections *Myth and Literature* and *The Scapegoat.*

Steven Webster teaches in the Department of Anthropology at the University of Auckland (New Zealand). He has published on the relation between ethnography, fiction, and cultural criticism in journals such as *Dialectical Anthropology, Man,* and *Cultural Anthropology.* He is currently completing a book entitled *The Ethnographic Avantgarde.*

Bibliography

Abercrombie, N., S. Hill, and B. S. Turner. 1980. *The Dominant Ideology Thesis*. London: Allen and Unwin.

Adorno, Theodor. [1935–38] 1977. Letters to Walter Benjamin. In *Aesthetics and Politics*. Edited by Livingstone, Anderson, and Mulhern. London: New Left Books.

Althusser, Louis. 1971. "Ideology and Ideological State Apparatuses." In *Lenin and Philosophy and Other Essays*. New York: Monthly Review Press.

———. 1977. *For Marx*. Translated by Ben Brewster. London: New Left Books.

Arato, Andrew. 1974. "The Neo-Idealist Defense of Subjectivity." *Telos* 21: 108–61.

Ardener, Edward W. 1971. "The New Anthropology and Its Critics." *Man* 6: 449–67.

———. 1985. "Social Anthropology and the Decline of Modernism." In *Reason and Morality*. Edited by J. Overing. London: Tavistock.

Arens, W. 1983. "Evans-Pritchard and the Prophets: Comments on an Ethnographic Enigma." *Anthropos* 87: 1–16.

Asad, Talal. 1973. *Anthropology and the Colonial Encounter*. London: Ithaca Press.

———. 1979. "Anthropology and the Analysis of Ideology." *Man* 14: 607–27.

Auden, W. H. 1966. *Collected Shorter Poems*. London: Faber and Faber.

———. 1968. *Collected Longer Poems*. London: Faber and Faber.

Augé, Marc. 1977. *Pouvoirs de vie, pouvoirs de mort*. Paris: Flammarion.

Austin, Diane J. 1979. "Symbols and Culture: Some Philosophical Assumptions in the Work of Clifford Geertz." *Social Analysis* 3: 45–59.

Austin-Broos, Diane J. 1987. "Clifford Geertz: Culture, Sociology, and Historicism." In *Creating Culture*. Edited by Diane J. Austin-Broos. London: Allen and Unwin.

Babcock, Barbara. 1986. "Not in the Absolute Singular: Re-Reading Ruth Benedict." Paper prepared for the Wenner-Gren Conference, *Daughters of the Desert: Women Anthropologists and the Native American Southwest*.

Bakhtin, Mikhail. 1968. *Rabelais and His World*. Translated by H. Iwolsky. Cambridge, Mass.: M.I.T. Press.

———. 1981. *The Dialogic Imagination*. Translated by C. Emerson and M. Holquist. Austin: University of Texas Press.

———. 1984. "L'Auteur et le héros." In *Esthétique de la création verbale*. Translated by A. Aucouturier. Paris: Gallimard.

———. 1986. *Speech Genres and Other Late Essays*. Translated by V. W. McGee. Austin: University of Texas Press.

Barthes, Roland. 1973. *Mythologies*. St. Albans: Paladin Books.

———. 1979. "From Work to Text." In *Textual Strategies: Perspectives in Post-*

Structural Criticism. Edited by Josue Harari. Ithaca, N.Y.: Cornell University Press.

Bataille, Georges. 1946. "Le sens moral de la sociologie." *Critique* 1: 39–47.

———. 1985. *Visions of Excess: Selected Writings 1927–1939*. Edited by Allan Stoekl. Minneapolis: University of Minnesota Press.

Baudelaire, Charles. n.d. "Le Peintre de la Vie moderne." In *Ouevres* vol. 2. Paris: Bibliotèque de la Pléiade.

Baudet, Henri. 1965. *Paradise on Earth: Some Thoughts on European Images of non-European Man*. Translated by Elizabeth Wentholt. New Haven and London: Yale University Press.

Baudrillard, Jean. 1972. *Pour une Critique de l'Economie Politique du Signe*. Paris: Gallimard.

Beer, Gillian. 1983. *Darwin's Plots: Evolutionary Narrative in Darwin, George Eliot, and Nineteenth-Century Fiction*. London: Routledge & Kegan Paul.

———. 1986. " 'The Face of Nature': Anthropomorphic Elements in the Language of *The Origin of Species*." In *Languages of Nature*. Edited by L. J. Jordanova. London: Free Association Books.

Bellah, Robert, ed. 1973. *Emile Durkheim. On Morality and Society: Selected Writings*. Chicago and London: University of Chicago Press.

Benedict, Ruth. 1924. "A Brief Sketch of Serrano Culture." *American Anthropologist* 26: 366–92.

———. 1930. "Psychological Types in the Cultures of the Southwest." In *An Anthropologist at Work: Writings of Ruth Benedict*. Edited by Margaret Mead. Boston: Houghton Mifflin, 1959.

———. 1932. "Configurations of Culture in North America." *American Anthropologist* 34: 1–27.

———. [1934] 1946. *Patterns of Culture*. Boston: Houghton Mifflin.

———. 1943. "Obituary of Franz Boas." *Science* 97: 61.

———. 1946. *The Chrysanthemum and the Sword: Patterns of Japanese Culture*. Boston: Houghton Mifflin.

Benjamin, Walter. [1929] 1979. "Surrealism: The Last Snapshot of the European Intelligentsia." In *One-Way Street and Other Writings*. London: New Left Books.

———. [1936] 1969. "The Work of Art in the Age of Mechanical Reproduction." In *Illuminations*. Edited by Hannah Arendt. New York: Schocken.

———. [1938a] 1973. *Charles Baudelaire: A Lyric Poet in the Era of High Capitalism*. Translated by Harry Zohn. London: New Left Books.

———. 1938b. "Reply." In *Aesthetics and Politics*. Edited by Livingstone et al.

———. 1983–1984. N [Theoretics of Knowledge: Theory of Progress.] *The Philosophical Forum* 15, no. 1–2: 1–40.

Bloch, Maurice. 1983. *Marxism and Anthropology*. New York: Oxford University Press.

Bloom, Harold. 1982. *Agon*. Oxford: Oxford University Press.

Boas, Franz. 1940. *Race, Language, and Culture*. New York: Macmillan.

Boon, James. 1972. *From Symbolism to Structuralism: Lévi-Strauss in a Literary Tradition*. Oxford: Basil Blackwell.

———. 1982. *Other Tribes, Other Scribes: Symbolic Anthropology in the Comparative Study of Cultures, Histories, Religions, and Texts*. Cambridge: Cambridge University Press.

———. 1983. "Functionalists Write, Too: Frazer / Malinowski and the Semiotics of the Monograph." *Semiotica* 46: 131–49.

Bottomore, Tom. 1984. *The Frankfurt School*. London: Tavistock.

Bourdieu, Pierre. 1977. *Outline of a Theory of Practice*. Translated by Richard Nice. Cambridge: Cambridge University Press.

Bruner, Edward M. 1986. "Introduction." In *The Anthropology of Experience*. Edited by V. Turner and E. M. Bruner. Urbana, Ill.: University of Illinois Press.

———. 1986. "Anthropology and Human Studies." *Cultural Anthropology* 1, no. 1: 121–24.

Buck-Morss, Susan. 1977. *The Origin of Negative Dialectics: Theodore W. Adorno, Walter Benjamin, and the Frankfurt Institute*. New York: The Free Press.

Bulfinch, Thomas. 1915. *Bulfinch's Mythology: The Age of Fable; The Age of Chivalry*. New York: Crowell.

Bullock, Alan. 1978. "The Double Image." In *Modernism*. Edited by Malcolm Bradbury and James McFarlane. London: Pelican.

Bürger, Peter. [1974] 1984. *Theory of the Avant-Garde*. Manchester: Manchester University Press.

Burke, Kenneth. [1935] 1984. *Permanence and Change*. 3d ed. Berkeley: University of California Press.

———. [1937] 1961. *Attitudes Towards History*. 2d ed. Boston: Beacon Press.

———. [1941] 1961. *The Philosophy of Literary Form*. 3d ed. New York: Vintage Press.

———. 1959. "On Catharsis, On Resolution." *The Kenyon Review* 21: 3.

———. [1961] 1970. *The Rhetoric of Religion*. 2d ed. Berkeley and Los Angeles: University of California Press.

———. 1968. "Dramatism." *International Encyclopedia of the Social Sciences*, Vol. 7. London and New York: Macmillan and Free Press.

———. 1972. "As I Was Saying." *Michigan Quarterly Review* 11: 9–27.

Caffrey, Margaret. 1989. *Ruth Benedict: Stranger in This Land*. Austin: University of Texas Press.

Callahan, Bob. 1981. "Introduction." Zora Neale Hurston. In *Tell My Horse*.

Callois, Roger. 1942. *Puissances du Roman*. Marseilles: Le Sagittaire.

Cassirer, Ernst. 1944. *An Essay on Man*. New York: Doubleday.

Caudwell, Christopher. [1937] 1973. *Illusion and Reality: A Study of the Sources of Poetry*. New York: International Publishers.

Clark, Katerina, and M. Holquist. *Mikhail Bakhtin*. Cambridge: Harvard University Press.

Clarke, A. 1805. *The Manners of the Ancient Israelites*. 2d ed. Translation of Claude Fleury. *Moeurs des Israelites* [1681]. Manchester: S. Russell, for Baynes, London.

Clifford, James. 1980. "Fieldwork, Reciprocity, and the Making of Ethnographic Texts: The Example of Maurice Leenhardt." *Man* 15: 518–32.

Clifford, James. 1981. "On Ethnographic Surrealism." *Comparative Studies in Society and History* 23: 539–64.

———. 1982. *Person and Myth: Maurice Leenhardt in the Melanesian World.* Berkeley: University of California Press.

———. 1983. "On Ethnographic Authority." *Representations* 1: 118–46.

———. 1986a. "On Ethnographic Allegory." In *Writing Culture: The Poetics and Politics of Ethnography*. Edited by James Clifford and George Marcus. Berkeley: University of California Press.

———. 1986b. "On Ethnographic Self-Fashioning: Conrad and Malinowski." In *Reconstructing Individualism*. Edited by T. Heller, D. Wellburg, and M. Sosna.

———. 1986c. "Introduction: Partial Truths." In *Writing Culture: The Poetics and Politics of Ethnography*. Edited by James Clifford and George Marcus. Berkeley: University of California Press.

———. 1988. *The Predicament of Culture: Twentieth-Century Ethnography, Literature, and Art*. Cambridge: Harvard University Press.

Clifford, James, and George Marcus, eds. 1986. *Writing Culture: The Poetics and Politics of Ethnography*. Berkeley: University of California Press.

Codere, Helen, ed. 1966. *Kwakiutl Ethnography: Frank Boas*. Chicago.

Codrington, Robert Henry. [1891] 1972. *The Melanesians*. New York: Dover.

Cornford, Francis M. 1907. *Thucydides Mythistoricus*. London: Arnold.

Courlander, Harold. 1938. Review of *Tell My Horse. Saturday Review*, 15 October, p. 6.

Crapanzano, Vincent. 1980. *Tuhami: Portrait of a Moroccan*. Chicago: University of Chicago Press.

Crick, M. 1982. "Anthropological Field Research, Meaning Creation, and Knowledge Construction." In *Semantic Anthropology*, Edited by D. Parkin.

———. 1985. " 'Tracing' the Anthropological Self: Quizzical Reflections on Fieldwork, Tourism, and the Ludic." *Social Analysis* 17: 71–92.

Cushing, Frank Hamilton. 1901. *Zuni Folk-Tales*. New York: G. P. Putnam's Sons.

de Certeau, Michel. 1980. "Writing vs. Time: History and Anthropology in the Works of Lafitau." *Yale French Studies* 59: 37–64.

Declaration of the College of Sociology on the International Crisis. Signed by Georges Bataille, Roger Callois, and Michel Leiris. Paris, 7 October 1938.

De Heusch, L. 1985. *Sacrifice in Africa*. Manchester: Manchester University Press.

del Bayle, Loubet. 1969. *Les non-conformistes des années trente*. Paris: Editions du Seuil.

de Man, Paul. 1979. *Allegories of Reading*. New Haven, Conn.: Yale University Press.

Derrida, Jacques. 1974. *On Grammatology*. Baltimore: Johns Hopkins University Press.

Diamond, Stanley, ed. 1979. *Toward a Marxist Anthropology*. The Hague: Mouton Publishers.

———, ed. 1980. *Theory and Practice: Essays Presented to Gene Weltfish*. The Hague: Mouton.

Douglas, Mary. 1973. *Natural Symbols*. London: Barrie and Jenkins.

———. 1975. *Implicit Meanings*. London: Routledge & Kegan Paul.

Dowling, William C. 1984. *Jameson, Althusser, Marx: An Introduction to the Political Unconscious*. Ithaca, N.Y.: Cornell University Press.

Downie, A. R. 1970. *Frazer and the Golden Bough*. London: Victor Gollancz.

Dreyfus, Hubert L., and Paul Rabinow. 1983. *Michel Foucault: Beyond Structuralism and Hermeneutics*. Chicago: University of Chicago Press.

Dumont, Louis. 1970. "Religion, Politics, and Society in the Individualistic Universe." Royal Anthropological Institute of Great Britain and Ireland, *Proceedings*.

Durkheim, Emile. [1912] 1965. *The Elementary Forms of the Religious Life*. Translated by J. W. Swain. New York: Free Press.

———. 1975. *Textes 2: Religion, morale, anomie*. Paris: Editions de Minuit.

Eagleton, Terry. 1976. *Marxism and Literary Criticism*. London: Methuen.

———. 1981. *Walter Benjamin: Or Towards a Revolutionary Criticism*. London: New Left Books.

———. 1983. *Literary Theory: An Introduction*. Minneapolis: University of Minnesota Press.

———. 1986. *Against the Grain*. London: Verso Editions.

Eichenbaum, Boris. 1965. "The Theory of the 'Formal Method.' " In *Russian Formalist Criticism*. Edited by L. T. Lemon and M. J. Reis. Lincoln, Neb.: University of Nebraska Press.

Eliot, T. S. 1952. *Complete Poems and Plays*. New York: Harcourt.

Evans-Pritchard, Edward E. 1940. *The Nuer*. Oxford: Oxford University Press.

Fabian, Johannes. 1983. *Time and the Other: How Anthropology Makes its Object*. New York: Columbia University Press.

Faulkner, William. [1936] 1951. *Absalom, Absalom!* New York: Modern Library.

Fee, Elizabeth. 1974. "The Sexual Politics of Victorian Social Anthropology." In *Clio's Consciousness Raised*. Edited by Mary S. Hartman and Lois Banner. New York: Harper and Row.

Feeley-Harnik, G. 1985. "Issues in Divine Kingship." *Annual Review of Anthropology* 14: 273–313.

Fergusson, Francis. 1953. *Dante's Drama of the Mind*. Princeton: Princeton University Press.

Fernandez, James. 1986. *Persuasions and Performances: The Play of Tropes in Culture*. Bloomington: Indiana University Press.

Firth, Raymond, ed. 1957. *Man and Culture: An Evaluation of the Work of Bronislaw Malinowski*. London: Routledge & Kegan Paul.

———. 1985. "Degrees of Intelligibility." In *Reason and Morality*. Edited by J. Overing. London: Tavistock.

Fischer, Michael M. J. 1986. "Ethnicity and the Post-Modern Arts of Memory." In *Writing Culture: The Poetics and Politics of Ethnography*. Edited by

James Clifford and George Marcus. Berkeley: University of California Press.

Fish, Stanley. 1985. "Consequences." *Critical Inquiry* 11: 433–58.

Fortune, Reo. 1932. *Sorcerers of Dobu*. New York: Dutton.

Foster, Hal, ed. 1983. *The Anti-Aesthetic: Essays on Postmodern Culture*. Port Townsend, Wash.: Bay Press.

Foucault, Michel. 1973. *The Order of Things*. New York: Vintage Books.

Fowler, Alistair. 1982. *Kinds of Literature*. Cambridge: Harvard University Press.

Frazer, Sir James G. 1907–1915. *The Golden Bough: A Study in Magic and Religion*. 3d ed. 12 vols. London: Macmillan.

———. 1918. *Folk-lore in the Old Testament: Studies in Comparative Religion, Legend and Law*. 3 vols. London: Macmillan.

———. [1922] 1955. *The Golden Bough: A Study in Magic and Religion*. New York: The Macmillan Company.

———. 1926. *The Worship of Nature*. London: Macmillan.

———. 1935. *Creation and Evolution in Primitive Cosmogonies*. London: Macmillan.

Freeman, Derek. 1983. *Margaret Mead and Samoa: The Making and Unmaking of an Anthropological Myth*. Cambridge: Harvard University Press.

Freud, Sigmund. [1918] 1960. *Totem and Taboo*. New York: Vintage Books.

Friedman, Jonathan. 1987. Review of Marshall Sahlins, *Islands of History*. *History and Theory* 26: 1.

Frye, Northrop. [1957] 1971. *Anatomy of Criticism*. Princeton: Princeton University Press.

Geertz, Clifford. 1968. "Thinking As a Moral Act: Ethical Dimensions of Anthropological Fieldwork in the New States." *Antioch Review* 28: 139–58.

———. 1973. *The Interpretation of Cultures*. New York: Basic Books.

———. 1980. "The Blurring of Genres." *American Scholar* 49: 165–79.

———. 1983. *Local Knowledge: Further Essays in Interpretive Anthropology*. New York: Basic Books.

———. 1984. "Anti Anti-relativism." *American Anthropologist* 86: 263–78.

———. 1985a. "Making Experiences, Authoring Selves." In *The Anthropology of Experience*. Edited by V. Turner and E. M. Bruner.

———. 1985b. "Waddling In." *Times Literary Supplement*. 7 June, pp. 623–24.

———. 1988. *Works and Lives: The Anthropologist as Author*. Stanford: Stanford University Press.

Gellner, Ernest. 1974. *Legitimation of Belief*. Cambridge: Cambridge University Press.

———. 1985a. *Relativism and the Social Sciences*. Cambridge: Cambridge University Press.

———. 1985b. "Malinowski and the Dialectic of Past and Present." *Times Literary Supplement*. 7 June, pp. 645–46.

———. 1986. "Original Sin." *Times Higher Education Supplement*. 10 October, p. 13.

Giddens, Anthony. 1979. *Central Problems in Social Theory*. Berkeley: University of California Press.

———. 1984. *The Constitution of Society: Outline of the Theory of Structuration*. Berkeley and Los Angeles: University of California Press.

Godelier, Maurice. 1977. *Perspectives in Marxist Anthropology*. Translated by Robert Brain. Cambridge: Cambridge University Press.

Goffman, E. 1974. *Frame Analysis: An Essay in the Organization of Experience*. New York: Harper Colophon Books.

———. 1981. *Forms of Talk*. Philadelphia: University of Pennsylvania Press.

Goldfrank, Esther. 1978. *Notes on an Undirected Life: As One Anthropologist Tells It*. Flushing, N.Y.: Queens College.

Goldman, Irving. 1980. "Boas on the Kwakiutl: The Ethnographic Tradition." In *Theory and Practice*. Edited by Stanley Diamond.

Goldmann, Lucien. 1980. "The Subject of Cultural Creation." In *Essays on Method in the Sociology of Literature*. Translated and edited by William Q. Boelhower. St. Louis: Telos Press.

Goldschmidt, Walter, ed. 1959. *The Anthropology of Franz Boas: Essays on the Centenary of His Birth*. The American Anthropological Association. Vol. 61. Memoir no. 89.

Goodenough, W. H. 1970. *Description and Comparison in Cultural Anthropology*. Cambridge: Cambridge University Press.

Graham, Patricia Albjerg. 1978. "Expansion and Exclusion: A History of Women in American Higher Education." *Signs* 3: 759–73.

Gurvitch, Georges. 1963. *La vocation actualle de la sociologie*. Paris: Presses Universitaires de France.

———, and Wilbert E. Moore, eds. 1971. *Twentieth Century Sociology*. Freeport, N.Y.: Books for Libraries.

Habermas, Jurgen. 1981. "Modernity versus Postmodernity." *New German Critique* 22: 3–14.

———. 1983. "Modernity: An Incomplete Project." In The *Anti-Aesthetic: Essays on Postmodern Culture*. Edited by H. Foster. Port Townsend, Wash.: Bay Press.

Halpern, Ben. 1961. " 'Myth' and 'Ideology' in Modern Usage." *History and Theory* 1: 137.

Handler, Richard. 1983. "The Dainty and the Hungry Man: Literature and Anthropology in the Work of Edward Sapir." *History of Anthropology* 1: 208–31.

———. 1984. "On Sociocultural Discontinuity: Nationalism and Cultural Objectification in Quebec." *Current Anthropology* 25: 55–71.

———. 1986. "Vigorous Male and Aspiring Female: Poetry, Personality, and Culture in Edward Sapir and Ruth Benedict." *History of Anthropology* 4: 127–55.

———. 1988. *Nationalism and the Politics of Culture in Quebec*. Madison: University of Wisconsin Press.

———. 1989. "Anti-Romantic Romanticism: Edward Sapir and the Critique of American Individualism." *Anthropological Quarterly* 62: 1–13.

Hanson, Allan, and L. Hanson. 1982. *Counterpoint in Maori Culture*. London: Allen and Unwin.

Harari, Joseu, ed. 1979. *Textual Strategies: Perspectives in Post-Structural Criticism*. Ithaca, N.Y.: Cornell University Press.

Hardin, Richard. 1983. " 'Ritual' in Recent Criticism: The Elusive Sense of Community." PMLA 98: 846–62.

Harris, Marvin. 1968. *The Rise of Anthropological Theory*. New York: Crowell.

Harrison, Jane E. 1912. *Themis*. Cambridge: Cambridge University Press.

———. 1913. *Ancient Art and Ritual*. New York: Henry Holt and Company.

Hastrup, Kristen. 1978. "The Post-Structuralist Position of Social Anthropology." In *The Yearbook of Symbolic Anthropology*. Edited by E. Schwimmer. London: Hurst.

Heller, Thomas, D. Wellburg, and M. Sosna, eds. 1986. *Reconstructing Individualism: Autonomy, Individuality and the Self in Western Thought*. Stanford: Stanford University Press.

Hemenway, Robert. 1977. *Zora Neale Hurston: A Literary Biography*. Urbana: University of Illinois Press.

Herskovits, Melville. 1927. *Life in a Haitian Valley*. New York: Alfred A. Knopf.

Hill, J. H. 1986. "The Refiguration of the Anthropology of Language." Review essay on Bakhtin's *Problems of Dostoevsky's Poetics*. *Cultural Anthropology* 1: 89–102.

Hirsch, E. D. 1983. "Against Theory?" *Critical Inquiry* 9: 743–47.

Hofmannsthal, Hugo von. 1969. "Reise im Nordlichen Afrika." *Das Erzählerische Werk*. Frankfurt am Main: Fischer Verlag.

Hollier, Denis, ed. [1979] 1988. *The College of Sociology*. Translated by Betsy Wing. Minneapolis: University of Minnesota Press.

Honigman, John Joseph. 1976. *The Development of Anthropological Ideas*. Homewood, Ill.: Dorsey Press.

Hooper, Antony, and J. Huntsman, eds. 1985. *Transformations of Polynesian Culture*. Auckland: *Journal of the Polynesian Society*. Memoir no. 45.

Horton, Robin. 1973. "Lévy-Bruhl, Durkheim and the Scientific Revolution." In *Modes of Thought*. Edited by Robin Horton and Ruth Finnegan. London: Faber and Faber.

Horton, Robin, and Ruth Finnegan, eds. 1973. *Modes of Thought*. London: Faber and Faber.

Huggins, Nathan Irvin. 1971. *Harlem Renaissance*. London: Oxford University Press.

Hurston, Zora Neale. [1935] 1978. *Mules and Men*. Bloomington: Indiana University Press.

———. [1938] 1981. *Tell My Horse*. Berkeley: Turtle Island Press.

Hyman, Stanley. 1962. *The Tangled Bank: Darwin, Marx and Freud as Imaginative Writers*. New York: Atheneum.

Hymes, Dell, ed. 1974. *Reinventing Anthropology*. New York: Vintage.

Jakobsen, Roman, and Morris Halle. 1971. *Fundamentals of Language*. The Hague: Mouton.

Jakubinskij, Lev. 1979. "On Verbal Dialogue." Translated by Jane E. Knox. Dispositio 4: 11–12, 321–36.

Jameson, Fredric. 1981. *The Political Unconscious: Narrative as a Socially Symbolic Act*. Ithaca, N.Y.: Cornell University Press.

———. 1983. "Postmodernism and Consumer Society." In *The Anti-Aesthetic: Essays on Postmodern Culture*. Edited by Hal Foster.

———. 1984. "Postmodernism, or the Cultural Logic of Late Capitalism." *New Left Review* 146: 53–92.

Jamin, Jean. 1981. "Quand le sacré devint gauche." *l'Ire des vents* no. 3 / 4: 98–118.

Jarvie, I. C. 1964. *The Revolution in Anthropology*. London: Routledge & Kegan Paul.

———. 1984. *Rationality and Relativism: In Search of a Philosophy and History of Anthropology*. London: Routledge & Kegan Paul.

———. 1986. "Anthropology as Science and the Anthropology of Science and of Anthropology." In *Philosophy of Science Association 1984*. Edited by Peter D. Asquith and Philip Kitchner. East Lansing: Philosophy of Science Association.

Johnson, Barbara. 1986. "Metaphor, Metonymy and Voice in Zora Neale Hurston's *Their Eyes Were Watching God*." In *Textual Analysis*. Edited by Mary Ann Caws. New York: Modern Language Association of America.

Jones, R. A. 1984. "Robertson Smith and James Frazer on Religion: Two Traditions in British Social Anthropology." In *Functionalism Historicized*. Edited by G. W. Stocking. Madison: University of Wisconsin Press.

Jorion, Paul. 1983. "Emic and Etic: Two Anthropological Ways of Spilling Ink." *Cambridge Anthropology* 8: 41–68.

Joyce, James. [1916] 1956; 1964. *A Portrait of the Artist as a Young Man*. New York: Viking.

———. [1922] 1961. *Ulysses*. New York: Modern Library.

Kaberry, Phyllis. 1957. "Malinowski's Fieldwork Methods." In *Man and Culture*. Edited by R. Firth. London: Routledge & Kegan Paul.

Karady, Victor. 1972. "Naissance de l'ethnologie universitaire." *l'Arc* 48: 33–40.

Kardiner, Abram, and E. Preble. 1961. *They Studied Man*. London: Secker and Warburg.

Kauffman, Robert Lane. 1981. "The Theory of the Essay: Lukács, Adorno, and Benjamin." Ph.D dissertation, University of California, San Diego.

Knapp, Steven and Walter Benn Michaels. 1982. "Against Theory." *Critical Inquiry* 8: 732–42.

Krader, Lawrence. 1974. *The Ethnological Notebooks of Karl Marx*. Assen, The Netherlands: Van Gorcum and Company.

Kristeva, Julia. 1980. *Desire in Language*. Translated by L. S. Rondiez. New York: Columbia University Press.

Kroeber, A. L. 1959. "Preface." *The Anthropology of Franz Boas*. Edited by Walter Goldschmidt. The American Anthropological Association. Vol. 61. Memoir no. 89.

Kuper, Adam. 1973. *Anthropologists and Anthropology: The British School, 1922–1972*. London: Allen Lane.

Kurtz, Paul W., ed. 1983. *Sidney Hook: Philosopher of Democracy and Humanism*. Buffalo, N.Y.: Prometheus.

La Capra, Dominick. 1972. *Emile Durkheim, Sociologist and Philosopher*. Ithaca and London: Cornell University Press.

Lamphere, Louise. 1986. "Gladys Reichard among the Navajo." Paper prepared for the Wenner-Gren Conference, *Daughters of the Desert: Women Anthropologists and the Native American Southwest*.

Lang, Andrew. 1911. "Mythology." *The Encyclopaedia Brittanica*. 11 ed. New York: Encyclopaedia Brittanica, Inc., pp. 128–44.

Langham, Ian. 1981. *The Building of British Social Anthropology: W.H.R. Rivers and His Cambridge Disciples in the Development of Kinship Studies, 1898–1931*. Dordrecht: D. Reidel.

Leach, Edward. 1957. "The Epistemological Background to Malinowski's Empiricism." In *Man and Culture*. Edited by R. Firth. London: Routledge & Kegan Paul.

———. 1961. "Golden Bough or Gilded Twig?" *Daedalus* 90: 371–87.

———. 1965. "Frazer and Malinowski: On the Founding Fathers." *Encounter* 24: 24–36.

———. 1966. "On the 'Founding Fathers.' " *Current Anthropology* 7: 560–67.

———. 1982. *Social Anthropology*. London: Fontana Paperbacks.

———. 1983. "Anthropological Approaches to the Study of the Bible during the Twentieth Century." In *Structuralist Interpretations of Biblical Myth*. Edited by E. R. Leach and D. A. Aycock. Cambridge: Cambridge University Press for the Royal Anthropological Institute.

———. 1985a. "Observers Who Are Part of the System." *London Times Higher Education Supplement*. 29 November.

———. 1985b. "Conclusion." In *Transformations in Polynesian Culture*. Edited by Hooper and Huntsman. Auckland: Journal of the Polynesian Society. Memoir no. 45.

Leach, Edward, and D. A. Aycock, eds. 1983. *Structuralist Interpretations of Biblical Myth*. Cambridge: Cambridge University Press for the Royal Anthropological Institute.

Lears, T. J. Jackson. 1983. "From Salvation to Self-Realization: Advertising and the Therapeutic Roots of the Consumer Culture, 1880–1930." In *The Culture of Consumption*. Edited by Richard Fox and T. Jackson Lears. New York: Pantheon.

Le Bon, Gustave. 1985. *Psychologie des Goules*. Paris: Alcan.

Lemon, L. T., and M. J. Reis, eds. 1965. *Russian Formalist Criticism*. Lincoln: University of Nebraska Press.

Lentricchia, Frank. 1983. *Criticism and Social Change*. Chicago: University of Chicago Press.

———. 1986. "The Return of William James." *Cultural Critique* 4: 5–31.

Levenson, Michael. 1984. *A Geneology of Modernism: A Study of English Literary Doctrine, 1908–1922*. Cambridge: Cambridge University Press.

Lévi-Strauss, Claude. [1949] 1969. *The Elementary Structures of Kinship*. Revised ed. Translated and edited by James Harle Bell, John Richard von Sturmer, and Rodney Needham. Boston: Beacon Press.

———. [1955] 1976. *Tristes Tropiques*. Harmondsworth: Penguin Books, Ltd.

———. 1950. "Introduction à l'Oeuvre de Marcel Mauss." In Marcel Mauss, *Sociologie et anthropologie*. Paris: Presses Universitaires de France.

———. 1963. *Totemism*. Boston: Beacon Press.

———. 1971. "French Sociology." In *Twentieth Century Sociology*. Edited by Georges Gurvitch and Wilbert E. Moore. Freeport, N.Y.: Books for Libraries.

Lévy, Bernard-Henri. 1981. *l'Idéologie française*. Paris: Grasset.

Lienhardt, G. 1966. 2d ed. *Social Anthropology*. London: Oxford University Press.

Lindberg, Kathryne. 1987. *Reading Pound Reading: Modernism after Nietzsche*. New York: Oxford University Press.

Livingston, Paisley. 1984. "Introduction." In *Disorder and Order: Proceedings of the Stanford International Symposium*. Edited by Paisley Livingston. Saratoga, Calif.: Anma Libri.

Livingstone, Rodney, Perry Anderson, and Frances Mulhern, eds. 1977. *Aesthetics and Politics: Debates between Block, Lukács, Brecht, Benjamin and Adorno*. London: New Left Books.

Locke, Alain. 1939. "The Negro: 'New' or Newer," *Opportunity* 17 (February): 38.

Lotman, Jurij. 1977. *The Structure of the Artistic Text*. Ann Arbor: University of Michigan Press.

———. 1985. *La semiosfera*. Translated by S. Salvestroni. Venice: Marsilio.

Lotman, Jurij and B. Uspensky. 1978. "On the Semiotic Mechanism of Culture." *New Literary History* 9, no. 2: 211–32.

Lowenthal, David. 1985. *The Past Is a Foreign Country*. Cambridge: Cambridge University Press.

Lubbock, J. 1875a. 3d ed. *The Origin of Civilization and the Primitive Condition of Man: Mental and Social Condition of Savages*. London: Longmans, Green.

———. 1875b. "Modern Savages." In *Science Lectures: Delivered in Manchester, 1873–4*. Science Lectures for the People. Manchester: John Heywood.

Lukács, Georg. [1922] 1971. *History and Class Consciousness: Studies in Marxist Dialectics*. Translated by R. Livingstone. Cambridge, Mass.: M.I.T. Press.

Lunn, Eugene. 1982. *Marxism and Modernism: An Historical Study of Lukács, Brecht, Benjamin, and Adorno*. Berkeley: University of California Press.

Lyotard, Jean-Francois. [1979] 1984. *The Postmodern Condition: A Report on Knowledge*. Minneapolis: University of Minnesota Press (English translation).

Macherey, Pierre. 1978. *A Theory of Literary Production*. London: Routledge & Kegan Paul.

Magarey, Susan, ed. 1984. *Changing Paradigms: The Impact of Feminist Theory upon the World of Scholarship*. Sydney: Hale and Iremonger.

Malinowski, Bronislaw. [1916] 1948. *Science, Magic and Religion*. Garden City, N.Y.: Doubleday.

———. [1922] 1961. *Argonauts of the Western Pacific*. New York: Dutton.

———. [1925] 1932. "Myth in Primitive Psychology." In *The Frazer Lectures, 1922–32*. London: Macmillan.

———. 1962. *Sex, Culture, and Myth*. London: Rupert Hart-Davies.

———. 1967. *A Diary in the Strict Sense of the Term*. London: Routledge & Kegan Paul.

———. 1944. *A Scientific Theory of Culture, and Other Essays*. Chapel Hill: University of North Carolina Press.

Manganaro, Marc. 1989. " 'The Tangled Bank' Revisited: Anthropological Authority in Frazer's *The Golden Bough*." *Yale Journal of Criticism* 3: 107–26.

Manning, F. E., ed. 1983. *The Celebration of Society*. Bowling Green: Bowling Green University Popular Press.

Marcus, George E. 1986. "Contemporary Problems of Ethnography in the Modern World System." In *Writing Culture*. Edited by J. Clifford and G. Marcus. Berkeley: University of California Press.

Marcus, George E., and Dick Cushman. 1982. "Ethnographies as Texts." *Annual Review of Anthropology* 2: 25–69.

Marcus, George E., and Michael M. J. Fischer. 1986. *Anthropology as Cultural Critique: An Experimental Moment in the Human Sciences*. Chicago: University of Chicago Press.

Marett, R. R. 1920. *Psychology and Folk-Lore*. London: Methuen.

Marx, Karl. [1857] 1973. *Grundrisse*. Edited by M. Nicolaus. London: Penguin.

———. [1867] 1983. *Capital*. Vol. 1. Moscow: Progress Publishers.

Mauss, Marcel. 1950. *Sociologie et anthropologie*. Paris: Universitaires de France.

———. 1967. *The Gift: Forms and Functions of Exchange in Archaic Societies*. Translated by I. Cunnison. New York: Norton.

———. 1969. *Ouvres* Vol. 3. *Cohésion sociale et divisions de la sociologie*. Paris: Editions de Minuit.

McLellan, David. 1986. *Ideology*. Minneapolis: University of Minnesota Press.

Mead, Margaret. 1928. *Coming of Age in Samoa*. New York: William Morrow and Company.

———. 1935. *Sex and Temperament in Three Primitive Societies*. New York: William Morrow and Company.

———. 1977. *Letters from the Field: 1925–1975*. New York: Harper and Row.

———, ed. 1959. *An Anthropologist at Work: Writings of Ruth Benedict*. Boston: Houghton Mifflin.

Mead, Margaret, and Ruth Bunzel, eds. 1960. *The Golden Age of American Anthropology*. New York: Braziller.

Menand, Louis. 1987. *Discovering Modernism: T. S. Eliot and His Context*. Oxford: Oxford University Press.

Merwin, W. S. 1970. *Carrier of Ladders*. New York: Atheneum.

Metz, Christian. 1982. *The Imaginary Signifier: Psychoanalysis and the Cinema*. Bloomington: Indiana University Press.

Mintz, Sidney. 1981. "Ruth Benedict." In *Totems and Teachers*. Edited by Sydel Silverman. New York: Columbia University Press.

Modell, Judith. 1983. *Ruth Benedict: Patterns of a Life*. Philadelphia: University of Pennsylvania Press.

Montgomery, David. 1987. *The Fall of the House of Labour: the Workplace, the State, and American Labour Activism, 1865–1925*. Cambridge: Cambridge University Press.

Mukarovsky, Jan. 1977. "Two Studies of Dialogue." In *The Word and Verbal Art*. Translated by J. Burbank and P. Steiner. New Haven: Yale University Press.

Nadeau, Maurice. 1965. *The History of Surrealism*. Translated by Richard Howard. New York: Macmillan.

Ogden, C. K., and I. A. Richards. 1972. *The Meaning of Meaning*. London: Routledge & Kegan Paul.

Overing, J., ed. 1985. *Reason and Morality*. London: Tavistock.

Owens, C. 1985. "The Discourse of Others: Feminists and Postmodernism." In *The Anti-Aesthetic*. Edited by Hal Foster. Port Townsend, Wash.: Bay Press.

Oxford English Dictionary (OED). 1971. Oxford: Oxford University Press.

Panofsky, Erwin. 1957. *Meaning in the Visual Arts*. Garden City, N.Y.: Doubleday.

Parkin, David, ed. 1982. *Semantic Anthropology*. London: Academic Press.

Peacham, Henry. [1593] 1954. *Garden of Eloquence*. A Fascimile Reproduction. Introduction by William G. Crane. Gainesville, Fla.

Peckham, Morse. 1962. *Beyond the Tragic Vision*. New York: Braziller.

Perelman, Chaim, and Lillane Olbrechtotyteca. 1958. *Traite de l'Argumentation*. Paris: Presses Universitaires de France.

Pickering, W.S.F. 1984. *Durkeim's Sociology of Religion: Themes and Theories*. London, Boston, Melbourne and Henley: Routledge & Kegan Paul.

Pierce, C. S. 1932. *Collected Papers*. Vol. 2. Cambridge: Harvard University Press.

Plekanov, George V. 1969. *Fundamental Problems of Marxism*. New York: International Publishers.

Potts, Abby Findlay. 1967. *The Elegiac Mode*. Ithaca, N.Y.: Cornell University Press.

Pound, Ezra. [1948] 1964. *The Cantos*. London: Faber and Faber.

Pratt, Mary Louise. 1986. "Fieldwork in Common Places." In *Writing Culture*. Edited by James Clifford and George Marcus. Berkeley: University of California Press.

Prattis, Iain, ed. 1986. *Reflections: The Anthropological Muse*. Washington: American Anthropological Association.

Prigogine, Ilya, and Isabelle Stengers. 1984. *Order Out of Chaos*. New York: Bantam Books.

Propp, Vladimir J. 1984. *Theory and History of Folklore*. Translated by A. Y. Martin and R. P. Martin. Minneapolis: University of Minnesota Press.

Rabasa, Jose. 1987. "Dialogue as Conquest: Mapping Spaces for Counter-Discourse." *Cultural Critique* 6: 131–59.

Rabinow, Paul. 1977. *Reflections on Fieldwork in Morocco*. Berkeley and Los Angeles: University of California Press.

———. 1983. " 'Facts Are a Word of God': An Essay Review." In *Observers Observed*. Edited by G. W. Stocking. Madison: University of Wisconsin Press.

———. 1986. "Representations Are Social Facts: Modernity and Post-Modernity in Anthropology." In *Writing Culture*. Edited by J. Clifford and G. Marcus. Berkeley: University of California Press.

Richman, Michèle. 1982. *Reading Georges Bataille: Beyond the Gift*. Baltimore: Johns Hopkins University Press.

———. 1988. "Introduction to the Collège de sociologie: Poststructuralism before Its Time?" Special Issue on Georges Bataille. *Stanford French Review* 12: 79–96.

Roberts, Julian. 1982. *Walter Benjamin*. London: Macmillan.

Rohner, Ronald, and Evelyn P. Rohner. 1969. "Introduction." *The Ethnography of Franz Boas*. Edited and compiled by Ronald Rohner. Chicago: University of Chicago Press.

Rorty, Richard. 1979. *Philosophy and the Mirror of Nature*. Princeton: Princeton University Press.

———. 1983a. *Consequences of Pragmatism*. Minneapolis: University of Minnesota Press.

———. 1983b. "Pragmatism without Method." In *Sidney Hook: Philosopher of Democracy and Humanism*. Edited by Paul Kurtz. Buffalo, N.Y.: Prometheus.

Rosaldo, Renato. 1989. *Culture and Truth: The Remaking of Social Analysis*. Boston: Beacon Press.

Runciman, W. G. 1983. *A Treatise on Social Theory*. Vol. 1. *The Methodology of Social Theory*. Cambridge: Cambridge University Press.

Russell, Frank. 1908. "The Pima Indians." *Twenty-sixth Annual Report of the Bureau of American Ethnology*. Washington, D.C.

Sacks, Peter. 1985. *The English Elegy*. Baltimore: Johns Hopkins University Press.

Sahlins, Marshall. 1976. *Culture and Practical Reason*. Chicago: University of Chicago Press.

———. 1981. *Historical Metaphors and Mythical Realities: Structure in the Early History of the Sandwich Islands Kingdom*. Ann Arbor: University of Michigan Press.

———. 1985. *Islands of History*. Chicago: University of Chicago Press.

Said, Edward. 1978. *Orientalism*. New York: Pantheon.

———. 1989. "Representing the Colonized: Anthropology's Interlocutors." *Critical Inquiry* 15 no. 2: 205–25.

Sangren, P. Steven. 1988. "Rhetoric and the Authority of Ethnography." *Current Anthropology* 29: 405–35.

Sapir, Edward. 1924. "Culture, Genuine and Spurious." In *Selected Writings of Edward Sapir*. Edited by D. Mandelbaum. Berkeley: University of California Press, 1985.

———. 1927. "The Unconscious Patterning of Behavior in Society." In *Selected Writings of Edward Sapir*. Edited by D. Mandelbaum. Berkeley: University of California Press, 1985.

———. [1949] 1985. *Selected Writings of Edward Sapir*. Edited by D. Mandelbaum. Berkeley: University of California Press.

Schwimmer, E. 1978. *The Yearbook of Symbolic Anthropology*. London: Hurst.

Shweder, Richard A. 1986. "Storytelling among the Anthropologists." *New York Times Book Review*, 21 September, pp. 1, 38–39.

Silverman, Sydel, ed. 1981. *Totems and Teachers: Perspectives in the History of Anthropology*. New York: Columbia University Press.

Singer, Milton. 1983. *Man's Glassy Essence*. Bloomington: Indiana University Press.

Sloterdijk, Peter. 1986. "Weimar et la Californie." *Critique* 42: 114–27.

Smith, Marilyn. 1959. "Boas' 'Natural History' Approach to Field Method." In *The Anthropology of Franz Boas*. Edited by W. Goldschmidt. The American Anthropological Association. Vol. 61. Memoir no. 89.

Smith, Paul. 1988. *Discerning the Subject*. Minneapolis: University of Minnesota Press.

Smith, William R. [1889] 1956. *The Religion of the Semites: The Fundamental Institutions*. New York: Meridian Books.

Solomon, Maynard. [1973] 1979. *Marxism and Art: Essays Classic and Contemporary*. Detroit: Wayne State University Press.

Sperber, Dan. 1985. *On Anthropological Knowledge*. Cambridge: Cambridge University Press.

Stocking, George W., Jr. 1968. *Race, Culture, and Evolution: Essays in the History of Anthropology*. New York: Free Press.

———. 1974. "The Basic Assumptions of Boasian Anthropology." In *The Shaping of American Anthropology, 1883–1911: A Franz Boas Reader*. Edited by George Stocking. New York: Basic Books.

———. 1976. "Ideas and Institutions in American Anthropology: Thoughts Toward a History of the Interwar Years." In *Selected Papers from the American Anthropologist, 1921–1945*. Washington: American Anthropological Association.

———. 1983. "The Ethnographer's Magic: Fieldwork in British Anthropology from Tylor to Malinowski." In *Observers Observed*. Edited by George W. Stocking. Madison: University of Wisconsin Press. (*History of Anthropology*, vol. 1).

———. 1984. "Radcliffe-Brown and British Social Anthropology." In *Functionalism Historicized*. Edited by G. W. Stocking. Madison: University of Wisconsin Press. (*History of Anthropology*, vol. 2).

———. 1988. *Victorian Anthropology*. Chicago: University of Chicago Press.

Stocking, George W., Jr., ed. 1974. *The Shaping of American Anthropology, 1883–1911: A Franz Boas Reader*. New York: Basic Books.

———, ed. 1983. *Observers Observed: Essays on Ethnographic Fieldwork*. Madison: University of Wisconsin Press.

———, ed. 1984. *Functionalism Historicized: Essays on British Social Anthropology*. Madison: University of Wisconsin Press.

Stoekl, Allan. 1985. "Introduction." In Georges Bataille, *Visions of Excess*. Minneapolis: University of Minnesota Press.

Strathern, Marilyn. 1984. "Dislodging a World View: Challenge and Counter-Challenge in the Relationship between Feminism and Anthropology." In *Changing Paradigms*. Edited by Susan Magarey. Sydney: Hale and Iremonger, 1984.

———. 1987a. "Out of Context: The Persuasive Fictions of Anthropology." *Current Anthropology* 28, no. 3: 251–82.

———. 1987b. "Partial Connections." Distinguished Lecture, 1988 Meeting of the Association for Social Anthropology in Oceania. In manuscript (to appear in ASAO special publication series, forthcoming).

———. 1988. *The Gender of the Gift*. Berkeley: University of California Press.

Strelka, Joseph P., ed. 1980. *Literary Criticism and Myth*. University Park and London: Pennsylvania State University Press.

Sullivan, Robert. 1987. *Christopher Caudwell*. London and Sydney: Croom and Helm.

Szwed, John F. 1974. "An American Anthropological Dilemma: The Politics of Afro-American Culture." In *Reinventing Anthropology*. Edited by Dell Hymes. New York: Vintage.

Thomson, George. 1941. *Aeschylus and Athens: A Study in the Social Origins of Drama*. London: Lawrence and Wishart.

Thornton, R. J. 1983. "Narrative Ethnography in Africa, 1850–1920: The Creation and Capture of an Appropriate Domain for Anthropology." *Man* 18: 502–20.

———. 1985. " 'Imagine Yourself Set Down . . .': Mach, Frazer, Conrad, Malinowski, and the Role of the Imagination in Ethnography." *Anthropology Today* 1, no. 5: 7–14.

Timpanaro, Sebastiano. 1970. 1975. *On Materialism*. London: New Left Books.

Tiryakian, Edward. 1979. "l'Ecole durkheimienne à la recherche de la sociologie perdue: La sociologie naissante et son milieu culturel." *Cahiers internationaux de sociologie* 66: 97–114.

Todorov, Tzvetan. [1982] 1984. *The Conquest of America: The Question of the Other*. Translated by Richard Howard. New York: Harper and Row.

Trilling, Lionel. 1971. *Sincerity and Authenticity*. Cambridge: Harvard University Press.

Tucker, Robert C., ed. 1972. *The Marx-Engels Reader*. New York: W. W. Norton.

Turner, Victor. 1974. *Dramas, Fields, and Metaphors*. Ithaca, N.Y.: Cornell University Press.

———. 1982. *From Ritual to Theatre*. New York: Performing Arts Journal Publications.

———. 1983a. "Body, Brain, and Culture." *Zygon* 3: 221–45.

———. 1983b. " 'Carnaval' in Rio." In *The Celebration of Society*. Edited by F. E. Manning. Bowling Green: Bowling Green University Popular Press.

Turner, Victor, and Edward Bruner, eds. 1986. *The Anthropology of Experience*. Urbana, Ill.: University of Illinois Press.

Tyler, Stephen. 1986a. "Post-Modern Ethnography: From Document of the Occult to Occult Document." In *Writing Culture: The Poetics and Politics of Ethnography*. Edited by James Clifford and George Marcus. Berkeley: University of California Press.

———. 1986b. "The Poetic Turn in Postmodern Anthropology: The Poetry of Paul Friedrich." *American Anthropologist* 84: 328–36.

———. 1987. *The Unspeakable: Discourse, Dialogue, and Rhetoric in the Postmodern World*. Madison: University of Wisconsin Press.

Tylor, Sir Edward Burnett. 1871. *Primitive Culture*. London: John Murray.

Urry, J. 1983. Review of I. Langham, *The Building of British Social Anthropology*. *Oceania* 53: 400–402.

Veltrusky, Jiri. 1977. *Drama as Literature*. Translated by J. Veltrusky. Lisse: Peter De Ridder Press.

Vickery, John B., ed. 1966. *Myth and Literature: Contemporary Theory and Practice*. Lincoln, Nebr.: University of Nebraska Press.

———. 1973. *The Literary Impact of "The Golden Bough."* Princeton: Princeton University Press.

———. 1980. "Literary Criticism and Myth: Anglo-American Critics." In *Literary Criticism and Myth*. Edited by J. P. Strelka. University Park and London: Pennsylvania State University Press.

Visweswaran, Kamala. 1988. "Defining Feminist Ethnography." *Inscriptions* 3 / 4: 27–44.

Vološinov, Valentin N. 1973. *Marxism and the Philosophy of Language*. New York: Seminar Press.

———. 1976a. "Discourse in Life and Discourse in Art." In *Freudianism*. Translated by I. R. Titunik. New York: Academic Press.

———. 1976b. *Freudianism: A Marxist Critique*. New York: Academic Press.

Wagner, Roy. 1986. "The Theatre of Fact and Its Critics." Review of *Writing Culture*. Edited by James Clifford and George Marcus. In *Anthropological Quarterly* 59: 97–99.

Webster, Steven. 1981. "Interpretation of an Andean Social and Economic Formation." *Man* 16: 616–33.

———. 1982. "Dialogue and Fiction in Ethnography." *Dialectical Anthropology* 7: 91–114.

———. 1983. "Ethnography as Storytelling." *Dialectical Anthropology* 8: 125–65.

———. 1986. "Realism and Reification in the Ethnographic Genre." *Critique of Anthropology* 6, no. 1: 39–62.

———. 1987. "Structuralist Historicism and the History of Structuralism:

Sahlins, the Hansons' *Counterpoint in Maori Culture,* and Postmodern Ethnographic Form." *Journal of the Polynesian Society* 96, no. 1: 27–65.

———. 1989. "A Zapotecan Meritocracy." *Cultural Anthropology* 1989 (November): 4.

White, Hayden. 1973. *Metahistory: The Historical Imagination in Nineteenth-Century Europe*. Baltimore: Johns Hopkins University Press.

———. 1978. *Tropics of Discourse*. Baltimore: Johns Hopkins University Press.

White, Leslie. 1963. *The Ethnography and Ethnology of Franz Boas*. Bulletin of the Texas Memorial Museum. No. 6.

Williams, Raymond. 1977. *Marxism and Literature*. Oxford: Oxford University Press.

———. 1981. 1983. *Culture and Society, 1750–1950*. New York: Columbia University Press.

Willis, Paul. 1977. *Learning to Labour*. Farnborough, Hants, U.K.: Saxon House.

Woolf, Virginia. [1937] 1958. *The Years*. London: Hogarth Press.

Yeatman, A. 1984. "Gender and the Differentiation of Social Life into Public and Domestic Domains." In *Gender and Social Life*. Edited by A. Yeatman. *Social Analysis*. Special issue 15.

———, ed. 1984. *Gender and Social Life. Social Analysis*. Special issue 15.

Young, M. 1983. Review of J. Clifford. *Person and Myth: Maurice Leenhardt in the Melanesian World. Oceania* 54: 169–70.

Index

Aaron's Rod (Lawrence), 144
Absalom, Absalom! (Faulkner), 55
Acéphale, 205
Adams, Henry, 136–37
Adorno, Theodor W., 44, 269, 274, 275–91, 294, 295–96, 298
Aeschylus and Athens (Thomson), 43
Aesthetics and Politics, 280
"African Elegy, An" (Duncan), 68
agonism, 222, 227
"Aims of Anthropological Research, The" (Boas), 142–43
"Aims of Ethnology, The" (Boas), 139–40, 141
Allegories of Reading (de Man), 17
Althusser, Louis, 247, 250, 257, 262, 265, 271, 274, 283
American Anthropological Association, 9
Americanness, 219
Anatomy of Criticism (Frye), 14
Ancient Society (Morgan), 250
animism, 12
anthropology: aims of, 142–43; collaborative, 11–12; and colonialism, 9, 27–28, 33, 99, 153, 155, 188–89, 266; comparative, 4, 19 n.9, 20, 21, 23, 32, 52, 87–88, 103, 137, 175, 177, 188; and cultural critique, 36–38, 43, 46, 185, 186, 249–50, 251; development of, 4, 29–30, 146–47, 219, 252; and evocation, 11, 32, 245, 268; modernism in, 4–8, 20, 23, 25, 95–96, 118–22, 266; as political, 35, 223 n.7; and pornography, 77–79; postmodernism in, 5, 6, 7–8, 9, 10, 11–12, 23, 25–26, 44–46, 108, 111–12, 113–17, 266, 269, 298–99; and power relations, 26–27, 33, 34, 146, 147–48; and pragmatism, 36, 217–18, 220–21, 222; and representation, 10–11, 18–19; as a science, 18, 52, 75. *See also* cultural representation; ethnography; ethnology
"Anthropology and the Abnormal" (Benedict), 172
Anthropology of Experience, The (Turner and Bruner), 39, 218, 221, 222
anti-aesthetic, 10
Aragon, Louis, 276
Ardener, Edward, 6, 25, 95, 96, 108, 110, 123, 129
Argonauts of the Western Pacific (Malinowski), 4, 24, 31, 32, 83, 302
Aristotle, 228, 230
Arnold, Matthew, 166, 271, 272
Asad, Talal, 26
Attitudes Towards History (Burke), 226, 228–29
Auden, W. H., 61–62, 68
Austin, Diane, 270
Austin, J. L., 220

Bachofen, Jacob J., 72 n.7, 77, 253
"Babylon Revisited" (Fitzgerald), 68
Bakhtin, Mikhail, 32, 33, 39, 40, 41, 46, 221, 224, 231–32, 233–34, 235, 237–38, 239, 241, 298
Barker, George, 68
Barnes, Djuna, 227
Barthes, Roland, 205, 212, 248, 253, 267, 270, 292, 296, 298
Bataille, Georges, 5, 23, 38, 44, 45 n.23, 183, 185, 204, 205, 206, 207, 208–9, 210, 211–12, 213, 214, 270, 272, 275, 276, 277–78, 279, 286, 292, 294, 295
Bateson, Gregory, 101 n.27
Baudelaire, Charles-Pierre, 17, 208, 212, 269, 277, 280, 285, 288, 289–90, 291, 292, 296, 301–2
Baudrillard, Jean, 205, 270, 271, 278, 296, 298
Beckett, Samuel, 141
Beer, Gillian, 93, 94, 113
Benedict, Ruth: as biographer, 168, 179; ethnography by, 19 n.9, 20–21, 31, 32, 133, 148, 149, 163–80, 272, 292, 295; poetry of, 5, 20, 30–31, 164, 165, 168, 179
Benedict, Stanley, 167

Benjamin, Walter, 23, 25, 44, 208, 263, 269, 270, 274, 275–91, 292, 294, 295–96, 298, 308
Bergson, Henry-Louis, 259
Berryman, John, 68
Beyond the Tragic Vision (Peckham), 60
Blackmur, R. P., 230
Blanchot, Maurice, 213
Bloom, Harold, 217
Boas, Franz: cited by Burke, 227; criticism of Frazer by, 21; as diffusionist, 4–5 n.1, 21, 170; and folklore, 160; and holism, 169–70; and New Negro, 158; opinion of amateurs, 147; provocation in texts of, 32; rejected in literary criticism, 13; seminal role of, 4, 19, 20, 31, 133–45, 272, 292; women students of, 148–49, 153, 154 n.9, 160, 165
Bonald, Louis-Gabriel-Ambroise de, 200
Boon, James, 15, 16, 17, 26 n.12, 90, 113–14, 118–19
Bourdieu, Pierre, 248, 265, 273
Brecht, Bertolt, 25, 44, 275, 276, 278, 279, 283–84, 286
Breton, André, 276, 277
"Brief Sketch of Serrano Culture, A" (Benedict), 165, 171
Bruner, Edward, 39, 218
Buck-Morss, Susan, 276, 280, 284
Bulfinch, Thomas, 72
Bullock, Alan, 134
Bunzel, Ruth, 133
Bürger, Peter, 274, 294, 298
Burke, Kenneth, 39, 223 n.7, 227–30, 231–33, 235, 236, 241, 257, 258

Caillois, Roger, 5, 12, 23, 183, 206, 208, 210–11, 213
Cambridge Hellenist school, 12, 13 n.4, 39, 41–42, 43, 51, 225, 227, 254, 258
Cantos (Pound), 56–57, 63, 71
Capital (Marx), 278, 281, 297
Carlyle, Thomas, 217
Carnegie, Andrew, 158
Cassirer, Ernst, 248, 249, 252, 255, 260
Castle, The (Kafka), 141
Caudwell, Christopher, 39, 41–42, 253
Charlevoix, Pierre-François-Xavier de, 188
Chateaubriand, François-Auguste-René de, 188
chronopolitics, 27
Chrysanthemum and the Sword, The (Benedict), 165, 175, 177, 179–80
Clarke, A., 81, 82
classical studies, 4–5 n.1
Clifford, James, 3, 5, 8, 12, 15, 18–19, 20, 23–24, 29, 32, 33–34, 46, 75 n.11, 79, 98, 108, 115, 116, 117, 128, 129, 130, 146–47, 244–45, 267, 269–70, 279, 292
Codere, Helen, 142
collective consciousness, 273–74
Collège de sociologie, 5, 37–38, 183–84, 186–87, 188, 193, 199–200, 205–8, 209, 212–13, 270, 274, 276
colonialism, and anthropology, 9, 27–28, 33, 99, 153, 155, 188–89, 266
Coming of Age in Samoa (Mead), 19 n.9, 37, 147, 149, 150, 157
Comte, Auguste, 197
Concept of the Guardian Spirit in North America, The (Benedict), 170
"Configurations of Culture in North America" (Benedict), 165, 173, 175, 178
Conquest of America, The (Todorov), 27
Conrad, Joseph, 8, 28, 135
consolidation, 31–32
Contribution to the Critique of Political Economy, The (Marx), 250, 252
conversationalism, 219, 220–21, 241
Cook, Stanley Arthur, 51
Cornford, Francis M., 12, 51, 225, 235
Crane, Stephen, 135, 136
Crapanzano, Vincent, 11, 129
Crick, M., 108, 110, 112, 117, 129
Criterion, The, 31
Croce, Benedetto, 272
cultural relativism, 28, 100, 137, 266, 268
cultural representation: and ethnocentrism, 19; and evocation, 11, 245; as problematic, 3, 18–19, 146, 244–45, 269; and text making, 16–17, 19–20, 267–68. *See also* representation
culture, 157; of African-Americans, 158–59, 160–61; and the individual, 163, 167, 178, 179, 198, 200–203; and social theories, 270, 271–74
Culture and Practical Reason (Sahlins), 271

Curtis, Natalie, 159–60
Cushman, Dick, 267, 269

Dahrendorf, Ralph, 262
Dante Alighieri, 69, 230
Darwin, Charles, 71, 93–94, 113, 250, 251
"Death of Europe, The" (Olson), 68
"Death of Parnell, The" (Yeats), 12
de Certeau, Michel, 77
deconstructionism, 16, 17, 45, 267, 268, 269, 270, 272, 274, 278, 280, 292, 293, 296, 298
de Man, Paul, 17, 136
Derrida, Jacques, 22, 75, 126, 136, 185, 212, 219, 224, 270, 298
Descartes, René, 243, 244
Descent of Man, The (Darwin), 71
Dewey, John, 218, 219, 221, 224, 225, 227
dialogue, in ethnography, 109, 115, 116, 231
Diderot, Denis, 185, 188, 199
diffusionism, 4–5 n.1, 21, 170, 172
Dilthey, Wilhelm, 172, 173, 174, 218, 272
Division of Labor in Society, The (Durkheim), 193
Douglas, Mary, 51
Downie, A. R., 85
dramatism. *See* performance, and theater
Dreiser, Theodore, 59
Driesch, Hans Adolf Eduard, 259
Dubliners (Joyce), 59
Dumont, Louis, 178
Durkheim, André, 191
Durkheim, Emile, 185; and collective religion, 39, 193–97, 199, 200–203, 207–8, 212, 214, 247, 273–74; influence of, 37, 38, 187, 190–91, 260; literary appreciation of, 13; and sociological methodology, 40, 42, 192–99, 203

Eagleton, Terry, 14
Economic and Philosophic Manuscripts (Marx), 250, 252
Education (Adams), 137
Einstein, Albert, 135
elegy, and anthropological text, 52
"Elegy on Dead Fashion" (Sitwell), 68
Elementary Forms of the Religious Life, The (Durkheim), 37, 38, 193, 194, 197, 198–99, 200, 201, 203, 204, 247
Eliot, T. S.: anthropological impact on, 4, 8, 12, 38, 39, 271; as literary artist, 31, 32, 43, 54, 63, 65, 68, 136, 144, 163, 225, 227, 230
Emerson, Ralph Waldo, 217, 218, 227
emic-etic dichotomy, 121 n.63
empiricism, 52
emplotment, strategies of, 15, 26 n.12
Engels, Friedrich, 41, 42, 43, 249, 250, 251, 253, 265, 277
epic form, used by Frazer, 71
epistemology, 215
ethnocentrism, 19, 21, 27–28, 35, 75, 81–84, 99, 121, 156, 170, 185, 261
ethnodramatics, 226, 231. *See also* performance, and theater
ethnographic allegory, 37, 38
ethnographic space, 93 n.16, 154
ethnographic surrealism, 4, 5, 23–25, 44, 185, 280
ethnography, 301; comparativism in, 4, 19 n.9, 20, 21, 23, 305; and disappearance of social forms, 29; of evocation, 11, 32, 275; experimental, 11, 266, 267, 269–70, 280, 292, 293, 296 (*see also* anthropology, postmodernism in); as literary, 18, 21, 147, 185, 222, 223–24, 226, 233, 235; methodology of, 19–20, 21, 84, 179–80, 279; postmodern (*see* anthropology, postmodernism in); and realism, 24, 25, 30–31, 266, 269, 303; and representation, 17; and structuralism, 267; styles of, 303; as text making, 15–16, 267–68. *See also* ethnology; monographs
ethnology: and colonialism, 27; knowledge of, 71 n.4; and symbolism, 192
Etruscan Places (Lawrence), 58
Evans-Pritchard, Edward E., 28, 86, 100, 197, 208, 224
evolutionary theories, of civilization, 21, 83, 84, 87, 94, 170, 193, 251
existentialism, 215

Fabian, Johannes, 27–28
fascism, 206, 213, 280
Fauconnet, Paul, 190
Faulkner, William, 54–55
feminism, 34
Fergusson, Francis, 230

Ferry, Jules, 189
fieldwork, development of, 86, 87, 95, 96, 97–99, 119, 147, 153–55, 162, 191
Finnegans Wake (Joyce), 60, 71, 137, 141
Firth, Raymond, 97
Fischer, Michael M. J., 6, 8, 11, 25, 26 n.12, 30, 150–51, 256, 260, 261, 262, 270
Fitzgerald, F. Scott, 68
Fleury, Claude (Abbé), 81, 82, 84, 90
folklore, 29 n.14, 159, 160–61, 235, 236
Folk-lore in the Old Testament (Frazer), 81, 85, 88, 94
Ford, Ford Madox, 54, 56, 58, 68, 135
Fortune, Reo, 178
Foster, Hal, 10
Foucault, Michel, 3, 16, 26, 133, 185, 212, 243–44, 245, 246, 252, 255, 270
Fowler, Alistair, 53
Frankfurt School, 262, 263, 271, 274, 276
Frazer, Sir James George, 301, 302; as celebrity, 84; comparativism of, 20, 21, 76 n.14, 87, 88–90, 104–7, 115, 305; criticism of, 21, 26, 69, 75–77, 80, 85–91, 97, 103, 197; and elegy, 62–68; ethnocentrism of, 13, 21, 28, 104; ethnographic methodology of, 19; and human sexuality, 78, 79; literary appreciation of, 21–23, 26, 31, 53, 69–79, 88, 91–95, 103, 126–28, 224, 225, 227, 235; manner of representation by, 92, 113–17; reappraisal of, 12, 22, 33, 86, 111, 112–13, 120–22, 248, 249; seminal role of, 4, 12, 15, 42, 85–91, 96, 252
Freeman, Derek, 150
Freud, Sigmund, 51, 62, 68, 71, 76, 78, 133, 135, 202, 217, 243, 250, 258–59
Friedman, Jonathan, 267, 271
From Ritual to Theatre (Turner), 222
From Symbolism to Structuralism: Lévi-Strauss in a Literary Tradition (Boon), 16
Frye, Northrop, 14–15, 26 n.12, 39, 257, 258
functionalism, 96, 101, 114, 123, 173

Gadamer, Hans-Georg, 221, 224, 270
Geertz, Clifford, 15–16, 19, 51, 83, 84, 117, 145, 224, 232 n.11, 260–61, 262, 264, 270, 271, 273, 293, 296
Gellner, Ernest, 122
German Ideology, The (Marx and Engels), 41, 250
Giddens, Anthony, 36, 264–65
Gift Essay (Mauss), 203
gift giving, 203, 204, 278
Gillen, F. J., 195, 198
Girard, René, 13
Giroux, Henry, 264
Gödel, Kurt, 134
Godelier, Maurice, 36, 271
Goffman, Erving, 226, 231
Golden Bough, The (Frazer), 4, 22, 51, 62–68, 69–79, 85, 94, 117, 227
Goldmann, Lucien, 256
Gordon, Deborah, 30
Gould, Eric, 13 n.5
Grammar of Motives, The (Burke), 226
Gramsci, Antonio, 274
Griaule, Marcel, 191
Grice, Paul, 220
Gurvitch, Georges, 204

Habermas, Jurgen, 24, 185, 212, 213, 215, 269, 294–95
Haddon, A. C., 96
Halpern, Ben, 247
Handler, Richard, 30, 32
Hardy, Thomas, 135, 136
Harris, Marvin, 134, 135
Harrison, Jane Ellen, 12, 13, 42, 51, 79, 85, 225, 227, 248, 249, 252, 254, 258
Hawthorne, Nathaniel, 71, 227
Heart of Darkness, The (Conrad), 28, 127
Hegel, Georg Wilhelm Friedrich, 208–9, 249, 250, 268, 278, 285
Heidegger, Martin, 219, 272
Heisenberg, Werner Karl, 135
Hemenway, Robert, 149, 154, 156, 159
Hemingway, Ernest, 68, 227
Herder, Johann Gottfried von, 271, 272
hermeneutic theory, 270
Hero, The (Raglan), 227
Herskovits, Melville, 148, 156
heteroglossia, 115, 232. *See also* polyvocality
Hill, Geoffrey, 68
historicism, 96, 99
history: as context for culture, 251; and cultural critique, 36; and elegy, 54–61; and golden age, 56–57; literariness of,

15; and myth, 14–15; and naturalized time, 28; and representation, 27, 34
holism, 96, 97, 99, 101, 163, 164, 169–70, 171, 172, 173, 176, 177, 179
Hooper, Antony, 267
Hughes, Langston, 161, 162
Hugo, Victor, 71, 289
Huntsman, J., 267
Hurston, Zora Neale, 20, 30, 147–48, 149–50, 154–62
Hyman, Stanley Edgar, 21, 251
Hymes, Dell, 227

Illusion and Reality (Caudwell), 42
incest, 78
individual, and society, 163, 167, 178, 179, 198, 200–203, 207, 243, 244, 246, 247, 249, 252–53, 254, 256, 261–62
inferencing, 52
interdisciplinary studies, 36, 38
"Ione, Dead the Long Year" (Pound), 68
irony, 113–17, 135–38
irrationalism, 185, 192, 195
Irving, Washington, 71

Jacobs, Melville, 133
Jakobson, Roman, 16, 74, 273, 295, 298
James, Henry, 62, 135, 137, 144, 230
James, William, 60, 217, 219, 220, 227
Jameson, Fredric, 6–7, 8, 9, 10, 14, 41, 45, 46, 115, 254, 257–58, 269, 273, 291, 294, 295
Jarvie, I. C., 86–87, 88, 96, 100, 102
Joyce, James, 4, 59–60, 63, 77, 136, 137, 141, 180
Jung, Carl, 12, 14, 172

Kaberry, Phyllis, 97
Kafka, Franz, 141, 284–85, 288
Karady, Victor, 192
Kaufmann, R. L., 280
Kluckhohn, Clyde, 45 n.23, 148–49, 271, 273
Knox, Jane E., 239 n.14
Kojève, Alexandre, 272, 278
Krader, Lawrence, 250
Kristeva, Julia, 205, 234 n.13, 270
Kroeber, Alfred L., 45 n.23, 133, 142, 148, 199, 271, 272, 273, 274
Krupat, Arnold, 32

Lacan, Jacques, 38, 243, 255, 257, 258, 259, 270
Lady Chatterly's Lover (Lawrence), 58
La Figlia (Eliot), 68
Lafitau, Joseph-François, 188
Lang, Andrew, 21, 51, 72
language: Darwin's use of, 114; native, 142; referentiality of, 17–18; social use of, 39, 40–41, 45–46, 119, 238, 239; as symbolic behavior, 231, 252, 253, 254–55, 259–60, 298; and theater, 229. *See also* conversationalism
Language and Symbolic Action (Burke), 226
Lawrence, D. H., 12, 57–58, 59, 63, 65, 144, 243
Leach, Edmund, 79, 84, 97, 99, 100, 267, 270, 273, 293
Le Bon, Gustave, 208
Leenhardt, Maurice, 108–9, 111, 116, 129
Leibniz, Gottfried Wilhelm, 202
Leiris, Michel, 12, 23, 183, 191, 206, 213, 214
Lentricchia, Frank, 223 n.7
Léry, Jean de, 188
Levenson, Michael, 31, 32, 163, 166
Levine, Stephen K., 261–62
Lévi-Strauss, Claude, 3, 10, 13, 16–17, 75, 76 n.13, 78, 108, 133, 184, 199, 200, 203, 204, 209, 247, 257, 258, 270, 272, 273, 293, 298. *See also* structuralism
Lévy-Bruhl, Lucien, 51
Lindberg, Kathryne, 163
Linton, Ralph, 148
literary criticism: as comparativist, 4–5 n.1, 219; and pragmatism, 217, 218, 221; primacy of ritual in, 12–13. *See also* New Criticism
Locke, Alain, 158, 160–61
logology, 229
Loriggio, Francesco, 36, 38–40
Lotman, Jurij, 236, 238, 240–41
Lubbock, Sir John, 81–82, 83, 84, 107, 250
Lukács, Georg, 9, 271, 274, 278–79, 281, 282, 283, 298
Lukes, Steven, 197
Lyotard, Jean-François, 8, 9–10, 23, 24, 30, 268, 270

Macherey, Pierre, 245
Maine, Sir Henry J. S., 42, 250

Malinowski, Bronislaw, 301, 302; appreciation of Durkheim by, 197; appreciation of Frazer by, 85; cited by Burke, 227; as classical anthropologist, 51, 248, 249; and cultural relativism, 28; and ethnocentrism, 83, 84; and human sexuality, 77–78; literary impact of, 4–5, 22, 23, 25, 32, 75, 97–98, 109, 114, 127–28; representation by, 92, 100–101; seminal role of, 4, 6, 15, 19, 20, 21, 24, 31, 52, 76, 85, 87, 90–91, 96, 97–99, 252; and theory of imagination, 92 n.14. *See also* functionalism
Malthus, Thomas, 71
Mann, Thomas, 59
Manner of the Israelites, The (Fleury), 81
Marcus, George E., 6, 8, 18, 25, 26 n.12, 30, 33, 150–51, 244–45, 257, 260, 261, 262, 267, 269, 270
Marcuse, Herbert, 274
Marett, R. R., 83 n.5, 85 n.6, 86 n.8, 89, 96
Margaret Mead and Samoa (Freeman), 150
marriage customs, 82, 87, 88–89, 92, 104–5
Marx, Karl, 41, 42, 43, 71, 247, 248, 249, 250–56, 264, 265, 268, 270, 274, 277–78, 280, 281–82, 283, 285, 289–90, 291, 296–97, 298
Marxism, 40–41, 42, 43, 45, 243–65 passim, 273, 275
Mason, Mrs. Rufus Osgood, 159–60, 161
Masters, Edgar Lee, 230
Mauss, Marcel, 4, 187, 188–90, 191–92, 193, 202–3, 204, 209, 210, 212, 270, 277, 278, 292, 295
Mead, George Herbert, 225, 227
Mead, Margaret, 18, 19 n.9, 20, 30, 37, 133, 147–54, 157, 158, 162, 164, 170
Melville, Herman, 71, 74, 227
Merwin, W. S., 68
meta-anthropology, 185
metaethnography, 7, 115
Metahistory (White), 223 n.7
metaphor, 17, 73–74
Miller, J. Hillis, 136
Milton, John, 136
Mintz, Sydney, 148
Mission Dakar-Djibouti, 23, 24
missionaries, as fieldwork sources, 188. *See also* colonialism, and anthropology
Modell, Judith, 168, 171, 172
modernism: in anthropology, 4–8, 20, 23, 25, 95–96, 118–22, 266; critique of, 279; and elegy, 53, 54, 60, 61, 62; and individualism, 164, 166, 167, 169, 178; in literature, 4–5, 8–10, 12, 31, 51–68 passim, 163, 266; Other in, 8–9; time frame for, 4, 6, 9; use of the term, 5–6, 46
monographs, 4, 5, 6, 10, 15, 18–32 passim, 98–99, 109, 123, 124. *See also* cultural representation; text; text making
Montaigne, Michel Eyquem de, 184, 188, 199
Montesquieu, Baron de La Brède et de (Charles-Louis de Secondat), 185, 188
Moore, Marianne, 227
Morgan, Henry Lewis, 41, 42, 248, 249, 250–51, 253
Mornings in Mexico (Lawrence), 58
Mukarovsky, Jan, 239 n.14
Mules and Men (Hurston), 149, 154 n.9, 158
Murray, Gilbert, 12, 51, 225, 227
Musée de l'Homme, 24
Myth and Literature, 22
Myth Criticism, 13–15, 22
mythic consciousness, 12
mythology: in anthropology, 13; comparative, 4–5 n.1; contextual analysis of, 98, 102; and society, 247

National Geographic, The, 77
New Anthropology, 299
New Criticism, 14, 22, 236
New Negro, 158
Nietzsche, Friedrich Wilhelm, 17–18, 19, 135, 136, 144, 172, 186, 217, 219, 227, 272, 277
Nisa (Shostak), 79
Noble savages, 28, 188
Norris, Frank, 59
novels, 231–32, 233–34, 239–40

Oakeshott, Michael, 220
objectification, 101–3, 109, 110, 119, 155, 175, 246, 305
observation, and fieldwork, 86, 87, 279
Olson, Charles John, 68
O'Meara, J. Tim, 11 n.3
On Grammatology (Derrida), 75
Order of Things, The (Foucault), 243–44
Orientalism (Said), 3, 35

Origin of the Family, Private Property, and the State (Engels), 41, 250, 253
Origin of Species, The (Darwin), 114, 251
Other: as a class, 233; and lessons for Western civilization, 37, 151–52, 156, 184–85, 186, 187, 199, 219; in modernism, 8–9; in monographs, 99; as participant-collaborator, 11; in postmodernism, 10–11; preservation of, 29; in structuralism, 10. *See also* cultural representation; objectification

Panofsky, Erwin, 58
Parade's End (Ford), 56, 68
Parsons, Elsie Clews, 168
Parsons, Talcott, 220, 273–74
Pater, Walter, 165–66, 169
Patterns of Culture (Benedict), 19 n.9, 20–21, 149, 164, 165, 167, 172, 175, 177–79, 272
Peacham, Henry, 136
Peckham, Morse, 60
Peirce, Charles Sanders, 218, 219, 220, 221, 227, 233
Pepe, C. F., 153
performance, and theater, 222–23, 225–26, 227, 228–30, 231–32, 233–34, 239, 275
phenomenology, 16, 266, 267, 270, 271, 278, 293, 296
philosophy, and anthropology, 215–17
Philosophy of Literary Form, The (Burke), 226, 227, 231
Piaget, Jean, 256
Pickering, W.S.F., 197, 198, 208
Plekanov, George V., 249, 253, 254, 259
Plumed Serpent, The (Lawrence), 58, 144
poetry: elegiac, 53; Frazer's literal reading of, 73; interpretation in, 216
Political Unconscious, The (Jameson), 14, 45, 257
polyvocality, 26, 33, 52. *See also* heteroglossia
Portrait of a Lady (James), 144
Portrait of the Artist as a Young Man, A (Joyce), 59, 77, 180
positivism, 21, 28, 45, 52, 138
Postmodern Condition, The (Lyotard), 9–10, 24
postmodernism: in anthropology, 5, 6, 7–8, 9, 10, 23, 25–26, 44–46, 108, 111–12, 113–17, 266, 269, 298–99; in literature, 7, 9–10; Other in, 10–11
poststructuralism, 270–71
Potts, Abby Findlay, 53
Pound, Ezra, 31, 32, 54, 56–57, 63, 68, 136, 163, 225, 230
power relations, 26–27, 146
pragmatism, 216, 217, 219–21, 222, 227, 231
Prague School, 273
Pratt, Mary Louise, 27
Predicament of Culture, The (Clifford), 19
primeval existence, 57–58
Primitive Culture (Tylor), 252
primitives: contrasted with the West, 151–52, 156; and cultural relativism, 28, 100, 268; disappearance of, 29; distanced from the present, 28–29, 82–83; ethnocentric representation of, 19, 21, 27–28, 81–82; lack of writing among, 75; as the Other, 3, 8–9, 99, 151, 156; as primal state, 13; sexuality of, 77–79, 152. *See also* Other
Prolegomena to a Study of Greek Religion (Harrison), 227
Propp, Vladimir, 235, 237, 240, 241
Proust, Marcel, 8
provocation, 31–32
"Psychological Types in the Cultures of the Southwest" (Benedict), 165, 172, 175

Rabasa, José, 27, 33
Rabinow, Paul, 7, 11, 26, 33, 34, 44, 115–17, 129, 269, 296
Race, Language, and Culture (Boas), 140, 143
racism, 141, 150, 158–59
Radcliffe-Brown, A. R., 86 n.9, 87, 96, 97
Radin, Paul, 133, 148
Raglan, Lord, 227
Rainbow, The (Lawrence), 58, 144
rationalization, 173
realism. *See* ethnography, and realism
Reflections on Fieldwork in Morocco (Rabinow), 11
reflexive anthropology, 109, 225
Reichard, Gladys, 148–49
religion: central role of, 194–96, 203–4, 210; group, 208; survival of, 197. *See also* Durkheim, Emile: and collective religion; theology, and language

representation: constructions for, 279, 282, 284, 286, 287–88; and control, 10–11; and ideology, 246–47, 262, 263–64; and language, 17–19, 91–93, 101, 109–11, 114, 120–22, 142, 260; multivocal, 118; of subjects, 244, 246; of the Other, 3. *See also* cultural representation
Rhetoric of Motives, The (Burke), 231
Rhetoric of Religion, The (Burke), 230, 231
Richards, I. A., 255
Richman, Michèle, 23, 37
Rickert, Heinrich, 272
Ricoeur, Paul, 267, 270, 293, 296
Rivers, W.H.R., 5, 86 n.9, 96, 97
Roberts, Julian, 281
Robinson, E. A., 230
Roethke, Theodore, 227
Rohner, Ronald, 142
Rorty, Richard, 215–16, 217, 218–19, 220, 224, 230
Rosaldo, Renato, 33 n.16
Roth, Marty, 22
Rousseau, Jean-Jacques, 185, 199, 258
Russell, Bertrand, 52, 64 n.1
Russell, Frank, 176

Sacks, Peter, 51
Sacred Fount, The (James), 137, 144
Sahlins, Marshall, 205, 267, 271, 273, 277, 293
Said, Edward, 3, 8–9, 26, 27, 33, 35
Sangren, P. Steven, 32–33
Santayana, George, 272
Sapir, Edward, 32, 45 n.23, 133, 163, 172, 173, 174, 178, 179, 227, 248, 249, 252, 254, 272, 292, 295
Saussure, Ferdinand de, 40, 45, 46, 73, 133, 135, 273, 292, 298
Schechner, Roy, 226
Schleiermacher, Friedrich, 127
scientism, 52, 303
Scott, Sir Walter, 71
Sea and Sardinia (Lawrence), 58
Sea and the Mirror, The (Auden), 61
Seabrook, W. B., 156
Searle, John, 220
Seligman, Charles G., 86 n.9, 96
semiotics, 15, 16, 145, 218, 235, 238, 239, 248, 267, 298
Sex and Temperament in Three Primitive Societies (Mead), 149
sexism, in anthropology, 147–49
Shore, Bradd, 261, 262
Shostak, Marjorie, 79
Simmel, Georg, 259
Singer, Milton, 218, 220
Sitwell, Dame Edith, 68
skepticism, 135, 266
Sloterdijk, Peter, 186
Smith, Elliot, 86 n.9
Smith, Paul, 245–46, 248–49, 264
Smith, William Robertson, 88 n.12
sociology: compared to anthropology, 225–26; French, 184, 190–91, 198, 199, 204
Solomon, Maynard, 42, 254 n.14
Soviet Union, anthropology in, 235–41
space, and time, 70
speech-act theory, 220, 221, 231
Spencer, Baldwin, 195, 198
Spencer, Herbert, 201
Spengler, Oswald, 172, 173, 174, 259
Spenser, Edmund, 60, 61, 62
Sperber, Dan, 224
Stevens, Wallace, 68
Stocking, George, 5, 15, 20, 21, 23, 97, 114, 133, 271, 272
Strathern, Marilyn, 10, 12, 15, 22–23, 25–26, 28, 31, 34, 75
structuralism: as comparativist, 4–5 n.1; and cultural rules expressed as signs, 203, 268; and culture history, 267, 272, 278, 280, 292, 293, 296; domination of French anthropology by, 204–5; in literature, 3, 16, 227; and modernism, 108; and Other, 10. *See also* poststructuralism
Studies in Classic American Literature (Lawrence), 144
"Study of Geography, The" (Boas), 138–39, 140, 141
subjectivity, 243, 245–46, 248–49, 258
Sullivan, Robert, 40–41, 43, 45
Sun Also Rises, The (Hemingway), 68
surrealism, 269–70, 274, 275, 276, 277, 278, 279, 281, 282, 294, 295. *See also* ethnographic surrealism
symbolism, 16
synchronism, 96, 97, 110, 121
systems, societies viewed as, 87, 98
Szwed, John, 158

Tartu School, 235, 238, 240
Tell My Horse (Hurston), 147, 154, 156, 157, 158, 160, 161
Tennyson, Alfred Lord, 64 n.1
text: in anthropological theory, 3, 7, 11, 15–16, 19–20, 267–68, 294; function of, 223; in literature, 12, 16. *See also* text making
text making: as focus of anthropology, 3, 15–17, 19–20, 109–10, 121, 147, 180, 267–68, 305–8; and French Symbolists, 16; polyphonic, 32. *See also* cultural representation; language; monographs; representation
theater. *See* performance, and theater
theology, and language, 229–30. *See also* religion
thick description, 33 n.16
Thomas, Dylan, 136
Thompson, E. P., 263, 271
Thompson, George, 227
Thomson, George, 39, 41, 43, 253–54
Thoreau, Henry David, 218, 221
Time and the Other: How Anthropology Makes Its Object (Fabian), 27
"To an Old Philosopher in Rome" (Stevens), 68
Todorov, Tzvetan, 3, 27
Toller, Ernst, 68
Totem and Taboo (Freud), 76, 78, 250
Totemism (Lévi-Strauss), 78
tradition, 218–19, 235
Trilling, Lionel, 180
Tristes Tropiques (Lévi-Strauss), 16, 17, 76 n.13
Tropics of Discourse (White), 14, 223 n.7
Tuhami: Portrait of a Moroccan (Crapanzano), 11
Turner, J.M.W., 72, 74, 75
Turner, Victor, 39, 40, 51, 218, 221, 222, 225, 226, 228, 230, 233, 235, 240, 241
Tyler, Stephen, 10–11, 32, 46, 111, 144, 145, 180 n.4, 224
Tylor, Sir Edward B., 86, 197, 248, 249, 252

Ulysses (Joyce), 4, 5, 31, 59, 60, 63, 64, 138

Van Vechten, Carl, 154
Veblen, Thornstein, 227
vegetation ceremonies, 12
vegetation deities, 51
Veselovsky, A. N., 235, 237
Vickery, John, 13, 22, 28
Vološinov, Valentin N., 234, 247, 256, 258–60, 261
Voltaire (François-Marie Arouet), 62, 185, 188
von Hofmannsthal, Hugo, 304
voyeurism, of anthropology, 77–79

Wahl, Jean, 183–84
Waiting for Godot (Beckett), 141
Walker, Alice, 149
Waste Land, The (Eliot), 4, 5, 12, 31, 54, 71
Waves, The (Woolf), 137
Webster, Steven, 25, 43–46
Wellek, René, 228
Weltfish, Gene, 133
West Germany, anthropology in, 186, 189
White, Hayden, 3, 14–15, 16, 17, 20, 26 n.12, 137, 223 n.7
White, Leslie, 134
Whitman, Walt, 227
Williams, Raymond, 29, 40, 41, 45, 144, 269, 271
Williams, William Carlos, 227, 230
Willis, Paul, 248, 263–65
Windelband, Wilhelm, 272
Wittgenstein, Ludwig, 220
women: in anthropology, 147–49, 150; and self-realization, 167–68
Women in Love (Lawrence), 58
Woolf, Virginia, 8, 61, 63, 68, 137
Wordsworth, William, 60
Works and Lives: The Anthropologist as Author (Geertz), 15
Worship of Nature, The (Frazer), 64
Writing Culture (Clifford and Marcus), 8, 18, 33, 34, 35, 78, 245, 246
Wyman, Lee, 148

Years, The (Woolf), 61, 68
Yeats, William Butler, 12, 62, 68
Young, M., 116

Zola, Emile, 59, 208, 277